Contents

Note on the 2013 Edition

When originally conceived, this book was not intended to be the first volume in a series. But that's how it turned out. It has been followed by *Rejoice! Rejoice! Britain in the 1980s* and *A Classless Society: Britain in the 1990s*, which continue the story of how the post-war consensus in British politics and society was finally destroyed, to be replaced by a new settlement, based on economic and social liberalism.

Running alongside that political narrative is another: the emergence of a cultural movement that was largely formed in the 1950s and 19'60s. Manifest in film and television, fashion and music, this was initially seen as being primarily the preserve of the working class and of youth and therefore of little serious interest. Over the period described in these books, the phenomenon matured, revealing itself to be sustainable and capable of crossing age and class lines: youth culture became national identity. That current intersects at crucial points with the world of politics, pre-empting, prompting and reflecting wider changes in the country.

When preparing this edition of the first volume in the trilogy, I have resisted the temptation to go back to the beginning and start again. The one exception is the final chapter. Since this was intended as a stand-alone book, I originally attempted to sketch in, very briefly, subsequent developments up to and including the Falklands War of 1982. Everything described in that chapter has now been treated more fully in *Rejoice! Rejoice!*, so I have cut much of the detail from here, and added instead a short note on the decade.

Crisis? What Crisis?

ALWYN W. TURNER is an acclaimed writer on post-war Britain. He is the author of *Rejoice! Rejoice! Britain in the 1980s* and *A Classless Society: Britain in the 1990s*, both of which are published by Aurum. His other books include *The Biba Experience, Glam Rock: Dandies in the Underworld, Halfway to Paradise: The Birth of British Rock* and *Terry Nation: The Man Who Invented the Daleks.* www.alwynturner.com

PRAISE FOR ALWYN W. TURNER

Crisis? What Crisis? Britain in the 1970s

'Turner has certainly hit upon a rich and fascinating subject, and his intertwining of political and cultural history is brilliantly done . . . This is a masterful work of social history and cultural commentary, told with much wit. It almost makes you feel as if you were there'
Roger Lewis, *Mail on Sunday*

'Turner appears to have spent much of the decade watching television, and his knowledge of old soap operas, sitcoms and TV dramas is deployed to great effect throughout this vivid, brilliantly researched chronicle. . . Turner may be an anorak, but he is an acutely intelligent anorak'
Francis Wheen, *New Statesman*

'An ambitious, entertaining alternative history of the 1970s which judges the decade not just by its political turbulence but by the leg-up it gave popular culture'
Time Out

'Entertaining and splendidly researched. . . He has delved into episodes of soap operas and half-forgotten novels to produce an account that displays wit, colour and detail'
Brian Groom, *Financial Times*

'Turner combines a fan's sense of populism (weaving in references to a rapidly expanding popular culture) with a keen grasp of the political landscape, which gives his survey of an often overlooked decade its cutting edge'
Metro

'Fascinating . . . an affectionate but unflinching portrait of the era'
Nicholas Foulkes, *Independent on Sunday*

Rejoice! Rejoice! Britain in the 1980s

'Put[s] into cold perspective what at the time we were too befuddled with emotion to understand. . . Turner has produced a masterly mix of shrewd analysis, historical detail and telling quotes. . . Indispensable'
James Delingpole, *Mail on Sunday*

'One of the pleasures of Alwyn Turner's breathless romp through the 1980s is that it overflows with unusual juxtapositions and surprising insights. . . The tone is that of a wildly enthusiastic guide leading us on a breakneck tour through politics, sport and culture'
Dominic Sandbrook, *The Sunday Times*

'This kaleidoscopic history . . . provides a vivid and enjoyable guide to these turbulent years. Ranging broadly across popular culture as well as high politics . . . Turner brings the period alive and offers insights into both sides of a polarised nation'
BBC History Magazine, Pick of the Month

'Turner's account of the 1980s is as wide-ranging as that fractured, multi-faceted decade demands . . . deft at picking out devilish details and damning quotes from history that is less recent than you think'
Victoria Segal, *MOJO*

'Turner does an excellent job in synthesising the culture and art of the day into the wider political discourse. The result is resolutely entertaining'
Metro

CRISIS? WHAT CRISIS?
BRITAIN IN THE 1970S

Alwyn W. Turner

Aurum

First published in Great Britain
2008 by Aurum Press Ltd
74–77 White Lion Street
London N1 9PF
www.aurumpress.co.uk

This revised and updated paperback edition first published in 2013 by Aurum Press Ltd

A catalogue record for this book is available from the British Library.

ISBN 978 1 78131 071 7

Design in The Antiqua by Richard Marston
Typeset by SX Composing DTP, Rayleigh, Essex
Printed and bound in Great Britain by CPI Group (UK) Ltd, Croydon, CR0 4YY

We're living on time we're having to borrow –
No one knows if we will live to see tomorrow.
People will say, when they look back at today,
Those were the good old, bad old days.
Anthony Newley, 'The Good Old Bad Old Days' (1972)

Howard turns and looks at Barbara, inspecting this heresy. He says:
'There may be a fashion for failure and negation now. But we don't have
to go along with it.' 'Why not?' asks Barbara, 'after all, you've gone along
with every other fashion, Howard.'
Malcolm Bradbury, *The History Man* (1975)

RIGSBY: This country gets more like the boiler room on the *Titanic* every
day: confused orders from the bridge, water swirling round our ankles.
The only difference is they had a band.
Eric Chappell, *Rising Damp* (1977)

Because the 1970s remain the subject of some dispute. S. Since the original publication of this book, there have been several other accounts of the period. As the decade slips deeper into history, there will be further such works and a more settled version of the times will becomes established. It is to be hoped that what emerges will judge the era on its own merits, rather than seeing it only as an appendix to the 1960s or a precursor of to the 1980s. In the meantime, the aim of this book, and its sequels, is to tell the story, insofar as it is possible, as it appeared at the time.

Alwyn W. Turner
June 2013

Seventies
'This is the modern world'

The lights were going out all over Britain, and no one was quite sure if we'd see them lit again in our lifetime.

That, at least, was one version of the period between Edward Heath's election victory in 1970 and that of Margaret Thatcher in 1979, the watershed years that saw the end of one Britain and the first tentative steps towards a new nation. As the amphetamine rush of the '60s wore off, the country was confronted by a series of crises that set the tone for the remainder of the century and beyond: crises about natural resources, about race and immigration, about terrorism and environmental abuse, about Britain's position within Europe and that of nationalisms within Britain, crises in fact about everything from street violence to class war and even to paedophile porn. It was a time when the certainties of the post-war political consensus were destroyed and it was unclear what would emerge to replace them.

For years afterwards, it was a decade that could scarcely be mentioned without condemnation, conjuring up images of social breakdown, power cuts, the three-day week, rampant bureaucracy and all-powerful trade unions. And then came the inevitable correction. In 2004 the New Economics Foundation constructed an analysis of national performance, based not on the traditional criterion of gross domestic product, but on what it called the measure of domestic progress, incorporating such factors as crime, family stability, pollution and inequality of income. And it concluded that Britain was a happier country in 1976 than it had been in the thirty years since.

For at least one generation, this was already common knowledge. To be young in that dawn might not have been very heaven, but sometimes it didn't seem too far off, despite the privations. The writer Philip Cato, who grew up in Rugeley in the West Midlands, commented that 'try as I might, I really cannot remember any truly bad times'. Even when his father, a postman, became involved in a bitter and unsuccessful seven-week-long strike in 1971, it was far from a disaster as seen through a child's eyes. 'I was well chuffed,' remembered Cato, 'because I was entitled to free school dinners which meant I was at the head of the queue in the canteen, clutching my little purple ticket with all the other kids whose dads were on the dole.' Similarly, the record-breaking long, hot summer of 1976 may have caused all manner of problems for the country's farmers, but for schoolchildren it was cherished as the time when head teachers were forced to admit publicly, in the first assemblies of the autumn term, that smoking actually existed, issuing warnings to be careful when disposing of cigarette butts.

By the time of that NEF research, the 1970s had also undergone a cultural reappraisal. No longer 'the decade that taste forgot', it was now seen as a golden age of British television, of popular fiction, of low-tech toys and of club football. The British film industry might have been in decline, but it was still capable of scaling new peaks with *Get Carter*, *Performance*, *The Wicker Man*. Even punk rock, which seemed at the time to be as limited in its commercial impact as skiffle had been twenty years earlier, had emerged as the only global rival to hip hop. Who would have predicted that in the twenty-first century, the legacy of the Sex Pistols would be more influential on new bands than that of the Beatles? Or that the prime minister would one day walk into his party's conference to the sounds of Sham 69 singing 'If the Kids Are United', as Tony Blair did in 2005? These things have become as significant in perceptions of the period as are the memories of political crises.

To some extent this is less a re-evaluation than a recognition of how significant they had been even at the time. In 1978 London Weekend Television launched a new series, *The South Bank Show*, to replace its existing arts programme, *Aquarius*. Presented by Melvyn Bragg, the new show announced that it was to cover 'the consumed arts', a term that embraced 'cinema, rock, paperbacks and even television'. It was an acknowledgement of how far the revolution in popular culture had come, and the extent to which it now permeated everyday life.

The greatest impact was made by television itself. The first *Social Trends* survey showed that in 1971 the average Briton watched 18.6 hours of television a week; by 1978 that figure had risen to 22 hours. And this was a shared culture, reaching the whole of society, so that over 95 per cent of all social classes acknowledged that they spent a considerable amount of their leisure time as viewers. There were still only three channels available, but between them they produced that decade both Britain's best-loved comedy act in Morecambe and Wise and its most revered sitcoms – *Rising Damp*, *Fawlty Towers*, *The Good Life* – as well as the great years of *Coronation Street* and *Doctor Who* and classic drama series from *I, Claudius* to *The Sweeney*. The growing strength of television was allied to the rise of colour broadcasting, still a novelty at the beginning of the decade, though the Ogdens did own a colour set in *Coronation Street*; sadly, it was repossessed because they failed to keep up the payments, leaving Hilda to testify how it had revolutionized her viewing: 'I loved that set, Stan. Everybody looked so bright and happy in colour. Even Sandy Gall.' It was not until 1977 that the number of colour sets exceeded that of black and white, and they remained something of a status symbol. 'I'm the proud owner of a colour television,' declared Rigsby in *Rising Damp*, refusing to turn on for a test match against the West Indies. 'I'm not watching something that looks the same in black and white.'

The messages carried by television were of central importance, even if they were not always explicit. A BBC survey in 1970 showed that less than half its audience regarded the Corporation as being 'always impartial', with some younger respondents pointing to coverage of Vietnam and Northern Ireland as the cause of their disillusion, while others saw excessive liberalism at work. But when it came to the really popular shows, the ones that were consumed by the huge audiences that BBC1 and ITV could then command, there was no doubt about their distortions. The broadcasters could still claim to offer a window on the world, and yet, when the biggest political issue of the day was the role of the trade unions, it is extraordinary how few union members – let alone officials – were depicted in the popular dramas and comedies of the '70s. While politicians of both left and right were quick to point to instances of perceived bias in news and current affairs, the real impact came elsewhere, in programmes that were not then deemed to be truly worthy of notice, but which have survived longer in the national consciousness than an edition of *World in Action* could ever achieve.

In terms of overt political reporting, the decade's major development came with the rise of the *Sun* newspaper, bought by Rupert Murdoch in 1969 and initially seen as a downmarket version of the *Daily Mirror*. As its sales rose to eclipse those of its elder rival, and its tone became increasingly aggressive, so it changed the nature of the popular press; its switch from supporting the Labour Party to backing the Conservatives proved to be a significant indicator of social change.

Less remarked upon, but also crucial to the period, was the phone-in radio show, which became the first interactive media format, allowing ordinary members of the public to participate directly in broadcasting. Although it was pioneered by BBC Radio Nottingham in 1968, the phone-in was to be exploited most heavily by the new independent stations. In 1971 the Conservative government introduced legislation to permit the launch of commercial radio and found the proposal attacked by the Labour Party, whose commitment to state broadcasting had resulted in opposition to commercial television in the 1950s and the crushing of pirate radio in the '60s. Now the Labour spokesman Ivor Richard warned that this new development would lead to the 'trivialization of broadcasting', and proceedings in the Commons were temporarily brought to a halt by protests led by Eric Heffer. Nonetheless the legislation was duly passed, and in 1973 London's LBC became the first legally approved commercial station in the country, with a schedule that relied heavily upon phone-ins. Informed by the newspapers they consumed, the listeners could now, to some extent at least, set the news agenda, establishing a circuit of feedback that has continued to develop. The result was not to everyone's taste: 'The more I hear commercial radio the more repellent I find it,' shuddered the comedian Kenneth Williams. 'The din created by the half-baked talking to the half-educated is horrible.'

Even so, the advent of the phone-in was a critical step towards the democratization of the airwaves. Its catchphrase was 'I'm entitled to my opinion' and it changed the nature of political debate. Revealing more sharply than ever before the divided nature of the country, it provided a voice for those who considered themselves to be part of the hitherto silent majority. There was some doubt how accurate that appellation really was – the numbers of those signing Mary Whitehouse's petitions against the degradation of television, for example, were massively outweighed by those who watched the shows of which she so heartily disapproved – but it nonetheless became part of the political vocabulary of the times. At the end of the '60s Enoch Powell had responded to the controversy caused by his speeches on immigration by talking about 'the staggering and dangerous gap between what is known by personal experience to a few millions of people and what it seems possible to bring home to the small minority – of course it's bound to be a small minority – who speak and write'. The phone-in went some way towards bridging that gap.

And, to a large extent, that gap was the story of the decade, for this was the era in which politicians lost the confidence of the public. Dismayed that their elected representatives did not seem to be responding to their experience, the people sought other means of articulating their discontent so that, to take the vexed issue of race, the National Front began to look as though it might rival the Liberal Party as the third force in politics, while at the same time the Anti-Nazi League and Rock Against

Racism were capable of staging the largest political rallies that the century had yet seen. And the clashes on the streets between these two forces, and between them and the police, added to the sense of impending social collapse.

Indeed it sometimes seemed as though Britain was effectively talking itself into having a crisis, as though it somehow felt more comfortable with its back to the wall, imbibing the spirit of the Blitz. Having spent the whole decade making its own flesh creep by telling horror stories about how bad things were, steeping itself in a popular culture that frequently verged on the apocalyptic, the nation finally found its nightmares coming true with the winter of discontent in early 1979. A T-junction seemed to have been reached, where continuing in the same direction was no longer an option, and the only issue that really had to be resolved was whether the country would take a sharp turn to the left or to the right, following the prospectus either of Tony Benn or of Enoch Powell. Conventional political wisdom at the time saw the former as being the more likely; all the indicators from popular culture suggested the latter.

This book is an attempt to depict both the high politics and the low culture of those times. The stories of the tabloid press, of soaps and sitcoms and of Radio One are represented alongside those of Westminster and Whitehall, because that was how the new world of the mass media reflected the nation's own experience to itself. Harold and Margaret were important, but so too were George and Mildred; the state of the national football teams was as much a cause of controversy as the state of the national economy; pop musicians had an influence upon the public just as politicians did. This is not therefore an insider's account, but rather one which – to use that phrase from *The South Bank Show* – considers politics as one of the consumed arts. And it is largely seen from the partial, subjective positions of the consumers.

The book is structured in three sections, broadly corresponding to the three prime ministers of the era: Edward Heath, Harold Wilson and James Callaghan. Each section starts with an overview of the period, followed by a series of chapters addressing contemporary issues. These latter are not entirely chronological but, it is hoped, will explore thematically a decade when it sometimes appeared that the nation was on the verge of a nervous breakdown.

PART ONE

HANG ON TO YOURSELF
1970–1974

Looking ahead, I said I thought one of our difficulties was that the Tories seemed to be thinking of the Seventies whereas the Labour Party looked as if it was just at the end of its period of office and didn't have much to say beyond that.
Tony Benn (1970)

Affluence is essential to Western societies, not an optional extra: without it, or the hope of it, they no longer possess any basis for social harmony.
Martin Pawley, *The Private Future* (1973)

JACK REGAN: 'There's an old Tory saying: switch off something now.'
Tony Marsh, *The Sweeney* (1974)

1

The Heath Years

'The party on the left is now the party on the right'

SHIRLEY: According to your master plan, you should have swept to power in 1967.
WOLFIE: I couldn't reckon on England winning the World Cup, could I? That sort of victory gives the proletariat morale.
John Sullivan, *Citizen Smith* (1979)

The swinging London of the '60s has given way to a London as gloomy as the city described by Charles Dickens, with the once imperial streets of the capital of a vast Empire now sparsely lighted like the slummy streets of a former British colonial township.
Der Spiegel magazine (1974)

In the '70s is there a different mood? My arse there is!
Pete Townshend (1970)

Harold Wilson was born in the West Riding of Yorkshire in 1916, which meant that he grew up in the glory days of his home-town football club. As he wrote on the very first page of his autobiography: 'When Huddersfield Town won the League Championship three years running and the Cup Final in two of those years, we felt we were the Lords of Creation.' Unfortunately his sense of grandeur was misplaced. Huddersfield did indeed win three League titles in a row from 1924 to 1926, with a team built by the great manager Herbert Chapman, but they have never in their history achieved the League and FA Cup double.

For a politician who was so celebrated for his prodigious memory and his obsession with trivial statistics, it's an intriguing error, suggesting that perhaps, like his fondness for HP Sauce and his public propensity to smoke a pipe rather than his preferred cigars, Wilson's enthusiasm for football was somewhat calculated, a learned behaviour designed to enhance his man-of-the-people image. Certainly he was aware, as no other politician before him had been aware, of the significance of football in the national psyche of Britain. In 1965 he awarded Stanley Matthews the first-ever knighthood given to a professional player, and he went on to honour in the same way England manager Alf Ramsey, for winning the World Cup in 1966, and Manchester United manager Matt Busby, for winning the European Cup in 1968. (Jock Stein, who had won the latter tournament with Celtic the year before Busby's triumph, got overlooked, despite lobbying from the Scottish secretary, Willie Ross, reinforcing the perception that Scottish football was less valued than its English counter-part.) And in the aftermath of England's 1966 victory, Wilson ensured that he accompanied the team onto the balcony of the hotel where they were enjoying a celebration dinner, determined to share their moment of glory as they took the cheers of the crowds gathered below. 'England,' he famously and fatuously remarked, 'only wins the World Cup under Labour.'

It was no great surprise, therefore, that the 1970 World Cup should be uppermost in his mind when considering how to secure an unprece-dented third general election victory in a row for the Labour Party. In March that year he remarked that 'he had thought about the date for the election for the last four years or more and the conflict with the World Cup had to be considered'. England, going into the tournament as defending champions and with a team that most commentators considered was even stronger than the 1966 vintage, were favourites to win and were certainly expected to reach the final. The election was accordingly called for Thursday 18 June 1970, the day after the semi-final matches, when English euphoria was predicted to be at its height. And, just in case the electorate had forgotten how integral the government was to the nation's sporting success, Wilson made an appearance on BBC1's *Sportsnight with Coleman* in April, 'ostensibly to comment on the cup final between Chelsea and Leeds United', though he slipped easily into discussion of the forthcoming international tournament.

Not knowing quite as much about the vagaries of football as he thought, however, he had made a profound miscalculation: England's campaign in the World Cup was to be plagued by bad luck and by (metaphorical) own goals, and Wilson himself was among the casualties. With the tournament due to be played in Mexico, the world champions had undertaken a 'good will' trip to that country in 1969, a visit on which Alf Ramsey had succeeded in alienating the local press by his perceived arrogance, adding insult to the injuries still nursed in Latin America after the bad-tempered

1966 quarter-final against Argentina ('not so much a football match,' wrote journalist Hugh McIlvanney, 'as an international incident'). In the build-up to the actual competition, captain Bobby Moore was arrested in Bogotá, following a warm-up match against Colombia, and charged with stealing a bracelet, while the host nation was again offended by England's insistence on travelling with their own bus and their own food, giving every impression of a colonizing force distrustful of local conditions. In the event, neither was a success – the coach broke down and most of the food was confiscated at Customs – but the tone was set, and at the opening ceremony the children who appeared in England team shirts were booed by the spectators. 'From the beginning,' reflected centre forward Bobby Charlton later, 'we got off on the wrong foot and we were unpopular throughout the country. Nobody wanted us to win.'

On the pitch, things were a little better. In the initial group stage of the tournament, England duly beat both Romania and Czechoslovakia by a goal to nil, but also came up against what is generally acknowledged to have been the best football team of all time, the 1970 incarnation of Brazil, and lost by the same score. ('The political effect of this can't be altogether ignored,' noted Labour cabinet minister Tony Benn.) Qualifying for the quarter-finals, to be played on Sunday 15 June, England were matched again with West Germany, who had been so memorably beaten in the 1966 final. With just over twenty minutes to play, England were 2–0 up and seemingly on course for their destiny, but, with Bobby Charlton substituted and with goalkeeper Gordon Banks sidelined due to a stomach upset, they proved vulnerable to a German counter-offensive, and went down 3–2 after extra time. The England team duly caught the next plane home, having played what turned out to be their last World Cup match not just of that campaign, but of the whole decade.

1970 was the first World Cup to be televised in colour in Britain and the viewing figures broke all records. The TV audience for the Brazil–England match exceeded that for the 1966 final, whilst the quarter-final was even more successful, attracting 30 million viewers for a game staged in the midday heat of Mexico to ensure prime-time coverage back in Europe. This was despite the fact that the public had been spared the worst excesses of jingoistic hype, thanks to a national newspaper strike that had wiped out coverage of the Czechoslovakia match and the entire build-up to the Germany game. Unfortunately for Wilson, the strike ended the day after the quarter-finals, just in time for the post-match analysis of England's exit from the competition, and for the full shock of defeat to be registered. And at least one person picked up on the parallels: 'Thinking of strange reversals of fortune,' wrote a correspondent to *The Times*, 'could it be that Harold Wilson is two-nil up with twenty minutes to play?'

The analogy was entirely appropriate. Wilson had gone into the election with every confidence. Both before and during the campaign the opinion polls – despite the usual inconsistencies – had suggested that a Labour Party victory was inevitable, and most of the media speculation concerned who would replace Edward Heath as leader of the Conservatives when the electorate rejected him for a second time. All the indications were favourable for Wilson and, to stack the odds still further in his favour, he was expected to be the beneficiary of the extension of the franchise to eighteen-year-olds (following the policies of Screaming Lord Sutch, who had stood against him in 1966 for the National Teenage Party), since it was thought that youth were more likely to vote Labour than Conservative; in fact, the additional 1.8 million voters made very little difference, save to reduce the turn-out to a record post-war low.

There were, however, dissenting voices. 'I have a haunting feeling,' wrote the outgoing employment secretary Barbara Castle in her diary the weekend before polling day, 'that there is a silent majority sitting behind its lace curtains, waiting to come out and vote Tory.' And it turned out that she was right and the pollsters were wrong. The Conservatives won a decisive victory, sending Heath into Downing Street and Wilson into confusion: 'The opinion polls have a lot of explaining to do,' he declared in the early hours of that Friday, as the extent of his defeat became apparent. Others too were feeling perplexed; typical was Annie Saunders, a fifty-five-year-old voter from Sheffield, who was quoted as saying: 'I would have voted Labour, but I saw in one paper that the opinion polls gave them a nine per cent lead. I didn't think, in view of the opinion polls, they would miss my vote. It just goes to show how misleading they can be.'

Apart from the false sense of security engendered by pollsters and the depression (south and east of relevant borders) at the World Cup failure, there were other explanations of what had gone wrong for Labour, mostly concentrating on the way that Wilson had alienated traditional supporters. In 1969 the government had published a White Paper, 'In Place of Strife', attempting to curb trade union powers, a move that had been soundly defeated by the lobbying of the unions even before it appeared as a parliamentary bill, but which had soured relations between the political and industrial wings of Labour. It 'had upset the entire trade union movement,' wrote left-wing MP Eric Heffer, 'and it was obvious to me that we would lose votes in the general election'. Also from the left, the newly elected Dennis Skinner cited the budgets of Labour chancellor Roy Jenkins as being too much concerned with appeasing the City of London and too little interested in the party's heartlands. Then there was the fact that the personal experience of the economy was unsatisfactory; put simply, 'People were fed up with rising prices and strikes.'

But above all else there was the complacency of Wilson himself. 'However tired people may be of me,' he commented in the run-up to the election, 'I think that most people will regard me as the lesser of the two evils.' It didn't sound much like a rallying cry and it failed to enthuse. The campaign was fought from the Labour side entirely around the figure of the prime minister, with as little discussion of policy as possible, an approach on which the *Daily Mirror*, loyal as ever to the Labour cause, tried to put a gloss: 'In an era when the principles of the political parties are not so far apart, the personalities and personal records of the leaders and their henchmen are even more important.' But it wasn't enough. ('What do you think this is?' demanded Enoch Powell. 'A contest between a man with a pipe and a man with a boat?')

Wilson had been the future once, carried to power in 1964 on the hopes of millions, ending a long period of Tory rule, and promising change in the form of a new socialism, this time forged in the white heat of a technological revolution. Now, though, he looked as though he was slipping into history along with the swinging sixties. Tainted by devaluation of the pound and by his perceived support of American involvement in Vietnam, he represented a mood of optimism that had failed, harking back to a time of suited mods rather than booted skinheads. His fading appeal was symbolized by a photo shoot of Sandie Shaw, a singer who had enjoyed her last-ever top 20 single more than a year before, appearing in a T-shirt designed by her then husband Jeff Banks proclaiming 'My Shirt's On Harold'. The message was clear: yesterday's pop stars were supporting yesterday's man.

That *Mirror* comment, however, has a greater significance. In January 1970 Edward Heath and the Tory shadow cabinet had held a policy meeting in the Selsdon Park Hotel in Croydon. Out of the weekend's discussion had emerged a set of proposals that were to become the bones of the Conservative Party's manifesto, *A Better Future*: tax reform, law and order, trade union legislation, immigration, a reduction in public spending, no government support for failing industries (so-called lame ducks) and no statutory incomes policy. It didn't, in truth, amount to a fully coherent philosophical platform, but Wilson was eager to give it that status. 'Selsdon Man is designing a system of society for the ruthless and the pushing, the uncaring,' he declared, as though outraged. 'His message to the rest is: you're out on your own.' It was intended as a scare tactic but it had the reverse effect, as the Tory education spokesperson, Margaret Thatcher, was later to note: 'It gave us the air of down-to-earth right-wing populism.' Right-wingers were to cite Selsdon Man for years to come as being evidence that Heath's agenda had prefigured the Thatcherite revolution, while Heath's own supporters insisted that it was all a figment of Wilson's fevered imagination.

That debate and its ramifications were to echo within the Conservative Party into the next decade and beyond, but in 1970 – as the *Daily Mirror* made clear – few people really noticed. The complaint was not that the Tories had adopted a hard-right position, but precisely the opposite, that there was so little to choose between the parties. The Liberal Party issued a campaign poster that depicted Wilson and Heath as identical twins, asking 'Which twin is the Tory?', and underground rock group the Edgar Broughton Band echoed the thought, producing a poster of a cartoon by Ralph Steadman that showed the two men's faces as a pair of buttocks, and the slogan 'Why vote? It's a double cross!' Delegates to the Labour Party's post-defeat conference at the end of September returned again and again to the same theme: 'When people say they could not distinguish between us and the Tories, it is a dreadful indictment, and it is vital that they be left in no doubt next time,' said one. 'If we are to get the votes back, we must establish a clearly defined sense of socialist purpose and ensure that the edges between the two parties are no longer blurred,' added another. Out of this confusion were to be born the moves to the left by the Labour Party and to the right by the Conservatives.

Meanwhile, the nation was adjusting to its new prime minister. Born just a few months after Wilson, and sharing his grammar school and Oxford background, Ted Heath seemed an extension of the technocratic meritocracy of his predecessor, though somehow even less rooted in a class system. He once admitted that he had 'a hidden wish, a frustrated desire to run a hotel', which made some kind of cultural sense: where Wilson self-consciously evoked the Northern humour and warmth of *Coronation Street* (he visited the set in the run-up to the 1970 election and sang a duet with Violet Carson, who played Ena Sharples), Heath seemed more akin to the soulless anonymity of the Crossroads Motel. He was also a much less familiar face for the general public, largely because his principal job in previous Tory governments had been as chief whip, though he had also led the unsuccessful negotiations to take Britain into the European Economic Community. All that was really known was that he had an interest in classical music and that he was the skipper of the

Morning Cloud, which in 1969 became the first British boat to win the Sydney–Hobart race since 1945, an achievement that, he said, had shown Australia that the British were 'not quite such a decadent people after all'.

It wasn't much of an image, but then Heath was apparently little concerned with image, keen instead to distance himself from the populist tendencies of Wilson in the 1960s. Certainly he had no interest in sharing himself with the public. 'I want to be feared,' he remarked privately, and he did dominate his cabinet to a remarkable extent, but to the country at large he was anything but fearsome. Rather, in the absence of any clear picture of the real thing, people turned instead to the portrayal of him by one of the rising stars of British comedy.

Impressionist Mike Yarwood had come out of the Northern clubs to secure his first headline TV series in early 1969, and was to prove a key figure in the political scene of the '70s. In an era of three TV channels, with very few appearances by politicians and no broadcasting of Parliament, it largely fell to him to present a human face for the sometimes rather remote figures governing the nation. Even so, he tended to play down any great significance to his work: 'I don't bear any malice,' he said. 'I have political views but I'm not fanatical either way. I don't do a *Private Eye* or an *Up Sunday*.' The latter reference was to a mostly forgotten satirical series on BBC2 – fronted by Clive James, John Wells and Willie Rushton – and Yarwood's relationship to the satire boom that preceded him, and that was now running out of steam, was revealing; like Peter Cook in *Beyond the Fringe*, he had impersonated Harold Macmillan in the early 1960s, though without the surrounding controversy, since his were essentially friendly portrayals. By the time he became a regular fixture on BBC1's Saturday night schedules in 1971, his impressions of Heath and Wilson were mixed with those of TV figures such as Michael Parkinson, Robin Day and both Steptoe and Son, implicitly suggesting that political leaders were no more than part of the broad sweep of light entertainment. 'The outstanding achievement I had brought off was to give politicians a sense of humour,' he wrote in his first autobiography; 'I have acted as public relations officer for them.' Ted Heath, in an incarnation that was chiefly notable for shaking his shoulders when he laughed, was the first great beneficiary of this gentle caricaturing, transformed in the public imagination from managerial autocrat to a strangely endearing and jovial uncle.

A parallel lack of public relations existed in terms of Heath's policies. His programme of technical reforms – the reorganization of local government, restructuring of Whitehall, reform of the tax system (including the introduction of VAT) – took up vast amounts of parliamentary time, but was of little or no interest to most of the population. Those measures that did resonate tended to be unpopular: changes to industrial relations legislation, adjustments to council house rents and entry into Europe. But beyond all this, his problem was that he simply didn't hold the initiative; the everyday political world was almost entirely dominated from the outset not by his actions but by those of the trade unions. Even as early as July 1970, less than a month after the election, he was obliged to declare a state of emergency in response to a strike by dockers.

The autumn of 1970 saw the first real slide into chaos with the so-called dirty jobs strike by local council workers in London. Refuse collectors seeking higher wages were joined by workers at refuse dumps, determined to prevent the public from disposing of their own rubbish, and by sewerage workers. By mid-October more than 60,000 workers were on strike, with solidarity action in the form of overtime bans and one-day stoppages pulling another 75,000 into the dispute. The effects spilled into unrelated areas – schooldays were lost and parks were closed when caretakers and park-keepers walked out – but the real danger came from the action at the heart of the strike. 'Millions of gallons of untreated sewage poured into the rivers Thames and Avon yesterday,' reported the press; 'only volunteers, working up to eighteen hours a day at pumping stations, were preventing serious flooding and the danger of many people being drowned in their homes.' Fish died in their thousands in the polluted rivers; swarms of flies, breeding in the Deephams sewage works in Enfield, descended on North London; and – as a foretaste of crises yet to come – Leicester Square became a temporary refuse tip, disappearing under a mountain of bin bags. There were even tinny echoes of the 1926 General Strike, as members of the upper classes demonstrated their opposition by symbolic action; one group of volunteers – which included the Duke of St Albans' daughter, Lady Caroline ffrench Blake – cleared up Downing Street, and their leader, an economist named Patrick Evershed, promised further such measures: 'Having successfully swept Downing Street the six patriots, plus some more friends, intend to sweep round the Cenotaph in time for the Remembrance service.' It was, he said, 'a disgrace that Mr Heath's visitors who come from all corners of the world should have to wade through debris on the way into No. 10'.

However grateful Heath may have been for the courtesy, it made no difference to the outcome of the dispute. The united front of the employers soon began to crumble, with first Barking Council and then Tower Hamlets reaching their own agreements, even before an independent committee, led by Sir Jack Scamp, concluded that 'a non-inflationary settlement was never in prospect', and accepted virtually all the unions' demands. That verdict brought a close to a six-week strike that offered little enough optimism for the immediate future, but the year was not yet over. Electricians began a work-to-rule that led to the first power cuts of Heath's government (and another state of emergency), and the parliamentary term ended with the House of Commons sitting in near-darkness, its proceedings illuminated by candles and paraffin lamps. 'Driving home through the darkened streets, which only weeks before had been littered with rubbish,' reflected the newly elected Tory MP Norman Tebbit, 'I wondered for how long this succession of strikes would continue.'

The answer was not very encouraging. Strikes, which had for some years been dominated by wildcat stoppages (in the mid-'60s 95 per cent of strikes were unofficial), became ever larger, ever more disruptive during Heath's period as prime minister. In 1970 the number of working days lost in industrial action was 11 million, the highest total since 1926, the year of the General Strike, and it was set to get worse; in 1972 the figure reached nearly 24 million days, ten times the level of the first year of Wilson's government back in 1964, with more than 10 million days accounted for by the first-ever national strike by the National Union of Mineworkers.

The NUM had been formed in 1945, when the mining industry was nationalized, and its quarter-century of relative industrial peace was primarily the result of its constitution, which called for a two-thirds majority in a poll of the members before a strike could be called. In 1970 this rule was amended so that a 55 per cent majority was sufficient, and the following year a 59 per cent vote was recorded in favour of action. The principal argument was over pay, which had slipped substantially relative to other groups of workers, but working conditions were also a factor: much of the industry was still unmechanized, whilst the annual holiday entitlement was just two weeks, at a time when the standard was three, and the TUC was pushing for four. Evidence was also given of pits that were so hot that the face workers were forced to work naked. 'It'll be a crime if you allow this strike to happen, because we shall win it, you know,' Heath was told by the newly elected NUM president, Joe Gormley. 'And when we have won, this will become the pattern for industrial relations for the next decade.'

The strike itself started in January 1972, with a warning by the government that it could last for up to a month. In fact it lasted seven weeks, though it did take Heath a month before he declared the now customary state of emergency. In the interim, floodlights on national monuments – including Big Ben, Marble Arch and the National Gallery – were turned off, along with the neon signs at Piccadilly Circus, and a rolling programme of power cuts was established.

The loss of electricity produced some unexpected consequences, with television series such as *Coronation Street* and *Doctor Who* being obliged to give a précis of the last episode before each new one, so that viewers who had been blacked out could catch up with the storylines. Elsewhere, Steve Jones, later to become a successful broadcaster, but at the time a working musician fresh from playing with skiffle king Lonnie Donegan, was the bassist in a band with a residency in a South London pub: 'We'd start at seven-thirty and play all this heavy stuff through to nine o'clock,' he remembered, 'and then bang, the lights would go out. So we'd put up Davy lamps, I'd take out the acoustic bass, the drummer would play with brushes, the guitarists would play acoustically and the singer sang through a megaphone. And you weren't getting that anywhere else in town, so the place was swinging from the bloody rafters.' More formal music was less successful in adapting to the new conditions, with concerts at the South Bank being cancelled.

When the state of emergency did materialize, it was the most severe yet. Thousands of factories were forced to close for up to four days a week, electric heating in shops, restaurants and places of entertainment was banned and people were urged to use electricity in just one room in their homes. Full-page adverts in the press outlined the extent of the restrictions and warned would-be offenders that 'conviction could mean three months in prison or a £100 fine or both'. The notices added a tug at the heartstrings: 'But even these penalties are small when compared to the hardships, possibly even tragedies, that could be brought about if thoughtless users were to overload the supply system.' More than a million workers in other industries were laid off as a consequence of the emergency regulations, and the home secretary, Reginald Maudling, was obliged to admit in the Commons that 'although the potential gravity of the situation was foreseen, no one could have been expected to know that the picketing would be quite as effective'.

The picketing was indeed the key to the success of the strike. Working on the (correct) assumption that the membership would be solidly behind the action, the NUM decided not to bother placing pickets at pits, but instead to concentrate on restricting the movement of coal around the country, preventing it from being unloaded at ports, leaving depots and reaching power stations. A new tactic emerged, the flying picket, whereby large numbers of miners would descend on an area, close the critical pressure points and depart for new territories, leaving a skeleton staff behind to ensure that facilities that had been closed remained so. And with the new approach came a new trade union hero in the form of Arthur Scargill, who led the Barnsley strike committee and whose name became synonymous with flying pickets: it was his men that closed down the transportation of coal by sea and rail in East Anglia, and who then moved on to fight the decisive action of the dispute, at the Saltley coke depot in Warwickshire. On 7 February some 500 pickets arrived at Saltley, to be confronted by 300 police. The following day the figures had grown to 1,000 and 400 respectively, and then on 10 February – with numbers swelled by car workers from Birmingham – 10,000 pickets turned up and the police admitted defeat, closing the gates to the depot and thereby shutting down what the papers called 'the only remaining source of coke in Britain'.

Television pictures of these massed ranks of workers confronting, and defeating, the police to bring yet another workplace into the strike gave a new image to British industrial disputes. Though it was entirely legal, the tactic amounted effectively to intimidation by sheer numbers and it provoked in some the suspicion that Britain was getting close to a pre-revolutionary situation. From one perspective, it was a key moment in the history of organized labour in Britain: 'Here was living proof,' reflected Scargill, 'that the working class had only to flex its muscles and it could bring governments, employers, society to a complete standstill.' On the other side, the government's mood was one of depression. Douglas Hurd, then Heath's secretary, noted tersely in his diary the enormity of the defeat: 'The government now wandering over battlefield looking for someone to surrender to – and being massacred all the time.' And his future leader was even more despondent: 'There was no disguising that this was a victory for violence,' wrote Margaret Thatcher in her memoirs. 'From now on many senior policemen put greater emphasis on maintaining "order" than on upholding the law. In practice, that meant failing to uphold the rights of individuals against the rule of the mob.'

In the wake of Saltley, the government capitulated (one of the crucial cabinet meetings was held in candlelight, 'because of a power cut') and set up an inquiry under Lord Wilberforce to resolve the dispute. That committee promptly produced a report that conceded virtually all the miners' demands, a decision which the union equally promptly rejected, arguing for more; the result was a wage rise three times as large as the 'final offer' tabled by the National Coal Board before the strike began, and a clear demonstration of the power of the unions.

'A national strike which doesn't enjoy similar support among the population in general,' said Gormley, 'is likely to be an unsuccessful strike.' And there is no doubt that the miners were then held in high public esteem, in recognition both of the dangers of the job and the moderation of their union (the following year they voted against their own executive in a call for further industrial action). Even the pictures of mass pickets could not erode popular sympathy for the justness of their claims.

So strong was the support that the dispute even turned up in the unlikely context of 'The Monster of Peladon', a 1974 *Doctor Who* serial. 'It was at the time of the great strikes,' reflected writer Brian Hayles, 'and I wanted to draw attention to the way the miners were being treated by the authorities.' In his earlier story 'The Curse of Peladon' in 1972, Hayles had depicted a remote planet that was emerging from a feudal structure and was trying to adapt to new technology as it joined the Galactic Federation, a storyline that reflected Britain's entry into Europe. In the sequel, set some fifty years later, the Doctor returns to Peladon to find that the working class is in a state of deep unrest: membership of the Federation has brought wealth and power to the ruling class, but has resulted only in an increased workload for the miners responsible for extracting trisilicate, the chief natural resource of the planet. The miners are, however, split between two leaders, clearly intended to evoke Gormley and Scargill: there is the venerated elder statesman, Gebek, who argues for strike action, and there is the younger, more extreme Ettis, 'one of the leaders of a resistance movement, sworn to drive the aliens from Peladon', who advocates armed revolution. The Doctor, in his thoroughly reasonable Jon Pertwee incarnation, sees his role as peace-loving honest broker, and urges Queen Thalira to look for compromise: 'Send for Gebek at once, your majesty, promise him a better way of life for his miners and see that they get it. That will cut the ground from under Ettis' feet,' he argues. 'You've got to convince your people that the Federation means a better way of life for everybody, not just for a few nobles at court.' By the time the series was broadcast, however, Heath had already fallen, having failed to follow the good Doctor's orders.

Perhaps the most significant aspect of the miners' strike was the way in which it ensured that the struggle against Heath's government was to be fought outside the confines of Parliament. 'I believe it is possible,' said Lawrence Daly, general secretary of the NUM, before the strike started, 'to create a broad unity in the trade union movement that will smash

Conservative economic policy and help to pave the way for the defeat of the Tory government and return a Labour government.' And his words proved prophetic: one of the main features of the early years of the decade was the way that the leadership of the working class shifted from the Labour Party to the unions.

In fact, the Labour Party itself was in no condition to offer such leadership. In 1951, the last time it had left office, the party had been able to look back on the Attlee government and its achievements with feelings of pride and accomplishment; in 1970 there was only disillusion and a suspicion of betrayal. And at the highest levels there was confusion about how to respond to the unexpected defeat.

On the left there was Tony Benn, who, even before the election, was becoming disenchanted with the government in which he served: 'I am absolutely sick,' he wrote in his diary, 'of the views of Harold Wilson, for whom I have in some respects the greatest contempt.' From his perspective, opposition was a time for serious rethinking, free from accusations that plain speech might rock the boat; as he pointed out in a shadow cabinet meeting in July 1970: 'When the boat is sunk, you can't exactly rock it.' He looked for inspiration to the increasingly militant unions and to the growth of new political groups centred on black rights, nationalism and students.

The leading figure on the right wing of the party, Roy Jenkins, was also clear about the need for developing new strategies, but found that the mood of Labour was firmly set against him. The 1973 party conference approved a programme that called for 'a fundamental and irreversible shift in the balance of power and wealth in favour of working people and their families', and Benn encapsulated the aspirations of the delegates with a speech that declared: 'We shall use the crisis we inherit as an occasion for making the fundamental changes and not as an excuse for postponing them.' It was left to Jenkins to suggest that the opinion polls didn't exactly encourage such lofty aspirations. 'It is not much good talking about fundamental and irreversible changes in our society and being content with a 38 per cent Labour voting intention,' he pointed out, to a noticeably more frosty response than that enjoyed by Benn. 'Democracy means that you need a substantially stronger moral position than this to govern effectively at all, let alone effect a peaceful social revolution.'

Above the squabbling princes, Wilson was demonstrating little of the populist flair that had made him such a formidable figure in the previous decade. In the immediate aftermath of the 1970 defeat he was virtually absent from centre stage as he wrote up his account of the 1960s government, and he then found himself embroiled in trying to keep the party together as rival factions fought each other over the future of socialism and – more pressing – the correct position to take on Europe. Unexpectedly it was his wife, Mary, the very epitome of the reluctant political spouse, who captured the public attention at this point, when her volume of *Collected Poems* made her the biggest-selling poet in the country (though Marc Bolan was soon to overtake her).

By the spring of 1972 there were rumours of a leadership challenge to Wilson, with the names of backbench MPs Willie Hamilton and Christopher Mayhew being touted around Westminster. 'One estimate,' reported *The Times*, 'was that Mr Mayhew, if he accepted the role of standard-bearer for the critics, would get more than 100 votes.' No such contest materialized, but the position failed to improve, and a series of poor showings in by-elections later that year prompted the disrespected elder statesman George Brown to join the fray: 'The nation,' he thundered, 'simply will not have the Labour Party, my party, with its present policies, present associations, present leadership.' At a time when the government was struggling, the opposition was uncertain how to oppose.

The fraying of the fabric of the Labour Party was replicated in the country, where for many people change seemed to be coming both too thick and too fast. Membership of the EEC was linked in the popular consciousness with what seemed like an assault on traditional images of Britain, in particular the introduction of decimal coinage in February 1971. Dismay at the disappearance of the familiar, if implausible, system of twelve pence to the shilling and twenty shillings to the pound was compounded by a not irrational suspicion that the change had been used as an excuse to raise prices. Inflation was – along with the trade unions – becoming the dominant story of the decade, and the government's figures were treated with some scepticism, as they failed to match the daily experience of life; according to *The Grocer* magazine, 1971 saw fresh food prices rise by an average of over 12 per cent with particularly steep rises in butter (48 per cent), fish (43 per cent), cheese (38 per cent) and fruit (32 per cent). A discrepancy between the retail prices index (RPI), the official measure of inflation, and the high-street reality was to become common: in October 1973, for example, food prices rose by 3.3 per cent, considerably faster than the already worrying RPI increase of 2 per cent. ('I must dash,' says a housewife in the sitcom *George and Mildred*. 'Get my shopping in before the pound slides again.')

Alongside this steady erosion of certainty about tomorrow's shopping basket was a sense of loss as Heath's restructuring of local government erased historic counties – including Huntingdonshire and, most famously, Rutland – and removed the autonomy of towns such as Plymouth and Bristol that had long prided themselves on their civic identities. And the belief that things were getting out of hand received further support from press reports that in Dudley a new system of metric street numbering was being given a trial: the first house in a street was given the number one, with the next being numbered according to how far away it was – if it was 12 metres from door to door, then it would be number thirteen, and so on. There were further historical losses as yet another wave of regimental amalgamations in the British Army saw the departure, in particular, of the senior Scottish cavalry regiment, the Scots Greys, who dated back to the seventeenth century, and who now disappeared into the Royal Scots Dragoon Guards. The band and pipes of the new regiment recorded an elegiac album, *Farewell to the Greys*, from which came a version of 'Amazing Grace' that topped the singles charts for five weeks in 1972.

Amongst Heath's other changes was the Housing Finance Act of 1972 which sought to address the system of council housing. The provision of low-cost rented accommodation by local authorities had been a key plank in the building of the post-war welfare state, but there had always been a gap between promise and delivery. The novelist James Herbert grew up in London's East End in the 1950s in a house that had been condemned by the council: 'We expected to be moved in six weeks; we ended up living there for fourteen years.' Such problems did not fade and by the 1970s, as the pace of new-build failed to meet demand, the allocation of homes was causing considerable disquiet. In a 1974 episode of the TV series *Special Branch*, Dennis Waterman played Frank Gosling, a character who steals a rocket launcher from an Army base and announces to the press that he did it in protest at the appalling housing conditions he and his family are being forced to live in; their street had been condemned by the council eight years previously and they'd been promised flats on a new estate, but nothing had ever materialized. His father explains what drove Frank to such a desperate act: 'Look, I fought in a war, all through. My lad did five years in Malaya, Kenya, Aden. We never asked for no favours, never been on the assistance or the welfare. Then what happens? They give council houses to any old scroungers that cons them with a hard-luck story and leave us, the real British, in the slums.'

The new Act attempted to address such concerns by introducing a system of fair rents to both council housing and private tenants. It was argued that the existing system forced tenants in privately rented accommodation, however great their need, to pay for those in council homes, regardless of their economic conditions, and that this was manifestly unfair, since it directed subsidies to buildings rather than human beings. Logical though the assertion might be, however, it was undermined by a perception that the Tories didn't actually believe in social housing at all, as demonstrated by their 1970 initiative to sell council homes to tenants, and by Norman Tebbit's declaration in the same year: 'Ideally I would like to see councils out of the business of housing completely. After all, if you can rent a TV set or a car, what is immoral about renting a house?'

Heath had undoubtedly entered Downing Street with every intention of turning around the ship of state. 'God knows we needed a captain,' novelist Peter Van Greenaway had recently written. 'We tacked from left to right under a succession of first mates drunk and incapable on conference wine bottled in Brighton and Blackpool. The ship was adrift and most of the crew didn't give a damn – there were some who'd watch it sink rather than cross a demarcation line to plug the hole.' But the events of the first half of his stewardship demonstrated beyond argument that Heath was not going to be that captain. Industrial disruption was increasing, inflation was rising, the nation was ill at ease and then, in January 1972, the unemployment figures topped 1 million, the worst seasonal figure since the war. For the first time in the century, Prime Minister's Questions had to be suspended, amidst scenes of parliamentary pandemonium. 'You ought to be ashamed of yourself,' shouted Dennis Skinner as he shook his fist in Heath's face. 'You're better fitted to cross the Channel and suck President Pompidou's backside.'

Confronted with a return to mass unemployment (the great fear of Heath's generation, who had lived through the 1930s), with a work-in at the Upper Clyde Shipbuilders, where the workforce were attracting widespread support for their refusal to accept the bankruptcy of the company, and with the bitter taste of defeat at Saltley still in its mouth, the government scrambled to abandon its previous positions. In March 1972 Tony Benn noted in his diary that John Davies, the trade and industry secretary, 'made a great U-turn speech on the budget in which he totally withdrew everything he had ever said about lame ducks, and the House just roared with laughter'. In November the final breach was made with the announcement of a ninety-day statutory freeze on pay and prices, a policy that had hitherto been explicitly ruled out. Enoch Powell, Heath's greatest enemy on his own backbenches, adopted the role of the small boy pointing out the Emperor's intellectual nakedness; had the prime minister, he asked, 'taken leave of his senses?'

It was, even by Powell's standards, a ferocious attack, couched in barely parliamentary language, but he was unrepentant: 'It is fatal for any government, party or person to seek to govern in direct opposition to the principles with which they were entrusted with the right to govern.' And while, as Norman Tebbit recalled, Tory MPs 'rallied reluctantly to the government flag', Powell's intervention struck a chord; these were 'the words that were in the mind of many of us'. Margaret Thatcher was to echo the sentiment: 'He was publicly cold-shouldered, but many privately agreed with him.' The seeds of future discontent were sown here.

And then things got worse. In October 1973 Syria and Egypt launched a coordinated invasion of Israel in what became known as the Yom Kippur War, that being the Jewish holy day on which the attack started. The conflict lasted for under three weeks, but its ramifications were to be felt into the next century.

Britain's immediate response, set by the foreign secretary Alec Douglas-Home, was to suspend arms sales to all the nations involved, seeking a position of neutrality. It wasn't a policy that enjoyed all-party support: Harold Wilson urged solidarity with Israel ('a democratic socialist country'), whilst there were even a few in his party who supported the cause of the Arab peoples, with Labour MP Andrew Faulds arguing that 'it is Israel's intransigence which has made the fourth round of the Arab–Israeli conflict inevitable'.

It was indeed yet another phase in a long-running dispute but, unusually in modern times, the UK had this time played its cards correctly. The Arab nations, perceiving yet again a pro-Israeli bias in the West, determined that they would use their economic muscle to redress historical grievances. 'All Arab Oil Exporting Countries,' announced notices in the newspapers, 'shall forthwith cut their production respectively by no less than 5 per cent of the September production, and maintain the same rate of reduction each month thereafter until the Israeli forces are fully withdrawn from all Arab territories occupied during the June 1967 war, and the legitimate rights of the Palestinian people are restored.' The statement singled out the USA and the Netherlands as being especially pro-Israel, but Sheikh Yamani, the Saudi oil minister who suddenly found himself the most powerful man in the world, took care to exempt Britain from the worst effects of the new restrictions, citing it as having been a friendly nation ever since Douglas-Home had called in 1970 for an Israeli withdrawal from the territories it illegally occupied.

There were a few politicians prepared to celebrate the Arabs' action ('the world underdog has at last risen', exulted the Labour foreign spokes-person, Lord Kennet, before being obliged to apologize), but mostly the attitude was a sudden, shocked sobriety as the country snapped out of its hangover from the '60s. Because, although oil supplies were still reaching Britain, the price for crude oil rose steeply from $2 a barrel in January to $7 in December, adding massively to the inflationary pressures already present in the British economy. And, to exacerbate matters, the miners began another overtime ban on 12 November 1973, pursuing a pay claim in defiance of the government's wages policy, and squeezing energy supplies still further.

Two days later, even as the country took a holiday to celebrate the wedding of Princess Anne to Captain Mark Phillips, and as the worst trade deficit to date was announced and the lending rate rose to a record high of 13 per cent, there dawned Ted Heath's fifth and final state of emergency. This time it was deadly serious, the longest-running such emergency since 1926. Street lighting was ordered to be cut by half, electric heating was forbidden in workplaces, a 50 mph speed limit was imposed on motor-ways, and floodlighting was banned at sports events; the latter prompted the football league to break a taboo by introducing Sunday matches to replace those on weekday evenings: 'We are still against the principle,' said league secretary Alan Hardaker. 'But it is obvious that clubs are losing spectators and this is one way to help them.'

As the crisis dragged on over the winter, further restrictions were announced, including a 10.30 p.m. curfew on television broadcasts that generated a great deal of hostility. (In practice, it worked out that BBC and ITV alternated between 10.20 and 10.30 closedowns, in an attempt to limit the power surge as the entire nation switched on its kettles.) And when the TV was on, there was no escaping the despondency. 'Keep your fingers crossed against a power cut tonight,' advised the *Times* television listings, with a note of heavy sarcasm. 'You can then watch an extensive, exhaus-tive, investigative and no doubt authoritative Energy Crisis Special.' The two-and-a-half-hour show didn't set many pulses racing. Even the most remote context offered little relief; a January 1974 episode of *It Ain't Half Hot Mum*, a sitcom set in India in 1945, depicted a British Army camp blacked out as electricity and telephone workers go on strike in protest at punkawallahs being made redundant.

Britain, of course, was not uniquely hit by the oil crisis. West Germany outlawed Sunday driving, while Holland, having all oil supplies from the Middle East cut off, appealed for help to the other members of the EEC in the vain hope that they might share their allowances; with no such solidarity having been received, the country introduced petrol rationing, a move that proved too far even for Heath, though ration books were distributed just in case. (The first to arrive in the hands of the general public were those stolen by a gang of thieves, who broke into an Eltham sub-post office for the purpose of being first on their block with the coupons). Despite such measures by other countries, though, nowhere were the difficulties seen in such traumatic terms as they were in Britain. Partly this was the result of the industrial action by the miners, soon to be compounded by an overtime ban by power engineers and a rail workers' strike; partly it was because of the state of unease induced by the spread of the Irish civil war to the mainland – bombs were going off at the rate of one a night in London over Christmas 1973; but mostly it was due to the loss of nerve by a government so used to living in a state of panic that it now seemed determined to enlist the whole nation in its struggles, perhaps in the hope that the spirit of the Blitz might yet be rekindled. (The French magazine *Paris Match* echoed the thought by talking of the mood of the nation as 'the three-day spirit'.)

During the 1972 miners' strike, the government had urged the nation to restrict energy use at home with the slogan 'Think before you switch on'; now it was sounding even more desperate: 'SOS – Switch Off Something now,' it pleaded in full-page newspaper adverts. 'Please heat only one room,' it added. 'If you don't, power cuts could soon be blacking out whole areas for hours on end.' Energy minister Patrick Jenkin even suggested that everyone should brush their teeth in the dark, until the resultant outcry made it clear that there were limits beyond which even the British people could not be pushed, and he was forced to climb down: 'The suggestion I made on radio the other day was not a practical one,' he was heard to mumble, as he tucked into his humble pie. The obsession with controlling consumption at the most trivial level extended as far as telling people not to iron underwear and to use a clothesline to dry clothes 'when the weather's fine'. This was, in short, a government in crisis, an administration that – uniquely in the industrialized world – felt the necessity to put its country's industry on a three-day working week, starting on 2 January 1974 (New Year's Day had newly been designated as a bank holiday in England and Wales).

The effect on the population was mixed. In Clay Cross, Derbyshire, the council responded by defying Heath and keeping street lights on full power: 'Why should we help the government?' asked council leader David Skinner. 'Why bother saving electricity? It only saves the government talking to the men who deserve a better deal.' A similar attitude was evident in a February 1974 episode of the TV sitcom *Till Death Us Do Part*, written and recorded as near to transmission as possible. 'We're helping the miners,' cried Alf Garnett's daughter, Rita, as she and her socialist husband Mike rushed around the house, turning on every electrical appliance they could find, and launching a counter-slogan to the government's SOS: 'Don't save fuel – use it up!'

In general, however, the attitude seemed to be a determination to eat, drink and be as merry as possible, in the face of adversity. 'Bad news all the time,' noted the National Theatre director, Peter Hall, in his diary. 'An economic slump threatens. The bomb scares go on. The miners continue their go-slow. The trains are in chaos. Meantime the nation is on a prodigal pre-Christmas spending spree.' There were reports that sales of wines and spirits were hitting an all-time high for early December, while bicycle shops were also experiencing a huge increase in business, and chef Jennifer Paterson was discovering that nothing rounded off a blacked-out dinner party quite so well as setting light to a crêpe Suzette. And for those too young to worry about being laid off from work, Christmas 1973 was actually a very happy time. The use of candles, albeit arising from necessity, simply meant fun if you were a child, and there was even the possibility that the start of the next school term might be delayed due to the crisis (sadly, it was not to be). It was also the high point of glitter pop, with the top five singles including records by Wizzard, Gary Glitter, Alvin Stardust and, at #1, Slade with what was to become the best-loved song of the era, 'Merry Xmas Everybody'. 'We were right in the middle of a disastrous period politically. There were power cuts every day and half the work force seemed to be on strike,' remembered the band's singer and lyricist, Noddy Holder. '"Merry Xmas" was a happy uplifting record. I'm sure that's part of the reason why so many people liked it.' His contemporaries too were busy producing foot-stomping singalongs delivered in ever more extraordinary costumes, as though they wished to be the antidote to the gathering gloom.

But the music industry was itself hit hard by the crisis. Californian-born Russell Mael was the singer with the band Sparks, who – after two unsuccessful albums in America – had finally got their big break, signing with a British company, to their great joy: 'We'd moved to England and this was our dream. We were always Anglophiles.' But when the group came to record *Kimono My House*, their first album for Island Records, they were surprised to find that sessions in the studio were severely curtailed by the power cuts. 'We thought, okay so you just work around that,' Mael recalled, but as the recording schedule dragged on, they were told that worse might yet come: 'Well lads, even if the record does get finished, there may not be enough vinyl to go around.' Since vinyl was an oil product, there were fears of shortages, and some of the leading record companies announced that they would issue no new releases in January 1974. (It was from this time that records became noticeably thinner.) The Sparks album did emerge in due course, but even then the problems continued; as the single 'This Town Ain't Big Enough for Both of Us' entered the charts, the band turned up to record their appearance on *Top of the Pops* and were promptly thrown off the show for not having Musicians' Union clearance. With blackouts, a vinyl famine and union disputes to contend with, and remembering too the experience of shopping by candlelight during a power cut, Mael was left somewhat bemused: 'It wasn't part of our dream of coming to Britain.'

Having already seen its economy become something of a laughing stock in Western Europe, Britain now found in the winter of 1973–74 that its reputation had fallen so low that it could be patronized by its former colonies. Idi Amin, who had seized power in Uganda in 1971, was still at this stage regarded more as a comic buffoon than as the brutal dictator he actually was, but he had become for the British public the best-known ruler of an African nation, thanks to his expulsion of Asians from the country and to his headline-grabbing publicity coups. In December 1973 he wrote privately to Heath, regretting 'the alarming economic crisis befalling on Britain', but reassuring him that: 'I have decided to contribute 10,000 Ugandan shillings from my savings, and I am convinced that many Ugandans will donate generously to rescue their innocent friends who are becoming victims of sharp tax increases, tighter credit squeeze and a possible pay squeeze.' The British government declined to respond, so Amin upped the ante by publicly initiating a Save Britain Fund to 'save and assist our former colonial masters from economic catastrophe'. The place chosen for the fund's launch was deliberately symbolic: in 1893 Kampala Hill had seen the Union Flag raised for the first time in Uganda; now it witnessed an auction that raised £2,400 for the old country. Dean Acheson's old comment about Britain having lost an empire but having yet to find a role seemed ever more apposite. Or perhaps, suggested despairing commentators, Britain had indeed found a role, this time as 'the sick man of Europe'.

In this context, there were many who saw ahead only an ever greater crisis, and who reached for the most terrifying historical parallel they could find: Germany in the pre-dawn of the Nazis. Environment secretary

Geoffrey Rippon commented in December that Britain was 'on the same course as the Weimar government, with runaway inflation and ultra-high employment at the end'. Sadly, it was not even an original observation, with Labour cabinet minister Richard Crossman having made the same comparison in 1970: 'the situation was like the early days of the Weimar Republic, he could see democracy coming to an end'. And the image was to recur throughout the decade; in 1977 the revolutionary communist Tariq Ali, responding to an *ad hominem* attack by a columnist in *The Times*, invoked it yet again: 'If Bernard Levin were to visit some of the more deprived areas of the midlands, the north-east or London, he would be able to get a smell of Weimar in the air.'

No mere politician, however, captured the sense of decadence and decline that descended on Britain in the latter part of Heath's premiership quite as comprehensively as did David Bowie, the most significant figure to emerge in the artistic world during that period. Having spent eight years desperately trying to become a star by any means at his disposal, but with only the novelty hit of 'Space Oddity' in 1969 to sustain him, Bowie went for broke in 1972, relaunching himself as the latest and last rock messiah in his alter ego of Ziggy Stardust. His first appearance on *Top of the Pops* with his new backing band, the Spiders From Mars, was to become enshrined in music mythology as the high point of that programme's long history. Clad in a sequinned jumpsuit and platform boots, with his arm draped lovingly around his beautiful guitarist, Mick Ronson, the frighteningly thin and self-proclaimed bisexual Bowie told his tale of salvation in the shape of a 'Starman' who'd 'like to come and meet us, but he thinks he'd blow our minds'. There wasn't a member of his instantly acquired following who didn't recognize that he was the subject of the song as well as its narrator: he looked and sounded like nothing else on Earth.

The album whence that single came was *The Rise and Fall of Ziggy Stardust and the Spiders From Mars*, which opened in appropriately apocalyptic manner with 'Five Years' ('that's all we got'), and went on to revive the spirit of Weimar cabaret reincarnated as rock & roll: 'People stared at the make-up on his face,' began 'Lady Stardust', adding that 'femmes fatales emerged from shadows to watch this creature fair' who 'sang songs of darkness and disgrace'. The album never got higher than #5 in the charts, but it did spend two years in the top 50 and brought Bowie the stardom he had long craved. The title track of its sequel, *Aladdin Sane* (1973), added to its punning name a subtitle – '1913-1938-197?' – that reiterated the pre-war implications of his work, while keeping alive the theme of celebration in the face of catastrophe ('Battle cries and champagne, just in time for sunrise'). By the time of *Diamond Dogs* (1974), the sense of complete collapse had moved into the present, as the spoken introduction made clear: 'And in the death, as the last few corpses lay rotting on the slimy thoroughfare . . .'

Bowie's success in 1972–74 was primarily based on his musical vision, but to a generation whose older brother was 'back at home with his Beatles and his Stones', he was also the first rock artist to speak directly of the chaos that was modern Britain, to admit the failure of post-war dreams of progress and to offer instead an escape into fantasy. 'Bevan tried to change the nation,' he shrugged, but 'I could make a transformation as a rock & roll star.'

2

Rivals

'This town ain't big enough for both of us'

Apart from the wilder fringes, political extremism in Britain today is represented by Powellism and Baden-Powellism, with Mr Benn as Labour's Boy Scout.
Terence Lancaster, *Daily Mirror* (1975)

I think our hope for the future is that England remains a moderate country. But moderates are easily taken advantage of by extremists. Enoch Powell is nuts, but it is evident that he's nuts. Tony Benn is nuts, but appears dangerously sane.
Peter Hall, diary entry (1975)

In the case of two noteworthy contenders of our time, J Enoch Powell and Anthony Wedgwood Benn, the reason for their failure to reach the top is surely obvious. They both look barmy.
Kingsley Amis, *Memoirs* (1991)

Ever since 1964, when *That Was the Week That Was* had its third series cancelled because of the forthcoming general election, British broadcasters have been convinced that the country is particularly sensitive to the effects of television during campaigning, capable of having its votes switched by an unanswered argument. 1970 was no exception. As soon as the election was announced by Harold Wilson, ITV responded by saying that it would postpone its broadcast of 'Amos Green Must Live', the latest instalment of the thriller series *Callan*.

The episode in question starred Corin Redgrave as the eponymous Amos Green, 'a politician who believes that coloured immigration is dangerous to Britain and must be stopped'. Smoothly persuasive, he is building a large following with his TV appearances: 'The people in this country know what they want,' he declares. 'What they want is not statistics, not facts dressed up, they want action. They want themselves;

no visitors, no immigrants.' As a prospective parliamentary candidate, he finds himself under threat from a rogue member of a radical civil rights group known as Black Glove. 'We do not as an organization believe in violence,' insists Anna, the leader of the group (Nina Baden-Semper). 'England is not yet America. But, one day if things don't change and it comes to violence, to protect ourselves and our interests, we must be ready.' One of the group's adherents, however, believes that the time has indeed now come, and David Callan, the secret service agent portrayed by Edward Woodward, is sent in to protect Green from the would-be killer.

The reason for the programme's ban during the campaign required little explanation in the press. The anti-immigration stance, the populist appeal, the Old Testament first name – no one could be in any doubt about the real-life model for Amos Green, nor of his significance. In that 1970 election, it was reported, the Press Association sent one correspondent to cover Harold Wilson and one for Edward Heath; Enoch Powell, on the other hand, was assigned two journalists just for him. That was how important Powell had become, though he held no position save that of backbench MP for a Wolverhampton seat: 'Enoch has had more effect on the country than either party,' said Tony Benn, in admiration rather than anger, as he assessed his own position after the government's defeat.

The idea of a Powell figure being assassinated, and the official terror at the ramifications of such an event, was not confined to *Callan*; a fuller exploration of the same theme came in Arthur Wise's 1970 novel *Who Killed Enoch Powell?* The story starts in a small, unnamed Yorkshire town where Powell's speech in a village hall ends in tragedy when a bomb explodes beneath the platform, killing the MP outright and sparking a sense of panic in Westminster. 'There are millions that think he's given them an identity,' argues the leader of the Labour opposition. 'And there are nearly as many who think he's a kind of Messiah.' As word spreads of the assassination, despite an attempted news blackout by the government, large areas of the country witness spontaneous demonstrations that rapidly degenerate into rioting and violence, and the home secretary begins to wonder who might fill this vacuum: 'What's been the pattern of public life these past few years?' he asks rhetorically. 'Student unrest – violence in every shape and form – near civil war in Ulster – this Glasgow business. The country's sick of it. Sick of permissiveness, sick of teenage drug merchants, sick of youth-worship, sick of being "swinging". You know what it wants? It wants a strong man – the iron fist.'

That strong man turns out to be Colonel Monkton (his name conflating those of the Commonwealth generals George Monck and Henry Ireton), a controversial war hero who is called out of retirement by the prime minister to take control of the situation. Unfortunately for his political masters, he is determined also to take advantage of the confusion caused by Powell's death by broadening the issue: 'His vision did not restrict the situation to the assassination of Enoch Powell and the nationwide unrest that it had triggered off. He saw deeper causes behind it. He saw a country losing its shape and coherence, a country in desperate need of discipline. He saw mass immigration as a principal cause of that lack of coherence – "this injection of foreign bodies" as he called it.' Exploiting the racial tension, he sets about staging a military coup.

The fact that such a novel could be written, and be received so well, was testament not only to Wise's skill as a writer, but to the very plausibility of the plot: 'Frightening,' said the *Morning Telegraph*, 'all this could happen if EP was assassinated for real.' The book was nominated for an Edgar Award as best novel of the year, but lost out to Frederick Forsyth's *The Day of the Jackal*, the story of an assassination attempt on another controversial right-wing leader; it wasn't the last time that Powell and General de Gaulle were to be linked.

The object of all this attention was perhaps the most extraordinary figure in post-war British politics. Dressed with severe correctness at all times, and in his trademark Homburg hat, Enoch Powell already looked in the mid-1960s like a throwback to an earlier era, evoking a formality that was slightly at odds with his educated Black Country accent; his most famous photo opportunity saw him in topcoat and hat bouncing on a pogo stick, an Edwardian bank clerk adrift in swinging London. As long ago as 1955, the *Spectator* journalist Henry Fairlie had correctly identified him as 'old-fashioned' and pinned down his eccentric political style: 'He simply believes in Order and Authority and is always prepared to offer a half-brilliant, half-mad, intellectual defence of them.' Even so, he was clearly one of the future Tory stars who emerged during the long period of Conservative rule in the '50s, and despite resigning as a treasury minister in 1958 over the issue of increased public expenditure, he returned to the government, serving in the cabinet as health secretary in 1962–63. In the party's leadership election of 1965 he unexpectedly stood as the standard-bearer of the right, and though he attracted a mere fifteen backers (Heath beat Reginald Maudling by 150 votes to 133), his support did include the likes of Nicholas Ridley and John Biffen, later to become cabinet ministers under Margaret Thatcher. His reward was the defence portfolio in the shadow cabinet, appropriately enough for a man who had enlisted as a private in the Royal Warwickshire Regiment in 1939 and had risen to become the youngest brigadier in the British Army by the end of the war.

This mostly steady advance through the party ranks was halted sensationally one Saturday lunchtime in April 1968, when he delivered the 'rivers of blood' speech that transformed him, literally overnight, into the most controversial politician in the country. The speech was not his first venture into the charged area of immigration, but it raised the stakes massively, representing a complete break from the established consensus on the subject. His essential argument was, he insisted, 'the official policy of the Conservative Party' – a reduction in the rate of future immigration and the encouragement of those immigrants already in Britain to return to their countries of origin – but the language he used was far removed from anything that the Tory leadership could possibly countenance. In particular, he cited a white constituent's comment that 'In this country in fifteen or twenty years' time the black man will have the whip hand over the white man,' and he quoted in full a letter that claimed to recount the experience of another constituent of his, an elderly white woman terrorized by her black neighbours: 'Windows are broken. She finds excreta pushed through her letterbox. When she goes to the shops, she is followed by children, charming, wide-grinning piccaninnies. They cannot speak English, but one word they know. "Racialist," they chant.'

To these comments, reported by Powell without qualification or attribution, he added his own gift of oratory, derived in part from his status as a leading classical scholar. The speech was studded with phrases that would reverberate for years to come: 'Those whom the gods wish to destroy, they first make mad. We must be mad, literally mad,' he exclaimed, in wide-eyed, disbelieving wonder. 'It is like watching a nation busily engaged in heaping up its own funeral pyre.' And he saved the best for last: 'As I look ahead, I am filled with foreboding. Like the Roman, I seem to see "the River Tiber foaming with much blood".' In fact, he didn't quite say that, since his quote from Book VI of Virgil's *Aeneid* was delivered in its original Latin (and thus passed over the heads of most of the local Tories gathered in Birmingham to hear him), but he helpfully translated the phrase in his press hand-outs to ensure maximum coverage in the media, and an adaptation of the phrase became the shorthand way to refer to Powell's position: he was widely understood to have predicted 'rivers of blood' flowing through Britain's streets as a result of racial conflict.

The reporting of the Birmingham speech in the Sunday newspapers sealed his immediate fate, while revealing how far the political elite had drifted from the population. Heath was horrified and sacked him from the

Conservative front bench, to which he was never to return, saying that his words were 'racialist in tone', even as the first of tens of thousands of letters were being written in support of those words. In a subsequent speech, Powell claimed that there was a 'gulf between the overwhelming majority of the country on the one side, and on the other side a tiny minority, with almost a monopoly hold upon the channels of communication', and there was much truth in his assertion. A Gallup poll in the *Daily Telegraph* a fortnight after the 'rivers of blood' showed 74 per cent support for his views, with 69 per cent saying that Heath had been wrong to dismiss him; just before the speech, a poll asking who should become Tory leader in the event that Heath stepped down had given Powell just 1 per cent support, now he was the front-runner with 24 per cent. And to confirm the allegation of media bias came this testimony: 'Television programmes deliberately underplayed the strength of racist feelings for years, out of the misguided but honourable feeling that inflammatory utterances could do damage,' admitted *Panorama* producer Jeremy Isaacs in late 1968. 'But the way feelings erupted after Enoch Powell's speech this year was evidence to me that the feeling has been under-represented on television, and other media.'

The fallout from that single speech changed British politics entirely. There was a huge groundswell of support in the parts of the country most affected, with many believing that immigration had been forced through without consultation: 'Surely only very clever people could fail to understand so simple a point,' said Powell, conveniently forgetting his own position as the cleverest of all Tory MPs. This paradox was reflected in Arthur Wise's novel, as a man in the crowd queuing to hear Powell's speech complains about 'bloody long-haired intellectuals', and a journalist reflects: 'Doesn't that throw some light on something? Because here he is queuing to hear one of the purest intellectuals. And when he's heard him he'll clap and cheer with the rest. But will he be quite sure what it is he's cheering? Or will it perhaps be something else he's cheering, something that hasn't been said?' It was a prescient observation, for the response to the 'rivers of blood' also changed Powell himself; he was, wrote sometime Tory MP Matthew Parris, 'a once-bisexual man, free-thinking and sensitive, seduced and finally trapped by the cheers of the mob: a free spirit cast in the role of populist bigot'. Meantime, he became the most famous politician in Britain, despite never achieving the final accolade of the times: 'The one I really can't do at all is Enoch Powell,' admitted Mike Yarwood. 'I put on a moustache and a Homburg but I can't get the voice right.'

What is sometimes forgotten is the immediate context in which the speech was delivered. Powell had recently returned from a trip to America, where city after city was enduring race riots on a scale never experienced in Britain; indeed, less than three weeks earlier, Martin Luther King had been assassinated in Memphis, sparking a new wave of unrest. These were the rivers of blood that Powell prophesied, as Callan's boss, Hunter, made clear: 'If Green dies, there'll be a real mess-up. We'll have a riot like Watts on our own back-door.' In his election address to his Wolverhampton constituents in 1970, Powell emphasized the same point: continued immigration, he warned, 'carries a threat of division, violence and bloodshed of American dimensions, and adds a powerful weapon to the armoury of anarchy'.

That haunting image from the other side of the Atlantic had been articulated in fiction even before Powell: 'The government is a bit slow in linking the outrageous activities of the Black Muslims in America with the black threat at our own front door,' notes the eponymous anti-hero of Robert Muller's 1965 novel of future fascism *The Lost Diaries of Albert Smith* (later retitled *After All, This Is England*). Indeed, the storyline of that book has uncanny pre-echoes of Powell's split with the Tories. 'Sir Charles Crossmere, MP, that excellent speaker and VC, who has always struck me as a man of great common sense, courage and dignity, has left the Conservative Party,' reports Smith. 'This has been brewing for a long time, of course. Crossmere has been attacking the Tory leadership for its tepid opposition policies for as long as I can remember. I fancy he's a man to be reckoned with now that he's out in the political wilderness.' Crossmere goes on to launch a new party whose seizure of power replicates the rise of the Nazis, a process that leads our narrator to become a clerk in a concentration camp on the south coast. As democracy is being systematically destroyed, the emergence of strong leadership is celebrated by the *Daily Mirror*: 'We are lucky to have men in charge today who are determined to clamp down on wranglers and lead-swingers, on Edwardian fuddy-duddies, who have for far too long held on to office through the old-boy network, and on the professional "England-is-never-right" brigade.'

The coup against democracy had been a recurrent theme in popular literature for many years, but had reached a new level of paranoia in the late 1960s. At the start of that decade, Constantine Fitzgibbon's *When the Kissing Had to Stop* had told of a left-wing takeover of Britain backed by Moscow, a tale which had sufficient resonance to see the novel reissued in 1971 and 1978, key moments of trade union activity. But as the years wore on, the politics began to change, and Gillian Freeman's *The Leader* (1965),

Peter Van Greenaway's *The Man Who Held the Queen to Ransom and Sent Parliament Packing* (1968) and Robin Cook's *A State of Denmark* (1970) – amongst others in the genre – all concerned the rise of right-wing figures. Although the narrative tone was in general disapproving, the motivation was clearly spelt out and sympathetically understood: a sense that the country was slipping out of control, that the system itself had failed. 'Britain today is a land without purpose, without hope, without a will of its own. The political system creating this state of affairs has much to answer for,' wrote Van Greenaway, and the same note was struck in novel after novel of the period. 'England was impotent now, but talkative, petulant, critical and, in decline, intellectually arrogant,' argued James Barlow's crime classic *The Burden of Proof* (filmed as *Villain* in 1970 with Richard Burton). 'Nobody could do anything now without being accountable to the scorn of the liberal intellectuals in print or on television. England was too articulate at the top. Nobody, even in a Socialist liberal permissive society, had the slightest notion of the wishes of the people, out there beyond the great conversational shop of London.'

This distrust of London began almost where the city's borders ended. Michael Palin, visiting friends in Guildford in 1971, noted in his diary: 'They talked about "London" as a descriptive term for all rather suspect, critical, left-wing, un-British opinions.' This was very much Powell's potential constituency. In this version of modern British history, society had moved too far, too fast, and the metropolitan elite, seduced by the post-war consensus in Westminster and Whitehall, had lost touch with the people it claimed to represent. Disillusionment with parties, with the very structures of politics, was growing apace and Powell was seen by millions to be the only hope, the man who expressed the rage of Caliban at not seeing his own face in the mirror.

In the 1970 election, Powell's contribution was the subject of huge press coverage. With Heath widely expected to lose, there was little doubt among commentators that Powell was positioning himself for a leadership challenge in the aftermath of defeat. His words were superficially supportive of the party, but his colleagues were not fooled as to their intent: 'I hope and believe that Mr Enoch Powell will learn to support the policy of the Conservative Party,' warned Quintin Hogg, 'but the Conservative Party does not support Mr Powell.' Meanwhile, so intense were the feelings that he stirred that he had a police guard mounted on his home, and at the local Conservative Association all the signs identifying the building were taken down: 'Bolts are on the front door, and sticky tape criss-crosses all the ground-floor windows – to stop the glass shattering if bricks are thrown.'

Harold Wilson, well aware of the populist potential of Powell, instructed that Labour politicians should simply avoid all reference to him, in the hope that race would not become an issue in the campaign. But there was one man who was prepared to break the embargo, and who ensured front-page headlines both for himself and, more especially, for his target: AMAZING ATTACK ON ENOCH screamed the *Sun*; THE ENOCH PERIL warned the *Daily Mirror*, while the *Daily Telegraph* clarified the source of the outrage: 'BELSEN FLAG' JIBE BY BENN AT POWELL. 'The most evil feature of Powell's new Conservatism is the hatred it is stirring up,' Tony Benn said in a speech that received saturation coverage. 'It has started with an attack on Asians and blacks. But when hate is released it quickly gets out of control. Already Powell has spoken against the Irish. Anti-Semitism is waiting to be exploited as Mosley exploited it before. Every single religious or racial minority can be made the scapegoat for every problem we face.' Invoking Mosley was bad enough, but Benn went further with a particularly personal attack that he regretted almost immediately: 'The flag hoisted in Wolverhampton is beginning to look like the one that fluttered over Dachau and Belsen.'

The severity of the charge, linking a former cabinet minister to the Holocaust, was without parallel in British politics and it 'changed the whole emphasis of the Labour campaign'. Actual supporters of Powell were thin on the ground in the media, save in the self-proclaimed reactionary world of the *Daily Telegraph*'s Peter Simple column (which claimed that the metaphorical flag was 'beginning to look, from some angles, uncannily like the Union Jack'), but the condemnation of Benn was close to universal: a 'grotesque exaggeration' said Sir Keith Joseph, 'savage and senseless' said the *Mirror*, 'silly and extravagant' said *Sun* columnist Jon Akass. Powell himself had the most authoritative response of all: 'In 1939,' he replied, with seething dignity, 'I voluntarily returned from Australia to this country to serve as a private soldier against Germany and Nazism.'

With the benefit of hindsight, some of the responses to the Benn–Powell clash are rich in irony. 'Mostly he talks about money,' Akass wrote dismissively of Powell's then unfashionable monetarist arguments. 'He has an arid and austere gospel, a theory that the Labour Government is ruining the country by printing money. I do not think that this proposition will win many votes.' Meanwhile the former BBC Sports Personality of the Year, and now Tory MP, Christopher Chataway, mocked Labour's attempt to paint Powell as a future leader of the party: 'It is nonsense, of course. It would make as much sense for us to try to threaten the nation with Michael Foot as leader of the Labour Party.' Thirteen years later, Powell's monetarist god-daughter was to trounce the Labour leader, Michael Foot, at the polls.

Beyond these diversions, Benn's speech was one of the crucial events of the campaign. As the psephologists, in the wake of Wilson's unexpected defeat, desperately attempted to explain what had happened, the Harris polling organization 'reckoned that Benn made the biggest mistake of the campaign by attacking Powell, since immigration was almost the only issue on which the Tories had a better poll rating than Labour.' For Powell as a constituency MP, the election was a triumphant vindication, despite the claims of commentators that 'what he is saying will not swing votes among intelligent people.' ENOCH DOUBLES HIS MAJORITY read the second-tier headline on the front page of the *Sun*'s post-election issue, but it was a pyrrhic victory. The power of his appeal was critical in swinging working-class votes to the Tories, thereby ensuring the success of his arch-enemy, Ted Heath, and guaranteeing that he, four years older than Heath, would be frozen out of the Conservative leadership. His popularity had effectively destroyed his own ambition. Unless, of course, the situation in the country degenerated to such an extent that he was called upon as a strongman figure, much as Colonel Monkton had been in *Who Killed Enoch Powell?* Which scenario was not far from his own thinking.

Effectively Powell was going into internal exile. In the early 1960s he had been compared to Robespierre, in tribute to his incorruptible intellectual certainty; now he was hoping that parallels might be found with another French figure, aiming at the model of Charles de Gaulle, who ostentatiously retired to his estate in Colombey-les-deux-Eglises in 1953, only to be recalled to become president when the Fourth Republic collapsed. Shades of de Gaulle were everywhere apparent in Powell's position during the Heath years. In 1972 he visited Alan Clark, then a young right-wing Tory MP, who recorded in his diary that Powell 'would not say how he hoped to attain power'; his only strategy appeared to be that 'the Lord will provide.' Another diarist, Tony Benn, noted in 1973: 'At the Commons I saw John Biffen who told me, "Enoch Powell is waiting for the call."'

That call never did come, but the image of the politician who wouldn't be silenced, who spoke the truth at the expense of his career, proved remarkably resilient, even if it was almost exclusively associated with his arguments about race and immigration. In 1977, just as the Tories were moving towards the sound-money economics he had long preached, a spin-off novel from the TV series *The Sweeney* was demonstrating how his name had already passed into the language. 'Joe's as straight as a die,' says a long-distance trucker. 'He's also very right-wing, a right Enoch-Poweller. Me, I don't mind the Pakis coming in to join their husbands and fathers. I agree with you it's a crying shame to keep families apart – let one in, you've got to let them all in. But Joe won't see it that way.' Such followers seldom worried about the finer points of Powell's intellectual rationalizations, instead invoking his name as a talisman to support primitive prejudice. In one of the *Hazell* novels by Gordon Williams and Terry Venables, a minicab driver dismisses the driving ability of 'nig-nogs': 'Not their fault I suppose, they just ain't got the brains for it. Enoch Powell, squire, he knows the score.' His other reputation was as a great pontificator; in *Coronation Street* Ena Sharples once complained that Albert Tatlock was too opinionated: 'You're worse than Enoch Powell.'

The extensive references in the fiction of the period demonstrate that, despite his dry-as-a-bone faith in the capitalist market – except where it touched the free movement of labour – Powell had an appeal and a public recognition that reached into the unlikeliest of places.

The comedian Charlie Williams was born in Yorkshire in 1929, the son of a white woman and a Barbadian ex-soldier; at 14 he went to work as a miner, before spending twelve years as a professional footballer with Doncaster Rovers. He subsequently turned to the club circuit, singing and telling jokes, the punch-lines of which he would invariably greet with a raucous cackle. 'He had great energy,' Lenny Henry wrote in a personal tribute on his death. 'When he came on stage, you were swept away by his good will and his grown up-ness. He had been poor, he had been a part of this country, and he had seen and endured things that people in the audience would never know about because they hadn't been in his skin.' When in 1971 ITV picked up a handful of club comics and put them together on the show *The Comedians*, Williams became an instant star and probably the most recognizable black Englishman. As such, his attitude to Powell was ambivalent. 'It sounds daft coming from me,' he argued, 'but in some ways you've got to go along with Enoch Powell. I reckon that immigration should be on a measured scale and under proper control.' It was a different version of Powell, however, that featured regularly in Williams's routines, one that was transformed into a nightmarish figure with a psychopathic hatred of Pakistanis:

> Enoch Powell went to the prime minister and said: 'After I'm dead, I'd like you to get 300 Pakistanis, and I want them all to stamp on my grave.'
> Prime minister: 'Are you sure, Enoch?'

Enoch: 'I'm quite sure. In fact 400, if you can round them up.'
Prime minister: 'Fair enough. Where do you want to be buried?'
Enoch: 'At sea.'

Jos White, another black stand-up who broke out from working men's clubs to make a name for himself on *The Comedians*, told gags in a similar vein:

Enoch Powell was seen crying on top of a cliff. Someone said: 'Why are you crying?'
He said, 'I just saw this bus load of Pakistanis go over the edge of the cliff.'
The other replied, 'And you're crying about it? Why?'
Enoch said, 'There were two empty seats.'

While this public perception was developing, Powell himself was proving to be the gadfly of the Tory party, and, as Clough Williams-Ellis, the architect of Portmeirion, once noted: 'There is nothing weighty or authoritative about a gadfly, yet for all that its sting has sometimes so tickled or exasperated the noblest of the brutes that his plunging reactions have changed the very course of history.' Powell voted against his own party on 115 occasions in the lifetime of the Heath government, more than any other MP, and kept a small but dedicated group of followers who, like him, hoped that his day might yet come. He also provided inspiration for the man who would become his greatest rival as a populist but controversial political figure, capable of attracting the most extreme of reactions from friend and foe alike. 'Tony Benn,' wrote Susan Crosland, 'saw himself as the left-wing answer to Enoch Powell calling in the wilderness.'

Though he would sometimes appear on the same side of a political debate, Benn shared none of Powell's principles, save those of courtesy, calmness and a fiercely proclaimed devotion to both Parliament and the power of reason. Characteristic of their differences was their attitude to Christianity: on the one side, Benn came from a Congregationalist background and found little problem in reconciling the message of the Gospels with a socialist interpretation of society; on the other, Powell was the most unorthodox of modern Anglicans, insisting that 'I find it insuperably difficult to draw deductions from my Christian religion as to the choices which lie open to me in my political life.'

In his approach to seeking political influence, however, Benn drew heavily on Powell. Like him, he too was compared to Robespierre and sought instead the more comforting example of de Gaulle: 'I should give serious and thoughtful lectures and try to get my message across that way,' he wrote in his diary on New Year's Eve, 1975. 'That is the Colombey-les-deux-Eglises strategy of waiting and arguing because the media have made me out to be destructive and fanatical, just as they did Enoch Powell. Yet I have slogged it out and soldiered on. I am not what they make me out to be and truth will out . . .'

One other thing was shared by the two men: the sense of exasperation they inspired in their colleagues, who struggled to understand what it was that drove them to adopt so cheerfully the label of maverick. The Tory minister Ian Gilmour saw in Powell's stance on immigration 'some combination of ambition, frustration and lack of judgement', a view echoed by Labour MP Austin Mitchell when he wrote of Benn: 'Whether the motive was ambition, incompetently pursued, or a propensity to take intellectual enthusiasm to absurd conclusions, was never clear.' As Michael Foot was later to point out: 'Tony fell out with his colleagues in almost every group he ever worked with.' In both cases, at a time when the choice of party leader was decided by sitting MPs, their ability to antagonize their immediate electorate did little to enhance their prospects of achieving the highest office.

A third-generation MP, Tony Benn came from a family of established radicalism and, having fought long and successfully to rid himself of the title of the 2nd Viscount Stansgate that he had inherited on his father's death in 1960, he emerged as the very epitome of Harold Wilson's technological socialism. As postmaster general and then as minister of technology, he flung himself into a series of initiatives that seemed to reflect his fascination for gadgetry of all kinds, from the Post Office Tower to Concorde, from colour television to the Giro Bank. Amongst his many contributions to the everyday life of the nation, commemorative stamps and postcodes were introduced, telephone numbers lost their three-letter area codes and pirate radio stations were outlawed.

Even during this period of office, however, Benn was beginning to feel the need to spread his wings. The election defeat offered him the opportunity so to do; he spent 1970–73 in the cocoon of opposition, entering it as a Wilsonian caterpillar espousing the virtues of efficiency and modernization, and emerging as a socialist butterfly. Determined to reforge the links between the party and the working class, he displayed a passionate espousal of workerism: 'This is the way forward in industry. I have no doubts about it,' he noted just before the 1970 election. 'You have got to recognize that the shop stewards do now represent power in factories and you have to deal with them and give them higher status in your thinking than the customers or the shareholders because they are the guys that build the product.' By 1973 he was firmly fixed on his future course: 'The most significant development in my own thinking in the last three years,' he told his diary, 'has been a recognition that the trade union movement not only has to defend its own rights and should be supported by us but ought to have a joint programme with the party.'

During this period too, he became the chairman of the party, taking office in October 1971 and chairing the 1972 conference. His tenure coincided with a wave of discontent from the constituency members, following what was seen as the elitism of the Wilson government. 'At present the upper reaches of this party seem to resemble a vast bed where the privileged indulge in an orgy of self-congratulation, while participation is by invitation only,' said a delegate at the 1970 conference, adding hopefully: 'The rest of us want to join in the fun.' The response of Benn, who had already argued that 'leadership does come from below', was to launch a campaign known as Participation 1972, an early attempt to build what would later become known as a rainbow coalition, bringing in pressure groups, single-issue campaigners, churches and others to help debate the future of Labour politics. ('Why not add Women's Lib and the "gay" groups?' a party official was heard to sneer, emphasizing how much work had yet to be done.)

Of these two strands in Benn's thinking – the celebration of the working class and the embrace of new political forces – it was the former that was to attract the most suspicion in the '70s, even within the labour movement, where his background was never entirely forgotten. 'Benn has an aristocratic disdain for British workers which he skilfully camouflages with empty rhetoric,' wrote Frank Chapple, leader of the electricians' union. 'He dismisses the views of the great bulk of workers and shop stewards and blames the media for brainwashing them.' Chapple went on to say that 'there was no one for whom I felt such a profound contempt over the years as I did for Benn.' (Benn's own feelings for Chapple were less combative: 'I like him, in a curious way, though he's a thug.') Austin Mitchell similarly pointed to his origins, saying that Benn venerated 'the working class, its traditions and institutions and particularly the trade unions, as only someone from a genuine upper-class background can'. And even those who had kinder words to say didn't fail to mention class: 'Tony's weakness was his inordinate love of the working-class Party members, and they loved and adored him in return,' noted Labour MP, Joe Ashton. 'He had the natural charm of a polite public schoolboy.' It was an image enhanced by a deceptively youthful complexion and by clear, teetotal eyes that seemed permanently widened in an attitude of frank amazement at the state of the world.

Aware of these charges that he was, in the phraseology of the 1930s, little more than a Bollinger Bolshevik, Benn underwent a personal as well as a political change in the early 1970s. In the words of Michael Foot, he 'was transformed – the word is too weak; *reincarnated* might be better.' He began with his name. He had never used the title Lord Stansgate, but through the 1950s and '60s he had been known as Anthony Wedgwood Benn, commonly abbreviated to Wedgie; now, as his move leftward became more pronounced, so too did his desire to divest himself of the clearly non-proletarian moniker. 'Today I had the idea that I would resign my Privy Councillorship, my MA and all my honorary doctorates in order to strip myself of what the world had to offer,' he wrote in 1972, 'but whether this would be a good idea, I don't know. But "Wedgie Benn" and "the Rt Honourable Anthony Wedgewood Benn" and all that stuff is impossible. I have been Tony Benn in Bristol for a long time.' He informed the BBC the following year that that was how he was to be referred to in future.

Meanwhile, he was busy editing his background in the pages of *Who's Who*. His entry in the 1970 edition of the directory dropped the previous reference to his education at Westminster School, while the 1974 edition still included his Presidency of the Oxford Union, but deleted the fact of his MA, instead noting of his education: 'still in progress.' By 1976 the whole entry had been reduced to just two lines, simply pointing out that he was an MP and the secretary of state for energy. The following year, his entry disappeared entirely and for six years he was absent from the book altogether. When he did return, in 1983, he was finally listed as Tony Benn, rather than Anthony Wedgwood Benn, and there was no indication at all of his education, whether at public school or at Oxford; furthermore, his service record, which once had read 'Pilot Officer RAFVR 1943–45; Sub-Lieutenant (A) RNVR 1945–46', now dropped any mention of his rank. What is odd about this entire process is merely the fact that he cared sufficiently to engage in such a procedure; the pages of *Who's Who* have often been used to proclaim eccentricity, even to pursue the occasional vendetta, but Benn's recreation of himself was, and remains, unique.

The rebranding was not universally acknowledged. Just as those with an agenda to pursue still called Muhammad Ali by his original name, Cassius Clay, long after his conversion to Islam, so most newspapers continued to refer to Tony Benn as Wedgwood Benn, or Wedgie in the case of the tabloids, for years to come (some older Tories were still doing so three decades later). In the short term at least, it simply became another weapon with which his enemies could attack him.

And enemies he certainly had. In 1974 the novelist Kingsley Amis referred to him as 'the most dangerous figure in British politics today,' and even earlier he had himself been shocked by the tone of the Thames TV programme *Today*: 'I was asked by Llew Gardner how it felt to be the most hated man in Britain,' he noted, 'to which the answer was, of course, that I was only hated by Fleet Street. I didn't think it was true that I was universally loathed, and I said that nothing would ever change in Britain if people weren't prepared to disregard pressure and criticism.' He was right on both counts, but even so it was quite a reputation for him to have acquired, particularly in so brief a time, having been the golden boy of Labour politics just a few years before.

Benn's great crime in the eyes of the press and of the establishment was to take up the cause of the unions at the precise moment when they were in the ascendancy. He rapidly became the public face of the new militancy, the representative of what was seen by many commentators as an extra-parliamentary threat to democracy. Typical of these critics was *Times* columnist David Wood, who wrote in millennial terms of 'a resort to anarchy in the name of democracy or so-called participation. The national identity is coming increasingly under threat.' And chief amongst the examples that he cited of this trend – alongside the defiance of the Industrial Relations Court by the Transport and General Workers' Union and the IRA's creation of no-go areas in Londonderry – was Benn's support of the Upper Clyde Shipbuilders' work-in. The demonization was such that he was sometimes seen as being personally responsible for all the nation's ills, an attitude widespread enough to be satirized in the sitcom *George and Mildred*; Jeffrey Fourmile, a stalwart of his local Conservative Association, reads in his paper that unemployment has reached one and a half million, and comments: 'I blame Anthony Wedgwood Benn.' 'Oh, Jeffrey,' his indulgent wife replies, 'you blame him when you get dandruff.'

As the hostility towards him increased, and as he began to attract the unfriendly attention of the unelected sections of the state, so Benn became aware of the power of the forces ranged against him, with the consequence that his position of democratic socialism became more and more radical; having started down a leftward path, he found, by an inexorable logic, that his pace was hastening at every turn.

'The more I think about this, the more I see that if you are going to have socialism, you have to have a secondary power structure in which ministers sit in but are not the dominant figures,' he wrote in 1974. 'This concept of a working-class power structure, democratic and organized in parallel with the Government structure – in effect joint government of the country by the Labour Party and the trade unions – makes an awful lot of sense.' Unfortunately, to an awful lot of people whose grasp on power was inevitably threatened by such a concept, it made no sense at all. They did not share his conclusions ('I think it is wholly compatible with all that is best in parliamentary democracy'), nor did they see the justice of his comparisons: 'we should govern in conjunction with the trade unions just as the Tories have always governed in conjunction with the City and big business.'

Even within the leadership of the Labour Party, such thinking was viewed at best with a barely tolerant contempt, summed up by Harold Wilson's famous put-down, that he 'immatures with age'. But the Labour leadership was itself only a minor, junior player in the establishment. Elsewhere, among those who were capable of believing that even Wilson himself was a dangerous socialist, Benn had wandered so far beyond the pale that he had to be fought tooth-and-claw: he was, it was regularly claimed, bent on revolution and on turning Britain into an Eastern Bloc nation. 'The tasteless self-parody of Mr Benn ceases to be funny and becomes frightening,' claimed Dick Taverne who, although he was now sitting as a Democratic Labour MP, was voicing the thoughts of many still in the Labour Party. Such was the growing fear of union power that the charge began to stick, and had Benn's diaries been published at the time, there is little doubt that not only Fleet Street, but the wider public, would have found him guilty on at least some counts: 'I also have to confront the genuine fear that state socialism, run by the shop stewards, will destroy individual liberty,' he wrote. 'I don't think there is anything in it, but people are afraid of it and I have to ensure that my socialism is lubricated with the old democratic ideals.'

But these were the private thoughts of a man looking to his future ('If I want to do anything other than frolic around on the margins of British politics,' read the same entry, 'I must be leader of the Labour Party and prime minister'), and of a man setting himself perhaps the biggest task ever undertaken by a senior peacetime politician: nothing less than a democratic revolution that would bring accountability to education, to the media, to the machinery of the state and, above all, to the workplace. By the mid-1970s Benn's programme for change embraced virtually every institution that made up public life in Britain; had it ever been implemented, it would have transformed the nation for ever. There was no other political figure of such seniority who came even close to the challenge he presented, to his demand that the very principles of the parliamentary system as currently constituted should be remade and remodelled. Nor has there been since.

Unique though his position was, Benn's real significance lay not so much in his own arguments, but in his role as the man who articulated an existing trend in society. He was no Leninist figure placing himself in the vanguard of the masses (there were plenty of Mao manqués in the country already), but rather a mouthpiece for a section of the working-class already engaged in struggle, a delegate rather than a leader. His endorsement gave a legitimacy to left activists, perhaps, as well as a presence at the cabinet table: his strength, however, the reason he was feared, came from below. Arthur Wise's novel had described Enoch Powell as 'a man whom thousands felt had spoken up for them when they were unable to speak for themselves,' and the same could have been said of Benn. He too was 'someone they felt had answered the question: What does it mean to be a Briton in the middle of the twentieth century?'

The solutions the two men offered to the malaise of British society were radically different. Powell's appeal was primarily to those who felt that the country had been somehow more secure, more at ease with itself in the 1950s, while Benn called out to those who felt that capitalism had failed to deliver on its promises and looked forward to a promised land run by and for workers. But both were responding to an incipient crisis of national self-confidence, an underlying loss of certainty, a sometimes inchoate belief that things could not continue on the same path and that consensus was not the answer. And both had their own band of devoted followers, who shared their sense of destiny.

These two diametrically opposed visions of Britain's possible future came to dominate much of the underlying political discourse of the 1970s. While centrist politicians of both parties engaged in fire-fighting, seeking day-to-day to manage the recurrent economic crises into which the country was plunged, Powell and Benn took up positions to right and left of the fray, offering instead purer, ideological answers. Sometimes it was their interventions that shaped the debates; on other occasions they resembled nothing so much as Statler and Waldorf, the ageing cynics in *The Muppet Show*, throwing disparaging comments from their private box at Kermit and Fozzie Bear, the performers on the main stage.

Harold Wilson and Edward Heath spent a total of ten years squaring up to each other over the dispatch box in the Commons, but the real battle for the soul of the nation was being fought between the forces represented by their dissident rivals.

3
Environment
'All I need is the air that I breathe'

> All other elil do what they have to do and Frith moves them as
> he moves us. They live on the earth and they need food. Men
> will never rest till they've spoiled the earth and destroyed the
> animals.
> Richard Adams, *Watership Down* (1972)

> VICAR: It came to me the other day, about pollution. It's the
> modern rediscovery of sin. Well, it's the only form it can take in
> a materialist world. All the rubbish, the mess – now, that's the
> new wickedness.
> Nigel Kneale, *The Stone Tape* (1972)

> TERRY COLLIER: We've always had pollution. We invented pollu-
> tion long before it was fashionable.
> Dick Clement and Ian La Frenais,
> *Whatever Happened to the Likely Lads?* (1973)

The refuse collectors' strike of autumn 1970 was an early indication of the inability of the Heath government to manage industrial relations, but it also provoked other, more atavistic fears, as Graham Don, a lecturer in environmental health at London University, pointed out: 'If the failure to collect rubbish goes on for any length of time there will be a build-up in the rat population. At the moment, we are retreating and the rats are advancing . . .'

This reminder of the struggle for coexistence between humanity and its oldest urban enemy, the rat, was guaranteed to send a shiver through society. It was also the main reason for the government taking the unusual step of using soldiers to deal with the effects of a strike, when the Army was sent into Tower Hamlets to clear the rubbish that had become a health hazard. Similar measures were called for in 1975 when an unofficial strike in Glasgow resulted in even worse conditions: 'In some places the piles of rotting garbage rise as high as 20ft,' reported the press. 'More than 50,000 tons of uncollected refuse are now polluting Glasgow.' When the troops were eventually called upon, it took them over a month to clear the streets, working in terrible conditions: 'The biggest hazard the soldiers face is the swarms of rats at every temporary rubbish dump.'

In between these two strikes, the animal in question had made a sensational reappearance in popular culture with James Herbert's first book, *The Rats*, in 1974. For some years British horror fiction, which had once driven the evolution of the novel, had been in danger of dying through neglect, reduced to little more than Dennis Wheatley's effete tales of Satanism among the upper classes. Herbert reversed that decline with a proletarian prose style that combined episodic narrative with an unflinching eye for visceral violence. The first chapter set out his stall, introducing us to a middle-aged salesman named Henry Guilfoyle who falls in love with a younger colleague and is hounded out of his job by homophobic bullying. Six years, and six pages, later he has become an alcoholic vagrant in the East End of London, which is where he finds himself attacked by a pack of huge rats: 'The dim shadows seemed to float before him, then a redness ran across his vision. It was the redness of unbelievable pain. He couldn't see any more – the rats had already eaten his eyes.' The unfortunate Guilfoyle was the first of many characters to make such brief appearances in the work of Herbert and his imitators, introduced as narrative cannon fodder and destined to be dead by the chapter end.

The success of *The Rats* – and it was hugely successful, particularly among secondary schoolchildren, who passed it on from hand to hand with salivating enthusiasm, so that its readership massively out-numbered even its sales figures – inspired publishers to take horror fiction seriously again. It also inspired a host of lesser writers to take up the causes of other animals that could turn against humanity, from slugs and maggots to pigs and pike, with Guy N. Smith's series of killer crab novels proving the most durable entry in the field. None, however, could match the original, partly because Herbert was a much better writer than his successors, and partly because rats have more resonance than jellyfish could ever achieve.

At the time of the novel's publication, Herbert was working in advertising as an art director, but he had grown up in the East End (next to Petticoat Lane market, where the troops had been sent to clear refuse in 1970) and knew well the bomb-sites and wastelands that were 'invisible to the authorities'. The story was, he said, set in 'the London I lived in' and it brought to British horror a distinctively urban dimension. Mutated animals had been a staple of the movies for decades, but Herbert's creatures were of a different order altogether. These rats came clawing out of the pages of Dickens and *Dracula*, dragging with them folk memories of Pied Pipers and plagues; reeking of urban decay, they descended on a recidivist society that had lied with its promises of a better life. Harris, the schoolteacher hero of the book, has no hesitation in apportioning blame, as he rages against 'the councils that took the working-class from their slums and put them into tall, remote concrete towers, telling them they'd never been better off, but never realizing that forty homes in a block of flats became forty separate cells'. And as if the dehumanizing tower blocks were not enough, 'these same councils could allow the filth that could produce vermin such as the black rats'.

This was the back-street horror that the slum clearances had supposedly eradicated, now reborn as grotesque nightmare, and it coincided with the city described by David Bowie's *Diamond Dogs*, where 'fleas the size of rats sucked on rats the size of cats'. The rat soon became a common shorthand for social decline, particularly in rock & roll, from the Stranglers' debut album *Rattus Norvegicus* (1977) to the Woody Guthrie-derived name of the Boomtown Rats, though none reached the histrionic magnificence of the Doctors of Madness, whose 1976 song 'Mainlines' had the opening line: 'This is the place the rats come to die.'

On television too the animal became a familiar presence, giant versions appearing – in somewhat unconvincing form – in the *New Avengers* episode 'Gnaws' (1976) and the *Doctor Who* story 'The Talons of Weng-Chiang' (1977). As in 'Tomorrow, The Rat', a 1970 episode of the series *Doomwatch*, though, these were still echoing a pre-Herbert theme of science gone wrong, a theme derived ultimately from the Frankenstein legend (and lampooned in the 1972 Goodies show 'Kitten Kong', which ended with an attack by oversized mice). Combining the two was the 1976 TV play *During Barty's Party*, which saw a middle-class couple, Roger and Angie Truscott, move into the country, only to find a hostile world, symbolized by the marauding terror of a tribe of super-rats with a taste for human flesh. 'They've always been afraid of people; we've always poisoned them and killed them and they knew we could,' argues Angie, in the throes of a near-breakdown. 'Now our most deadly poison doesn't work on them any more, so won't they know that too? So now we're the enemy that doesn't always win, so they don't have to be afraid of us. And if that happens, if they stop being afraid . . .' Even when trying to escape the city, its dwellers found themselves trapped in its entrails. Written by Nigel Kneale, who had scripted the classic 1954 BBC production of *1984* with its controversial rat sequences in Room 101, *During Barty's Party* had the most creative approach to rodents on TV: it simply didn't show them, leaving the viewer's imagination to fill in the gaps.

The recurrence of the rat in the mid-1970s thus came to represent two aspects of the crisis of modern society: on the one hand the disaster of social planning, and on the other the inability of science to deliver a brave new world.

Even so, the allure of science and technology, which had been so hopeful in the 1960s, took some time to lose its sheen. This was an era that cherished the marvels of human ingenuity almost without question, a feeling that reached its finest expression in the enthusiasm for the 1969 Moon landings (the TV broadcast of which even co-opted David Bowie's dissenting fable 'Space Oddity'), and survived well into the early '70s. The media-endorsed memory of the time conjures up images of shops full of synthetic products, all available in a range of colours seldom seen in nature. It's a vision enshrined in the TV adverts for Cadbury's Smash, in which a group of friendly, if metallic, Martians fell about laughing at the way in which primitive Earthlings cooked their own potatoes, rather than simply pouring boiling water onto a packet of chemicals. In 1999 that Smash series was named commercial of the century by *Campaign* magazine, and to celebrate the award, the 1974 original was rescreened on Channel 4 in the final advert break of the twentieth century.

Less successful, and much less cherished, however, was Cadbury's other major venture into nutritional substitutes with its Soya Choice range of tinned foods, including imitation mince and stewed steak. The appearance on the British market of soya products like TVP (textured vegetable protein), Protena and Kesp (both brand names) was initially aimed at the catering industry – an estimated 20 million school dinners were made using Kesp in 1977 – where the appeal was straightforward: the substitutes were simply cheaper than the meat equivalent. Similarly, when TV scientist Dr Magnus Pyke suggested in 1975 that pet food would become more dependent on TVP in the future, it seemed a logical idea, particularly as he pointed out that 'Three times as many puppies as babies were born in Britain last year.' But when supermarkets tried to sell such delights as tinned Kesp & Kidney Pudding or Kesp Curry to individual consumers, they found far fewer takers. The campaign wasn't helped by the fact that the products were so lacking in flavour that they had to be augmented: 6 per cent of the weight of the Cadbury's mince was animal fat, while the

Kesp version of a roast joint was similarly covered in a layer of succulent beef fat. Any potential vegetarian market, as well as those with religious dietary requirements, was thus excluded from the outset. Nor was the environmental argument – that soya produced around twenty times as much protein per acre as meat – sufficiently promoted to consumers. Instead the selling point was purely budgetary and, although such products 'became fashionable in the mid-1970s when meat prices rose sharply', they had no longevity. By 1977 soya beans had become so associated with cheap imitations that Morecambe and Wise could joke about them being used to make a new currency for Britain in an attempt to salvage the devalued economy (to be promoted under the slogan: 'You've never had it – so what!').

Kesp had been created in 1972 by Courtaulds, a company best known for its synthetic fabrics, and a spokesperson explained that, although the manufacturing process was an industrial secret, it 'was much the same as that for making textiles'. The belief that the public would joyously embrace such substitutes was evident in another Courtaulds product of the period: Planet cigarettes. Launched in 1973, and made in equal parts from tobacco and from cellulose derived from eucalyptus and wattle trees, Planets cost the same as normal cigarettes and were aimed at the social smoker, rather than the nicotine addict. Despite the reduction in tobacco content, they were attacked by the anti-smoking pressure group Action on Smoking and Health, and criticized by the health secretary, Keith Joseph, for being marketed 'before the relative safety of the product has been fully appraised'. He need not have worried; Planets were an unmitigated commercial flop. The idea didn't disappear, though, and in 1977 a new version of Player's cigarettes was launched by Imperial Tobacco with 25 per cent NSM (New Smoking Material), whilst Silk Cut also appeared with a tobacco substitute: 'It offers smokers a touch more flavour than conventional Silk Cut,' claimed the adverts. 'And, as you would expect, a touch less tar.' Despite heavy advertising, the idea of a tobacco substitute was not popular, and the brands soon dropped all reference to its presence.

The intention behind such products was obvious at a time when the dangers of smoking were becoming more widely known. Cigarette advertising had been banned on television in 1965, a move which had in turn produced the growth of sports sponsorship, however inappropriate the connection might be – snooker was an obvious choice, Formula 1 less so. In 1972 there was a proposal to rename the British Grand Prix as the John Player Grand Prix, which provoked the motor-racing legend John Surtees to protest in the pages of *Autosport* magazine: 'This is a disgusting insult to all those who still put British first.' Even less relevant sponsorship also materialized, notably the Benson & Hedges Gold Award for concert singers, launched in conjunction with the Aldeburgh Festival, while the auction house Sotheby's lent their prestigious name to a new upmarket brand from Wills, Sotheby's Special Reserve cigarettes, which debuted in 1971, retailed at one and a half times the normal price, and disappeared rapidly. The truth was that, despite a 1975 Gallup poll showing that '30 per cent of British smokers do not believe that cigarettes can kill', the tide was beginning to turn against tobacco, with the New Inn, Appletreewick, West Yorkshire claiming the distinction of being the first British pub to ban smoking, in 1971; being a little too far ahead of the game, however, it saw an immediate slump in bar takings.

The failure in the marketplace of TVP and NSM indicated a shift in public attitude during the 1970s away from synthetics and their promise of an artificial future, a trend that perhaps reached its defining moment in February 1976 when Brentford Nylons went into receivership. Eight years earlier the company, founded by Armenian businessman Kaye Metrebian, had been greeted enthusiastically when it opened a £24 million plant outside Newcastle, a project described by the Board of Trade as 'one of the biggest – in terms of money – to come to the North-East for a long time'. By the early '70s it had branched out from production into retail, and was fast becoming one of the most distinctive presences on ITV, with a series of adverts voiced by Radio One disc jockey Alan 'Fluff' Freeman. 'I've got Brentford Nylons sheets on my bed at the moment,' he gushed to the press. 'Their stuff is fantastic. I bought it with my own money.' The impression given was that this was the future, but in fact the business model (who needed a chain of shops that sold nothing but nylon products?) was as flawed as its bedclothes were uncomfortable, and the commercials became almost the primary output of the company: at its peak, Brentford Nylons managed to spend £3.3 million on advertising while its profits amounted to under £1 million. Following its collapse, the firm was bought up by Lonrho, best known at the time for having been described by Ted Heath as 'the unacceptable face of capitalism', who got a £5 million loan from the government for the purpose. Even so it was subsequently 'acknowledged by Lonrho directors as far from a good buy'.

The same month that Brentford Nylons went bust, a review in the rock weekly *NME* gave the first mention in print of a new band, the Sex Pistols. The punk movement that the group inspired, and which impacted on the country's culture in complete disproportion to its sales figures, was characterized by the gleeful war that it waged on its own heritage, so that

Jamie Reid's artwork for the Pistols took the Union Flag that had been emblematic of mod in the '60s, cut it up and reassembled it with safety pins. Similarly there was a mocking celebration of the artificial in opposition to the natural, encapsulated in the stage name adopted by Marianne Elliott, who became Poly Styrene, the singer of X-Ray Spex, and in the reinvention of teen-pop band Slik to become the punk-friendly PVC2. The ironic adoption of artificial fabrics as the standard uniform simultaneously scorned the '60s enthusiasm for plastic futurism, and rejected the alternative hippy ideals of authenticity; in common with the other early symbols of punk, it taunted society with a caricature of itself.

And, also in common with other aspects of punk, it was soon assimilated into the mainstream, with Zandra Rhodes the first to pick up on the possibilities. Having made a name for herself as a textile designer in the '60s, Rhodes had then reinvented herself as a fashion designer in the '70s, celebrated for bringing ethnic influences from America, Australia, Japan and elsewhere onto the catwalk. Now she saw the London punk scene as another source of anthropological inspiration: 'The kids were wearing black plastic garbage bags tied up with safety pins, torn rubber t-shirts, black suspenders, laddered stockings, bondage strips of dread black vinyl,' she noted. 'It was a revolution – it was repugnant – it was exciting, it was there, a point of no turning back in style.' By the time the ripped clothes, safety pins and bathroom chains had been absorbed into her Conceptual Chic collection (1977), they were being displayed against a much less aggressive set of fabrics – silk, satin, jersey – and a skirt would set you back £125, with a top coming in at £250.

The uncertain and ambivalent attitudes towards synthetic products reflected a shift in the culture. Although nothing was to be settled in the 1970s, the decade can be seen in retrospect to have represented a transition from space age to new age. The catalyst for such a change was the awakening of interest in environmentalism, itself partially caused by the culture shock of seeing the pictures of Earth taken from the Moon, the solid certainties of life replaced by images of a fragile planet hanging in space. To the existing fear of nuclear destruction was now added a new sense of vulnerability, and, for some, the determination to protect what we had. There was, though, some doubt at the outset whether this interest in sustainability could itself be sustained: 1970 was declared European Conservation Year, and in a speech that February Prince Charles worried about 'the whole thing being a temporary craze which reaches a peak of over-emphasis and then deflates itself rapidly'. The economist

E.F. Schumacher echoed his concerns: 'Is this a sudden fad, a silly fashion, or perhaps a sudden failure of nerve?'

As it turned out, such apprehension was unnecessary. There was in due course an inevitable falling-off in media interest in ecology, but by the end of the century, the decline had turned out to be temporary, as stories of climate change moved from the scientific press to the news pages, causing even governments to profess themselves concerned about the environment. In the '70s the agenda was related but slightly different, as set out by another royal contributor to the debate, Prince Philip: 'Problems of overpopulation, environmental pollution, depletion of finite resources and the threat of widespread starvation.'

Different too was the political response. Tony Benn was one of the very few senior politicians to acknowledge 'the real challenge of the ecologists, who are now saying that there must be a major cut in the population, a major reduction in growth, if humanity is to survive'. There was little evidence in his actions as a minister to suggest that he had been much affected by such ideas, but he did at least recognize that environmentalism was an intellectual threat to the growth-based economy, on which the Labour Party had been relying since Anthony Crosland's 1956 book *The Future of Socialism*. 'The traditional social democratic view that if we are going to get socialism now, we must have growth and distribute it fairly,' Benn wrote in 1972, 'has got to be re-examined in the light of a possible ban on growth. This will drive us towards redistribution without being able to give us the excess that would make that redistribution painless.'

Crosland himself clearly understood the same point and, turning defence into attack, was, according to his widow, quick in his condemnation of those whose 'attitudes, in his view, were anti-democratic, springing – probably unconsciously – from a common enough middle-class and upper-class bias (he threw in princely bias while he was about it)'. As far as he was concerned, environmentalists were 'kindly and dedicated people, but were usually affluent and wanted to kick the ladder down behind them'. The same attitude was still evident a decade later in the words of union leader Frank Chapple. 'We cannot afford to dice with the political and technological uncertainties of low-energy options. My members have achieved decent living standards and they want further improvements.' He added scornfully: 'They can identify with the advance of new technology and its benefits, not with the muesli-eaters, ecology freaks, loony leftists and other nutters who make up the anti-nuclear brigade. That is surely true of most of our citizens.'

From an environmentalist perspective, such arguments were danger-ous in the extreme. In 1975 some 30 per cent of the British population didn't have access to a car, but if the socialist argument was that everyone had a democratic right to enjoy the privilege of personal motoring, at the expense of public transport, then something had gone wrong with the priorities of socialism; the greater good of society was being sacrificed on the altar of individual freedom. In this respect, ecology was the most radical challenge to orthodoxy that the '70s produced, a threat to the assumptions held in common by market capitalists and social democrats alike. And when environmentalists talked of crisis, it was not simply a return to mass unemployment that they predicted, but the destruction of humanity itself, as witnessed by a spate of prophetic, if Cassandraesque, books with titles like *Can Britain Survive?* (1971), *A Blueprint for Survival* (1972) and *The Death of Tomorrow* (1972). Most influential, and most hopeful, was *Small Is Beautiful*, the 1973 work by Dr Schumacher, who had spent twenty years as economic adviser to the National Coal Board; its subtitle spelt out his intention: *A Study of Economics as if People Mattered*.

There was at the time a minority position of deep ecology (the concept that humanity should not be the prime concern of environmentalist thinking), but the principal line of attack was to accumulate the evidence necessary to prove that we were despoiling nature in a way that would ultimately destroy us. To take one example, Schumacher analysed at length our profligate use of fossil fuels: 'If we treated them as capital items,' he argued, 'we should be concerned with conservation; we should do everything in our power to try and minimize their current rate of use.' Instead we saw the consumption of this finite and irreplaceable source of energy as a kind of social virility symbol, demonstrating that our civilization was technologically superior to that of 'undeveloped' nations. Drawing inspiration from the teachings of Gandhi as much as from his own training as an economist, he put forward a case for the reduction in scale of human endeavour so that we might learn to 'understand the great rhythms of the universe and to gear in with them'.

This appeal to reconnect with nature found a receptive audience amongst the British public, as seen in the phenomenal success of Richard Adams's novel *Watership Down* (1972), which spent thirty weeks at the top of the *Sunday Times* best-seller lists, even though that chart didn't make its first appearance until two years after the book had been published. This epic tale of rabbit mythology, drawing on Homer, Virgil, Norse legends, even *King Lear*, begins when the runt of a litter experiences a sense of impending doom, and persuades a small group of bucks to leave their warren at Sandleford and to embark on a hazardous journey to found a new home. The disaster that is about to befall Sandleford, we learn, is the clearing of the ground in order to build a new housing estate, and humanity is seen throughout the novel as a lurking danger, unpredictable and devastating in its actions.

So dominant has this single species become that all nature is shaped by it; the rival warrens that the band of wanderers encounter, and that act as alternative societies, are characterized entirely by their attitudes to human beings. The first such community is Cowslip's warren, which has made its peace with *Homo sapiens*, accepting both its food and its snares; as long as the fatalities aren't too frequent, the rabbits are content to live a comfortably decadent life of aestheticism, creating art and poetry and drifting ever further from traditional leporine ways. The second is Efrafa, a military dictatorship presided over by General Woundwort, and again the distance from nature is stressed, symbolized by the fact that the rabbits here have learnt to bury their droppings in order to conceal themselves from humans. The inhabitants of both warrens are seen as being incomplete, alienated from their true selves: 'There are rabbits there,' reflects one of our heroes, 'who'd be the same as we are if they could only live naturally, like us.' By contrast, the group we follow are not only at peace with themselves but with nature more generally, befriending other creatures across the species divide, though the mice they meet are, for no immediately apparent reason, depicted as having an Italian accent, while the bird who helps them appears to speak in a mutated East European voice. Despite the awkwardness of this transcription of 'the very simple, limited *lingua franca* of the hedgerow', the key is the fact that all the animals can converse with each other, with the one exception of humans.

In retrospect, though, the enduring popularity of *Watership Down* can be seen as being due as much to its archetypal characters of king, soldier, priest, and intellectual – Hazel, Bigwig, Fiver and Blackberry respectively – as to the immediacy of its environmental message. Adams's subsequent novel, *The Plague Dogs* ('a Doomsday Disney', said the *Daily Mail*), was similarly a tale of animals fleeing the harmful presence of humanity, in this case two dogs escaping from a research laboratory. It too sold well but failed to make the same cultural impact, perhaps because the satire was too heavy-handed with the unsubtle naming of the laboratory as Animal Research (Scientific and Experimental), or ARSE for short, where experiments are performed 'for the good, or the advancement, or the edification – or something or other, anyway – of the human race'.

The Plague Dogs did, however, add to the growing sense of outrage at what were seen as the abuses of scientific research on animals. In 1975 the story broke that the development of NSM involved laboratory beagles smoking thirty cigarettes a day, to ensure (following Keith Joseph's complaints about Planets) the safety of the new tobacco substitute, and the resultant image came to dominate public perceptions of animal experimentation, despite assurances from Sir Jack Callard, chairman of ICI, that 'there was no cruelty, and the beagles did not mind being made to smoke'. Labour MP William Molloy suggested that those conducting such experiments should volunteer to be bitten by dogs to aid research into rabies, while Lady Parker, the elderly widow of a former Lord Chief Justice, announced that she was willing to do the requisite amount of smoking herself, if it would spare just one of the dogs. And when, later in the year, a couple of animal rights campaigners were jailed for three years after admitting arson attacks on targets connected with animal research, the controversy over the smoking beagles helped provoke 'a flood of letters to the *Sun* – almost all in support of the two protestors'. For those who regarded such expressions as being little more than anthropomorphic sentimentality, the equivalent shock image came in 1977 when anti-hunting enthusiasts dug up the grave of nineteenth-century huntsman John Peel in the Lake District.

What was notable about such issues was that the initiative came from below, from grass-roots campaigning groups. In his satirical novel *Experiment at Proto* (1973), Philip Oakes had depicted a maverick right-wing MP, Guy Afton ('he volleyed and thundered: repatriate our coloured brethren, penalize strikes, make students toe the line'), who seizes, for reasons of cynical politicking, on the use of chimpanzees in a scientific project: 'People loved the chimpanzee – visitors to London Zoo had voted it their favourite animal. To champion its cause against the demon research was a simple but symbolic act.' But in reality such politicians were few in number; this was essentially a movement of activists, who found that they enjoyed a remarkably high degree of public sympathy, however passive that might be. The fear that this support might be extended beyond animals to more global economic concerns was expressed in *Hollow Target* (1976), Paul Bryers's tale of environmental terrorism: 'There are people who seem to feel that the major oil companies are a greater threat than the extremists,' laments the fictional home secretary. 'It is only a matter of time before misguided people come to regard them as working class heroes fighting the capitalist juggernauts.'

This sensitivity towards oil companies was, of course, not unrelated to the imminent advent of North Sea oil, the proceeds of which were seen as the fabled pot of gold at the end of the '70s rainbow. Even here, though, there were potential ramifications to be explored by popular fiction: 'Nature abhors a vacuum,' explains a character in Walter Harris's *The Fifth Horseman*. 'We're taking out oil and gas, and putting nothing back.' Sure enough, the seabed collapses as a result of the drilling, and sends a tidal wave across northern Europe. Harris's book was one of a brace of environmental disaster novels in 1976 that concerned the flooding of Britain, the other being Richard Doyle's *Deluge*, which centred on an entirely natural freak weather system, albeit one whose effects could have been avoided: 'The great barrier project at Woolwich was designed to prevent all this, but since it had been paralysed by strikes, it was now two years behind schedule.' (Work on the Thames Barrier began in 1974, and it was officially opened in 1984.)

The reaction against technology was also evident in one of the best-remembered *Doctor Who* storylines. 'The Green Death' (1973) told the story of a multinational company, Global Chemicals, using a disused mine in South Wales to dump the waste from their new oil-refining process. An exploration of the pit reveals a lake of green slime in which a mutated species of giant maggots is growing; these prove to be lethal to humans and almost – though not quite – indestructible. The theme was far from original, but the series did add a couple of radical new threads to the tradition. First, there is a group of environmentalist campaigners, led by a Nobel Prize-winning biologist, Clifford Jones, who are allowed time and space to put their arguments against the destruction of the Earth. Their approach is strictly scientific, and Jones's own work centres on developing an alternative protein source to meat, based on fungi. That they are to be seen as the good guys is made explicit by the fact that the Doctor's companion, Jo Grant (Katy Manning), is on their side, even before she meets Jones and decides to marry him: 'It's time to call a halt, it's time that the world awoke to the alarm bell of pollution instead of sliding down the slippery slopes of, of whatever it is,' she declares, in slightly unconvincing tones.

Second, there is a serious ratcheting up of anti-capitalist sentiments with a direct linkage of big business to fascism. The story opens with Stevens, head of Global Chemicals, addressing a group of miners left without jobs after the National Coal Board closed down the pit where they had worked: 'I have in my hand a piece of paper which will mean a great deal to all of you,' he says; 'wealth in our time.' Having registered the overt association between Stevens and the appeasement policy of Neville

Chamberlain after Munich in 1938, we eventually get to see who he is appeasing: a megalomaniac computer which makes repeated Hitlerian references to Wagner, Nietzsche and the concept of the Superman. (In this context, the manner in which Jones comforts Jo after the death of a miner – saying that the dead man was unique in the whole history of the world, and would remain so even if the Earth lasted for a hundred thousand years – can only be seen as a very obscure reference to, and rejection of, Nietzsche's theory of eternal recurrence.)

Just to add further resonance, the controlling computer is named BOSS, which stands here for Biomorphic Organizational Systems Supervisor, but which also carried echoes of the Bureau of State Security, the secret police of apartheid South Africa. But there is in any event no question of where our sympathies should lie once Stevens tells the Doctor that he intends to create freedom from pain and fear, and the Doctor snorts derisively: 'Freedom from freedom!' It was a sign of the politically charged times that such a clearly anti-business storyline was considered appropriate for children's television.

On a fluffier level, 1973 also saw the arrival on TV of the proto-recyclers *The Wombles*, based on characters created by Elizabeth Beresford. These small but long-nosed creatures inhabited Wimbledon Common and spent their time, in the words of the theme song, 'making good use of the things that we find, things that the everyday folk leave behind'. That song was written by Mike Batt, who, having walked into the offices of CBS Records in a Womble suit made by his mother, managed to negotiate a contract for the 'band'. A succession of hit singles followed, all of them perfect pop parodies, from the calypso of 'Banana Rock' to the bubblegum punk of 'Super Womble'; as the guitarist on the records, Chris Spedding, pointed out: 'Mike was very ingenious with his little pastiches of music.' (At the same time that he was appearing on *Top of the Pops* in a Womble suit, Spedding was also turning down an invitation to join the Rolling Stones.)

Bizarrely the Wombles became the biggest-selling singles act in the country in 1974. Even more bizarrely they provoked a series of near-riots when thousands of children turned up that Christmas to see what they thought were going to be gigs by their furry heroes and were instead confronted by a shoddy musical. 'They had one director and nine casts all in this one rehearsal room,' said Batt. 'They rehearsed this really awful show, gave them a load of crap costumes and told them to go out and do it.' The result was hordes of kids screaming for their mummies, hordes of mummies screaming for their money back, and a deluge of bad publicity for the Wombles that probably prevented them from taking the coveted

Christmas #1 spot on the charts with 'Wombling Merry Christmas', instead allowing in Mud's 'Lonely This Christmas'. Those who went to the Manchester show could at least comfort themselves that they had seen the ironic '80s pop star David Van Day of Dollar in an early incarnation as American Womble, Captain Yellowstone, as well as hearing music played by future members of the soft-rock band Sad Café, but it was clearly a traumatic event for many: 'That was the straw that broke the camel's back,' regretted Batt. 'The other Wombles were out of my control.' The band split up soon afterwards, though Wellington Womble did release a solo single, 'Rainmaker', during the great drought of 1976.

From terrorists to Wombles, there was for a while what seemed an almost insatiable appetite for eco-fiction of all shades. How much the concern was matched by individual changes of behaviour on a wide scale was more arguable. The split between private concern and public self-interest was evident in the growth of out-of-town superstores, or hypermarkets as they were originally known, following the Continental model. For those in doubt, *The Architect* magazine provided a definition: 'An isolated store sited either in a green field location or a suburban or new town district centre. It will have a total floor area of between 60,000 and 100,000 square feet, of which about sixty per cent will be sales area.' The size was crucial. In 1972 the Department of the Environment issued a circular requiring any local authority receiving a planning application for a store of 50,000 square feet or above to refer the application to central government; it wasn't long before a way around the regulations was found as 'one local authority issued planning consent for the development of a supermarket occupying 49,999 square feet of space'.

The message was anyway somewhat confused, for the previous year government had given 'the go-ahead to local authorities to grant permission for out-of-town hypermarkets provided they presented no environmental problems'. Under this guidance, the French retail group Carrefour had obtained permission for Britain's first hypermarket, a 60,000-square-feet store in Caerphilly, 'which during its initial period was besieged by traffic jams, resulting in appeals to people to keep away'. The definition of 'environmental problems' was to evolve in later decades, but what was clear from an early stage was the demand from retailers for such developments and, it had to be assumed, from the public as well. By March 1972 it was being reported that Lancashire alone had received sixty planning applications for such hypermarkets, and despite reservations in some quarters – a spokesperson for *Which?* warned that 'consumers have to be careful about the concentration of power in large retail groups' – it was evident that this was the future face of shopping. The erosion of the high street and the encouragement of excess traffic were fears yet to come.

Indeed, what is notable about this first eruption of environmentalism, in light of future concerns, is the priorities it established. As early as 1970 the Labour conference was passing a motion that 'viewed with alarm the increasing pollution of land, sea and air and called on the Labour Party to demand the necessary controls', while earlier in the same year Prince Charles had written to the prime minister complaining that salmon stocks were in danger of being overfarmed in the Atlantic and that the species was threatened 'by modern methods which give it no chance'. He added: 'People are notoriously short-sighted when it comes to questions of wildlife, and several species have been wiped out because no one has woken up in time to the danger.' Even the fictional detective James Hazell was aware that something was happening: 'My dad says the weather's changed because they're cutting down forests in Brazil.' But in political terms, such voices were way ahead of their time; much more typical was the Liberal Party spokesman, John Pardoe, arguing in 1977 against further taxation on motoring: 'Liberals, he said, had always been opposed to higher petrol prices and car taxes because of their effect on low-earning rural areas, where cars were essential for people to get to work.'

What was clear even at this stage, however, was the scientific warning of imminent catastrophe. Professor Dennis Meadows of the Massachusetts Institute of Technology was reported in 1971 to have produced a computer model showing 'that man is using up his natural resources too quickly, that population is growing too rapidly and that economic growth is leading to pollution levels which will end in disaster'. The reports added that: 'If present trends continue, it is estimated, the disaster will overtake the world in thirty years.' In a foretaste of political short-sightedness to come, government scientists were said to be supportive of Professor Meadows, but to have been overruled by Ted Heath, who was in a state of panic over unemployment and remained committed to growth. The conflict between immediate economic crisis and medium-term environmental catastrophe was already evident.

As the decade continued and the economy showed little prospect of improving, so the initial wave of enthusiasm for environmental issues receded somewhat. In 1975 the BBC launched what was to become one of its most cherished sitcoms, *The Good Life*, in which Tom and Barbara Good (Richard Briers and Felicity Kendall) opt out of the middle-class rat race to take up a life of self-sufficient farming in the garden of their Surbiton home. Inspired by the likes of smallholder John Seymour, author of *The*

Complete Book of Self-Sufficiency – which sold remarkably well in the wake of the TV show – *The Good Life* was intended to tap into a public desire for a less stressful life, partly in response to the message that small was indeed beautiful. The most revealing feature of the series, though, was the way in which it drifted from its ecological roots, and turned into a much more conventional domestic sitcom, as the Goods' next-door neighbours, Jerry and Margo Leadbetter (Paul Eddington and Penelope Keith), still fully immersed in the suburban mainstream, emerged as figures of equal standing to the Goods. So powerful a figure was Margo in particular, displaying both ludicrously exaggerated levels of snobbery and genuine warmth, that by the end she dominated the programme.

And as she grew in stature, so too did the viewing figures: the first episode to attract an audience of over 10 million was significantly also the first to centre on a Leadbetter story. That was towards the end of the second season, and the lesson was clearly learnt; from the third series in 1976, the relationship between the two couples had become the focus, with the result that one of the episodes that year reached the giddy heights of 17.7 million viewers. With yet another immediate economic crisis to be faced, the nation evidently found conventional comedy easier to digest than purer pro-environmentalist fare.

4
Violence
'It's the only thing that'll make you see sense'

> It can generally be assumed that demos, in the liberal sense, are no longer ways of 'voicing our opinion', but ways of showing our collective strength and solidarity.
> Agitprop Collective, *The Bust Book* (1971)

> Whatever these bimbos were protesting about, it was obviously something they were taking to heart rather. By the time I had got into their midst not a few of them had decided that animal cries were insufficient to meet the case and were saying it with bottles and brickbats, and the police who were present in considerable numbers seemed not to be liking it much. It must be rotten being a policeman on these occasions. Anyone who has got a bottle can throw it at you, but if you throw it back, the yell of police brutality goes up and there are editorials in the papers next day.
> P.G. Wodehouse, *Aunts Aren't Gentlemen* (1974)

> These boots were made for stompin', and that's what they'll do,
> One of these days these boots are gonna stomp all over you.
> Symarip, 'These Boots Are Made for Walkin'' (1969)

'You're a big man, but you're in bad shape.' The most famous line in the 1971 film *Get Carter* sees Michael Caine as London gangster Jack Carter seeking to avoid a fight with the decidedly portly Bryan Mosley (here playing Brumby, though better known as Alf Roberts in *Coronation Street*). More revealing is Carter's next thought: 'For me, it's a full-time job.' He's not bragging about his propensity for violence, merely stating a fact: he's a professional who earns his living by his ability to inflict harm on others. And it's not something of which he is particularly proud. He has come back to his home town of Newcastle – or Scunthorpe, in the original Ted Lewis novel, *Jack's Return Home* – to investigate the murder of his brother, a decent, ordinary citizen who he acknowledges to have been the better man of the two: 'I'm the villain in the family,' he says, recognizing that his need for vengeance is the tribute that vice pays to virtue.

This self-awareness is crucial to the film named as the best British movie of all time by *Total Film* magazine in 2004. *Get Carter* shows in close-up a collection of singularly unappealing thugs, killers and pornographers; with scarcely a redeeming feature between them, they live in a relentlessly vicious world of their own making, devoid of humanity or decency. Behind this amoral group, however, in the background to the action, there is another world entirely, a city that remains untouched by their activities; we see pubs, a dance hall, a bingo hall, a kids' marching band in the streets, a whole community going about its everyday business and sharing nothing in common with the parasites who prey upon it. It is this community that Carter left behind him when he moved to London, and he is painfully aware of his distance from it. Early on in the film, as he's leaving a pub, a fight breaks out between two women, a fight that won't result in anyone's death or even in serious injury, but is a simple statement of honour. It's a lifetime away from the industrialized violence of the central characters, and Carter's spontaneous smile at the uncomplicated honesty of the dispute makes it clear that there's a part of him that yearns for this society where he no longer belongs.

At the time, the cold brutality of the film's violence captured the attention of critics and audiences, but in retrospect *Get Carter* can be seen almost as an elegy for a passing world, one where there was still an absolute demarcation between the villain and the citizen. Already such innocence was being challenged in fiction, with a spate of crime novels that questioned the complacency of Britain. James Barlow's *The Burden of Proof* (1968) drew on the story of the Kray twins to depict a country where a bent lawyer can blackmail an MP into committing perjury, and thereby ensure that a violent thug gets off any charge brought against him. Over this travesty of justice presides an elderly and blinkered judge, who smugly believes 'that England was unique because her Government and Law were not corrupt. But neither was true any more.' As the dedication to the novel ('To the policemen of England, who are still the salt of the earth') makes clear, however, there is at least one institution on which we can depend: the star of the book, if not the subsequent movie *Villain*, is an incorruptible copper, representative of one of the last bastions of decency.

G.F. Newman had no such illusions. Rejected as a writer for the TV series *Z-Cars* because his script showed a police officer accepting a bribe, he made his name with his first novel *Sir, You Bastard* (1970), which sold 200,000 copies and spawned two sequels (*You Nice Bastard* and *You Flash Bastard*). Its anti-hero is Terry Sneed, an intelligent young man with a Nietzschean sense of his own destiny: 'Power, he decided, was the only worthwhile thing having; some thought money, but money amounted to power; others intelligence, but intelligence equalled power, too.' Sneed would have been plausible as a serial killer or as a putative fascist leader, but instead he becomes a CID officer, ruthlessly ambitious and, inevitably, corrupt as well. For, while he's clearly a potential high-flyer from an early stage, he's in no way seen as being different in kind from his colleagues; in fact he's accepted by them precisely because of what they have in common: 'Corruption in the CID had reached saturation point and an uncorrupt detective might easily blow the whistle.'

What had changed between these two novels was the first serious indication that the police might not be as honourable as the public had naively assumed. A 1969 investigation by journalists on *The Times* had uncovered (with tape recordings to back up the story) three separate detectives taking bribes from a professional criminal in return for dropping charges and allowing him to continue in his chosen career. The traditional excuse in such situations, that there might be the occasional bad apple, seemed to have been undermined from the start when one of the policemen pointed out to the criminal: 'We've got more villains in our game than you've got in yours, you know.' To the relief of the police force, however, an internal inquiry under the leadership of Detective Chief Superintendent Bill Moody, which investigated dozens of officers, could find no traces of widespread corruption; with the exception of one demoted detective, no disciplinary action was deemed necessary.

For those inclined to take comfort from such a verdict, there was a rude awakening to come. In 1977 Moody himself was given a twelve-year jail sentence for bribery and corruption in his capacity as head of the Obscene Publications Squad, a position he had held even while carrying out his inquiry. In the intervening period, much had been done by Sir Robert Mark, Commissioner of the Metropolitan Police from 1972 to 1977, to clean up the force, but even he was perhaps a little too inclined to understand the bent copper, using the argument implied in *The Burden of Proof*; there is, he wrote in his autobiography, 'a widespread general acceptance that in London, at least, the system of justice is weighted so heavily in favour of the criminal and the defence lawyer that it can only be made to work by bending the laws. In fairness to the CID that view is not confined to them.'

Faith in the police was not destroyed by the scandals of the early and mid-1970s. They added to the background noise, to the sense that something was not quite right in Britain, but the force still tended to get the benefit of the doubt. In 1975 *The Sweeney* erupted onto TV screens, depicting members of Scotland Yard's Flying Squad as boozing, womanizing brawlers, and taking televised violence to new levels for both police and villains, though there were limits; the briefing paper for writers on the series advised, with an implied regret, that 'Four-letter words are not permissible, nor can we indulge in "souped up" horror, e.g. represent, in slow motion, a security guard having his head blown off by a shotgun.' Even here, however, the tone was entirely supportive, and a 1975 episode that centred on allegations against a senior Squad officer made explicit reference to the *Times*-prompted investigation, whilst emphasizing that what we were watching was yet another case of a decent copper being stitched up by villains.

For the public, acceptance of police corruption was still perhaps a step too far (a 1977 opinion poll showed that only 15 per cent thought the police weren't honest), for there remained a need to believe that someone somewhere was holding the line, defending society against what was seen as a rising tide of violence. Because, as the '70s dawned, the media were awash with tales of our descent into brutality. The term 'mugging' was imported from New York to describe the crime of street robbery, and although the practice was not exactly unknown in Britain, muggers sounded both more contemporary and more dangerous than footpads and highwaymen; the word could also, some noted, be subtly nuanced towards black criminality more than anything in the previously existing vocabulary had been. There was also the increasing focus on football hooligans at the same time and, allied to this, the emergence of the skinheads.

Descended from the mod culture of the early 1960s, but stripped of that movement's art school pretensions, skinheads were an uncomfortable sight for the general population. Working-class youths with hair shaved to within a quarter-inch of its life, clad in boots, braces and rolled-up jeans, they came to represent the nihilistic antithesis to the idealism of the late '60s. 'What are we for? Nothing really,' commented one. 'We're just a group of blokes. We're not *for* anything.' They made early appearances at the 1968 Grosvenor Square demonstration against the Vietnam War (chanting in support of Enoch Powell) and at the Rolling Stones' free concert in Hyde Park the following year, but it was the '70s that saw them transformed from a style-conscious London scene into a national movement; by 1972 it was being argued that they 'constitute by far the biggest single group among this country's teenagers'. And their image was one of mindless violence, aimed at rival gangs, especially in football grounds, and at ethnic minorities.

'We're being exploited, the working class,' explained one skinhead from London's East End. 'It's hard for us to fight for our job and our house, but with them here as well, trying to get our houses, it's another opposition.' In case his meaning wasn't entirely clear, he added, 'I'll tell you another thing, when you stand next to these people that have just come over here, they fucking stink.' The same rage was evident in the words of a Birmingham skin: 'Have you ever been in their restaurants? Have you seen the way they *grovel* round you, the way they're always trying to please you? I hate them, that's all.'

In so far as this racial hatred had a political expression, it was manifested in support of the one politician who spoke out against immigration. 'You don't see no blacks in China,' argued one, with contorted but rigorous logic. 'That's what we need – a Chinese Enoch Powell.' For those who lived in Powell's heartlands, the original was quite sufficient. SKINHEAD BODYGUARD FOR ENOCH read a 1970 *Daily Mirror* front-page headline, claiming that forty skins had surrounded Powell at an election rally in Smethwick, and quoting sixteen-year-old Neil Sandford as saying: 'We heard that long-haired people and students were coming to cause trouble. No one causes trouble to our mate Enoch. And if there is any trouble we will soon sort it out.'

By this stage, assaults on British Asians had already become common, initially in Brick Lane in London where a wave of attacks had claimed their first fatality in April 1970, and the expression 'Paki-bashing' was gaining currency in the media. The following month, Pakistan's High Commissioner to the UK met the home secretary, James Callaghan, to protest at the violence and to point out the damage the skinheads were doing to relations between the two countries. Meanwhile, in Wolverhampton, the convener of a meeting of concerned groups threatened that: 'It would also be possible to arrange retaliation against English people in India and Pakistan. This could be a reaction.' In fact, there had already been reports in the London-based publication *Mashriq* of assaults on British people in Pakistan.

A related phenomenon of the time, though one less likely to cause international tension, was the victimization of gay men under the banner of 'queer-bashing'. In 1970 a gang of twelve youths, aged between fifteen and eighteen, were sentenced for an attack on Michael de Gruchy, a twenty-nine-year-old solicitor's clerk, that left him dead on Wimbledon Common. Four were convicted of murder, amongst them eighteen-year-old butcher's assistant Geoffrey Hammond, whose father – in an early example of what would one day be called blame culture – knew who was responsible, and it wasn't him or his boy: 'The first part of a policeman's job is crime prevention. They know queer-bashing on the common has been going on for years and failed in their duty for not stopping it. All the parents have been let down.' The class division between killer and victim was typical of such violence; in 1978 two youths, a bricklayer and a hod carrier, were jailed for life for the queer-bashing murder of Peter Benyon, a thirty-two-year-old librarian.

The skinhead cult had started as an obsessively working-class fashion statement, but by 1970 it had mutated into something far nastier: 'Every other schoolboy in England was reading scabby little exploitation paperback novels called *Skinhead* and *Skinhead Escapes*, following the tawdry exploits of Joe Hawkins, tooled-up, blood-spattered thug in a Harrington,' recalled former skin and future style writer Robert Elms; 'the whole thing was well on the way to parody'.

The paperbacks in question were written by James Moffat, the most successful, if not the most talented, pulp author of his time. Churning out a bewildering number of books, under a variety of pseudonyms and at great speed (he claimed that his record was writing a novel in 36 hours), Moffat struck gold in 1970 with *Skinhead*, published by the New English Library under the name Richard Allen. The story concerns Joe Hawkins, the leader of a small skinhead gang in the East End, and follows him through a week of violence and sex, taking in the full range of standard settings – football match, Brighton, youth club, pubs – visits to all of which provoke outbreaks of fighting with opposing gangs, public transport employees, hippies, Asians, and the police. In an attempt to provide him with some context, we first meet his father, a distant relation of Alf Garnett, a dock worker who doesn't quite have the courage of his convictions: 'He was completely disillusioned with this Labour government – but he wouldn't abstain nor vote Tory. He would vote Labour as he always had; as his dad and his granddad had.' But this background soon fades in favour of a denunciation of Joe's discredited culture: 'His was a senseless world of violence for the sake of violence; his ideal devised by those wishing the end of civilized behaviour patterns; his the star-struck era of pop and pot and the belief that might is right even if might has to play games and call itself right.' In this world Hawkins and his gang are seen as little more than animals, depicted in a way that prefigured the rats of James Herbert: 'They swarmed over him, knocking him to the ground, kicking and gouging and slashing with all the ferocity of their ugly minds.' And if there is a character articulating the authorial voice, it's the doctor who stitches up one of the victims. 'I'd like to see what a dictator could do in this country,' he despairs. 'Slums wiped out, harsh measures to curb the grab-all boys, savage sentences for injury to persons, hanging for child rapists and cop-killers, the birch for young offenders like these skinheads.'

Despite this wholly negative portrayal of its subjects, and much to the publisher's surprise, the book was a huge success, selling a reported million copies (given how rapidly it was passed around classrooms, it must have been read by millions more), and spawning a series of sequels that started with *Suedehead* and included *Skinhead Girls*, *Boot Boys*, *Smoothies* and *Terrace Terrors*. In a preface to *Suedehead*, Allen spelt out his own position, that skinheads were a product of 'our permissive society which has, rightly or wrongly, encouraged the growth of off-beat cults within a framework peopled by law-abiding, decent, sometimes dull citizens'. Claiming the pulp privilege of having his cake and selling it, he blamed 'mercenary-minded rag-trade merchants, a soft-pedalling attitude by politicians who look for teenage votes to save their seats, and an overwhelming pandering by the news media', and he warned that 'Britain cannot survive long in a climate of anarchy.'

Youth violence was far from a new development, of course, but skins were of a different order from those that had recently gone before, primarily in being so self-contained in their negativity; for all its aggression, skinhead was a curiously passive phenomenon with no obvious interest in interacting with, let alone changing, society. And, in a first for a post-war youth cult, it didn't even produce its own music, preferring to dance to the early versions of reggae that were coming out of Jamaica. The result was that, with the exception of a few imported records making the singles charts, this was a cult that had virtually no impact on a wider culture, save in the sense of instilling despair in those 'sometimes dull citizens' who Allen claimed to have close to his heart.

This majority – or at least those within it who paid attention – worried about the soil wherein this nihilism had grown, and perhaps the most commonly identified cause was the breakdown of discipline in schools, a development popularly linked to a decline in the physical chastisement of pupils. A 1968 survey showed that 40 per cent of primary school heads had unilaterally banned the use of the cane, and the Inner London Education Authority built on this trend towards liberalism, decreeing that, from 1973, corporal punishment would be outlawed in its primary schools (towards the end of the decade, Labour's education secretary, Shirley Williams, announced that the government was planning to abolish it in all primary schools, as well as special schools for the handicapped). That meant that it still remained in most secondary schools, though here problems arose as a result of the Sex Discrimination Act, passed in 1975. To comply with the new legislation, Heaton Park School in Newcastle upon Tyne, amongst others, announced that henceforth the strap, formerly used only on misbehaving boys, would now be applied also to girls; in response, some 200 girls walked out of their classrooms, and proceeded to vandalize property to such an extent that the police had to be called in to prevent a riot. Labour MP Renée Short protested that 'The aim of the Act was to bring the disadvantaged sex up to the standards of the advantaged, so we should be seeing that boys are no longer caned,' but she was then in a minority, even in Parliament. An attempt to ban all corporal punishment was voted down in the Commons, where Tory MP Patrick Cormack explained that his opposition to abolition was based on the fact that 'juvenile vandalism was costing the country £8.5m a year'. It didn't exactly speak well of the existing system, though a survey of teachers by the *Times Educational Supplement* in 1977 showed a clear majority still in favour of retaining corporal punishment, and the fear of even greater disorder was genuinely held.

Symptoms of this supposed fall in standards included reports of a game known as Potter, which achieved a degree of popularity with Putney schoolchildren in 1970. Named after the caretaker of Fenn Street Secondary Modern School in the sitcom *Please Sir!*, as played by Deryck Guyler, the practice involved 'harassing school and library caretakers, putting sticks through their bicycle spokes, and using accents similar to those of the television character'. Also causing concern was a new generation of toys that could be used in playground violence, starting with clackers (two solid plastic balls on either end of a piece of string; the string was held in the middle and the balls bounced together, as a kind of yo-yo for thugs). A succession of injured children, some of them hurt intentionally, prompted many schools to outlaw clackers, while the Home Office launched an investigation in 1971 into whether they should be banned outright. The following year, however, the craze ended as abruptly as crazes generally do, leaving the manufacturers, James of England, with 400,000 clackers in their warehouses and 170 workers redundant. Trivial though these stories might have sometimes appeared, the wider picture to which they contributed had serious implications; in 1975 it was reported that numbers of male applicants for teacher training courses had fallen by a third in just two years, with classroom discipline being the most frequently cited reason.

If the skinheads were one violent manifestation of the splintering of 1960s youth culture, then another was the Angry Brigade. A London-based anarchist organization of limited but uncertain strength, the Angry Brigade engaged in a series of bomb attacks in 1970–72, a campaign that resulted in a five-month trial at the Old Bailey, with four defendants convicted and another four acquitted. The targets of their actions were for the most part related, at least tangentially, to the political mainstream of the times – two bombs exploded at the house of employment secretary Robert Carr on the day of a mass demonstration against the Industrial Relations Bill, another at a Territorial Army recruitment centre following the introduction of internment in Northern Ireland – but the agenda was not always so clear. There was, for example, the strange case of the attack on the Biba shop in Kensington on 1 May 1971.

Biba had been present at the birth of swinging London – indeed the *Daily Telegraph* article by John Crosby that launched that phrase had named Biba's founder, Barbara Hulanicki, as one of the 'people who make London swing' – and it had since grown to become a fully fledged department store, run almost entirely by women and celebrated by its mostly female customers as a place of glamorous liberation. In its final incarnation, from 1973 to 1975, it would create an escapist paradise, a version of retail theatre that owed more to Busby Berkeley than to the high street, and that offered glam heaven to its customers and habitués: 'You can be Garbo! You can be Marilyn!' enthused the store's designer, Steve Thomas. 'It took girls out from being second-class citizens, secretaries and shopgirls, to being stars.' It also attracted the fashionable end of the middle-ageing '60s generation; the caftan-wearing wife of *The History Man*, in Malcolm Bradbury's satire of radical intellectuals, regularly disappears off to London for a 'Biba weekend', occasions for her to go shopping and meet up with her lover (she has, it need hardly be said, an open marriage).

Biba had thus emerged from the same cultural explosion that produced both the Angry Brigade and its supporters in the underground press and beyond, even if their paths had subsequently diverged. The *Guardian* was later to claim that it was 'some kind of macabre tribute' that Biba should be targeted by the bombers 'to protest the rising tide of capitalist female deco-decadence', though those who worked at the store, particularly the security officer, John Evans, who was injured in the blast, did not entirely appreciate the compliment. The May Day attack was allegedly ordered by feminist associates of the Brigade, angered by Biba's decadent appeal, and the admission of guilt issued in the wake of the bombing contained the one great slogan produced by the organization in its entire existence: 'If you're not busy being born, you're busy buying.' There was a certain irony, therefore, in the fact that the terrorist campaign itself inspired a new line of clothing. Craig Stuart Fashions Ltd, a strictly non-political company which 'had the dubious claim to fame of inventing loon pants' (the heavily flared jeans that became the uniform of 1970s hippies), went on to create a trouser in tribute to the Angry Brigade. 'Angry pants were introduced to follow up the phenomenal success of loons and were made in various shades of brushed denim,' remembered company founder Craig Austin. 'They sold quite well but never really took off in anything like the same incredible way as loons. Great name though.'

The bombs of the Angry Brigade were, as it turned out, only the prelude to the wave of political violence that was to engulf mainland Britain. Much more serious was the struggle by the Catholic minority in Northern Ireland, which had re-emerged in the late 1960s, and which became the source of terrorist attacks that lasted through to the end of the century. The scale of the problem was such that troops were sent into Ulster in 1969, with the intention that they might assist the police and step between the factions; or as folk singer Harvey Andrews put it in his 1972 song 'Soldier':

> Then came the call for Ireland as the call had come before,
> Another bloody chapter in an endless civil war.

It wasn't an appealing proposition, and Andrews's gloomy assessment was shared by Lieutenant General Sir Ian Freeland, the first commanding officer to be appointed to the province: 'Why won't they realize we are on the brink of civil war?' he asked in despair at his superiors in July 1969. For most of the UK population, however, a more typical response was summed up in the reported words of the home secretary, Reginald Maudling, on the plane back from his first visit to Ulster: 'What a bloody awful country!' he remarked to an air stewardess. 'For God's sake bring me a large Scotch.'

Maudling it was who made the most profound mistake of the period when, on 9 August 1971, he authorized the introduction of internment without trial for suspected terrorists and their sympathizers. The decision was made in the context of enormous pressure from the Protestant-dominated Parliament of Northern Ireland in Stormont, which still nominally controlled policing policy, but in the face of advice from Lt. Gen. Sir Harry Tuzo, who had taken over the military command: 'Other possibilities for disrupting the IRA should certainly be tried first,' he warned, adding that it would have a 'harmful effect'. In fact, the effects were beyond harmful and more akin to calamitous, with massive resentment at both the measure itself and its illiberal and incompetent implementation – amongst those imprisoned without charge was a seventy-seven-year-old blind man, who had last been arrested in 1929. Before internment, thirty-one people had been killed in the province in 1971; between then and the end of the year, the death toll rose by a further 150. The following year was the worst of all, with nearly 500 killed, and ten times that number injured; there were 'almost 2,000 explosions and over 10,000 shooting incidents, an average of around thirty shootings per day'.

In the midst of this mayhem, the Army itself had become complicit, firmly identified in the minds of Catholics with the repressive tactics of the Protestant state. As barricades went up in the streets of Belfast and Londonderry, creating no-go zones for the forces of law and order, and a virtual state of siege for some communities, reports spread of Army brutality and of simple callousness. 'She didn't have to tell me the story about the dead dog. I'd heard it,' reported Michael Walsh in *Tribune*; 'how soldiers had shot someone's pet, brandished the carcass before a Catholic crowd that hadn't been able to buy food for two days, and told the crowd, "Here's your fresh meat".'

From the point of view of the soldiers, they were engaged in an undeclared war with the IRA, one in which, they felt, their actions were constrained by civilian concerns. On one of the rare occasions when their grievances were aired publicly, Lord Richard Cecil, formerly a captain in the Grenadier Guards with three tours of the province, told the press that the troops were 'frustrated by the politicians' failure to combat the terrorists with strength'. And, he added rhetorically: 'What can you say to one of your men when he asks, "Which side are the politicians on, sir?"' With such public outlets few and far between, the barrack-room culture of the time was dominated by a grim humour, mostly at the expense of the untrained amateurs on the other side; a contemporary collection of 'Rhymes From Ulster' includes this typical example by a serving soldier:

> Jack and Jill went up the hill
> To plant a claymore mine,
> But got their neg and pos mixed up,
> The clever little swine.

> A great big bang spread them around
> Up in a cloud of smoke.
> I wish I could have been there,
> I do enjoy a joke.

The most significant deaths in that appalling tally for 1972 came on 30 January, 'Bloody Sunday', when thirteen unarmed civilians on a civil rights demonstration were shot dead by members of the Parachute Regiment. The horror of that day inaugurated a new, wider phase of the conflict, first with a 30,000-strong mob burning down the British embassy in Dublin, 'already blackened and damaged from petrol bomb attacks on two previous nights', and then with a bomb attack in Aldershot that killed seven people and brought the spectre of terrorism to England. In vain did A.W. Anderson, the home affairs minister in the Stormont government, try to put the Bloody Sunday deaths in perspective: 'Let us remember that terrorism has led to the deaths in only one year of seventy-two innocent civilians, forty-three soldiers, eleven policemen and five men of the Ulster Defence Regiment.' His pleas were futile, not least because in March, Edward Heath announced that the Northern Ireland Parliament was forthwith suspended, to be replaced by direct rule from Westminster, under a new secretary of state, William Whitelaw. So extreme had the situation become that the transfer of power was by no means assured: 'In the general turmoil and emotional upheaval,' wrote Whitelaw of his arrival in the province, 'even the long-established loyalty to the Crown of the civil service and the police could not be taken for granted.'

Although the levels of 1972 were never again to be reached, the remorseless cycle of killings and revenge killings, reprisals and counter-reprisals continued through the decade, as did the frustration amongst politicians and public alike on the mainland at the apparently irreconcilable historical grievances. 'There are two rival slogans to be seen around Belfast,' reported the press at the end of 1976: 'the Peace Movement's "Aren't Seven Years Enough?" and the Provisionals' "Aren't Seven Hundred Years Too Much?".' The bitterness of the religious divide between the two communities also left the rest of the country bewildered: a 1969 survey showed that 25 per cent of Britons declared no religious affiliation, while the comparable figure in Northern Ireland stood at just 2 per cent. In an increasingly secular society, the fact that three-quarters of the local population thought it important that the province 'should be a Christian country' was hard to comprehend.

The violence reached a new low in November 1974 when the Provisional IRA planted bombs in two Birmingham pubs, the Mulberry Bush and the Tavern in the Town, killing twenty-one members of the public and injuring another 182. Years later, after the release of the six men who had been wrongfully convicted of the murderous attacks, Birmingham-born Lawrence Hayward of the band Denim captured the still raw emotions of those in his home town: 'All around the people say, we hate the IRA, and we asked for justice but it never came . . .'

The fact that one has to reach into the 1990s to find a song articulating such feelings is indicative of one of the most notable aspects of the civil war raging in the United Kingdom: its virtual absence from the popular culture of the time. At the peak of the troubles, in the early '70s, Northern Ireland was the dog that didn't bark in the night. Despite the precedent of the politicization of American rock, for example, there was little response by musicians, save for a small handful of records in the early days: McGuinness Flint's 1971 single 'Let the People Go', John Lennon's Dylanesque album track 'Sunday, Bloody Sunday' in 1972 and, in the same year, 'Give Ireland Back to the Irish', a minor hit for Paul McCartney's band Wings, also written in response to Bloody Sunday:

> Great Britain, you are tremendous
> And nobody knows like me,
> But really what are you doing
> In the land across the sea?
> Tell me how would you like it
> If, on your way to work,
> You were stopped by Irish soldiers?
> Would you lie down, do nothing,
> Would you give in, or go berserk?

For those who thought this represented a low point in McCartney's lyric writing, the follow-up single, 'Mary Had a Little Lamb', was to demonstrate that there was further yet for the ex-Beatle to fall. Such was the nervousness of the times, however, that even the triteness of 'Give Ireland Back to the Irish' was banned by the BBC on political grounds. The Corporation did broadcast two interviews with David O'Connell, a self-professed member of the IRA, around the same time, but found itself in a running battle with the government for allegedly giving succour to Britain's enemies. 'They want us, in effect, to conduct a propaganda campaign for the Army, and for the government of Brian Faulkner, and against the Catholics,' a senior BBC executive, John Crawley, complained. 'We say we should be wrong to do that.' It was a short-lived protest. In 1971 the telecommunications minister, Christopher Chataway, pointedly remarked that the BBC should remember 'the values and the objectives of the society that they are there to serve', and the following year – with the pressure intensifying – the organization issued a statement explaining that while impartiality was important 'between the two communities in Northern Ireland', there were limits: 'between the British Army and the gunmen the BBC is not impartial and cannot be impartial'.

Over on ITV there was likewise little inclination to provoke a full-scale confrontation with the government by discussing the issues at stake, though again there were early exceptions. In a December 1970 edition of *Coronation Street*, during a discussion in the Rovers Return on the image of America overseas, Len Fairclough pointed out that 'ours isn't looking too good in Belfast at the moment, is it?' Similarly 'The Blue and the Green', a storyline in the children's series *The Tomorrow People*, sees civil disorder break out between two groups, identified by blue and green badges, and the parallels are spelt out: 'If you think there's no harm splitting people up into factions of any kind, religious or just the colour of a badge, well, look at Northern Ireland.'

The more common response, however, was simply an increase in the number of Irish jokes turning up on comedy shows and in society more generally. A typical example, taken from a 1975 student rag mag, shows every sign of having being amended from Catholic to Protestant terrorists, presumably in the interests of balance: 'Two UDA men were driving through Belfast, one of them with a bomb on his lap. "Patrick, I'm sure this thing's going to go off." "Don't worry, Mick. I've got a spare one in the boot."' The gags were, for the most part, non-political in nature, but the relentless mocking of the supposed stupidity of Irishmen acquired a certain edge in the '70s, as some noticed even at the time: 'Irish jokes are getting boring,' comments the narrator of Gordon Williams's 1974 novel *Big Morning Blues*. 'If they're so fucking dim, how come the whole British Army can't beat 'em?'

Apart from the self-censorship of the broadcasters, there was another key factor in the difficulty of portraying the conflict: the absence of any recognizable figure who could represent the Catholic minority. The biggest constitutional party, the SDLP, had been founded in 1970 with Gerry Fitt as its first leader, but he made little impact in most of the UK, while the IRA was pictured primarily as an anonymous, balaclava-wearing gunman. Certainly there was no face that could come close to matching the public profile enjoyed by Ian Paisley, who had emerged as the voice of the

Protestant working class in the 1960s, and who was elected to the Westminster Parliament in 1970 as MP for North Antrim amidst much local rejoicing: 'This day,' he announced in his stentorian tones, 'it is known in North Antrim that there is God in heaven.' Elsewhere, his election was greeted with more trepidation. The *Sun* advised the new prime minister to steer clear of any deals, linking the new MP with a more established rabble-rouser; Heath, it urged, 'must not compromise with Powellites and Paisleyites, however popular they may be with some voters'. It wasn't long before a single shout of the word 'No!' in a Northern Irish accent was sufficient to constitute an impression of Paisley and, by extension, of the Protestant majority. For those seeking 'impartiality' there was no Catholic equivalent until the rise of Gerry Adams a decade later.

In the absence of commentary from TV, cinema or rock music, the one area of culture that could freely address Northern Ireland was popular fiction. Among the first entries in the field was Peter Leslie's *The Extremists* (1970), which was advertised as 'a sensational novel of riot-torn Belfast', though it failed to deliver on the promise; by chapter three, it had become sufficiently aware of its clichés that it was abbreviating the phrase 'riot-torn Belfast' to 'RTB'. Later novels, most of them thrillers, had a broader perspective, while sharing a sense of weariness and exasperation at the intractability of the situation. 'The real agony for Christie was that he belonged to an establishment which, with the situation steadily deteriorating, was being brought increasingly under the control of London,' wrote John de St Jorre and Brian Shakespeare of a Protestant police officer in *The Patriot Game* (1974). 'And there was no way out even though, in common with many Ulster Protestants, he disagreed almost as much with Whitehall as he did with the declared enemies in the IRA and Republic.'

In Brian Freeborn's *Good Luck Mister Cain* (1976) a senior officer in the Royal Ulster Constabulary travels to London to hire a hitman prepared to kill a leading member of the IRA; 'I don't concern myself with politics,' warns Harry Grant, the small-time villain whom he recruits, but even he later confesses: 'I don't know what the British think they're doing over there.' And Graham Lord's *The Spider and the Fly* (1974) shows a British MP drinking in a Dublin pub: 'He felt a sudden anger at the blatant racialism, the powerful ignorance of a people drugged with legend. Who did they think they were, these leeches swollen with the very blood they denigrated? A rabble that had gnawed for centuries at England's breast, singing *Roisin Dubh* in English, a whole race denying its dependence with melancholy jests and a mawkish way with words.'

Despite the explosions in Birmingham, Guildford, Aldershot and London, the real tragedy of Northern Ireland was of course primarily played out in the province. But, more widely, the sense of incipient civil war provided a terrible counterpoint to the tensions engendered by strikes and blackouts. Mark Patterson, chairman of the Film Viewing Committee at the Greater London Council, warned in 1972 that 'We are going to have to consider the social and political implications of certain films.' He was being interviewed by critic Alexander Walker, who noted: 'Dr Patterson was at pains to stress that political censorship was not sought by his sub-committee, but I formed the impression that its members, disturbed by chaos in Ulster, the Aldershot outrages and violence in the picket lines during the miners strike, are tending to sharpen and harden their attitude to films that reflect anarchy without providing answers.'

The movie that was causing such soul-searching was Stanley Kubrick's *A Clockwork Orange*, a shockingly violent film based on Anthony Burgess's 1962 novel. 'It is not, in my view, a very good novel,' commented Burgess himself, but even if one accepts his self-criticisms ('too didactic, too linguistically exhibitionist'), there is no doubting its power or its influence. The plot concerns a small-time gang leader named Alex, who loves Beethoven and thuggery in equal measure and, having been convicted of murder, finds himself being reprogrammed through a form of aversion therapy to reject violence, before reverting to type. In the last chapter of the novel Alex decides that he wants to settle down to raise a family, and while it's far from a conventional happy ending – since he's also aware that his own children will have a similar phase of development to pass through – it does change the nature of the story, by recasting the earlier violence as a disorder of male adolescence. Kubrick, however, jettisoned this chapter in his adaptation, a decision that brought forward a more immediately troubling, though more superficial, theme: that violence is an essential part of humanity.

The film was supposedly set in the future, but there was actually little to distance it from contemporary Britain, a fact which made it all the more disturbing when it premièred in January 1972 at the height of the first miners' strike. It also attracted much negative criticism since its stylized visuals, invented slang and gang costumes had an enormous fascination for the youth market, for the very people that Burgess had warned were prey to violent tendencies. In particular, the set pieces in the first forty minutes – the almost balletic scenes of Alex and his droogs on the rampage, staging a fight with a rival gang, committing a rape and then a murder – imprinted themselves so strongly on the imagery of British youth culture that they show no signs of being forgotten.

The press campaign against the film centred, as such media controversies invariably will, on the supposed possibilities of copycat violence, and the usual search for related incidents was undertaken. One of the most publicized was the murder of a tramp in Buckinghamshire, which appeared to mimic a scene in the movie, though the manufactured outrage fell a little flat when it was discovered that the killer, while he had read the book, had never actually seen the film. Even so, the hostile reception persuaded Kubrick, apparently fearful that he would become a target for violent attacks by anti-violence campaigners, to withdraw the film from public screenings in Britain in 1974, a decree that lasted until his death. This unprecedented act of self-censorship enshrined the movie's status as a key work of rebel art. Just as it became important in the mid- to late '70s for any poseur worth his salt to claim a long-standing love of commercially unsuccessful bands like Iggy and the Stooges and the Velvet Underground, so too was he obliged to have seen *A Clockwork Orange*, preferably at the time, but if that couldn't be made credible, then at least in Paris, where it proved a popular tourist attraction for visiting British youth.

A simultaneous controversy engulfed *Straw Dogs*, another film by an American director – Sam Peckinpah – that was based on a British novel and filmed in Britain. Dustin Hoffman played David Sumner, a mild-mannered mathematician seeking refuge with his wife (Susan George) in an apparently idyllic Cornish village. From this distance, his native America is perceived as a society in crisis: 'Bombing, rioting, sniping, shooting the blacks – can't walk down the streets, they say,' comments one of the locals, a man who will later be seen throwing live rats at Sumner's terrified wife during a night of siege and slaughter. Rural England turns out to be every bit as brutal as downtown Los Angeles or Detroit, and ultimately Sumner has to turn to the violence within himself simply in order to survive and to retain any sense of self-worth. 'I care,' he declares defiantly, when he finally decides to take a stand against the thugs who have been taunting and persecuting him throughout the long build-up and who have, though he isn't aware of the fact, also raped his wife. 'This is where I live. This is me. I will not allow violence against this house.'

Even more than Kubrick, Peckinpah took considerable liberties with the source material, Gordon Williams's novel *The Siege of Trencher's Farm*. 'They've added a rape scene, an act of buggery and lots of violence that was not in the book,' complained Williams, though Peckinpah was unrepentant: 'I think Mr Williams has a penchant for his own work,' he chuckled. 'I don't.' His gleeful transfer of the Wild West to the West Country was far from everyone's taste – critic Pauline Kael called it 'the first American film that is a fascist work of art' – but *Straw Dogs* remains a compelling vision of a man driven to extremes by a society that has abandoned order.

The ultimate theme – that civilization hasn't obviated the need for violent self-defence, or even simply violence itself – was to become a standard feature of '70s cinema, from *Taxi Driver* to *Death Wish*, the latter neatly reversing the journey of Kubrick and Peckinpah, as British director Michael Winner showed the Americans the horrors of their own society. None, however, made quite the same impact as *A Clockwork Orange* or *Straw Dogs*. After them, mainstream cinema toned down its most violent impulses, but beyond even the sight of extreme horror, the timing was crucial: the two films were released just as Britain began to fear its own disintegration. The buttons they pushed – youth gangs, the besieged middle class, the need for uncompromising measures to deal with decadence – encapsulated so much of the period that their unflinching depiction on a big screen was guaranteed to amplify society's fears for the worst.

5

Unions
'I can ruin the government's plan'

Only one thing can threaten our future. That is our continued
tragic record of industrial strife. We can't afford the luxury of
tearing ourselves apart any more. This time the strife has got to
stop. Only you can stop it.
Edward Heath (1974)

Don't YOU ever feel like shooting a Union Leader?
George Shipway, *The Chilian Club* (1971)

Rigsby: Don't you know what's behind all these strikes? All this
political unrest? Russian gold!
Eric Chappell, *Rising Damp* (1974)

'This coal strike is the beginning of a revolution,' warned the foreign
secretary; 'power is passing from the House of Commons to the trade
unions.'

Sir Edward Grey was speaking in 1912, but sixty years later his words
would still have found a ready audience. For if there was one theme that
dominated politics in the 1970s it was that of the untrammelled power, as
it was seen in certain quarters, of the trade unions, and the terrible
consequences that would surely result. 'To some of us, the Shrewsbury
pickets had committed the worst of all crimes, worse even than murder,
the attempt to achieve an industrial or political objective by criminal
violence, the very conduct, in fact, which helped to bring the National
Socialist German Workers Party to power in 1933,' wrote Robert Mark.
'Conduct of that kind kills freedom, and there are still people who feel that
freedom is more important than life itself.' The fact that one of the
Shrewsbury Two – building workers imprisoned in 1972 for 'conspiracy to
intimidate' on the picket line – later turned out to be the affable, banjo-

playing actor Ricky Tomlinson from *The Royle Family* suggests that Mark may have misplaced his apocalyptic indignation, but his argument was not untypical of its time.

The popular image of the trade union activist had been fixed as long ago as 1959 with Peter Sellers as Fred Kite in *I'm All Right Jack*, forever calling his men out on strike and dreaming of the paradise that was the Soviet Union ('All them corn fields and ballet in the evening'). His would-be 1970s equivalent was Vic Spanner, the Zapata-moustached shop steward in a lavatory factory, played by Kenneth Cope in *Carry On at Your Convenience* (1971), an unlovable figure who signally fails to represent his members. 'All we want is an honest day's work,' they plead, to which he responds: 'Listen, brother, it's Bolshie talk like that that got this country in the mess it's in today.' Similarly, when one of the workers complains about a proposed strike, Spanner replies, 'If you'll pardon me, you don't have a say. This is union business.' 'But it is our union, isn't it?' protests another worker. 'Exactly,' snaps Spanner. 'And for that reason you'll do as I bloody told you.' The tension between leader and led reaches a peak towards the end of the film when Spanner is organizing a picket: 'All right brothers, we have got to keep a full picket line today because I have heard that some of the men want to come back to work.' His henchman Bernie Hulke (Bernard Bresslaw) asks: 'Well, if they want to, how are we going to stop them?' 'Force!' replies Spanner grimly, handing out baseball bats to the picketers.

If none of this sounds typical of the cheerful, saucy spirit of the *Carry On* movies, that's probably because it wasn't; this was a film that took the series into the troubled waters of industrial politics and left the cast floundering out of their depth. It could, though, have been worse. The working title was *Carry On Comrade*, and in the original cut it also featured Terry Scott in an unsympathetic portrayal of a union boss named Mr Allcock. That character was lost in the editing, which helped tone down the anti-union sentiments, but even so actor Richard O'Callaghan (who played Lewis Boggs, the boss's son) was unimpressed: 'I personally was very embarrassed by what I was doing,' he commented later. 'It was all so right-wing, presenting the unions as complete asses – when, in fact, the unions were protecting millions of people's security in this country at the time. I believe the box-office takings reflected this.' He was quite correct about the takings; in general, the barrel-scraping budget of *Carry On* meant that a film could recoup its costs in three days at the box office – it took *Carry On at Your Convenience* nearly five years to do so. It was not much of a surprise that after this disaster, the team scuttled back to safer ground in their next outing, *Carry On Matron*, the fourth medical setting for the series.

The problem was that, although they were subsequently adopted as an emblem of British culture, the appeal of the *Carry On* movies in their own time was strictly to a working-class audience, and *Convenience*'s middle-class assault on unions was wildly inappropriate. This was, after all, 1971, when Edward Heath's government was attempting to limit by law the activities of the trade unions, and when the fightback began in earnest.

The success in 1969 of the trade union leadership in defeating 'In Place of Strife' – the Labour plan to impose legal restrictions on union activity – had strengthened the resolve of the Heath government to make changes to legislation; the result was the 1971 Industrial Relations Bill, described by miners' leader Joe Gormley as the 'unexpurgated copy' of 'In Place of Strife', which passed through Parliament, but was never fully implemented. And the motivation behind both sets of proposals was the same: a fear of the growing militancy of shop stewards.

Traditionally, unions were organized on geographical and occupational bases, with a hierarchy of officials at branch, district and national levels. Separate from this structure, though, were the shop stewards, who represented union members within a specific workplace and whose primary job was to liaise between the workforce and management. There were in 1975 an estimated 300,000 shop stewards in Britain. It was this alternative power base that became the preoccupation of industry, and therefore of politicians, as the number of small-scale, unofficial strikes grew steadily through the 1960s. The growing power of the shop stewards was where Tony Benn saw hope for the future of socialism, but for many others, it signified potential peril: Fred Kite, Vic Spanner and their ilk, it was believed, were threatening to wrest control of the union movement from the decent, moderate leaders, who were considered to have been a mostly responsible force, at least since the crushing defeat of the 1926 General Strike. And the elections of left-wingers Jack Jones and Hugh Scanlon ('the terrible twins', as they were nicknamed) to head the transport and the engineering unions respectively led to fears that the militancy was becoming contagious.

Certainly, argued sometime employment secretary Norman Tebbit, this was Heath's misguided view, that the leaders were reasonable men, while everyone on the shop floor was a rabid militant. And the legislation he brought forward was founded on this belief: a complicated structure of union registration, with unofficial strikes made illegal, and the whole thing to be controlled by the new National Industrial Relations Court. But the TUC, having seen off the Labour government on the issue, was in no mood to submit docilely to the Tories. In September 1971 it voted for a policy of non-cooperation, simply refusing to allow its member unions to enter themselves on the official register, and threatening those which did with expulsion; thirty-two unions, few of even moderate size or strength, were in fact expelled and there seemed no obvious way for the government to compel cooperation on those remaining.

In 1972 it was the turn of the NIRC to face – and fail – its first great test. Two companies running container depots found their premises being picketed by dockers, concerned at the loss of jobs that would be caused by containerization of the ports; the firms applied to the NIRC for an injunction against such action, and the court found in their favour, ordering the arrest of five of the pickets. Vic Feather, the general secretary of the TUC, had predicted that 'as soon as the first trade unionist goes to prison, all hell will be let loose', and he was to be proved right; the Pentonville Five (that being the jail in which the dockers were imprisoned) became an instant cause célèbre, 'like modern-day Tolpuddle Martyrs'. The TUC voted to stage a one-day general strike, but it didn't prove necessary in the face of a vacillating government. A hastily called protest march on Pentonville took on something of the air of a triumphal procession, so certain were its participants of victory: 'I can still feel the electricity going through my body,' remembered Dennis Skinner, the only MP on the demonstration, thirty-five years later. 'I'd been on many marches, but I could see this was something different.' And indeed the show of strength proved sufficient; the next day a very questionable legal loophole was uncovered that allowed the release of the five men, a move that effectively ended the possibility that the Act was ever to be of any use. While the government claimed to have had no involvement in the legal arguments, it was widely considered to have been behind the Five's release, choosing to run rather than fight and lose; 'Their protests were not credible,' insisted another Labour left-winger, Eric Heffer. 'Working-class solidarity had inflicted its first major defeat on the Heath government. It was not long before it struck again.'

The Act was to be repealed by the next Labour government in 1974, and its ignominious ending ensured that there would be no further legal moves to limit union activity until the Thatcherite onslaught of the early 1980s. Public concern, however, showed no signs of abating. As the dust settled on the traumatic events of 1971–72, when the miners and the Pentonville Five had won broad support and sympathy, the sober realization began to dawn that there was a force in the land capable of inflicting serious policy defeats on democratically elected governments of either colour. Henceforth union leaders were almost invariably referred to in the press as trade union barons, evoking images of medieval struggles between rival power bases, though, as Tony Benn pointed out, the terminology was inaccurate: 'Barons aren't elected'.

Although the likes of Feather, Gormley, Jones and Scanlon became household names, the most commonly depicted union figure in popular culture remained the shop steward. Following on from Fred Kite, the BBC sitcom *The Rag Trade* (1961–63) established a basic workplace format with Peter Jones, as the eponymous boss of Fenner Fashions, engaged in a war of attrition with the shop steward, Paddy (Miriam Karlin). It enjoyed enormous success – twenty-five years later *The Listener* was to refer to it as 'the most popular TV series of all time' – and the template was copied by several subsequent sitcoms including *On the House* and *Up the Workers*. The original was even revived itself on ITV in 1977, after a proposed spin-off movie – *The Rag Trade Goes Mod* – had failed to get off the drawing board at Hammer Films.

What was noticeable in all these blue-collar workplace sitcoms was their lack of engagement in political argument. The one major exception was *The Dustbinmen*, created by Jack Rosenthal. Here the central character, Cheese and Egg (Bryan Pringle), is not a shop steward, but rather a highly articulate barrack-room lawyer with anarchist inclinations, more used to ducking and diving than he is to organizing; essentially he is the descendant of Alfred Doolittle, as portrayed by Stanley Holloway in *My Fair Lady*, with a strong side helping of Sgt. Bilko, though the class politics were much sharper than anywhere else in the TV comedy of the time. A 1970 episode revealed a binman from another team in the depot to be a Tory voter ('You can get ten years for that!'), and in the resultant argument Cheese and Egg lambasts the members of his own crew: 'There's always been thick buttocks like you, full of gripe and argument, but not prepared to do anything,' he rages. 'I reckon I know how the Tolpuddle Martyrs felt, shipped abroad like convicts because unions were illegal in those days. And now you've got the benefit. So next time, don't blame the government, don't blame the bosses, because it's your own pigging fault.'

That episode came from the third, and final, series of *The Dustbinmen*, broadcast just before the 1970 dirty jobs strike that brought refuse collection so sharply into the public domain. According to an official in NUPE (the union that was primarily involved) that was in fact the deliberate intention of the action: to make people aware 'of dirt below the surface'. The public, he pointed out, 'don't want to know about hospital porters having to take arms and legs from operating theatres to the furnaces, or crematoria workers having to put burnt bones into grinding machines, or gravediggers, or what it's like down the sewers'.

Less spectacular strikes, especially those concentrated on a single small employer, generally went unrecorded, but could still cause huge distress to those concerned, and cumulatively offered little hope for the future of British industry. 'The funeral will take place on November 10 of Tina Transport which died of strangulation by the Transport & General Workers Union,' read a bitterly ironic notice issued by a Norfolk haulage company, closing down after a seven-month dispute. 'The immediate mourners are Miss Christine Brown, aged 11, and Miss Beverley Brown, aged 3, whose future depended on Tina Transport. The TGWU choir will render "The fight is o'er, the battle won".'

Pop music too was touched, even if only peripherally, by the upheavals of the time. In 1974 Alan Price, formerly of Newcastle band the Animals, scored a top 10 hit with 'The Jarrow Song', inspired by the great crusade of the unemployed in 1936, and taken from his album *Between Today and Yesterday*:

> My name is little Billy White,
> and I know what's wrong and I know what's right,
> and the wife says 'Geordie, go to London Town!
> And if they don't give us a couple of bob,
> won't even give you a decent job,
> then Geordie, with my blessings, burn them down.'

The parallels with the contemporary situation were made explicit in the bridge passage: 'I can see them, I can feel them, and I'm thinking nothing's changed much today.' Diametrically opposed to Price's supportive stance, and even more successful and enduring, was 'Part of the Union', a hit for the Strawbs in early 1973:

> So though I'm a working man,
> I can ruin the government's plan;
> Though I'm not too hard, the sight of my card
> Makes me some kind of superman.

Clearly intended as a parody of union power, the piece has enjoyed a chequered life, surely the only song to have been covered both by comedian Jim Davidson (as the B-side to his hagiographic 1985 single 'Maggie') and, at a 2006 gig, by New York poet-rocker Patti Smith. Most notable has been its unusual drift across the political spectrum from right to left. The tub-thumping, singalong chorus ensured that, despite the ironic tone of the lyrics, the song was soon to be annexed by those it was satirizing; barely a year after its release, it was to be heard pumping out of loudspeakers mounted on the car of the future Labour leader Neil Kinnock, as he toured his South Wales constituency during the first election of 1974. Thirty years later it was to be played at the funeral of the militant Nottinghamshire miner Keith Frogson, its status as a workers' anthem seemingly assured.

The humour of the Strawbs' single was not unrelated to the curious relationship that rock stars enjoyed with the rules of their own organization, the Musicians' Union. All fans knew – or thought they knew – that when appearing on TV shows such as *Top of the Pops* the artists mimed to their hit records, but in fact this wasn't quite the case; as Don Smith, then the sessions organizer of the MU, explained, the actual rule was that 'no records could be used as the basis of a mimed performance'. If a band was asked to appear on *Top of the Pops*, therefore, it was given a three-hour studio session, in which to re-record the relevant song, and it was this tape to which the group would then mime on television. (The time limit was fixed by the BBC, and reflected the fact that the Corporation had to pay the musicians, even if only at the standard union rate.) The intention was that musicians wouldn't lose work through gramophone records being broadcast on TV, when their members could have been playing live, and the result was supposed to be that the people you saw on your screen were the actual people who made the music, even if it had been pre-recorded a few hours, or even a few weeks, earlier. It was, though, a system that was widely abused, with producers pretending to make a new recording, whilst actually using a tape of the original single. As Chris Redburn, formerly of the band Kenny, recalled: 'There was a famous MU guy – Dr Death, they used to call him – who would come to the studio to watch you record, and they'd get him wrecked. He was pissed as a newt by the end of it, and they used to switch the tapes. It was ridiculous, a real farce.' Even so, there were bands prepared to take the proposition seriously; Smith was present at a session in which Queen knocked out a version of the ferociously complex 'Killer Queen' in under three hours.

A similar situation arose over 'needle time', the name given to the agreement between the union and the BBC over how much radio airtime was permitted to be taken up with the broadcasting of records – the 1973 settlement allowed 97 hours a week across what were then the four national stations. Again the intention was to create work for MU members, by encouraging the use of almost-live performance. To cut down on the number of records played, bands would be invited to record songs for John

Peel or one of the other Radio One shows, so that, for example, David Bowie would record four tracks in three hours for the standard fee of £12 a session, to be broadcast on a specified programme. Here there was no cheating and, as it happened, out of the practice came some of the best music of the era, particularly when Peel gave the opportunity to an unsigned band like Roxy Music or Siouxsie and the Banshees to record and broadcast for the first time. For the artists, the major handicap was learning not to offend the engineers and electricians in the strictly unionized BBC studios: 'You weren't even allowed to plug your own guitar amp into the mains socket, or adjust a microphone to your height,' recalled Bowie's producer Tony Visconti. 'Any transgression of the rules threatened a union walkout.'

The Musicians' Union was an unusual case, of course, a body that included in its ranks both unemployed craftspeople and the biggest stars of the entertainment world. The same was true of Equity, its equivalent for actors, though this tended to attract a more vociferous far-left element than almost any other union. When Vanessa Redgrave, an active member of the Workers Revolutionary Party, was rehearsing her appearance on the Morecambe and Wise show, she attempted to engage the two men in political debate, arguing that they too were part of an exploited working class. 'Do you *own* the BBC?' she asked fervently. 'No,' replied Ernie Wise, casting a casual glance around the studio, 'but we're willing to make them an offer.'

Even so, the regulations of the MU and Equity typified what became known as restrictive practices – or protective practices, as the docker Jack Dash insisted they be called – of the unions. Demarcation disputes, over which group of workers did which job, were reported endlessly in the press, while the newspaper industry itself was notorious for its 'outrageously high manning levels', as the unofficial history of the *Sun* noted: 'members of the same basic workforce signed on twice for the same job, using false names to get a second wage packet'. Amongst the pseudonyms typically used by these phantom print workers were the likes of Mickey Mouse and Lester Piggott. The perceived obsession with rules and regulations, with the implication of work-shy workers and far-left shop stewards, was such that mere mention in a comedy of the union rule book could guarantee a laugh. The stand-up comic Bernard Manning used to tell a joke about Alexey Kosygin being shown round a British factory by Edward Heath, and being shocked by the slack working hours and the prevalence of tea breaks: 'In Russia,' he boasts, 'we work from six in the morning till ten o'clock at night.' 'You couldn't get these lads to do that,' says Heath. 'Why not?' demands the Soviet premier, and Heath replies: 'Because they're all communists.'

The spectre of communism was indeed then haunting political debate in the country. Following the traumatic events of its first quarter-century – the Berlin airlift, the Hungarian uprising, the Cuban Missile Crisis, the Prague Spring – the Cold War spent the 1970s at an unprecedented level of calmness. It appeared for a while as though the conflict had been fought to a standstill, that the West and the East had settled for coexistence, or at least were catching their breath before resuming hostilities. But to a society that had been brought up to fear an external threat, in the form of Marxist expansionism, this sudden thawing of the Cold War was strangely disconcerting, and in its confusion the nation appeared to turn in on itself, to internalize the fear. The hatred that had been directed at Moscow was transferred to the supposed traitors in our midst; it wasn't invasion but internal corruption that now captured the fevered imagination, a tendency that reached its most extraordinary manifestation in the belief amongst sections of the security services that Harold Wilson himself was a Soviet agent.

Those who denounced 'the communist menace to British industry and the country' were at this stage more concerned with the Communist Party of Great Britain than with the various Trotskyist groups that were later to attract so much attention. And while politically the CPGB hadn't had an MP since 1950 (the best it managed in the 1970s was the 6,000 votes registered by Jimmy Reid, who had led the work-in at the Upper Clyde Shipbuilders), there was, it was suggested, a serious industrial threat. In this interpretation of society, the party was believed to have worked tirelessly for several decades to get its men placed high in key unions, with the intention of destabilizing the nation. And when someone like Hugh Scanlon, a former party member, argued that the job of the unions 'must be to change society itself, not merely to get the best out of existing society', there were plenty who saw their fears confirmed.

In the winter of 1973–74, as it became apparent that Heath's government was heading for a decisive showdown with the unions, the red scare spread like a rash, with particular attention being focused on Mick McGahey, the vice-president of the National Union of Mineworkers and a member of the CPGB's executive. When suggestions arose that troops might be sent in to deal with the imminent miners' strike, it was McGahey's contribution to the debate that captured the headlines, calling on soldiers who were placed in this situation to disobey orders. Harold

Wilson put down a Commons motion condemning his comments, and the right-wing press denounced furiously this incitement to mutiny. 'Tiny in numbers, the communists have nonetheless achieved a crippling grip on vital industries,' claimed the *Daily Express*, 'so that again and again we have missed our expansion targets and have been dragged down by industrial strife and sabotage. Whoever wins this election must make sure the communists lose.'

Coming up fast behind McGahey as a communist bogeyman was Arthur Scargill, who was elected leader of the Yorkshire miners in 1973 and would become perhaps the most famous, certainly the most controversial, union leader in British history. He had been a member of the national committee of the Young Communist League, though whether he progressed into adult membership of the CPGB was never entirely clear. Certainly he never seemed to feel the need for a revolutionary party in the Leninist mould: his strategy, his style, his politics were all his own, not the product of a committee or a party position. Even so, he was widely considered to be a communist in all but name by his many enemies, amongst them Scargill's own NUM president, Joe Gormley, who was secretly reporting back to the security services. ('He loved his country,' commented Gormley's handler in Special Branch on his client. 'He was a patriot and he was very wary about the growth of militancy within his union.') An alternative, possibly more damaging, account of Scargill was that he was a self-publicizing grandstander. Ian MacGregor, who was chairman of the National Coal Board during the great strike of 1984–85, was later to write that the 1972 dispute gave Scargill 'his first taste of three drugs, the effects of which were to addict him for ever. They were the glamour of leadership in battle, the power of the revolutionary mob and the magic of performing on television.'

Some things are unarguable about Scargill. First, he was an effective public speaker, rising to the big occasion, even if his technique varied little – he started loud and angry, then increased the volume. Second, despite failing to communicate any clear programme for change, he was at heart a revolutionary: 'It's no good compromising. History is littered with abortive attempts to reform capitalism,' he declared. 'What we need is a complete and utter change in this society.' And third, in the medium term he failed not only to instigate such a change, but also to secure the jobs and future of his members. The official account of his career notes that 'In 1953, at the age of 15, he left school and went to work at the (now closed) Woolley Colliery which at that time employed 3,000 miners.' Coincidentally, when he finally stood down as president of the NUM, after twenty years in office, the entire membership of the national union now stood at 3,000. It had numbered 700,000 on its creation in 1945.

The truth was that, although communists were undeniably represented in the ranks of trade union officials to an extent that belied their numbers in society, and although there was undoubtedly a longer-term political agenda in the minds of some, the vast majority of union members embarked upon industrial disputes, as they always had, simply because they wished to defend their livelihoods, and because they thought they were in with a decent shout of winning. The unions were not revolutionary institutions, but precisely the opposite; despite the rhetoric of Scanlon and Scargill, the function of trade unions was to achieve an accommodation within a capitalist society to the advantage of their members, and there was little appetite for anything more. 'There isn't a Lenin lurking in the wings,' wrote Benn at the height of the struggle against the Industrial Relations Act in 1972. 'The Angry Brigade couldn't pick up a hundred votes in any constituency.'

Furthermore, the popular 1970s perception that union members were, like the troops of the Great War, lions led by donkeys, tended to obscure the fact that, even in those militant days, unions did not exist simply to go on strike. The historic task of fighting to improve wages and conditions, in the face of continuing opposition by employers, was as vital a part of national life as ever it had been. The more mundane day-to-day concerns of unions were centred on their members' welfare (in 1971 the General and Municipal Workers' Union 'spent £3.3 million on funeral benefits, considerably more than its total spending on strike pay'), and on issues like health and safety at work, a serious concern, as Benn noted when reporting the 1976 figures: 'Eight workers a day are killed in industry, there are 3,000 accidents a day, 23 million man days lost by accidents – which is four times as many as by strikes.'

There was one major exception, a strike that was purely and explicitly political from start to finish, but since it fitted into the mythology of neither right nor left, it has tended to be played down in industrial history. In 1973 representatives of the British and Irish governments, together with those of some parties in Northern Ireland, signed the Sunningdale Agreement (named after the civil service training centre in Berkshire, where the discussions took place). At the heart of the agreement was a proposal for a Northern Ireland Assembly that would represent both Protestant and Catholic parties in a power-sharing coalition government, and the Assembly did in due course come into being. Unfortunately, its very existence was opposed both by the IRA and, more importantly, by a majority of senior Protestant politicians. In the February 1974 general election the United Ulster Unionist Council, an anti-Sunningdale alliance, won eleven of the twelve Westminster seats for Northern Ireland, and it reasonably interpreted this as a popular vote against the Assembly. In May of that year a general strike in the province was called with the avowed intention of bringing down the Agreement.

Initiated by the Ulster Workers' Council, the strike was supported by the Ulster Defence Association, a recently launched umbrella organization of paramilitary loyalist groups, whose contribution in the form of road-blocks and armed threats ensured a huge response. 'There was relatively little overt violence, but then there did not need to be,' noted one account. 'It was intimidation on a huge scale.' And despite the declaration of a state of emergency in the Six Counties, there was little appetite for intervention by the armed forces, whose leadership allegedly had some sympathy for the strikers. As an army officer commented: 'For the first time, the Army decided that it was right and that it knew best and the politicians had better toe the line.'

As industrial output fell in the province, and the inevitable power blackouts began, the newly elected prime minister, Harold Wilson, made a wildly inflammatory TV broadcast, denouncing the strikers as 'people who spend their lives sponging on Westminster and British democracy and then systematically assault democratic methods'. A new phenomenon was born on the streets of Northern Ireland: people wearing little pieces of sponge in their buttonholes, to demonstrate that they were the spongers of whom he so disapproved, and that they remained defiant. After two weeks, Brian Faulkner, the man who had already had the dubious honour of being the last-ever prime minister of Northern Ireland, resigned as the chief executive of the Assembly, and the Sunningdale Agreement fell in ruins.

Wilson's fear and fury when confronted with the Protestant workers' strike was perhaps understandable. He had, after all, been returned to Downing Street in a general election sparked by what was widely seen as a politically motivated strike; such action having brought down the previous government, he was more aware than anyone of the power of a mobilized working class.

That election of February 1974 proved to be one of the great miscalculations of British political history. Edward Heath had a substantial parliamentary majority, despite the backbench sniping of Enoch Powell and his consorts, and was not obliged to call an election until the following year. But as the oil crisis worsened, and as the miners voted, by over 80 per cent, to extend their overtime ban into a full-scale strike, Heath decided that enough industrial militancy was enough, and that the country should make its mind up on a fundamental issue. 'Do you want a strong government which has clear authority for the future to take the decision which will be needed?' he asked in his television broadcast announcing that there would be an election. 'Or do you want them to abandon the struggle against rising prices under pressure from one particular group of workers?'

It was clearly intended as a rhetorical question, but the electorate took it as a serious enquiry. If the issue was 'Who governs Britain?' then the answer was self-evidently: 'Not the man who can't control the unions'. By polling day the country had endured two months' worth of the three-day week and patience was running thin: wage packets were being hit, a million people had signed on the dole as the cutbacks started and there was a serious shortage of bread and other staple goods. It was, fortunately, the mildest January since 1932, which eased some of the pain, but even so everyone was being squeezed both at work and at home, and blame was being apportioned to the Arabs, the unions and the government; the only question, for electoral purposes, was: in what proportion?

The press reported that the coming miners' strike could make 4 million workers unemployed, and cause the deaths of up to 1 million pensioners, while Michael Chapman, the president of the Confederation of British Industry, said that the country was facing a crisis 'almost as serious as the outbreak of war'. The government's own pronouncements were simply self-contradictory: on 18 January the minister of power, Lord Carrington, announced the return of a four-day week, which never materialized; instead, within a fortnight, he was warning of a possible two-day week. In the midst of such extremities and such confusion, a prime minister who appeared to doubt his own authority was of little obvious use to the nation.

The torment of the Tories was played out in the fifth series of the BBC sitcom *Till Death Us Do Part*, which aired in those crucial months of January and February 1974. The central character, Alf Garnett, a Conservative-supporting docker played by Warren Mitchell, had become a huge TV hero in the mid-1960s by articulating the fears and failings of the traditionalist white working class, whilst engaging in a perpetual struggle with both his subtly subversive wife, Else (Dandy Nichols), and his socialist son-in-law Mike (Anthony Booth). Now, as the government he had advocated through the years of Wilson's administration began to disintegrate, he was left isolated, adrift in a sea of confusion, losing touch completely with his family: Else is more withering in her put-downs, Mike is mockingly triumphant, and his daughter Rita (Una Stubbs) has become vocal about the subjugation of women.

Alf, who is himself working a three-day week, finds his world of certainties crashing about him. 'You've got a little boy and you'll find you'll have to bring him up the same, the best way you know,' he appeals tearfully to Rita, clutching at an analogy between parenting and Mike's politics: 'You'll make mistakes. I suppose I have. I'll admit some of my ideas might be wrong, I'll admit that. But are his ideas right, eh? Can his lot prove that their way's the right way? Can they prove that they know better than the rest of us?'

But his opponents are not in the mood to give any quarter. 'Everyone wants to get back on the job, everyone,' seethes Rita, in an explosion of hatred at Heath. 'And everyone wants to pay the miners. But old fatso won't, oh no. He makes me sick, every time I see him on there with his great porky face wobbling with fat.' Her husband meanwhile is exultant: 'These are the greatest days England's ever gone through,' crows Mike. 'The people are rising at last, they're rising at last and they've said: We don't want any crumbs from your economy.'

And finally, on the edge of a nervous breakdown, Alf Garnett spits out the truth he has so long hidden even from himself: 'Sod Mister Heath!'

PART TWO

GOLDEN YEARS
1974–1976

While everything, all forms of social organization, broke up, we lived on, adjusting our lives, as if nothing fundamental was happening. It was amazing how determined, how stubborn, how self-renewing, were the attempts to lead an ordinary life.
Doris Lessing, *The Memoirs of a Survivor* (1974)

FLETCHER: Do you know this country is on the verge of economic ruin? This once-great nation of ours is teetering on the brink of an abyss.
Dick Clement and Ian Le Frenais, *Porridge* (1975)

Goodbye, Great Britain. It was nice knowing you.
Wall Street Journal (1975)

6

The Wilson Years

'Did you miss me?'

> Do you think a Labour government these days can have a member who's rumoured to be a Red? Not any more it can't. You know what the Party's like these days – it's more conservative than the bloody Tories.
>
> Graham Lord, *The Spider and the Fly* (1974)

> Kramer had grown tired of London which was no longer the swinging city of the sixties. All the best people had gone. Heading for the next fashionable hot spot. London, and indeed the whole of England, was on the scrapheap. It reminded him of Eastern Europe. Creeping socialism, high taxes, austerity, cold porridge and power cuts.
>
> Paul Bryers, *Hollow Target* (1976)

> Democracy is dead. Take what you need.
>
> graffito in Kentish Town, London (1974)

A *Sunday Times* cartoon by Calman on the weekend after the February 1974 general election sarcastically showed a man celebrating the results: 'Hurrah! Everyone's won!' The rest of the world was even less impressed. 'The Sick Man of Europe seems to have become even sicker overnight,' noted the Austrian newspaper *Kurier*, and it had a point. After all, the great virtue of having a first-past-the-post electoral system, rather than one of the various forms of proportional representation favoured by most democratic nations, was supposed to be that it produced a decisive result. Yet here was an election, fought in the most dire circumstances since the Second World War, and the result was the very definition of indecision.

The response from the electorate had reflected the gravity of the situation, setting a new record for the number of votes cast, and registering the highest percentage turn-out since the 1950s, but the outcome was a hung parliament, with no party commanding a majority of seats. The Conservatives had 297 MPs, while the Labour Party had 301, even though the Tories actually achieved a slightly higher proportion of the votes. Elsewhere, the Liberals turned in their highest post-war level of support (nearly 20 per cent of those who voted) and in the south of England, excluding London, they even managed to outpoll Labour; their reward was an increase from six to a plainly unfair fourteen seats. For four days, as Edward Heath attempted in vain to stitch together a deal with one of the minor parties, Westminster hung in limbo. And on the fifth day, Harold Wilson rose again.

One thing was certain: Heath had gambled and lost. For all the talk of the miners bringing down the government, it was he who had chosen to call an election, and he who had failed, his negotiating hand forced by his own rhetoric and by a fear that, as Conservative MP Piers Dixon calculated: 'If the government gave way, the Tory Party would disintegrate and Enoch Powell would take over.' From the miners' side, Joe Gormley was emphatic: 'it was *not* a political dispute but an industrial one', he insisted. 'It was *not* the miners, but Ted Heath who brought himself down.' In 1972 it had clearly been the union that had won; now it was Heath who surrendered almost before battle was joined. 'The fact that Britain seemed almost ungovernable at the time,' reflected erstwhile Liberal Peter Hain, 'had more to do with the Tories' policies than any desire by the unions to overthrow a constitutionally elected government.'

As in 1970, however, the incumbent prime minister had had some cause for optimism, for it was the government that had been odds-on favourites to win. Bookmakers William Hill were offering 4–7 on a Conservative victory in mid-January, with Labour out on 5–4; three weeks later, after the election had been called, Joe Coral were still quoting exactly the same odds. But, again as in 1970, there was a shift in voting intentions during the course of the campaign, with Wilson apparently convincing sufficient numbers that he represented a slightly safer pair of hands. He was not, though, endorsed with much enthusiasm by the press. The *Daily Mirror* did its duty with an election-day headline that had vague echoes of wartime – FOR ALL OUR TOMORROWS VOTE LABOUR TODAY – but the *Sun*, which, under its new owner and jockey (Rupert Murdoch and Larry Lamb respectively), had recently galloped ahead of the chasing pack to rival the *Mirror* as Fleet Street's front-runner, broke with tradition and said that it was reluctantly going to support Heath. Significantly, it added a caveat that if Labour had James Callaghan as leader, and even more so had it been Roy Jenkins, then the position might well have been different.

Amongst the electorate, there was scarcely more passion for Wilson, despite some appearances to the contrary. At one of his final rallies, it was reported, he had to fight his way through a massive crowd of well-wishers even to get into the Fairfield Halls, Croydon. It wasn't until after the election that a letter corrected what might have been a misleading impression: 'I must point out,' wrote Jeffrey McKenzie of the London County Council Tramways Trust, 'that the "hundreds of people outside" were not waiting for the political meeting but for the film programme *Trams, Trams, Trams* in the main concert hall.' Wilson, it transpired, had attracted an audience of just 450 people, while some 1,700 others – seemingly unimpressed by this life-or-death struggle over Britain's future – were blithely gathering to celebrate the transport of the past. As W.H. Auden once pointed out, even the most momentous event 'takes place while someone else is eating or opening a window or just walking dully along'.

Of the two supporting players who had upstaged their principals in 1970, one at least was absent from centre stage. In November 1973 Tony Benn had gone to a Labour Party fête in Ilkeston, Derbyshire where a constituency worker, appearing in the guise of a fortune-teller named Madame Eva, had looked into her crystal ball for him. 'You are going to have a great shock in February,' she predicted. 'You are going to get the blame for something you haven't done. Then in September, it will be all right again.' Displaying that vein of superstition that so often accompanies a man's love of gadgets and technology, Benn couldn't rid his mind of her warning. 'This woman's wretched words preyed on me all winter,' he wrote later, 'and then as the election got nearer and nearer, I became convinced we were going to lose, and I was going to get the blame.' As it happened, despite a prominent role during the early days of the miners' dispute, Benn was not a very visible figure in the national media coverage, save in the Tories' rhetoric, where he remained a bogeyman. The Labour campaign chose not to focus upon him.

Enoch Powell, on the other hand, set new standards by which to judge those who wish to be considered a political maverick. His long-nurtured hatred of Heath now reached fruition, as he derided the very calling of the election, and sensationally announced that he himself would not be standing as a candidate. I QUIT SAYS ENOCH, proclaimed the front page of the *Sun*, overshadowing the announcement of the election itself. The paper made the now customary comparison with de Gaulle, but also pointed out that, even at sixty-one, he was younger than Churchill, Attlee and Macmillan were when they became prime minister; a comeback was still possible. The fact that he was not even contesting the election did nothing to prevent him from making speeches, or from providing the one dramatic moment of the campaign. Back in 1966, at the Free Trade Hall in Manchester, the most famous heckle in rock & roll history – a solitary cry of 'Judas!' – had greeted Bob Dylan's appearance with an electric band. 'I don't believe you,' Dylan had exclaimed, after a shocked pause. 'You're a liar!' Now, just over the border in Shipley, Yorkshire, the same insult ('Judas!') was flung at Powell as he denounced the Tory government for having taken Britain into membership of the EEC. His response was even more withering than Dylan's had been; with arm outstretched, his finger pointing out the offender, he hissed: 'Judas was paid! I am making a sacrifice.'

Despite the authoritative put-down, the heckler spoke the truth. For Powell had followed his retirement as an MP with heavy hints in public that he might break entirely with the Conservatives, while in private he was secretly keeping Wilson's inner circle fully informed of his move-ments, urging them to dovetail their own campaigning with his own. Indeed he later claimed that he had been discussing his strategy with the leader of the opposition since the previous June, chatting over the urinals in a House of Commons lavatory: 'There were half a dozen meetings with Wilson in the loo,' he said. And then, in the final week of the campaign, he detonated his ultimate weapon, revealing that he had already cast his vote by postal ballot, and that he had voted for the Labour Party. He stopped just short of calling on his followers to do the same, but that was the clear implication of his words and actions.

Tories were thus entitled to feel betrayed, and all the more so when the election results were pored over: while there was a national swing from Conservative to Labour of around 1 per cent, that in the West Midlands was 4 per cent, rising to 10 per cent in the immediate vicinity of Powell's old constituency. The authority that he wielded regionally was truly extra-ordinary. Even more so, however, was a subsequent in-depth analysis of voting patterns, which suggested that the huge vote for the Liberals was also attributable in part to his intervention, with many Tories unable to follow him all the way across the political spectrum and instead stopping off halfway: 'There seems little doubt,' wrote the authors of the study, 'that many of the six million Liberal voters of February 1974 might have preferred to cast a vote for Enoch Powell but, *faute de mieux*, "com-promised" by voting for Jeremy Thorpe.'

There was some irony in such electoral behaviour. For the issue on which Powell broke with the Tories was Europe – so intense was his objection to EEC membership that he was seduced by the Labour promise of holding a referendum on the question – and yet the Liberals, who benefited from his apostasy, were the most Europhiliac of the major parties. In the event, Britain's position in Europe was entirely unaffected by his actions, but he could, and did, claim to have destroyed Heath's premiership: 'I put him in and I took him out,' he boasted. And of the Labour governments that resulted from the two 1974 elections, he said that he viewed them 'as one might look on one's children. You may not admire them, or even like them very much, but you cannot escape the fact that without you they would not be there.'

Within that Liberal vote there were also many making a positive decision in support of what appeared to be an intriguing new develop- ment in British politics. The party's assembly in 1966 had seen the emergence of the Young Liberals as a radical force, submitting motions that called for workers' control in industry, for a US withdrawal from Vietnam, for Britain to leave NATO and for an expanded EEC to take in the communist states of Eastern Europe. This was the voice of the '60s student generation, outflanking Labour on the left, and although the leadership never fell under its spell, an alliance was forged in the new decade between the Young Liberals and grass-roots activists in the urban North, united by attitudes that were a long way removed from the slightly rakish style of the Old Etonian party leader, Jeremy Thorpe. This contradiction seemed of little concern to the public, who instead responded enthusiastically to the sight of a reinvigorated party; in 1972 Cyril Smith overturned a Labour majority in Rochdale to record the first of five Liberal by-election gains in little more than a year. Smith, by virtue of his enormous size and his blunt manner, rapidly became one of the most recognizable MPs in Westminster and a useful, if sometimes infuriating, foil to Thorpe. He was the closest thing that the Liberals had to a Benn or a Powell, a man who spoke his mind heedless of consequences; as the country's problems mounted during the winter of 1973–74, Smith issued an open letter demanding that Thorpe 'come down off the fence', and asking: 'When the hell are we going to do something?'

The split personality of the Liberal Party became crucial in the immediate aftermath of the February election, as Heath tried to woo them into a coalition government. Thorpe was keen to accept an invitation that would probably have seen him installed as home secretary, but the party was disinclined to act as a life-support system for his ambition, and insisted that the price of any deal must be the introduction of propor- tional representation for Westminster elections. Unable to provide such a pledge, Heath turned next to the Ulster Unionists, who had traditionally taken the Tory whip but whom he had alienated, first with direct rule and then with the power-sharing agreement struck at Sunningdale. Their price too – the abandonment of Sunningdale – proved beyond him, and he finally accepted defeat, making way for the return of a slightly surprised Wilson to Downing Street at the beginning of March. 'It is,' snorted the actor Kenneth Williams, 'an unsatisfactory and muddled result of a stupid election fought on unsatisfactory and muddled issues.'

Much had changed in the ten years since Wilson had first won power. The optimism of 1964 was but a distant memory, long replaced by a grim fatalism. The three-day week and the miners' strike were still in place (though television had been given special dispensation to resume normal broadcasting, so that politicians be not deprived of the oxygen of publicity), and the old triumphalist, presidential style, derived from John F. Kennedy, would clearly be inappropriate in this bleak new world. This time therefore, Wilson resolved, he would occupy a different role in government. Reaching for his book of football metaphors, he decided that while in the '60s he 'had to occupy almost every position on the field, goalkeeper, defence, attack', he would now play at centre-back, 'letting his ministers score the goals'.

Coincidentally, in the real world of football, the English FA was also staging a momentous changing of the guard at exactly the same moment, the state of the national game having declined steadily since that 1970 defeat to West Germany. In 1973 England were obliged to play in a qualifying competition for the World Cup for the first time in twelve years (previously they had been excused, first as hosts and then as champions), but, at least on paper, it didn't look like too difficult a proposition. Drawn in a group of three nations with Wales and Poland, however, England underperformed, achieving a win and a draw against Wales and losing away to Poland. That left the final fixture, against Poland at Wembley, to decide who topped the group and thereby progressed to the tournament proper.

Played in October 1973, as the first implications of the fallout from the Yom Kippur War were becoming evident, the match has gone down in English footballing folklore as a disaster to be mentioned in almost the same breath as the defeats by the USA in 1950 and by Hungary in 1953. England needed a win, but despite having thirty-five shots at goal, compared to Poland's two, emerged with just a 1–1 draw; not unreasonably, the man of the match was the Polish keeper, Jan Tomaszewski (referred to in advance as 'a clown' by Brian Clough, a man not known for bottling up his opinions and who had earlier that week sensationally resigned as manager of Derby County). For the first time since England had deigned to recognize the World Cup in 1950, they had failed to qualify for the tournament. And in March 1974 the FA sacked Sir Alf Ramsey as the national manager and installed Joe Mercer in a caretaker capacity; his first words to the squad suggested that his was a poisoned chalice to rank with becoming prime minister at a time of economic crisis: 'I didn't want this bloody job in the first place.'

The man chosen as Ramsey's permanent replacement was Don Revie, an appointment that seemed somehow symbolic of a coarsening of public life in Britain. Ramsey had been criticized for being overly defensive and for not giving sufficient opportunities for flair players. Revie, however, had an entirely different reputation: he had coached the Leeds United side that dominated the English League in the early '70s with what many considered deliberate brutality, turning gamesmanship into a martial art. Clough, who briefly succeeded Revie as the club's manager, called them 'the dirtiest and most cynical team in the country', a judgement that was more accurate than his description of Tomaszewski. In later years Revie was to reflect that his biggest mistake with England was not to instil the same values in the national side: 'I should have forgotten all about trying to play more controlled attractive football and settled for a real bastard of a team.' Given that he was also accused of trying to bribe opposing clubs to throw matches, it is perhaps just as well that he didn't entirely succeed in remaking the team in his own image, though his stewardship was to prove controversial enough.

With Ramsey's departure, a key cultural link with the glory days of Wilson's first premiership was broken. Wilson himself, however, remained and, amidst the upheavals of 1974, that in itself was some achievement. By the end of the year, America, West Germany, France and Israel all had new leaders, following the exits of Richard Nixon, Willy Brandt, Georges Pompidou and Golda Meir respectively, while the Carnation Revolution in Portugal had seen a dictatorship overthrown in a bloodless coup, timed to start when the first notes of the Portuguese entry were heard in the always political Eurovision Song Contest.

Just as important as his own remarkable talent for survival, Wilson brought with him perhaps the most experienced and impressive team of any newly elected prime minister since the war. An opinion poll on the eve of the election had asked who should succeed him as Labour leader if he were to lose: the front-runners were (in order of preference) Roy Jenkins, James Callaghan, Denis Healey, Tony Benn and Anthony Crosland. If one adds Michael Foot, now given his first front-bench job as employment secretary, it shows a field of six potential leaders for the future, who would form the nucleus of the new cabinet. Confident in his colleagues' capabilities, and calculating correctly that the Tories would not be prepared to risk another election by rocking the boat too soon, Wilson spurned any possible coalitions and formed a minority administration.

In its first few days the Labour government settled the miners' strike and ended the state of emergency, and then turned to the serious task of addressing two perhaps incompatible tasks: first, trying to rescue the economy and second, providing enough goodies for its supporters to ensure a decisive victory in a general election that could not be held off for very long. The first goal was compared by Healey, now chancellor of the exchequer, to cleaning the Augean stables, though not even he claimed he would be able to replicate Hercules' feat in the same timescale of a single day. Every economic indicator was in the danger zone, and the legacy of his predecessor, Anthony Barber, ensured that inflationary pressures would be felt for a long time to come. Having warned at the previous year's party conference that 'there are going to be howls of anguish' from the rich, Healey now set about his mission of redistributing wealth at a time of recession. Public spending was increased, council rents were frozen and sales of council houses ended, basic foodstuffs were subsidized by the state to the tune of £500 million (though VAT was added to ice cream, crisps and sweets), and unemployment payments and pensions were substantially increased. To help pay for such a package, the top rate of income tax was increased to 83 per cent. These changes, together with comprehensive wage rises, represented substantial socialist achievements by a minority government. Or, depending on one's persuasion, they were nothing more than simple bribery in an attempt to get re-elected with a more convincing mandate.

If the intention had been to buy off the electorate with its own money, then it was not a notable success. When the widely anticipated election came, in October 1974, it did manage to produce a Labour government with a majority, but a majority that amounted to just three seats over all other parties.

The campaign, as well as the result, was lacklustre. There was no appetite for a return of Heath – memories of the three-day week were too fresh – while the Liberal turn-out also fell, for reasons best articulated by fashion designer Ossie Clark, who had previously supported the party: 'I didn't vote because I couldn't be bothered and it all seems so pointless.' There was a feeling that the Liberals stood no chance until either hell froze over, or a system of proportional representation was introduced, whichever came the sooner. Labour picked up a handful of constituencies in a desultory kind of way, but the only real beneficiaries were the Scottish National Party and Plaid Cymru, who saw their share of the vote rise to 30 and 11 per cent respectively within their territories; the SNP actually outpolled the Tories in Scotland, though they won fewer seats.

Tony Benn was virtually invisible during the campaign, kept firmly out of the spotlight in case he frightened the horses, while Enoch Powell, whose name had been touted as a possible Conservative candidate for various English seats, instead surprised many when he re-emerged as the Ulster Unionist MP for Down, South. In fact it was as logical as were most of his decisions. Passionately committed to the unity and independence of the United Kingdom, Powell saw Northern Ireland as 'the test of Britain's national will to live' and he undertook his campaign as though it were his last crusade: 'I am like Saint Paul,' he declared to his prospective constituents (who included the Sunningdale-tainted Brian Faulkner). 'I was born elsewhere, but I have come here to say what needs to be said.' His return to the Commons meant that his threatening shadow would hover over the leadership issue for as long as Heath remained *in situ*; Lord Plowden, a veteran of the British establishment, predicted that 1975 would see 'some kind of authoritarian government of the left or right', adding that 'the latter is more likely and that Enoch may well lead it'.

The lack of appetite for the October election sprang perhaps from a feeling that really nothing much had changed. Strike levels were certainly down, but only at the cost of pay rises that were clearly no kind of long-term solution; in 1974 wages rose by 28.5 per cent, massively outstripping inflation, which itself stood at a worrying 19 per cent. Worse was to come, as the twelve months to July 1975 saw prices rise by a record 26 per cent, though still outstripped by wages.

The beneficiaries were primarily those in unions, which now represented more than half the workforce, though their strength was concentrated in the nationalized industries and in the biggest companies: only 17 per cent of all union members were employed by private firms with fewer than 2,000 employees. For other sections of society – the 2 million self-employed, the elderly, those on a fixed income, even those in non-unionized workplaces – these were difficult days, with threats coming from all directions. 'The electricity board caused great distress last year,' wrote Tory MP Rhodes Boyson in 1975, 'by raising the cost of electricity for night storage heaters which threatened to bankrupt pensioners who had sunk their retirement capital into such well-advertised forms of central heating.' The same year the Greater London Council announced that it owed international bankers some two billion pounds and was therefore obliged to increase its rates demands by 80 per cent.

The state of uncertainty was articulated in *Coronation Street*, always one of the nation's key weather vanes: 'I have one hundred pounds I want to save, invest for a rainy day, and I honestly don't know what to do with it,' worried Annie Walker, landlady of the Rovers Return (played by septuagenarian Doris Speed). 'I don't trust the government. Industry is either a playground or a battleground, according to the whim of the week. And inflation could make the whole question academic anyway.' Annie had long struggled to reach just the genteel lower slopes of the middle class, but even at the remote summit of that amorphous social grouping, far beyond anything to which she could ever aspire, the top rate of tax ensured problems with any new financial commitment: 'It's going to cost £1,500 a year to send Christopher to Cambridge,' reflected theatre director Peter Hall, 'which I suppose means earning another £7,000 or £8,000 to have that clear after tax.' A sobering illustration of the same calculation was offered by the proprietor of Wedgie's nightclub on the King's Road, Chelsea, who used to point out to his customers that every time they ordered his champagne at £17 a bottle, they needed to earn a hundred pounds to pay for it; his mark-up was high, but couldn't rival Healey's 83 per cent income tax.

There was, in any event, little enough to celebrate, even for those with a taste for champagne. The most important exhibition of 1974 was 'The Destruction of the Country House', staged at the Victoria and Albert Museum by the gallery's new director, Roy Strong. Overtly polemical in its attack on inheritance and wealth taxes, the show centred on a full-size model of a stately pile's crumbling façade, adorned with photographs of a thousand such houses that had been demolished in the previous century; 'in the background a tape conveyed the sound of burning timbers and crashing masonry, while a voice read the names of those houses like a litany'.

Even as the stately homes of England were thus falling, a similar fate was descending on the Biba store. It had achieved unparalleled heights of popularity (up to a million visitors a week) by providing the public with romantic escapism in the same way that Hollywood had done during the depression of the 1930s. But, while the economic crisis might have created a need for such fantasy, it also spurred a crash in the property market, and in 1975 British Land, the property company that had bought Biba, with its shares now in freefall, closed the doors on what had been called 'the hallowed Mecca of the near-decadent'. During its brief existence, the final incarnation of Biba had acquired a reputation as 'the glam party centre' and its passing was somehow emblematic of a new, less frenetic era in which glam and partying were no longer on the agenda. Indeed glam rock itself predeceased Biba; by the end of 1974 its chief practitioners, David Bowie and Bryan Ferry, had drifted away, lured by the mirror ball of disco, leaving behind a music scene that, for eighteen months or so, was very clearly bereft of inspiration. The celebration of decadence had lost its appeal.

So too had glam rock's kid brother, glitter pop. The acts that had brightened up *Top of the Pops* in the days of the Heathite power cuts were struggling to make the charts at all, let alone the high placings to which they had become accustomed. Even those who wrote their own material – Marc Bolan, Slade, Gary Glitter – suffered from the shifting of fashion, their eccentric excesses looking ill at ease in a world of increasing uniformity and drabness. They had offered a short-term escapism, but weren't built for the long haul that was clearly required.

For these were dour, sullen times. Wilson's government seemed somehow satisfied that it had, if only temporarily, averted the complete catastrophe implicit in Heath's final months, and did little more than attempt to steady the ship a touch, while doing nothing to address the problems that had led to that predicament. Unemployment, which had gradually been falling, began to creep up again and would have officially hit three-quarters of a million in January 1975, save for the fact that the civil servants responsible for collating the figures were engaged in industrial action, so the numbers weren't published. At the same time Chrysler reduced its workforce to a two-day week (by the end of the year, the government was providing massive hand-outs to prevent the UK division of the company from going bankrupt), and many other firms were also cutting down the working week 'in the desperate hope that the economy will pick up'. The public, even more desperate, tried simpler forms of hope, with half the adult population turning to games of chance: 'Betting on the pools has gone up by eighty per cent in the last four years,' reported the press. 'Gambling on horses, bingo and fruit machines has increased by nearly half.' Six million Britons were now regular visitors to the bingo halls. Alcohol consumption had also increased, up from 6.7 per cent of household expenditure in 1966 to 8 per cent in 1976, even though the relative price had fallen in that period.

It appeared that the nation had lost faith in itself. The events of the winter of 1973–74, and the background to them, were so traumatic that they had shaken confidence in the future of Britain, and there was a fear that disaster still lurked around the corner, a suspicion of crisis post-poned. There was a danger too that the situation might deteriorate simply through lack of will to resist. The *Daily Mail* journalist Terry Coleman toured the country in early 1975 to gauge the national mood, and detected 'not a sense of approaching cataclysm, but of increasing erosion'. Earlier Lord Longford had staged a conference in London titled 'The Crisis Deepens: What Can I Do About It?', to which the answer appeared to be 'nothing much' – despite an expected attendance of 3,000, only 400 actually turned up.

It was an attitude identified by the Hungarian-born conductor Sir Georg Solti in 1975, when he 'bewailed the collapse of all the democratic and liberal values of England; how we were letting 400 years of achievement slither down the drain through ineptitude and apathy'. Similar despon-dency was evident everywhere during Wilson's second stint in Downing Street. The last episode of the ITV soap *Crossroads* for 1974 saw Hugh Mortimer (played by John Bentley) looking back on the year with some distaste: 'Two elections, a disastrous summer, one crisis on top of another . . .' Hughie Green, the host of TV talent show *Opportunity Knocks*, clearly agreed but took a broader political stance in his own final broadcast of the year, delivering a straight-to-camera state of the nation address. 'Let us work with all our might to see that 1975, with the gathering storm of despair ahead, will not be the end of our country,' he urged, in his most sincere tones. 'Lest we perish, friends, let us all together say in 1975, both to the nation, to each other and to ourselves: For God's sake, Britain, WAKE UP!' At which the orchestra of Bob Sharples, which had been playing mood music behind his words, swelled, the timpani rolled and a choir broke into a rousing rendition of 'Land of Hope and Glory'.

The confused paralysis that seemed to have descended was depicted in Margaret Drabble's novel *The Ice Age*, in which a cast of middle-Englanders – a property developer who has been jailed, another recovering from a heart attack, a woman who has lost both her husband and her foot in an IRA bomb attack – attempt to understand the calamities that have befallen them. 'All over the country, people blamed other people for all the things that were going wrong – the trades unions, the present government, the miners, the car workers, the seamen, the Arabs, the Irish, their own husbands, their own wives, their own idle good-for-nothing offspring, comprehensive education.' And as the storm clouds show no sign of dissipating, the tone becomes almost eschatological: 'England, sliding, sinking, shabby, dirty, lazy, inefficient, dangerous, in its death throes, worn out, clapped out, occasionally lashing out.'

Somewhat more cynically, in the first episode of the prison sitcom *Porridge* the old lag Fletcher (Ronnie Barker) attempts to cheer up Richard Beckinsale's character Godber, who had just been sent to jail for the first time: 'Cheer up, could be worse,' he says. 'State this country's in, you could be free. Stuck outside, with no work and a crumbling economy. How horrible that'd be. Nothing to do but go to bed early and increase the population.' (There had, predictably, been a rise in the birth rate in the autumn of 1974, some nine months after the TV curfew of the previous winter.) Indeed the power structure of the fictional Slade Prison demonstrated the contemporary conviction that leaders were of diminishing importance: 'Officially, as we know, this hotel is run by a governor appointed by the Home Office,' explains Fletcher. 'In truth, we know that genial Harry Grout could bring this place to a standstill if he so wished.' Grout was another of the prisoners, a ruthless but mostly amiable gangster, who was serving his time in a fully furnished and decorated cell, and whose word was seldom questioned by either screw or con. He was the real authority in the jail, just as much of the media believed that Tony Benn and the unions were the organ-grinder to Harold Wilson's monkey.

The problem was that virtually no one now believed Wilson was the solution to the nation's ills. Politically, he was seen by most as a spent force whose sole attraction was that he wasn't Heath, and would therefore not antagonize the unions too much, even if some critics claimed there was the whiff of Danegeld in his policies. 'What is most damaging to your reputation and position in the country,' Roy Jenkins had told him as far back as 1971, 'is that you are believed, perhaps wrongly, to be devious, tricky, opportunistic.' (That masterly dig, '*perhaps* wrongly', was entirely characteristic.) Even in his own inner circle, defeatism was rampant. 'Britain is a miserable sight. A society of failures, full of apathy, and aroused only by envy at the success of others,' reflected Wilson's policy adviser, Bernard Donoughue. 'This is why we will continue to decline. Not because of our economic or industrial problems. They are soluble. But because the psychology of our people is in such an appalling – I fear irretrievable – state. Meanness has replaced generosity. Envy has replaced endeavour. Malice is the most common motivation.'

In May 1975 came the sound of a door being firmly shut on an era when Tony Crosland announced bluntly: 'We have to come to terms with the harsh reality of the situation which we inherited. The party's over.' Such an admission coming from the prophet of revisionist socialism, the great advocate of growth and spending, was the political equivalent of John

Lennon bidding farewell to the '60s counter-culture in his 1970 song 'God', an impression emphasized by the phrasing, redolent of Lennon's own line: 'The dream is over.' And Donoughue concluded, in Voltairean terms: 'It is time to go and cultivate our gardens, share love with our families, and leave the rest to fester.'

The unsettled state of public life was reflected in the saga of the National Theatre, even if this was not exactly a new story. The campaign for a national theatre, intended at that point to promote the work of Shakespeare, had been initiated in 1848 (further back, the eighteenth-century actor David Garrick had made similar calls) and seemed to have made a breakthrough in 1913 when a private member's bill was passed, authorizing the establishment of such a venture, with a proposed budget of a third of a million pounds. Then the First World War intervened. And then the Second World War. In 1949 a parliamentary bill was again passed, this time promising a million pounds, and the project got as far as the Queen Mother laying a foundation stone two years later. It was not until 1962, however, that Laurence Olivier was appointed the first director of the National Theatre, and even then there was no physical building in which to house the company, with productions staged instead at the Old Vic in Waterloo. Finally, in 1969, construction began on the new home for the NT, designed by architect Denys Lasdun, on a South Bank site adjacent to the Royal Festival Hall, with the first cement shovelled in by arts minister Jennie Lee. (The following year, she lost her parliamentary seat in Staffordshire, and had no doubt who was responsible: 'I blame my defeat on Powellism,' she declared unequivocally.)

The 1970s should therefore have been the coming of age for this long-dreamt-of showcase for the nation's drama, with the new building scheduled to be occupied in spring 1974. But obstacles still remained; construction delays, rising costs (eventually reaching £16 million) and serious illness left Olivier in the position of a latter-day theatrical Moses, destined never to lead his people into the promised land. His successor was Peter Hall, who had founded the Royal Shakespeare Company in 1961, and under whose leadership the National Theatre did finally emerge, roughly as conceived, with the South Bank complex in full operation only three years behind schedule, though for some time a succession of strikes by technical staff meant that there was an element of pot luck when buying a ticket for a performance. Even before those disputes, though, the recurrent delays, the media sniping at Hall's policies and the interminable debates about whether Britain really needed a national theatre, whether it could afford such a thing, and whether the post-war dramatic renaissance was finished anyway – all these revealed an unattractive and querulous spirit amongst the country's artistic elite.

Hall himself, provoked by the strikes, was ultimately to vote for Margaret Thatcher's Conservative Party in 1979. ('It wasn't at all difficult,' he noted. 'In fact it positively felt good.') But at this stage he was still a nervous moderate in the Labour ranks, one whose wishes in the October 1974 poll were granted by the electorate: 'I want Labour to win with a very small majority so that their dogmatic excesses are kept in check.'

Those excesses were, to all intents and purposes, represented by Tony Benn. The two most controversial issues of the Wilson government were both initiated by him: the referendum on whether to remain in the EEC, and the Industry Bill. This latter was to become the touchstone for the left in its evaluation of Labour's performance in the 1970s, the key issue in the alleged betrayal of socialism, and thus the prime factor in the drive towards internal democracy that ultimately led to the 1981 split in the party and the creation of the SDP. In essence the argument was this: The 1973 Labour Party conference had called for – in those famous words – 'a fundamental and irreversible shift in the balance of power and wealth in favour of working people and their families', and the manifesto of February 1974 had reflected that aspiration. The October election campaign had even used as its slogan 'Labour Keeps Its Promises', and Benn, as industry secretary, was determined to do just that. But he was thwarted by what was seen as the leadership's collaboration with the class enemy.

Benn's proposed industrial strategy had three central planks: the expansion of state ownership with, if necessary, the compulsory purchase of firms by a new National Enterprise Board; the adoption of planning agreements across all the key sectors of the economy; and the involvement of trade unions in decision-making, with a tripartite structure of government, management and workforce. All of this was precisely what the Labour movement had voted for and expected to happen, yet none of it was achieved. Instead Wilson himself personally intervened to have the proposed legislation completely rewritten, with the result that the bill that finally emerged was, as Eric Heffer, one of Benn's ministers, put it, 'emasculated out of all recognition', so much so that it was barely worth the parliamentary time spent on it.

The problem, as Benn and the left soon identified, was structural. The annual conference of the Labour Party, dominated by the massive block votes of the big trade unions, was supposed to be the primary policy-making body of the movement, but in reality it lacked the power to hold the leadership of the party to account. Instead the Labour MPs, who had little or no influence on the conference, simply went their own way, and – when in power – the prime minister and his cabinet went *their* own way, sometimes not even in accord with the wishes of the backbench MPs. For much of the post-war period, when the unions were led by right-wingers, this was not a problem save for the more radical grass-roots members, in whom no one was much interested: 'You don't need to worry about the outside left,' Wilson had said. 'They've got nowhere else to go.' But with the leftwards drift of the unions in the early '70s, the gap between them and the Parliamentary Labour Party, let alone the cabinet, became a major issue. Frustrations simmered as Wilson, in the words of veteran left-winger Ian Mikardo, took to treating the Labour Party 'as one would treat an elderly, boring maiden aunt, sending her a birthday card (in October) every year but never inviting her to visit and never listening to what she said'. MPs on the right of the party countered that their job was to respond to the wishes of their electorate, not simply to those of their local activists, and certainly not to those of Jack Jones and Hugh Scanlon. All of which made it nigh on impossible to reconcile the resolutions of conference with the practice of government.

Because even if Wilson had wished to defer to conference decisions (and there was little indication that he did), the government was in too precarious a position, with too slender a mandate, to afford the luxury of ignoring the electorate. And there was by this stage a very definite public reaction against the left and the unions that worried many of the social democrats within Labour.

Back when popular novels like *The Leader*, *The Lost Diaries of Albert Smith* and *A State of Denmark* had been written in the 1960s, warning of right-wing reactions against union power, the selling point had been 'it could happen here'. Since then, there had been a marked change. In George Shipway's *The Chilian Club* the message was more akin to 'it *should* happen here'. The four heroes of the book are a group of retired Army officers who believe that Britain is on a downward slope, and resolve to do something about it on behalf of decent citizens everywhere, regardless of the laws of the land: 'The laws imprisoned worthy citizens for momentary lapses on motorways,' they argue; 'the laws protected wildcat strikers, agitators, anarchic students and such allied vermin whose only object was destruction.' Most importantly, they claim, the rise of the unions will undermine democracy. 'If you rule industry you rule England,' explains one of the protagonists. 'The Russians have been fighting for years, and it seems they've won. Every union is now communist-controlled, and extremely – what's the word? – militant.' And so the four men resolve upon a programme of assassination, murdering key shop stewards, Moscow-controlled politicians and black rights leaders, a programme which is depicted with apparent enthusiasm and approval. The novel's popularity was such that in 1975 a forthcoming film adaptation was announced, to be produced by Michael Klinger, who had earlier been responsible for *Get Carter* (though his stock had fallen somewhat since, for he was then in the midst of producing the *Confessions* series); the seemingly terminal decline of the British film industry meant that the movie never materialized.

In fact it was not simply the unions that were pursuing extra-parliamentary methods at this point. In an essay contributed to the collection *Why Is Britain Becoming Harder to Govern?*, the Labour MP John Mackintosh pointed out that breaking the law had acquired a new popularity in recent years: 'People at once say: "It worked for the miners. Why not for us?"' And, he added, such campaigns were achieving success in a way that conventional action simply didn't: 'The individuals who ruined the test match cricket pitch in order to draw attention to what they believed was the wrongful conviction of a Mr George Davis obtained an immediate home office inquiry into the case.' Similarly, in relation to another recent campaign of non-violent direct action, 'the fishermen never had such concern shown about their problems as was forthcoming when the blockade of the ports was undertaken'.

Employers too were beginning to push beyond normal lobbying practices, as they concentrated their fire on Benn's Industry Bill. Even as the leaders of the CBI held private meetings with Wilson, demanding the watering down of the bill, a twin-track strategy of propaganda and thinly veiled threat was adopted to strengthen their hand. The firm Bristol Channel Repairers took out full-page newspaper adverts to protest at the nationalization of the ship-repairing industry, and included Benn's home address, suggesting people visit him to discuss their opposition. ICI, concerned that it was one of the targets for future nationalization, relied on financial brute force to ensure that its message got through, spending '£60,000 writing to its 600,000 shareholders, 132,000 employees and 43,000 pensioners explaining why the NEB should not buy ICI'. Lord Watkinson, former head of Cadbury Schweppes, warned of conflict as employers 'may be driven to develop industrial muscle power', and threatened a policy of 'confrontation and non-cooperation'. And a representative of the CBI told a parliamentary committee that its members would simply refuse to cooperate with any clauses that required the disclosure of information, while Sir Alistair Pilkington, chairman of the country's largest glass company, declared that 'he would go to prison rather than conform with the provisions in Tony Benn's Industry Bill about disclosing information to the government and unions'.

These suggestions of lawlessness from the upper ranks of the business establishment were among the pressures that were piling on Wilson in an attempt to stop Benn's plans. They were, however, as nothing compared to the personal pressures on Benn and his family; amongst the many death threats they received was a letter addressed to his wife: 'We regret that your husband is going to be killed and that you will be a widow, but it is in the public interest.'

As the referendum campaign built up to its inevitable climax that would see Britain remain in the EEC, the newspapers stepped up their calls that Wilson take the opportunity of the vote to remove Benn from office, with coverage that was probably more hostile than any cabinet minister had previously faced: SACK BENN! was the stark front-page headline in the *Sun*, and the *Sunday Mirror* chipped in gleefully with BYE BYE BENN. 'It is obvious,' the man himself noted bitterly in his diary, 'that there has been heavy briefing by Number 10.' When the move did eventually come, it was not a sacking, nor even officially a demotion, rather a move sideways to become energy secretary, but no one was in any real doubt what it meant, or what the future of the Industry Bill would be. 'What you are doing,' Benn told Wilson, 'is simply capitulating to the CBI, to the Tory press and to the Tories themselves, all of whom have demanded my sacking.' And Neil Kinnock, later to become the *bête noire* of Benn's supporters but at this stage still regarded as a left-winger, denounced the surrender in *Tribune* magazine: 'We are now in the extraordinary and dangerously undemocratic situation where our foes have a direct influence on the selection of Labour ministers.' (The objection was to the party's enemies, not to external influences; after the February 1974 election Jack Jones had decided that the shadow employment spokesman, Reg Prentice, should not get the equivalent government post and had his own suggestion: 'We needed a man at the employment post who was sympathetic to our views. We agreed that Michael Foot would be the ideal choice.')

Wilson's work was now essentially complete. In 1973 the Labour Party had adopted a left-wing programme, but with Britain now securely part of Europe and with industrial policy reduced to something less than a shadow of its former self, he had done all he could to ensure that radical policies were off the agenda. He had but one last card to play in his remarkable political career.

In March 1976, a few days after his sixtieth birthday, Wilson announced that he was resigning as leader of the party and as prime minister. He informed the cabinet of his decision, setting in motion a frantic race for the succession, and then went off to Parliament for his scheduled appearance at Prime Minister's Questions, where he took the opportunity to attack the Labour left, while Enoch Powell – never one to miss a chance of slipping the knife into another former leader – praised him for 'bringing peace to Ireland in contrast to the appalling policies of the previous government'.

Rumours and theories to explain the shock announcement began to spread immediately, and the atmosphere of conspiracy and semi-scandal was compounded when his resignation honours list (swiftly, though erroneously, nicknamed 'the lavender list') was published. Widely seen as repaying personal favours, no matter the calibre of those who were rewarded, the list was described by Benn as comprising 'inadequate, buccaneering, sharp shysters', though family favourite Mike Yarwood did manage to slip in between the industrialists and impresarios and secured an OBE. Despite the whispers of scandals yet to break, however, none stood up to the mildest of scrutiny, particularly after Wilson's press secretary, Joe Haines, revealed that the resignation had long been planned. Had the 1970 election gone according to plan, Wilson would have stood down a couple of years into that parliament 'so that he wasn't just another defeated prime minister'. Haines added, 'I think he had run out of ideas on what he could do for Britain.' Bernard Donoughue expressed much the same sentiment in his diary: 'He has nothing else to give: just like an old boxer shadow-boxing. He knows the moves and goes through the motions, but he has lost his punch and the appetite to fight.'

On Wilson's last day in office, Donoughue noted that the outgoing prime minister had 'No regrets. No proud memories. No lasting traces. Ultimately, he sees himself, as he sees others, in his own words as "a ship that passes in the night".' And indeed he passed very quietly, slipping peacefully away into nonentity and making no attempt to build a position as an elder statesman of the party from which he had become so estranged. In what looked like an act of auto-Stalinism he airbrushed himself out of existence. However history might judge him in future years, the immediate impression was that he had simply ceased to be a part of politics; the waters closed above him and he was gone. Just a week after his departure, Benn wrote: 'I saw Harold tonight wandering round the House and he has absolutely shrunk; it shows that office is something that builds up a man only if he is somebody in his own right. And Wilson isn't.'

7

Opposition
'I think I got something to say to you'

MARGO LEADBETTER: **The day of the woman is coming.**
John Esmonde and Bob Larbey, *The Good Life* (1976)

JEFFREY FOURMILE: **Once upon a time there was this golden-
haired Thatcher, who was wise and good and had magical
powers ...**
Johnnie Mortimer and Brian Cooke, *George and Mildred* (1977)

**Keith Joseph smiles and a baby dies
in a box on Beasley Street.**
John Cooper Clarke, 'Beasley Street' (1980)

In 1970 the *Daily Mirror* ran a competition to celebrate the role of working
women, asking readers to send in a description of their experience of
being female in the workplace. The prize was to be 'the difference between
her pay and a man's rate for the same job for three years', and the winner
was Ivy Williams, a welder from Hemel Hempstead, who had been in her
job for twenty-eight years and who earned 7s. 5½d. an hour, three-quarters
of the wage of her male colleagues. As a means of illustrating the
employment inequality of the sexes, at a time when over 40 per cent of
married women had jobs, it could scarcely be improved upon.

The rise of feminism – or women's liberation, as it was then known –
was one of the more far-reaching developments of the early 1970s, though
inevitably it was one that attracted a great deal of suspicion in a society
that was still male-dominated. 'It only dawned on me recently but
Englishmen don't like women. It's not British reticence or any of that
baloney at all, it's that they plain don't like them,' says the heroine of Dee
Wells's 1973 novel *Jane*. 'To them, women are the enemy. Crazy things you
have to humour along like drunks or village idiots and that you escape
from every chance you get. That's what soccer games and pubs and

men-only colleges and those dirty old clubs on Pall Mall are for.' Wells was an expatriate American journalist, married to the philosopher A.J. Ayer, and therefore perhaps moved in somewhat exclusive circles (her appearance at a party was once memorably described by Roy Strong as 'all cleavage, like a vampire on her night off', which did nothing to invalidate her argument), but there was no doubt that she touched on something of a raw nerve. This was a country in which, until forced to change its policy at the end of 1971, the Wimpy burger chain banned women from entering their premises after midnight unless they were accompanied by a man, on the grounds that only prostitutes would be out alone in public at such an hour.

Much of the argument in Wells's novel derived from Germaine Greer's incendiary 1970 book *The Female Eunuch*. It wasn't the first work of modern feminism, but it was the first to make a major impression on the British market and to become a best-seller, thanks to Greer's own persona as the articulate, sexy incarnation of the underground, to her instantly quotable prose style, and to John Holmes's startling illustration for the paperback cover: a female torso with handles on the hips, hanging empty like a bathing costume on a clothes rail. Greer went beyond the public position of women to examine the private realm of oppression and complicity, and in so doing changed thousands of lives; '*The Female Eunuch* dramatically altered what I believed and the way I led my life,' testified Dale Spender, another Australian expatriate living in London. As she ranged freely and widely over literary criticism, personal experience and the politics of self-liberation, Greer's idiosyncratic iconoclasm made her an atypical feminist, but her readability and her acute insights – particularly into the everyday marginalization of women – made her the most famous of them all. She was to retain that position for the remainder of the century, existing as the media shorthand for the women's movement, even as feminism drifted further and further away from the flamboyant counter-culture from which she had emerged.

Despite Greer's analysis of family and sexual life, there was truth too in the memory of Labour MP Joe Ashton, looking back on the '70s: 'No one ever really doubted that it was women who ran every establishment from Buckingham Palace to the Rovers Return. Basil Fawlty never ran Fawlty Towers. Nor did Alf Garnett run his house in Wapping.' His focus on soaps and sitcoms was entirely appropriate. The soap opera, which in those days primarily meant *Coronation Street* and *Crossroads*, was essentially a female genre, with the latter centred on the figure of Meg, played by Noele Gordon, who was voted Female TV Personality of the Year right through the decade.

Coronation Street was even more the province of strong women, dominated by the likes of Annie Walker, Elsie Tanner, Hilda Ogden, Rita Fairclough and – above all – Ena Sharples. 'A woman needs a good, strong voice,' Ena once declared. 'It makes up for lack of muscle.' Similarly, a recurrent theme in sitcoms, from *Love Thy Neighbour* to *The Good Life*, was the solid common sense of the female characters, as contrasted to the foibles of the men; Sybil Fawlty may have been seen as a ball-breaking battle-axe by Basil, but she was almost always in the right, and her impatience with her incompetent, arrogant husband was entirely justified.

These, however, were the traditional and accepted images of women in the domestic sphere. The increasing demand for a female voice in public politics was more confusing, and it spawned a spate of novels that showed the gender tables being turned. The exploitative end of the market included such titles as *The Droop* (1972) by Ian Rosse (a pseudonym of J.F. Straker), which concerned a worldwide outbreak of male impotence, and *W*I*T*C*H* (1971) by Jane Harman (a pseudonym of Terry Harknett), the blurb for which promised 'hordes of bare-breasted, shaven-headed girls on motorcycles', but which was mostly about a radical feminist group attempting to seize power and being defeated when 'every decent, law-abiding woman' mobilizes in opposition. Then there were two books by science fiction writer Edmund Cooper, *Five to Twelve* (1968) and *Who Needs Men?* (1972), which offered satirical portraits of future societies in which women had achieved the upper hand; indeed *Who Needs Men?*, set in the twenty-fifth century, after men had almost destroyed the world in a terrible war, sees the male population of Britain reduced to a few thousand outlaws in the Scottish Highlands, while the rest of the country has become exclusively female. Sometimes seen as anti-feminist, Cooper's novels are in truth witty burlesques (a typical joke sees the renaming of Nelson's Column as Germaine's Needle) that reaffirm humanity in the face of doctrinaire attitudes. More immediate depictions of the rise of women to political prominence came in Pamela Kettle's *The Day of the Women* (1969), which depicted a new all-female party, IMPULSE, sweeping to power in a general election, and in Walter Harris's *The Mistress of Downing Street* (1972), which starts with the assassination of the prime minister and his replacement by his young widow, Viola Jones; both purported to show the first female prime minister.

What all these fictional accounts failed to allow for was the possibility that a woman might rise in the normal way to become the leader of a major political party and thereafter prime minister. And yet, of course, that was precisely what happened.

Perhaps the gap between fiction and reality was not too surprising, for the arrival of Margaret Thatcher as the leader of the opposition was far from being an inevitable development in British politics. The pre-eminence of Edward Heath was such that even after the disaster of February 1974 he remained unchallenged as Conservative leader, despite having now lost two of the three elections he had contested. Few at the time registered the deep-running feelings of the right wing of the party, the hopes for Selsdon Man and thus the smouldering sense of betrayal when the principles outlined therein were betrayed. 'I naively assumed that the conversion of both Ted Heath and the Party to the Selsdon programme was one of deeply rooted conviction,' remembered Norman Tebbit. 'In doing so I overestimated Ted Heath's conviction.' He was not the only one.

'We believe the Conservative Party now has an opportunity, indeed a duty,' Rhodes Boyson had written after Heath's 1970 victory, 'to govern our people in such a way that they will so consciously enjoy the benefits of the free market in a free society that the only chance for Labour to return to power will be when that party ceases to be socialist in its aims.' He went on to outline many of the issues that would become closely associated with the social agenda of Thatcherism: low taxation is a moral imperative; private schooling and healthcare are virtues that demonstrate self-reliance; choice is inherently good; patriotism is to be encouraged; welfare provision was out of control and was fostering dependence; permissiveness had gone too far and freedom become licence; the views of ordinary folk on Europe and immigration had been ignored. Underlying it all was a belief that the silent majority of middle England was crying out for a strong, right-wing brand of Toryism. 'We shall not have completed our work,' declared Boyson, 'until a future leader of the Labour Party in an election broadcast can proclaim with moral fervour: "We are all capitalists now."' That may have seemed absurdly ambitious at the time, but ultimately the dream was very nearly realized; in 1998 (shortly before his first resignation from Tony Blair's cabinet) the Labour Party strategist and trade secretary Peter Mandelson wrote an article for the *Daily Telegraph* about his proposals on competitiveness, which he heralded as 'the most business-friendly document any Labour government has ever produced', and which the newspaper felt able to summarize with the headline: WE ARE ALL CAPITALISTS NOW.

Tebbit and Boyson were then in a minority, and for the moment they were powerless. The absence of Enoch Powell from the short parliament of 1974 temporarily strengthened Heath's hand, removing his most acerbic critic, though there were mutterings of dissident voices to be heard for those who were listening. Alan Clark argued that there was an urgent need for 'a rethinking of Tory Party attitudes and philosophy', while Edward du Cann, chairman of the 1922 Committee of backbench Tory MPs, insisted that: 'In the eyes of the general public, our party seems to lack a clear philosophy and therefore credibility. So intellectually bankrupt have we become that the language of most political debate, in university or public bar, is now habitually the socialistic language of the left.' And one of the journalists most in tune with the malcontents, Peregrine Worsthorne, identified the roadblock on the path to the future: 'The personality of Mr Heath does not make it easy for the Tory leaders to engage in the kind of policy reappraisal which the party so urgently requires. In the frosty climate created by his company, ideas do not burst into blossom.'

Most importantly, the current of pure monetarism that Powell espoused was to make its presence felt in the shape of former social services secretary Sir Keith Joseph. In a series of speeches over the summer of 1974, Joseph broke ranks with Heath's vision of Conservatism to announce that 'Inflation is threatening to destroy our society,' and that the only way forward was the rigid control of the money supply. For those who didn't entirely grasp the essence of this new creed of monetarism, the most succinct articulation had come even before the February election from the most unlikely of sources, Alf Garnett's socialist son-in-law, Mike: 'You want to know something about inflation and what causes it?' he asked. 'It's *them* printing more of their paper money than we've got goods for in the shops.' Joseph arrived at the same conclusion slightly later, but he did so with all the fervour of a convert. ('I have heard of death-bed repentance,' sneered Powell about his distanced disciple, 'but it would perhaps be more appropriate to refer to post-mortem repentance.')

Joseph's campaign over those months was the clarion call that was to usher in the Thatcherite revolution, and in the context of the subsequent agenda there's a certain irony that his motivation was an awareness of Europe: 'I never focused on America – I thought they were outside our culture and our reach,' Joseph said later, 'but our ruddy *neighbours*. Why should they do so much better, particularly when they had been prostrate and flat on their back after the war?' And in the speech launching the Centre for Policy Studies, the think tank which was to provide the intellectual backbone for Thatcherism, he elaborated on the theme: 'Compare our position today with that of our neighbours in Germany, Sweden, Holland, France. They are no more talented than we are. Yet, compared with them, we have the longest working hours, the lowest pay and the lowest production per head. We have the highest taxes and the lowest investment. We have the least prosperity, the most poor and the lowest pensions.' The impoverished position of Britain relative to its nearest competitors was by now recognized everywhere, it seemed, except at the very highest political level: 'He never goes abroad other than under the artificial circumstances of a prime ministerial visit, so he is unaware of the growth and strength of countries like France,' wrote Bernard Donoughue despairingly of Harold Wilson. 'He takes his holidays in the Scillies, which is unchanged since 1950, so he thinks the world is unchanged.'

Joseph's emphasis on the defeat of inflation being the absolute priority was intended as a rejection of the previous administration, and was taken as such. 'Your analysis of the government's record has left me heartbroken,' Heath told him, in unusually emotional terms. But Joseph went much further, with a denunciation of the whole political consensus that had dominated British politics since 1945. 'The path to Benn,' he proclaimed, 'is paved with thirty years of intervention, thirty years of good intentions, thirty years of disappointment.' Boyson was subsequently to bring the two themes together, claiming that the Heath government had served as 'John the Baptist for Wedgwood Benn'. This obsessive focus on Tony Benn was crucial; politics in Britain were polarizing rapidly, and the right needed to find a rival who could present a coherent challenge to Benn's espousal of shop steward democracy in a centralized economy. In the vacuum created by Powell's defection, Joseph looked the only plausible standard-bearer for such a movement, despite his inability to rouse the public and despite his habitual appearance – as '80s impressionist Phil Cool pointed out – of being 'someone who'd put his finger through the toilet paper'.

Against this background of hardening positions, there was also a counter-demand for a moderate coalitionist force. In 1971, a full decade before the SDP came into existence, Benn had identified the trend that would lead to its birth. 'There is a small group of highly dedicated Marketeers led by Roy Jenkins,' he wrote of his colleagues in the Parliamentary Labour Party. 'This group, working with the conservative Europeans, really represents a new political party under the surface in Britain.' On New Year's Day 1975 Jenkins confided to his friend Ronnie McIntosh that he felt his moment of destiny approaching. 'He wants a coalition government and expects to see one in the first half of this year,' reported McIntosh. 'He wouldn't mind whether Wilson or Callaghan led the new government but made it clear that he would expect to succeed whichever of them took it on – and implied that he would expect to do this quite soon.'

The appeal of a new force was understood in many quarters. At one end of the social spectrum there was Len Fairclough in *Coronation Street*, who served as an independent on Weatherfield Council and who insisted that 'It's party politics that's strangling this country. It's out of date.' And at the other end there was the Queen herself. 'Different people have different views, deeply and sincerely felt, about our problems and how they should be solved,' she was to have said in her Christmas broadcast for 1973. 'Let us remember, however, that what we have in common is more important than what divides us.' Those words were never broadcast, because Heath asked that the passage be deleted, for fear of it being interpreted politically, but in the period between the two elections of 1974, there was renewed talk of the possibility of a government of national unity, bringing together Tories and Liberals, and possibly even the right wing of the Labour Party. Several leading Conservatives, including future members of Thatcher's cabinets like Nigel Lawson, Ian Gilmour and Peter Walker, floated the idea of a coalition, and Heath himself was clearly attracted to it. The problem was, of course, that the people were no longer attracted to him, and while he remained as Tory leader no such coalition was possible; he regarded himself as a unifying force in the country, but the country simply didn't agree.

Even so, the concept was to remain through to the next decade, sometimes lurking in the depths of political discourse, sometimes forcing its way to the surface. 'In November 1976,' wrote Cyril Smith, 'I called for the foundation of a new party of the centre to be joined, I hoped, by such political heavyweights as Edward Heath, Peter Walker, Shirley Williams, Reg Prentice, David Steel and John Pardoe.' And behind it all was the reality that this was to be in essence an anti-Benn alliance, so great was the fear of the forces he represented. 'For the last three years, ever since the miners brought down Ted Heath,' Smith claimed, 'there have been long and passionate discussions in all the rooms of Westminster except the chamber of the House of Commons, in the bars, in the restaurants, even in the splendid marble halls of the toilets, about the possibility of revolution in this country. I am by no means the only MP who thinks that it is not only possible, but, in fact, quite likely *if* the present situation is allowed to drift.'

The answer to this drift, however, was ultimately to be found not in vague proposals for coalition but in those speeches of Keith Joseph. The impact of his contribution was temporarily eclipsed by the October election of 1974, but once that was over, and the need for a regeneration of the Conservative Party had become clear (it had now shed 3 million votes since 1970, and achieved its lowest share of the poll since 1906), he resumed the offensive. 'He will have to go' was the *Daily Mail*'s verdict on Heath after he lost his second general election in a row, and his third in total, and Joseph was the right's front-runner in the succession stakes, an intelligent, if awkward, man who had already distanced himself from the failures of the past and who offered a clear, determined direction forward.

And then he threw it away. His first post-election speech was in Edgbaston, not far from the site of the 'rivers of blood', and it proved almost as significant as its predecessor in the outrage it provoked. Ever since his time in social services, Joseph had been concerned with what he referred to as 'cycles of deprivation', the way in which the stratum of society that would later be termed the underclass was becoming self-perpetuating, dependent on state benefits for generation after generation. 'A high and rising proportion of children are being born to mothers least fitted to bring children into the world and bring them up,' he now declared. 'Some are of low intelligence, most of low educational attainment. They are unlikely to be able to give children the stable emotional background, the consistent combination of love and firmness, which are more important than riches.' And, in the phrase that damned him, he warned that 'the balance of our population, our human stock, is threatened'. It was that 'human stock' that provided his enemies with the rope with which to hang him. Was this not, they asked, a call for eugenics, redolent of the policies of Nazi Germany? Not only that, but his argument was unashamedly based on class; he talked of problems in the socio-economic groups four and five, prompting Labour MP Renée Short to leap to the defence of their impugned honour, claiming that 'it is not those in the fourth and fifth groups who patronize call girls', a remark that perhaps revealed more about her knowledge of society than about society itself.

Stripped of its emotive phrasing, Joseph's Edgbaston speech identified an issue that was to become of ever greater significance to policy-makers over the coming decades. But his message was lost amidst the noise, partly at least because he had nothing to offer those on the right, who might otherwise support him, save remedies that they distrusted. 'The trouble was,' wrote Margaret Thatcher, his closest ally in the shadow cabinet, 'that the only short-term answer suggested by Keith for the social problems he outlined was making contraceptives more widely available – and that tended to drive away those who might have been attracted by his larger moral message.' The birth control pill was still then seen as a totem of the permissive society of the 1960s, and Joseph's pragmatic endorsement of it (he had made it available nationally on the NHS) failed to resonate with his natural constituency. Caught between the pill and the pillory, he was assailed on all sides. 'It's great fun to see somebody else getting into hot water over a speech,' chuckled Powell. 'I almost wondered if the River Tiber was beginning to roll again.' But unlike Powell, Joseph was ill-equipped for the media onslaught that ensued. 'Ever since I made that speech the press have been outside the house,' he told Thatcher. 'They have been merciless.' And, he added, he was no longer prepared to challenge Heath for the leadership of the party; he felt unable to put himself and his family under that kind of pressure permanently.

Joseph's moment had passed and he retreated with a great sigh of relief into the background, to become the *éminence grise* of Thatcherism. In her government he was to head the industry and education departments for seven years, but he was seldom a front-rank figure in public presentation, being seen primarily as the arid voice of ultra-orthodoxy. His image, such as it was, veered towards a caricature of the right-wing bogeyman, an ascetic fundamentalist nicknamed 'the Mad Monk'. When, in 1979, Leon Griffiths put together the concept of what would become the series *Minder*, he identified his two main characters in terms of their political allegiances: the decent, uncomplicated Terry McCann 'votes Labour because his dad was a docker and "We've always been Labour"', while the small-time crook and would-be businessman Arthur Daley 'admires Sir Keith Joseph'. Arthur's perpetual pursuit of a nice little earner was not necessarily what Joseph had in mind when he was so eloquently defending 'the wealth-creating, job-creating entrepreneur and the wealth-creating, job-creating manager', and arguing that 'If they are not treated reasonably, if they do not feel appreciated, they will quit either by way of the brain drain or by the internal brain drain which might be called switching off. There is a great deal of switching off in this country.'

With Joseph ruling himself out of the running, even before the race had started, Thatcher decided to rule herself in, on the grounds that 'someone who represents our viewpoint *has* to stand'. In November 1974 she announced that she would be challenging Heath for the leadership.

She was not an obvious choice, partly because she, following Joseph, had begun to espouse the unfashionable cause of monetarism, and partly because the policies she had pursued in her previous incarnation as education secretary under Heath had led to her being dubbed by the *Sun* 'the most unpopular woman in Britain'. In retrospect, given the controversy she subsequently attracted, this was something of an overstatement. Her supposed offence was absurdly innocuous – under pressure from the Treasury, the statutory provision of free milk for schoolchildren was ended on her watch – but the tabloid sobriquet 'Margaret Thatcher, Milk Snatcher' had a pleasing enough ring, and it lingered long in the memory. An entry in Kenneth Williams's diary in January 1972 captured some of the reaction to her time at education, as well as offering a foretaste of future protests: 'There were barriers at Downing Street and mounted police. It depressed me very much. The bawling long-haired youths shouting "Thatcher Out!" and carrying coffins expressing sentiments like "Maggie Dead" etc was the spectacle of only another form of fascism.'

Mostly, though, Thatcher was an improbable candidate for the simple reason that she was a woman. That was, for the media, the overriding issue, and coverage of her tended to be couched in terms of her appearance, with a particular focus on her headwear. When she was education secretary, the *Sunday Telegraph* had described her as being 'sometimes rather pretentious and given to the smart hat and neat pearls favoured by suburban ladies coming to Tory conferences for the first time', and the image still dominated the declaration of her candidacy. 'Try to forget her plummy voice and her extravagant hats and her Dresden-shepherdess appearance,' advised the *Daily Mirror*. 'She is the toughest member of the Shadow Cabinet, and even if she doesn't win the battle for the Tory leadership she may yet be responsible for bringing down Ted Heath.' But even Enoch Powell, who had as good a claim as any to be her trailblazer, had trouble forgetting these things, insisting that the Tories couldn't possibly elect her: 'They wouldn't put up with those hats and that accent,' he shuddered. It was an image of which she was well aware, describing herself defiantly as 'a middle-aged lady who likes hats'.

It was noticeable that when she did emerge as Heath's successor, in February 1975, it was the handful of women Labour MPs who were the first to celebrate the achievement. 'I am very pleased,' said Gwyneth Dunwoody, while Joyce Butler went further: 'Absolutely splendid. I am delighted. It is time we had women in the top jobs.' And Shirley Williams added, 'I cannot help admitting privately, as a woman, being pleased to see that in the Tory Party, of all parties, a woman has broken through.'

This latter argument, that somehow it was a remarkable step for the Tories in particular to have taken, was exploded by Barbara Castle, who had followed Joseph as social services secretary. Reflecting in her diary on the consequences of Thatcher, she wrote of the Labour Party: 'There's a male-dominated party for you – not least because the trade unions are male-dominated, even the ones that cater for women.' She went on to identify what was to become a key problem for Labour: 'The battle for cash wage increases is a masculine obsession. Women are not sold on it, particularly when it leads to strikes, because the men often don't pass on their cash increases to their wives. What matters to women is the social wage.' And she concluded, in very unBennite terms, that: 'To me, socialism isn't just militant trade unionism. It is the gentle society, in which every producer remembers that he is a consumer too.' Two years later, an opinion poll was to show that Thatcher's strongest lead over Labour was amongst working women.

Thatcher's victory in the 1975 leadership contest was no great endorsement of monetarism. Indeed it is doubtful how many of those who voted for her in the first ballot (when she defeated Heath), let alone in the second, when she saw off all other challengers, understood or believed her deeply held, if newly acquired, convictions on economics. The support was instead predicated on her courage in volunteering to bell the cat: 'She's the only man among them,' was the phrase going around Westminster. 'Suddenly Mrs Thatcher stands out among the Tory dwarfs like a life-size Snow White,' editorialized the *Daily Mirror* before the first ballot. 'A very tough Snow White.' But it warned that if she became leader, the Conservatives would be taking on an image that was 'Dominatingly middle-class. Suburban. Anti-union. Even more Southern English than it is now.' It was precisely this image that excited those who sought hope in Thatcher's election. The *Daily Mail* leader column that welcomed her arrival put it in the context of the great enemy of the right: 'The majority of the British people do not want socialism. They do not want Bennery.' The only question was whether this bold experiment of having a female leader might misfire and inadvertently hand the future to Benn.

Thatcher's appeal was to two separate, and perhaps contradictory, constituencies. On the one hand, she articulated the intellectual monetarism of right-wing groups such as the Institute of Economic Affairs, led by Ralph Harris, and the Centre for Policy Studies, which had Alfred Sherman as its director of studies. But to the country at large, she was also the woman who espoused common-sense virtues of good housekeeping, the embodiment of the old adage to be neither a borrower nor a lender. Where Benn offered the masculine logic of centralized planning, the state as rational father figure, Thatcher countered with the no-nonsense, class-defying home truths of matron. Meg Richardson, one felt, would have gone to hear her speak, while Ena Sharples would be watching on television at home, nodding in approval. Though her vision was not dissimilar to that of Powell, his had been predominantly a male following, while she brought to the kitchen table the superficially moderating fact of femininity.

She spelt out that vision in her first conference speech as leader: 'A man's right to work as he will, to spend what he earns, to own property, to have the state as servant and not as master – these are the British inheritance.' And she concluded with a peroration that explicitly turned its back on the post-war cross-party consensus: 'We are coming, I think, to yet another turning point in our long history. We can go on as we have been doing, we can continue down. Or we can stop, and with a decisive act of will we can say "Enough".' Joseph's speech on the same occasion elaborated on the theme, arguing that what was needed was a move not to the centre ground, but to the common ground.

Despite the support of right-wing think tanks, Thatcher, like Enoch Powell, was venerated primarily by a public that was mistrustful of intellect, and she took care to emphasize her remoteness from the political elite: 'I'm a plain straightforward provincial,' she told Anthony Sampson in 1977. 'I've got no hang-ups about my background, like you intellectual commentators in the south-east.' And her image as the suburban hat-wearing lady, a woman who could have been Margo Leadbetter's other next-door neighbour in *The Good Life*, was balanced by her perceived position as an outsider in Westminster, purely by virtue of her gender. This fact, that she was not part of an old school tie network, that she was not one of the boys, was a huge part of her attraction, and it played into one of the great myths of the 1970s: that of the outsider, the individualist, the rule-breaker with no time for bureaucracy and unearned authority.

The rebel was, of course, far from being a new theme in popular culture, but it was one that acquired a much wider currency in the period, moving from the cultic fringe into the mainstream. It became, for example, central to the culture of British sport. One could see it in boxer John Conteh, who won the world light heavyweight title in 1974, but discovered that partying was preferable to training. (When asked why, as world champion, he didn't work harder at boxing, he replied with admirable economy: 'It hurts.') Likewise a rebellious, mercurial brilliance was at the heart of the appeal of Alex 'Hurricane' Higgins, who arrived from nowhere to take the world snooker title in 1972 at his first attempt, and to win over a huge new audience for the game with a persona that mixed the gladiator with the kamikaze pilot, the soul of a poet with the appearance of a glue-sniffer. The following year, in response to his arrival, the BBC acquired the rights to the tournament, and the process of turning snooker into a major armchair sport was under way.

Higgins was following in the path of his fellow Belfast boy George Best. In the 1960s Best had been celebrated as the Fifth Beatle, but the off-pitch legend was really built later, amidst the alcoholic excesses and unpredictable brilliance that culminated in him being sacked by Manchester United in 1974. The boy wonder was transformed into self-destructive genius, and thereby acquired a much greater celebrity than he would had he followed his team-mate Bobby Charlton into elder statesmanship. A playground rhyme of the period was adapted from *Jesus Christ Superstar*:

> Georgie Best, superstar,
> Walks like a woman and he wears a bra.

His successors as the icons of the terraces were similarly nonconformist figures. There was Chelsea's Peter Osgood, the King of Stamford Bridge, whose fame was captured in the T-shirt worn by Raquel Welch that proclaimed 'I Scored With Osgood'. There was Rodney Marsh, whose England career ended when Sir Alf Ramsey threatened to pull him off at half-time, provoking the reply, 'Crikey, Alf, at Manchester City all we get is an orange and a cup of tea.' And there was Arsenal's Charlie George, the idol of the skinheads, despite his inappropriate haircut: 'They hate the opposition, and so does Charlie. They adore him for his V-signs and his tantrums, just as they adore kicking in the teeth of an enemy fan.'

Above all there was Brian Clough, the manager who took Derby County into the top tier of English football and then won the league title. The fact that he repeated the feat with Nottingham Forest (the first man to take the title with two clubs since Herbert Chapman), and went on to win the European Cup twice, convinced every England fan that he should be the next national manager, an opinion loudly shared by Clough himself. He was the single most opinionated figure in the history of English football, convinced, with good reason, that he was also the greatest manager of them all. And though much of what he stood for – old-fashioned virtues of team spirit, rigid discipline and a refusal to allow misbehaviour by his players – have come to look ever more appealing in ensuing years, his absolute arrogance and intolerance of any higher authority ensured he would never be appointed to the England job; the FA, as he admitted, wanted a diplomat, not one who denounced the Juventus team after a controversial European Cup semi-final as 'cheating, fucking Italian bastards'. He was wooed by the Labour Party, keen that he put himself forward as a parliamentary candidate, but fortunately for football – and perhaps for Labour – he turned them down. Intelligent and nonconformist, he spoke his mind at a time when football was generally considered mindless.

Similarly, in February 1975, the same month that Thatcher was elected Tory leader in the teeth of the old boy establishment at Westminster, *The Sweeney* started its first series on ITV. Here, in a radical break with previous TV police shows in Britain, John Thaw played Jack Regan, a maverick cop closer in spirit to Clint Eastwood's 'Dirty' Harry Callahan than he was to Sgt Dixon of Dock Green. *The Sweeney* had little or no interest in conventional themes of police procedure, detection or criminal master plans; instead it adopted a more aggressive, even bellicose, attitude, with protracted chases, shoot-outs and fist fights. 'You're building an image, Jack,' his boss warns him. 'A broken marriage, drinking, deliberate flouting of authority . . .' But Regan has no patience with older, more senior officers who don't approve of his style. 'They don't understand,' he snaps. 'It's war, it's bloody war now. When you stop a kid in a stolen car, you can't be sure he isn't tooled up and ready to blow your face off.'

At the emotional heart of the show was the male bonding of Regan and his sidekick George Carter (Dennis Waterman), as they lived cheek by jowl with London's criminals, and as they fought villains, cop-baiting journalists and even their own hierarchy on the fifth floor, to whom their immediate boss Frank Haskins (Garfield Morgan) is always answerable when they overstep the line yet again. 'I sometimes hate this bastard place. It's a bloody holiday camp for thieves and weirdos, all the rubbish,' Regan says of London. And then he gets personal: 'You try and protect the public and all they do is call you fascist. You nail a villain and some ponced-up pinstriped amateur barrister screws you up like an old fag packet on a point of procedure, then pops off for a game of squash and a glass of Madeira. He's taking home thirty grand a year, and we can just about afford ten days in Eastbourne and a second-hand car.' This was the world of James Barlow's *The Burden of Proof* replayed on a much bigger stage and inflated for more cynical times: the heroes are still the thin blue line, but now they are deeply flawed human beings, battling not only the criminal classes, with their bent lawyers and politicians, but also penpushing superiors who don't understand how desperately corrupt the world has become. In the words of the original brief for writers of the series: 'Regan is contemptuous of the formality and bureaucracy which characterizes much of the police service. His basic philosophy is "Don't bother me with forms and procedures, let me get out there and nick villains".' Or, as Carter was later to put it, 'You can't operate unless you break the rules. Everybody knows that.'

If the anti-authoritarian individualist was one of the key 1970s archetypes, then another was the malcontent, a figure particularly associated with sitcoms and derived directly from Tony Hancock's persona in the '50s; at a time when Harold Macmillan was telling the nation that they'd never had it so good, Hancock represented those who felt that they'd never had it at all. His descendants included Alf Garnett in *Till Death Us Do Part*, Basil Fawlty in *Fawlty Towers* and, most brilliantly, the seedy landlord Rigsby in *Rising Damp*, played by Leonard Rossiter: 'I think he really caught something about the English in Rigsby,' commented co-star Don Warrington of Rossiter, 'a sort of emotional incontinence which one can see in pubs. The one who knows it all and actually knows nothing.' All these were right-wing, quasi-Powellite characters, but the dissatisfied and disgruntled cynic, the personification of raging impotence, also had his counterparts on the traditional left, including the racist trade unionist Eddie Booth in *Love Thy Neighbour* and the intriguing figure of George Roper, portrayed by Brian Murphy.

Roper first appeared in *Man About the House* as a middle-aged, infantile miser. Living off his young lodgers, he spends most of his life, and all of his ingenuity, trying to avoid the clutches of his sex-starved wife, Mildred (Yootha Joyce), whilst still finding time to nurture a wide range of bigotries. In one of the best shows in the series – pre-dating the more famous *Fawlty Towers* episode 'The Germans' – the regular characters invite to dinner a German named Franz Wasserman (played by Dennis Waterman), which gives Roper the opportunity to indulge one of his most cherished prejudices. When he learns that Wasserman's father was in the Luftwaffe, he immediately asks, 'Was he ever over Putney on a Monday, bath night?', a reference to an alleged incident in Roper's childhood when a German bomb hit the area and blew him out of the bath. ('Always reckoned Hitler knew when it was bath night round our way,' he reflected. 'Very ruthless, these Krauts.') Throughout dinner, he needles Wasserman with tales of two world wars and one world cup, until the latter eventually explodes in rage and spits out the uncomfortable, and seldom spoken, truth: 'You're nothing but a bloody fascist!'

When the Ropers were given their own series, *George and Mildred*, they moved out of their Earl's Court home (compulsorily purchased by the council) and bought a new house in the distinctly middle-class Hampton Wick, despite George's misgivings about suburbia: 'All BBC2 and musical toilet rolls.' A new element was added to the existing mix in the form of naked class war between Roper and his next-door Tory neighbour, Jeffrey Fourmile (Norman Eshley). 'I'm working-class and bloody proud of it,' declares George, and the resultant tension between his determination to cling to his class roots and his wife's desperation to escape hers provided many of the series' sharpest lines. When Mildred tries to persuade him to join the local Conservative association – in the hope of getting a cheap holiday – she insists that the Tories are essentially a social organization who just organize events, at which he spits, 'Yeah, whist drives in aid of the death penalty.' Meanwhile the estate agent Fourmile was sitcom's first overt Thatcherite; '*Socialism: The Way Ahead*,' he says, reading the spine of a book as he sorts out a stall at a jumble sale. 'Hmm, put that with the fiction, I think.'

Despite his protestations, it's not hard to see Roper secretly putting his cross on the ballot paper for Thatcher, nor to see him joined in the polling booth by Garnett, Fawlty, Rigsby and even perhaps Eddie Booth. Alongside them would have been not only Fourmile, but also Margo in *The Good Life* and – from *Whatever Happened to the Likely Lads?* – Bob Ferris, an aspirant member of the middle class who might have voted Liberal in 1974, but would surely have opted for Thatcher in 1979. Against these massed ranks, British sitcoms in the '70s could offer few genuinely left-wing characters: possibly Wolfie, the parody of a revolutionary in *Citizen Smith*, certainly Mike in *Till Death Us Do Part*, who would ostentatiously read copies of the *Morning Star*, *Militant* and *Workers Press* in front of Alf Garnett, but there were very few others.

The numerical imbalance was striking. 'I certainly do notice,' mused Tony Benn in 1975, 'how wildly hostile the press is to everything to do with working people, trade unions and young people. It is an extremely dangerous tendency which I have noticed building up over the last few years. Whether it is a move towards fascism is perhaps too early to say.' He was, of course, referring to news coverage – Benn was seldom aware of anything as trivial as TV sitcoms – but his point had a wider application. Erstwhile critic Kenneth Tynan had earlier pointed out that the BBC drama series *The Trouble Shooters*, set in the boardroom of the Mogul International oil company, was 'naked propaganda for capitalism'. The same could have been said of others, including the 1960s ITV series *The Power Game*, which had started on the shop floor before shifting its focus to Patrick Wymark as the managing director of an aircraft company. Even when a new drama was launched in 1972 under the title *The Brothers*, it turned out to be not the story of trade unionists that one might have expected, but yet another tale of boardroom power struggles, this time in the context of a transport firm; the first series hinged on a dockers' strike, but it was presented almost entirely from the point of view of those prepared to break picket lines. There was no shop-floor equivalent to these shows, labour being instead relegated to the one-off play favoured by the politically committed dramatists; such work, though it tended to be more controversial and to attract more attention from critics, was marginal compared to the huge audiences guaranteed to the likes of *The Brothers*, with its prime-time slot on BBC1. As Tynan noted: '"Will he become boss?" is the question raised by this kind of series. "Will he go on the dole?" is a question raised by no TV programme known to me.'

Despite these product placements for capitalist enterprise, it was still the twin figures of the maverick and the malcontent that dominated much of '70s fiction. United by a feeling that Britain had been taken over by officious time-servers and placemen, they had something in common with the real-life equivalents of George Shipway's *The Chilian Club*, men like the retired NATO commander General Sir Walter Walker and SAS hero Colonel David Stirling, who proposed the creation of private armies of 'volunteers on call to the government in the event of a crisis'. Indeed the crisis was apparently pretty much upon us already: Benn's 'steady encroachment on the public enterprise system, together with the forcing of trade union members on to the executive board of companies', wrote Stirling, constituted a 'realizable threat of a magnitude this country has never faced before'. The fantasies of would-be power-brokers lusting after coups had been prefigured by newspaper proprietor Cecil King in 1968, when he made an abortive attempt to persuade Earl Mountbatten to lead such a rebellion, but again they became more prominent in the '70s. 'Two years ago we could have easily faced a coup in Britain,' wrote Jack Jones in 1977. 'The fear of hyper-inflation was strong. There was talk of private armies being assembled. There was talk of the end of democracy.'

Jones concluded that such threats had been curtailed by the public-spirited actions of 'trade unions and progressive management' working together to conquer inflation, but the best put-down of such fantasists came in the TV comedy *The Fall and Rise of Reginald Perrin* a year later. The focus here was on the mid-life crisis of Reggie himself (played by Leonard Rossiter), but his military brother-in-law, Jimmy Anderson (Geoffrey Palmer), is also struggling against modern society and confides that he's proposing to recruit a secret army for 'when the balloon goes up'. His targets are the 'Forces of anarchy, wreckers of law and order. Communists, Maoists, Trotskyists, neo-Trotskyists, union leaders, communist union leaders. Keg bitter, punk rockers, glue-sniffers, *Play for Today*, squatters, Clive Jenkins, Roy Jenkins, up Jenkins, up everybody's.' To which Reggie retorts: 'You know the sort of people you're going to attract, don't you,

Jimmy? Thugs, bully boys, psychopaths, sacked policemen, security guards, sacked security guards, racialists, Paki-bashers, queer-bashers, Chink-bashers, basher-bashers, anybody bashers, rear admirals, queer admirals, vice admirals, fascists, neo-fascists, crypto-fascists, loyalists, neo-loyalists, crypto-loyalists.' And Jimmy, with lugubrious enthusiasm, leaps at the vision: 'Really think so? I thought support might be hard to get.'

Jimmy Anderson too was probably to be found in the ranks of the comedy characters who would have voted for Thatcher (Reggie was more likely to have spoilt his ballot paper), reflecting a strand of middle-class disenchantment with modern Britain. Right at the end of his life in 1975, the great comic songwriter Michael Flanders said that 'it puzzled and saddened him to think that all the things he was, and had been brought up to be proud of – solid professional middle class, well-educated at non-snob public school, liberal with a small "l" in politics and morals – had suddenly become bad things, to be ashamed of'. For those like him, and for those, such as Annie Walker in *Coronation Street*, who aspired to such things, Thatcher appeared the most plausible chance for deliverance, as *The Times* pointed out in its description of her 1975 conference speech; it was, the paper said, 'a calculated call to political arms addressed to all those, in every socio-economic class, who identify themselves and their best interests with middle-class moral values'.

In preparing for that speech, Thatcher had instructed her team to broaden the focus beyond the economy, to look at values and philosophy. 'The economy had gone wrong,' she was convinced, 'because something else had gone wrong spiritually and philosophically. The economic crisis was a crisis of the spirit of the nation.' Whether she was correct or not, her analysis chimed with a great swath of public opinion. There was a perception amongst her supporters that a new establishment had some-how sneaked its way into existence, creating a society that elevated the rule-book mentality of Fred Kite and Vic Spanner to the status of standard practice, that bound traditional freedoms in red tape, that believed that the bureaucrat knew best. The trade union leaders, raised in profile by Mike Yarwood's impressions, were now seen by many as being part of the system, joining the ranks of the bosses, the bankers and the politicians; according to a 1976 Gallup survey, more than half the population saw Jack Jones as the most powerful man in the country.

Against this establishment the mavericks kicked, the malcontents raged and the fantasists plotted counter-revolution. And Thatcher, revelling in her status as the first woman leader of a major party, and taking on not merely the mantle but also the manner of Enoch Powell, began to build a reputation as one of the few politicians prepared to speak inconvenient truths, to question the very foundations of modern Britain. The Tories had finally found a credible champion who could offer a vision of the future entirely distinct from that of Tony Benn. Her constituency at this early stage was fragmented and fractured, and conventional wisdom still saw the prospects for the country as being dominated by the left, but on the right there was for the first time in a long while some semblance of hope, if only she were capable of bringing the disparate strands together. 'If this is "lurching to the right", as her critics claim,' said the *Daily Mail* of her 1975 conference speech, 'ninety per cent of the population lurched that way long ago.'

8

Obscenity
'I wanna take dirty pictures of you'

> FLETCHER: I'm talking about standards, moral standards. I mean,
> what do all these social commentators know, eh? They don't
> know nothing about the real world. They all live within a
> stone's throw of each other in North West One, don't they?
> Never been further north than Hampstead or further south
> than Sloane Square.
>
> Dick Clement and Ian La Frenais, *Porridge* (1975)

> Every night they watched television: comedy shows, plays,
> quiz games, anything they could get until the stations closed
> down for the night. Emily liked the plays, especially if there
> was what she called a bit of 'blue' in them but she wouldn't let
> Ernest watch BBC2 because there was every chance that there
> would be naked women in them, and that was taking things
> too far.
>
> Jack Ramsay, *The Rage* (1977)

> Last night I saw a (uh) strange movie (uh uh), everyone was in
> bed;
> Last night it made me (uh) feel groovy (uh uh), watching
> things that they did.
> There was Bill and Sue, checking Sid and Mandy too,
> And they went uh uh uh uh uh uh uh ohhh ...
>
> Troggs, 'Strange Movies' (1973)

In a 1977 storyline in the cartoon strip *Flook* the character Pru Scoop is
seen heaping relics from the previous decade onto a bonfire: a Union
Flag carrier bag, a copy of *Oz* magazine, a book by Germaine Greer, an
album by the Rolling Stones. Feeling that she and her generation were in
some way to 'blame for today's football hooligans', she is seeking to

absolve herself of the guilt she feels about the society she has helped bring into being. 'You are witnessing,' she proclaims loftily, 'the middle-class divesting itself of the decadent trappings of the Swinging Sixties.'

This retrospective dislike of what was pejoratively termed the permissive society became one of the key pillars of the right-wing renaissance in the '70s. 'The 1960s saw in Britain the beginning of what has become an almost complete separation between traditional Christian values and the authority of the state,' wrote Thatcher in her memoirs. 'People in positions of influence in government, the media and universities managed to impose metropolitan liberal views on a society that was still largely conservative morally.' The primary political cause of this supposed separation was the raft of legislation in the late '60s that legalized abortion and male homosexual acts, that ended capital punishment and the Lord Chamberlain's control of the stage, and that restrained racism and facilitated divorce. But there was too the wave of decensorship that had started with the trial of *Lady Chatterley's Lover* in 1960 and that had inadvertently democratized pornography, making available to the many what had previously been the province of the few. And here was the ground on which some of the key cultural battles were to be fought in the next decade, making some unlikely bedfellows along the way; the Tory minister Viscount Eccles declared in 1971 that 'Pornography is the ugly child of the permissive society,' a right-wing precursor to the radical feminist slogan 'Porn is the theory, rape is the practice.'

The rearguard fight against obscenity was led not by a politician, but by a woman who – in the mythically innocent days of the mid-'50s – had lived just two doors down from Enoch Powell in his Wolverhampton constituency. Mary Whitehouse was then an unremarkable teacher and mother, but in 1963 she was to launch herself on the public scene, leading a seemingly doomed campaign against the perceived permissiveness of the era and, particularly, against what she saw as an abandonment of standards at the BBC. By the 1970s, as the tide showed signs of turning against liberalism, she found herself – like Powell – hated and fêted in almost equal measure and, like him, seen by many as the spokesperson for ordinary decent folk feeling excluded from the political consensus. Even her most sympathetic biographer, however, felt the need to point out in 1975 that 'she was very definitely *not* a Powellite', an indication of how far beyond the pale Powell was by now deemed to have strayed.

The popular perception of Whitehouse was of a neighbourhood busybody in horn-rimmed glasses and surprisingly colourful print frocks, somewhat akin to Edna Everage before the damehood; she was a self-appointed censor, a woman who objected above all to the depiction of sex on television, in the cinema and in pop music. But that tells only part of the story. When she began her campaign, her primary target was not the presence of explicit sex scenes on TV, since these did not then exist; rather she was prompted by 'the irreverence of the late-night "satire" shows, and by the kind of plays put out by the BBC'; many years later she was still insisting that such programmes 'played havoc with everything that the vast majority of people hold dear'. The key, however, was that word 'irreverence', for Whitehouse was essentially a traditionalist, reflecting a middle-class, Anglican vision of Christianity that was rooted in social order and stability, a mindset that had reached its best-known expression in Cecil F. Alexander's hymn 'All Things Bright and Beautiful':

> The rich man in his castle,
> The poor man at his gate,
> God made them, high or lowly,
> And order'd their estate.

Or, in her own words, 'Freedom dies when moral anarchy takes over. It lives when citizens accept limitations upon themselves for the greater good of the community as a whole.'

This happy state of affairs was apparently threatened in 1963 by the arrival on BBC TV of the satirical show *That Was the Week That Was*, with its Oxbridge assaults on the establishment, by the Profumo scandal, and by the Bishop of Woolwich's book *Honest to God*. Convinced that this unholy trinity might shake the very foundations of civilization, Whitehouse initiated what was first known as the Clean-Up TV Campaign and later as the National Viewers' and Listeners' Association (VALA). She was thus amongst the first to register that the 1960s were marking a radical break from the past, and she was determined to do all that she could to put a stop to it. For much of the decade she was a thorn in the flesh of the BBC, denouncing perceived lapses of taste and judgement, expressing outrage, and arguing that licence-payers' money should not be spent on undermining the family values that she considered essential to a stable society. But a thorn was all that she was, for, despite the sound and fury, and despite the widespread exposure she received in the newspapers, she was then a marginal figure with few positive results to show for her efforts, save the support of those who thought of her as the voice of the silent majority – over a third of a million signed a petition in 1965 expressing concern at the 'low standards' of television. In the words of her friend Bill Deedes, Tory MP and future editor of the *Daily Telegraph*: 'The

1960s were rough times for people with the message Mrs Whitehouse sought to deliver.' The victories were not to come until the '70s.

By then she had become a figure of ridicule in the media. Indeed there had been those prepared to mock from the outset: the character of Mrs Smallwood, played by Margot Boyd in the 1964 serial *Swizzlewick*, with her advocacy of 'freedom from sex', was clearly based on Whitehouse. Later, thinly veiled depictions included the Sensational Alex Harvey Band's 'Mrs Blackhouse', Beryl Reid's incarnation as Desiree Carthorse in *The Goodies* – 'You mean you're going to condemn that film without even seeing it?' asks Bill Oddie, to which she replies: 'Why should I change the habit of a lifetime?' – and Norma Blackhurst in porn star Fiona Richmond's semi-autobiographical film *Hardcore*. (This latter was played by Joan Benham, better known as Lady Prudence Fairfax in the Whitehouse-approved *Upstairs, Downstairs*.) She was also the inspiration behind the ironic title of the pornographic magazine *Whitehouse*, and William Bennett's power electronics band of the same name, while Pink Floyd sang about her as a 'house-proud town mouse' on their album *Animals*: 'You gotta stem the evil tide, and keep it all on the inside.'

The most entertaining caricature of the attitudes Whitehouse was believed to embody was Pete Walker's exploitation movie *House of Whipcord* (1974), in which a nineteen-year-old French model (played by Page Three girl Penny Irving) is arrested doing a semi-nude advertising shoot in Kensington Gardens and fined £10 for behaviour liable to cause a breach of the peace. There the matter would normally rest, except that the film posits the existence of an alternative, unofficial prison, run by a retired judge and a trio of former prison wardresses. And it is here that our heroine is taken to be tried by the ex-judge: 'This is a private court. And we are constituted here by private charter within the walls of this fine, historic building, that was once a county jail, to pass what we regard as proper sentence on depraved females of every category, with whom the effete and misguided courts of Great Britain today have been too lenient.' It proves to be a rigorous regime; for a first offence of breaking prison regulations, the penalty is two weeks' solitary confinement; for a second offence, flogging, and for a third, hanging. In case the satire isn't entirely apparent in this women-behind-bars flick, the film starts with a written message: 'This film is dedicated to those who are disturbed by today's lax moral codes and who eagerly await the return of corporal and capital punishment . . .'

But derision was, some felt, scarcely necessary, when Whitehouse herself was so adept at self-parody; in 1972 she was to be found protesting against *Top of the Pops* playing Chuck Berry's #1 single 'My Ding-a-Ling', not on the grounds that such trite nonsense wasn't worthy of the man who invented the poetry and guitar style of rock & roll, but because she believed its schoolyard smut was obscene. The BBC chose on this occasion – as on so many others – not to follow her advice, but it could, with the other hand, point proudly to the way it assiduously banned every single record released by Judge Dread, a white British DJ born as Alex Hughes, who specialized in rude nursery rhymes set to ska rhythms:

> Two old ladies sitting on the dock;
> One put her hand up the other one's frock.

Dread ended the decade having sold more singles in Britain than any other reggae artist, up to and including Johnny Nash and Bob Marley, but so total was the prohibition on his work that even his 1973 single 'Molly', a benefit record for famine victims in Ethiopia, was banned from radio play despite its complete lack of any hint of offensiveness, simply because of the artist concerned. Such anomalies abounded at the BBC during the period, the most celebrated being Lou Reed's 'Walk on the Wild Side', a single that documented transvestism, oral sex, prostitution and drugs and still failed to earn itself a ban, for reasons that have never been entirely clear.

Meanwhile, amongst the many other targets at whom Mary Whitehouse thundered in the early '70s with equal futility, and with no apparent sense of priority, were *A Clockwork Orange* ('the most shocking film ever to be shown in England', she gasped in her habitually hyperbolic way), the swearing on the Rolling Stones' album *Exile on Main Street*, the horrific content of *Doctor Who* and the amorality of the BBC series *Casanova*, an attack that provoked writer Dennis Potter to call her 'an ignorant and dangerous woman'.

The repeated calls for the BBC to ban programmes and records that the Corporation decided not to ban might sometimes have given the impression of impotence, but Whitehouse was nonetheless an influential player in 1970s culture. There was, to start with, the long-term self-censorship achieved by her Fabian strategy, as TV writer Wilfred Greatorex pointed out: 'the sheer noise which has come from her has caused some writers to be inhibited'. Even when a writer was not thus subdued, even when a play was commissioned, accepted and recorded by the BBC, the fear of complaints could still cause panic, as Potter discovered with his 1976 piece *Brimstone and Treacle*, which was pulled by Alasdair Milne, then the director of programmes, less than three weeks before its scheduled broadcast. The plot centred on a disturbing character, who appeared to be the Devil in human form, visiting a suburban family and raping their brain-damaged daughter; as the BBC press release admitted, it was 'likely to outrage viewers', and certainly it's hard to imagine Whitehouse not turning it into a major tabloid issue. (In a complaint about Potter's later series *Pennies from Heaven*, VALA called him a 'brilliant playwright' but objected, in anatomically tautological terms, to the sight of a woman 'having painted round the nipples of her breasts with lipstick'.)

More than this occasionally suppressive effect, however, there was the fact that Whitehouse's absolute certainty in her own faith ensured that she wouldn't be deterred by short-term defeats; she was in for the long haul. In this respect she mirrored the ruthless dedication of those she considered to be her ultimate enemies, for behind her anti-permissive rhetoric was not simply a Christian defence of deference, nor solely a concern for the impressionable minds of children, but a passionate opposition to communism.

Though seldom expressed in the media, it was Whitehouse's conviction that the perceived assault by both the BBC and the pornography industry on the moral standards of British society was inspired and funded by Moscow, in an attempt to bring about the downfall of democracy. Her husband, Ernest, believed that the Book of Daniel in the Old Testament prophesied the (temporary) triumph of communism, and she herself had no hesitation in seeing reds both under and in the bed: 'They've infiltrated the trade unions,' she argued. 'Why does anyone still believe they haven't infiltrated broadcasting?' Whether or not she was correct in attributing a controlling interest in pornography – capitalism's most profitable industry – to the Soviet Union, at a time when that country was not renowned for its ability to foster enterprise, she herself was undoubtedly convinced of the truth of the claim, and her faith that she was struggling against the forces of evil sustained her through her long guerrilla war against modern culture. While public attention was focused on her criticisms of, for example, *Till Death Us Do Part*, for using the word 'bloody' and suggesting that the Virgin Mary might have been 'on the pill' (the BBC apologized for that one), there was also a strictly political agenda that was less noticed; a tough *Panorama* interview with the Northern Ireland prime minister Brian Faulkner prompted her to ask 'where the sympathies of the BBC lie in relation to Northern Ireland', while during the three-day week she complained that the Corporation was 'committed to polarization of public sentiment in favour of the miners'.

The twin themes of politics and obscenity came together when Whitehouse took on the new administration at the Greater London Council. Labour had captured the GLC in 1973 on its most radical ever manifesto, uncompromisingly titled *A Socialist Strategy for London*, and, amidst the promises of a massive programme of house building and a freeze on public transport fares ('as a first step towards their eventual abolition'), the most controversial aspect of its policy turned out to be its position on film censorship. The passing of movies for public screenings, and their classification, was primarily the responsibility of the British Board of Film Censors, but this was a self-governing body set up and run by the industry itself, and its decisions were always potentially subject to being overturned by local authorities, which had a statutory duty to license cinemas in their areas. And of those local authorities, the GLC was far and away the most important, with one seventh of the nation's cinemas coming under its jurisdiction. So it was a relatively big news story when Enid Wistrich was appointed the first female chairman of its Film Viewing Board (her vice-chairman was a newly elected councillor named Ken Livingstone), and even more so when, the following year, she volunteered the effective abolition of her own job; in her own words, she proposed 'that the Council cease to exercise its powers to censor films for adults over the age of 18 with the effect that any film which did not fall foul of the law could be shown in London's cinemas'.

By this stage Whitehouse had already come into conflict with the new regime. The full version of Marco Ferreri's 1973 film *Blow Out* (*La Grande Bouffe*) was refused a certificate by the BBFC, but Wistrich's committee passed it uncut, with a condition that a warning be displayed in the foyer of the cinema, together with a synopsis of the plot, to ensure that those liable to being shocked might be deterred from entering. As the dramatist Ted Willis had recently pointed out, however: 'People go to an extraordinary amount of trouble to be shocked.' Whitehouse duly went along to see the movie at the Curzon Cinema in Mayfair and, discovering that the warnings were indeed entirely accurate, she fulminated against such depravity to the press ('the most revolting film I have ever seen') and then 'dashed off to the nearest police station to lodge a complaint'. When the police declined to act, on the grounds that there was no law against it, she instead launched a private prosecution against the Curzon under the Vagrancy Act, arguing that this was indecency in a public place. The case was a failure – the magistrate reluctantly decided that a cinema did not constitute a public place as defined in law – but it gave her a taste for legal action that would become more apparent as the years went on, as well as alerting her to the dangerous subversives at the GLC.

When therefore the question of the abolition of censorship came before the Council in January 1975, it was a huge media event, billed as a heavy-weight title fight: Whitehouse vs Wistrich. For the first time ever a GLC meeting was broadcast on live radio, with Whitehouse being interviewed in the public gallery, whilst outside County Hall a Salvation Army band entertained the anti-porn demonstrators when they weren't praying for divine intervention. The four-hour debate encapsulated the long process of decensorship: on the one side was Wistrich citing John Milton's argument that 'When God gave Adam reason, He gave him freedom to choose, for reason is but choosing'; on the other were those who feared a 'vicious spiral of ever increasing violence' and the creation of 'cesspools of iniquity'. And behind it all was the much vaunted conflict of the elite and the silent majority; as far as Whitehouse was concerned, 'the Enid Wistrichs of this world are the elitist "experts" who are responsible to no one and whose expressed opinions are so far removed from the experience of the vast majority of people in Britain that their views amount to an almost complete distortion of the national will'. When the votes were counted, the proposal to allow adults to watch what they liked had been lost by 50 to 44, thanks to seventeen Labour councillors who voted against the motion, whilst only two Tories had broken ranks to support Wistrich; one of these latter, she noted, was a woman, and indeed female councillors 'voted for abolition by a proportion of two to one, demonstrating clearly that it was not women who felt the need to curb visual expressions of sexuality'.

The failure of Wistrich's bold initiative ensured that anomalies and absurdities would continue to exist in a way that reflected the law more generally. In the late 1970s the BBFC announced that it would in future allow depictions of homosexual intercourse on the same basis as it permitted depictions of heterosexual acts, though any film about homo-sexuality would still demand an X certificate. And thereby were ushered in all sorts of incongruities. Anal intercourse was then illegal between heterosexuals, however consenting they might be ('It is as serious as committing manslaughter or grievous bodily harm' commented a judge in 1974, suggesting that his technique was not all that it might be), whilst it was permissible between gay men over the age of twenty-one so long as it wasn't witnessed by a third party. No such act could therefore be performed at all by heterosexuals or, in the presence of a camera crew, by homosexuals, but the simulation of it could be viewed – though the reality not practised – by gay men between the ages of eighteen and twenty-one. Elsewhere, the abolition of theatrical censorship by the Lord Chamberlain in the Theatres Act of 1968 had permitted Kenneth Tynan's sex revue *Oh! Calcutta!* to become one of the great stage hits of the era, with over 2,400 performances in London, but the 1972 film of a New York staging was banned outright by the BBFC: it was permissible to show what many saw as filth in the theatre, but not the celluloid depiction of exactly the same filth in the cinema. (A British bookseller was also fined for importing copies of the book of the revue.) Similarly, the film of Pauline Réage's classic novel *The Story of O* was refused a certificate by both the BBFC and the GLC, whilst the book on which it was based was freely available in a Corgi paperback from 1972 onwards.

In the case of this latter, one can't help feeling that those who sought to protect society from itself had missed a trick. The movie, directed by Just Jaeckin, was an innocuous piece of high-gloss soft porn that allowed no room for imagination and did a great deal to defuse the power of the original. The book, on the other hand, which came complete with endorsements on the back cover from Graham Greene and J.G. Ballard, was much more disturbing and even downright incendiary. Beautifully written and entirely devoid of linguistic obscenity, it was the tale of a sexually submissive Parisian woman finding fulfilment, first in a secret brotherhood of men at the Château Roissy and then at the hands of an English gentleman named Sir Stephen (the film role was originally offered to Christopher Lee, though thankfully he turned it down). As the first, and most enduring, piece of sadomasochistic erotica to be widely available in high-street bookstores, the novel exerted a huge influence on many who had previously felt that their proclivities were inappropriate and wrong; 'When I first read *The Story of O*,' wrote the Danish feminist Maria Marcus, 'it filled me with a mixture of sexual excitement, horror, anxiety – and envy.' It also articulated the nascent sexuality of many thousands of young women who stumbled upon it on the bookshelves of their permissive parents.

Originally published in France in 1954, the novel benefited in Britain from appearing at a time when flagellation was edging its way into mainstream consciousness. When novelist Gillian Freeman was researching pornography in 1966, she reported a Soho bookseller having to disappoint a customer looking for depictions of straight sex: 'Sorry, mate, it's all got a bit of fladge in it.' Within a few years it appeared almost as though the same were true of novels generally, with erotic beating and binding to be glimpsed everywhere from Alec Waugh's semi-respectable comedy of manners *A Spy in the Family* (1970), through Christopher Nicole's black magic thriller *The Face of Evil* (1971), all the way down to Timothy Lea's sex farce *Confessions of a Window Cleaner* (1971). As Terry Collier put it in *Whatever Happened to the Likely Lads?*: 'I know I've been away for five years, but dear me, I never realized that bondage was that popular.' The lightweight simulations in the movie of *The Story of O*, however, were still considered too strong to be seen by a British audience, a situation that remained until the end of the century.

Despite all the foolish inconsistencies, progress was made in the '70s in terms of cinema regulations. The X certificate in film classification was revised in 1970 to an age limit of eighteen rather than the previous sixteen (the interim AA certificate, with an age limit of fourteen, was introduced at the same time), which allowed for a broader range of adult themes, and gradually a degree of common sense was introduced. In 1976, for example, James Dean's *Rebel Without a Cause* (1955) was finally passed in an uncut version and given an AA certificate; previously an edited version had only been available as an X film. This meant that it was now on the same footing as the final *Carry On* movie in the original series, *Carry On Emmannuelle* (1978), which had sufficiently broken with its nudge-nudge heritage to warrant an AA classification. Even so, the marginally increased raunchiness was insufficient to maintain the series in the face of the sex comedies that had emerged in response to the new X certificate, and that soon dominated the domestic film industry: *Come Play with Me* (1977), featuring Mary Millington, was said to be the most profitable British movie ever, while Martin Scorsese's 1975 urban masterpiece *Taxi Driver* was outgrossed in Britain by *Adventures of a Taxi Driver* in the same year.

On mainstream TV meanwhile, despite Whitehouse's fears of Sodom and Gomorrah in the homes of England's green and pleasant land, little had changed; it was not until 1977 that *Robin's Nest* – another spin-off from *Man About the House* – became the first British sitcom to depict an unmarried couple living together, and even then special permission had to be gained from the Independent Broadcasting Authority to show such a thing. Few noticed the storming of the ramparts.

The IBA's job was to ensure that suitable standards were maintained on ITV broadcasts, and the referral of *Robin's Nest* was therefore entirely proper, but an earlier decision by the authority was more tendentious and led to much adverse press comment. In 1975 ITV announced that it was to start showing films during the afternoon hours of children's broadcasting and the IBA approved the plan, but insisted that certain movies would be inappropriate, particularly those featuring the greatest of all the 1930s child stars: 'The Shirley Temple films are mawkish and sentimental,' said a spokesman. 'Today's youngsters are more sophisticated than those of forty years ago, even quite little ones aged five or six.' Quite how this decision fitted into the IBA's remit was unclear, particularly since they approved Will Hay's films of a similar vintage, and even allowed the frankly frightening drag act of Arthur Lucan as Old Mother Riley. 'Future historians will recall with amazement,' wrote a correspondent to the *Daily Mail*, 'the day when the permissive society was rampant, and film censorship practically non-existent, and a decision was made to ban Shirley Temple's films by branding them as unsuitable for children.'

In later years, of course, such an attitude would have been damned as political correctness, as would the 1973 decision of the Inner London Education Authority to end the decades-old custom of a schools' carol concert at the Royal Festival Hall. This, it was explained, was the result of a policy shift away from 'solemn and formal teacher-directed music' towards 'a child-centred creative exploration of the subject'. And instead of the carol concert, a programme by the Spinners, a folk group much in demand on light entertainment TV shows, was screened in all ILEA schools.

The media's happy indulgence in such horrors, however, was as nothing compared to the festival of fun that ensued when the former Labour cabinet minister Frank Pakenham, the 7th Earl of Longford, announced in 1971 that if the government wasn't going to establish a royal commission to investigate the effects of pornography, then he would jolly well set up his own inquiry to do the job for them. A convert to both socialism and Catholicism, Lord Longford was now in his late sixties and, with an unkempt ring of hair protruding from around his monkish pate and with a look of bespectacled bemusement, he was a gift to tabloid editors, who were quite prepared to attack the porn industry whilst reserving their right to mock those who sought to reform it, particularly when it came to the newly nicknamed 'Lord Porn'. (In later years, as Longford's interest in the reform of prisoners led him to call for the release of the Moors murderer Myra Hindley, he became simply a hate figure for the same newspapers.)

The committee of inquiry was, predictably, a farce from beginning to end. Its remit was to discover the 'means of tackling the problem of pornography', so no one was much surprised when the membership was packed with Christian cronies of the chairman, and excluded those who didn't see pornography as a problem in the first instance. And, since a survey in the '70s revealed that one in five men regularly bought pornographic magazines, it has to be assumed that there were many who didn't view it in the same negative light. Amongst those who were included, and who stayed the course, were singer Cliff Richard and Radio One DJ Jimmy Savile, alongside more obvious suspects like Malcolm Muggeridge (he had spoken at VALA's first convention, declaring that 'if *Till Death Us Do Part* is life, I cannot see that there would be anything to do but commit suicide') and the Rt. Revd Ronald Ralph Williams, the Bishop of Leicester, whose response to a Ken Russell film was truly magnificent in its acceptance of the divine will: 'I never thought that I should give thanks to God for being blind, but since my wife has told me what she has seen in the film, *The Devils*, I am genuinely grateful that I at least have been spared that.'

The high point of the exercise was undoubtedly a trip to Denmark to witness some of the famed live sex shows of that country, at one of which 'a beautiful young woman pressed a whip into Lord Longford's hand and invited him to beat her'. The *Guardian* report of the incident added: 'His Lordship declined.' As he beat instead a hasty retreat, he told his colleague, the future Tory MP Gyles Brandreth, that he 'had seen enough for science and more than enough for enjoyment'. In the circumstances, it was perhaps as well that he didn't recognize that the 'woman' was in fact a transvestite. On the plane over, Longford had been ostentatiously reading the Bible to put himself in the correct frame of mind, though perhaps he would have been better off having had a word with his newly acquired fellow campaigner, Mary Whitehouse. She had visited Denmark the previous year as part of a *World in Action* programme and had picked up a magazine in her hotel bookshop containing images so 'pervasive and corrupting' that she had to pray to 'ask the Lord to cleanse her'.

When the Longford report emerged in 1972, it was an immediate best-seller, largely because it was marketed as a fat paperback with the single word 'Pornography' in huge letters on the cover, and because it retailed at a very competitive 60p. Its contents, however, were disappointing in terms both of intellectual engagement with the subject (Bernard Levin dismissed it as 'heated amateurism') and of cheap thrills, though there were those who relished such passages as a lengthy account of sex and sadism in a boys' boarding school: 'Sometimes the prefects did a lot of the whipping; at other times they made the third-year boys do it as well, or the second-year boys whip the first years and the first years whip each other.' The most succinct response to the entire enterprise came when the actor Robert Morley told Longford that 'if somebody liked to dress up in chamois leather and be stung by wasps, I really couldn't see why one should stop him'.

Whether anyone did seek such an experience is perhaps doubtful, but had they done so, they would certainly have found a place to parade their penchant. As pornography began to move out from the Soho bookshops into more orthodox retail outlets, *Forum* magazine – which at this stage eschewed all photographic material in favour of text and journalism – acquired a reputation for the exploration of practices hitherto neglected in mainstream publishing; this was particularly true of its letters pages that were widely believed to have been written by its own journalists, seemingly in the spirit of running fetishes up flagpoles in the hope that the odd reader or two might salute. A single issue from 1970 included, for example, not only such well-known tastes as rubber but also a predilection for corduroy, as well as the employment during sex of – *inter alia* – a vacuum cleaner, wild honey and raw steaks ('which we beat well with garlic and herbs'). It also found room for the tale of eight men who attached the bells from cat collars to their genitalia and gave a performance of 'Bells Across the Water' in the men's toilets at Victoria Station, 'much to the enjoyment, if not edification, of many onlookers. The applause occasioned by this rendering encouraged us to attempt, with a notable measure of success, Schillenberg's mediaeval "Aquascutum in Plasticus".'

Because of its textual nature, *Forum* was generally considered to be a middle-class publication and therefore seldom of great interest to the law. Indeed it was never clear quite what was of interest to the law, since the legislation and the legal precedents were so confused and contradictory, but the fact that the law was interested could not be doubted. There were, estimated the *Observer* in 1971, around a hundred shops selling nothing but pornography, half of them in London and thus under the purview of the Obscene Publications Squad of the Metropolitan Police, colloquially known as the dirty books squad. The real profits here were to be made on imported material from Sweden and Denmark, as David Sullivan, the future newspaper proprietor and owner of Birmingham City Football Club, pointed out in 1975: 'I was offered 10,000 Scandinavian magazines for £2,500. That's five shillings a book. Well, they could be sold for not less than £3 to £5, so you've got a factor there of twelve or twenty times the buying price.' The potential profit on the deal (which Sullivan declined) was £47,500. In such a world it was hardly surprising that there was no shortage of people looking for their own cut of the action, a fact which the Met Commissioner, Robert Mark, the man who did much to clean up Scotland Yard, couldn't fail to notice: 'The real fear of the pornographers was not of the courts but of harassment, either by strong-arm men seeking protection money or by police doing, in effect, the same thing.'

When, however, the fact was revealed that members of the dirty books squad were taking massive backhanders from the proprietors of sex shops (and, in the case of the squad's operational chief, even offering to write for the spanking magazine *Janus*), the public and the courts were shocked. *The Sweeney* might show Flying Squad officers mixing with the criminal classes, but there was nothing in the series to indicate that, for example, James Humphreys, a leading Soho porn baron, 'was considered a suitable guest to be invited to the annual dinner of the Flying Squad in the autumn of 1970'. In a high-profile series of trials, five officers were sentenced in 1976, and a further ten the following year, for terms of up to twelve years, having been found guilty of conspiracy and other offences relating to bribery and corruption in the Soho porn industry.

With the association between pornography, the criminal underworld and bent coppers now in the public domain, an attempt to clean up the trade was launched. Several leading publishers came together to form the Kingsley committee in 1977 in the hope of regulating the industry on a voluntary basis; as a spokesman said: 'We have been going too far recently. We feel it is time to put our own house in order before the authorities impose their censorship upon us.' The resultant board of control was chaired by one of Whitehouse's long-standing foes, John Trevelyan, who had been a liberal figure at the BBFC. In reality, though, the whole enterprise might already have been too late for those who remembered the mega-profits that had been enjoyed at the start of the decade; a report the same year claimed that sales of porn magazines were down by 20 per cent.

But even if the feverish days of expansion were passing, there was some compensation in that pornography had by this stage become an established fact of British society, with the image of the consumer having moved on from earlier perceptions. In the television series *Budgie*, the eponymous hero Ronald 'Budgie' Bird (Adam Faith) spent much of his time hanging around a Soho bookshop, where in a 1971 episode, he encounters one of his former schoolteachers, Marcus Lake (John Franklyn-Robbins). 'It's a drug, pornography's a drug,' explains Lake, trying to justify his habit as much to himself as to Budgie. 'I'm not an adulterer. I don't visit prostitutes. I don't molest little boys or little girls. I don't make obscene telephone calls. I don't expose myself on canal banks. I have my secret, expensive little vice. And I fight it, I fight it.' A more extreme portrayal of the same attitude was to be found in *Last Bus to Woodstock*, the first novel featuring the detective Inspector Morse, as well as a character named John Sanders, who shared Lake's addiction: 'He realizes well enough that his dedication to pornography is coarsening whatever sensibilities he may once have possessed; that his craving is settling like some cancerous, malignant growth upon his mind, a mind crying out with ever-increasing desperation for its instant, morbid gratification. But he can do nothing about it.' As Morse puts it: 'He's sick, Lewis, and he knows he's sick . . .'

These, however, were extreme cases. Already a more tolerant attitude to the typical user was being expressed. When, in 1972, *Coronation Street*'s Stan Ogden was accused of being a peeping Tom, his wife Hilda reassures him that she doesn't believe him capable of such offences: 'I know you look at pin-ups and things like that, but then all men do, don't they? But that's different.' By 1977 even a mainstream sitcom like *George and Mildred* felt comfortable addressing the issue, in an episode where Mildred inadvertently donates George's collection of magazines – with such splendid titles as *Nudge*, *Wink* and *Titter* – to the vicar's jumble sale, much to her husband's dismay. 'It took me years, that collection,' he whines. 'Be hard to replace some of them. Especially the Swedish ones.' Even Jeffrey Fourmile next door is seen sharing his indulgence, and defending it to his own wife: 'It's not so much people like you or I,' he argues. 'I mean, we can handle it. It's the working class – salt of the earth, goes without saying – but they are easily inflamed. They don't have the training and self-control that we have.'

In political terms, of course, the whole issue of pornography remained a minefield to be avoided if at all possible, save by the most courageous. The great liberalizing moves of the 1960s had come when Roy Jenkins was home secretary, but his successor, Jim Callaghan, was much more concerned with the world outside fashionable London circles. 'What worries me about the libertarians is that they may lose our supporters,' he had mused; 'the people in the Cardiff back streets who I know and feel at home with.' He was not alone in his reservations, but it was still something of a surprise when Keith Joseph, as a senior front-bench politician, explicitly paid tribute to Mary Whitehouse in his 'human stock' speech at Edgbaston: 'We can see in her a shining example of what one person can do single-handedly when inspired by faith and compassion,' he declared. 'Look at the scale of the opposing forces. On the one side, the whole of the new establishment with their sharp words and sneers poised; against them stood this one middle-aged woman.'

In fact the conflict was somewhat greater than this; Whitehouse had had to endure more than 'sharp words and sneers'. The loathing she engendered was comparable to that inspired by Tony Benn, and she suffered much the same experience of obscene phone calls, death threats and media snooping on her children. The fact that she survived, despite her lack of preparedness for such hostility, was testament to the courage of the long-distance crusader. 'This is the Cross,' she wrote in her diary; 'to realize there is no glamour, no appreciation to be asked or expected, nothing but ridicule, pain and loss.' One didn't have to share her obsession with obscenity to recognize that, like Benn, she was something of a heroic figure.

Joseph's endorsement of Whitehouse on behalf of the Conservative Party was formalized when William Whitelaw, the deputy leader, spoke at VALA's 1978 conference. 'There will always be those who regard any action by the State to protect its citizens and maintain standards of society as unjustified censorship and interference,' he said. 'Such people regard as antiquated and prudish prigs those, among whom I include myself, who believe that we have a duty to conserve the moral standards on which our society has been based, and so preserve them for future generations.'

The real prize, of course, would have been the unequivocal backing of Margaret Thatcher, and here there were some grounds for hope. Her voting record on the liberalizing bills of the late '60s was mixed but promising: she had supported the legalizing of homosexuality and abortion, but opposed the divorce reforms and the abolition of capital punishment. This latter position was entirely in accord with what she boasted was her one rebellion against the party whip, when she had voted in 1961 for the reintroduction of 'birching or caning for young violent offenders'. Even so, her mostly tacit support for Whitehouse – the two women did meet and shared many of the same views – appeared to be based more on the common cultural assumptions of a decent, Christian society than on any active engagement with the issues that so troubled VALA. Indeed, while Whitehouse was only too aware of the failings of the flesh, a fact that helped make her so powerful a voice, Thatcher seldom gave the impression that she had entirely mastered the moral brief. When in 1973 Earl Jellicoe, the Tory leader of the House of Lords, resigned after admitting to having used prostitutes, it was reported that she had asked her permanent secretary at the education department in naive amazement: 'Do men really pay for that kind of thing?' For those who sought the rolling back of the permissive society, it was not an entirely auspicious comment.

9
Nostalgia
'Driving me backwards'

> JUAN: Remember, we opened in 1974. That was a long time ago.
> It was the heyday of the elegant renaissance – Bryan Ferry in
> his white dinner jacket, a great era.
> Howard Schuman, *Rock Follies* (1976)

> TOM BATES: I simply want the world to stop just where it is. And
> go back a bit.
> Dennis Potter, *Brimstone and Treacle* (1976)

> I guess I really learned a lot since then,
> Cause I can really do it now it's back again.
> The Rubettes, 'I Can Do It' (1975)

As Britain drifted into crisis, three of the country's most creative and innovative rock musicians appeared to take a step backwards, recording albums that consisted entirely of cover versions: David Bowie's *Pin-Ups*, Bryan Ferry's *These Foolish Things* and John Lennon's *Rock 'n' Roll* (the first two were released in 1973, while the third – containing tracks from sessions in that year – did not emerge until 1975). The motivations behind the three records, however, were quite distinct. Lennon's album was an act of simple homage and affection, revisiting the records of his adolescence, the first-generation rock sounds that he had fallen in love with, while Ferry's eclectic exploration of the history of popular songs, stripped of their original context, had the effect of establishing an alternative, solo career, one with better long-term prospects than his arty day job in Roxy Music could ever provide.

Bowie, on the other hand, was doing something very different. The music he covered on *Pin-Ups* was that of his near-contemporaries, the bands that – in his fantasies – he would have liked to consider his peers when he was starting his career. Three of the songs date from 1964, the year he released his first single, with all but one of the remainder from 1965–66. This was a harking back to the very peak of '60s creativity, a time when Britain's pop culture was at its most optimistic and confident, when mod briefly ruled the world of cool in the shape of the Who, the Yardbirds, the Kinks and the Pretty Things. The cut-off point of 1967 (the Pink Floyd's 'See Emily Play', included to provide financial support for its drug-damaged composer, Syd Barrett) was significant, for that was the year when the peacock-proud pantheon of Swinging London began to lose its sense of progress, as the Beatles adopted antique uniforms and music hall elements on *Sgt. Pepper's Lonely Hearts Club Band*, as the influence of Aubrey Beardsley sparked a reawakening of interest in art nouveau and as *The Forsyte Saga* became the BBC's biggest drama series. It was also when the wheels came off Harold Wilson's modernizing bandwagon, the year of his 'pound in your pocket' devaluation of the currency and of the rejection – again – of Britain's entry into the EEC. In December 1967 Biba moved from the mini- to the maxi-skirt, and the fashion press reported that hemlines were falling 'as swiftly as the pound sterling'.

This turn to the past continued for a while to spark artistic exploration, but it also suggested a certain nervousness, a loss of faith in the present and of hope for the future. Over the next few years, the element of nostalgia in popular culture continued to grow, so that by the time Bowie released *Pin-Ups* the album looked as though it were part of the prevailing mood; in fact, though, by providing a reminder of the last time that British pop had been entirely forward-looking, it was precisely the opposite – an implicit rejection of the revivalist trend, an attempt to reconnect to the creative impulses of a more optimistic era.

Nonetheless, the nostalgia continued. The rock & roll revival that was heralded in Britain by Dave Edmunds's #1 cover of the Smiley Lewis song 'I Hear You Knocking', and that was manifest in a 1972 gig at Wembley Stadium (the first rock show there) starring Chuck Berry, Jerry Lee Lewis and Little Richard, became an established feature of cultural life. A new self-awareness of rock's own history was now evident, reflected in David Hare's play *Teeth 'n' Smiles*, first staged in 1975 but set in the dying days of the '60s; as a band falls apart, their manager recalls the glory years: 'It'll never get better than 1956,' he reflects. 'Tat. Utter tat. But inspired. The obvious repeated many times. Simple things said well. Then along came those boys who could really play. They spoilt it of course. Ruined it.'

At its peak in 1972–73 the glam rock movement led by Bowie and Roxy Music had drawn on this mood, though it blended its love of 1950s rhythms and its pre-Beatles celebration of artificial stardom with a diversity of other influences, from Dylanesque wordplay to Warholian pop art to Berlin cabaret. But as the moment passed, and the leading artists departed for fresh territory, what remained was little more than a pale pastiche of the past, with groups such as Showaddywaddy, the Rubettes and Mud dominating the singles charts with recreations of American high school pop from the Kennedy years. The most successful of these post-glam bands were the Bay City Rollers, whose four top 10 singles in 1974 provoked a wave of teen hysteria (swiftly named Rollermania, in the hope of evoking Beatlemania) and were followed the next year by a brace of #1 hits, starting with the old Four Seasons song 'Bye Bye Baby'. This was a perfectly fine pop record, and in its own way it did mark a new era for the band – not least because they actually played the music on it, the earlier hits having been the work of seasoned session men like Clem Cattini and Chris Rae – but the choice of material merely maintained the image conjured up by their previous songwriting team of Bill Martin and Phil Coulter: 'Remember (Sha La La)', 'Shang-a-Lang', 'Summerlove Sensation'. So adept had the British music industry become at reworking the history of American pop that when Brian Wilson heard the Beach Boys-derived sounds of 'Beach Baby' (1974) by studio band the First Class, he assumed it was an original piece of Californian pop from the early '60s, a misunderstanding which session singer Tony Burrows cited as one of his proudest moments.

The fact that the Rollers got to #1 with an old song was hardly noteworthy in 1975. Within weeks it was followed at the top of the singles charts by Mud's slowed-down version of Buddy Holly's 'Oh Boy', and by Windsor Davies and Don Estelle's comic rework of the Inkspots' 'Whispering Grass'. In between those two came Tammy Wynette's 'Stand by Your Man', a track recorded seven years earlier, signalling another trend of the year – the reissued record from the '60s – which brought new life to hits by Chris Farlowe, the Small Faces and even Bowie ('Space Oddity' finally gave him a #1, six years after its original release). Even older stars, who thought their chart career had ended with the Beatles, also found their way back to the *Top of the Pops* studio in the persons of Chubby Checker, Duane Eddy and Brian Hyland. And for those who found all this too modern, there was that Christmas a debut hit single for Laurel and Hardy, while the hippest clubs were busy exploring a Glenn Miller revival. It was also a golden age for novelty singles, with Telly Savalas, Billy Connolly and Typically Tropical reaching the top with 'If', 'D.I.V.O.R.C.E.' and 'Barbados' respectively. Meanwhile Englebert Humperdinck, Jim Reeves and Perry Como all had greatest hits albums at #1 that year, followed in 1976 by Roy Orbison, Slim Whitman, Bert Weedon and Glen Campbell, and in 1977 by Frank Sinatra, Johnny Mathis and Connie Francis. It was entirely in keeping with the spirit of the times that 5,000 latter-day Teddy boys should march on Broadcasting House in May 1976, demanding that Radio One play more rock & roll.

What all this amounted to was a crisis of confidence in the future of British pop music. Ten years earlier it had been a radical, vital art form, the driving force that sold British culture around the world – even three or four years earlier, glam had restored some much needed vigour to the format of the 7″ single – but now it seemed moribund, sinking into an inherited dotage. (So desperate had the situation become that the nation's teenyboppers began to turn their attention to the Swedish tennis player Björn Borg, upsetting traditionalists at Wimbledon by screaming at their idol.) There were new acts being promoted, but there was a distinct nervousness in the approach of the record companies; John Miles, who had built a local cult following in Newcastle with singles on the independent Orange label, was signed to Decca in 1975 and launched with *Rebel*, an album whose title and cover photograph – by Terry O'Neill – saddled him with a gimmicky James Dean image that was entirely inappropriate and from which he struggled to escape. The one truly revolutionary hit of 1975 was Kraftwerk's 'Autobahn', imported from Germany, and even that was at the time regarded as yet another novelty.

Rock was not alone in being in thrall to the past. It was unusual perhaps only in that its own timeline was so short (barely two decades), while much of the rest of British culture had considerably longer memories. A new-found and seemingly insatiable public appetite for nostalgia could be discovered at every turn. On television there was a ten-year waiting list to be in the audience for the music hall revival show *The Good Old Days*; the hugely popular ITV drama series *Upstairs, Downstairs* spent five years recreating the world of a wealthy family in Belgravia between 1903 and 1930; and Dennis Potter's *Pennies from Heaven* attracted critical acclaim and sizeable audiences with its characters miming to popular hits of the 1930s, even though Potter claimed to hate nostalgia, calling it 'a very second-order emotion'. In the world of publishing, Alf Wight became a best-selling author under the pen name James Herriot, with episodic, autobiographical tales about his life as a vet in Yorkshire from 1939 onwards that spawned movie and TV adaptations, and Edith Holden, who had died as a little-known artist in 1920, became a posthumous star when her notebooks from 1907 were published as *The Country Diary of an Edwardian Lady*. In fashion, Laura Ashley's rustic romanticism took her fabrics business from a turnover of a third of a million pounds at the decade's start to £25 million by its end, and even Vivienne Westwood, later to be canonized as the patron saint of *enfants terribles* everywhere, started in 1971 with the shop Let It Rock, selling sacred relics from 1950s Britain. Similarly the ceramics firm Portmeirion Pottery, which had achieved a certain vogue in the 1960s with its 'daring originality and confidence in its own tastes', really became a household name in 1972 when its founder, Susan Williams-Ellis, bought a copy of Thomas Green's nineteenth-century book *The Universal Herbal* and began to reuse its colour plates, printing them on tea and dinner sets; the resulting range, known as Botanic Garden, was one of the successes of the decade ('shops find it difficult to keep enough stock to satisfy the demand', reported the press), bringing old-world charm to the suburban dining table.

All this was presented, and for the most part accepted, as harmless escapism, though it would be naive to assume that it had no ideological content. In late 1975, for example, television viewers were presented with two sharply different visions of the General Strike, on the eve of the 50th anniversary: on BBC1 there was *Days of Hope*, written by Jim Allen and directed by Ken Loach, while over on ITV *Upstairs, Downstairs* tackled the same subject in the episode 'The Nine Days Wonder'. *Days of Hope* was a four-part series that covered the period 1916–26 via the experience of a working-class family, and came with an unashamedly left-wing agenda: 'I've never seen a more truly subversive work for TV,' wrote Kenneth Tynan. Parallels were made, and immediately recognized, between the current situation and the political compromises made by reformist Labour politicians in the 1920s, both centring on industrial action by the miners. A storm of protest ensued at what some saw as a prima facie case of BBC socialist bias, culminating in Margaret Thatcher's first conference speech as Tory leader, where she denounced 'those who gnaw away at our national self-respect' and, in case her target wasn't entirely clear, accused them of depicting 'days of hopelessness, not days of hope'.

Unsurprisingly, such outrage was much less visible, in fact non-existent, when James Bellamy in *Upstairs, Downstairs* made points that were equally intended to draw comparisons between the two periods: 'A small group of people are directly challenging the authority of the government,' he fumed. 'They are deliberately trying to cripple our economy and drive us to the point of surrender.' Despite the token presence of the maid Ruby and a brief appearance by her miner uncle, the only real counterbalancing voice here was that of Lord Richard Bellamy, who shared the King's distaste at imprisoning the strike leaders: 'His own subjects thrown into prison for their beliefs! That would be the end of this country.' Together with his endorsement, in principle at least, of the concept of unionism ('You must have strong unions for the future good of this country'), he made a strong case for moderation, but these were sentiments coming from a fictional Tory MP at a time when moderate Toryism was already looking out of fashion.

Much of this yearning for yesterday reached back to a long-lost and semi-mythologized society of harmony, deference and stability, to a time before the war to end all wars ended all prospects of peace. When E.M. Forster looked back on his novel of homosexuality *Maurice*, written in 1914 but not published until 1971, he wrote that the story was set in 'the last moment of the greenwood' and he dedicated the book 'to a Happier Year'. It was a sentiment that was perfectly in keeping with the Britain into which it finally – posthumously – emerged, where the Edwardian era was increasingly seen in idealized form. For those who sought something more achievable, the 1950s (sans rock & roll) were acquiring something of the same status, a touchstone for many who felt that Enoch Powell and Mary Whitehouse had the answers to the country's woes. Ironically, it was Harold Macmillan, prime minister during the last years of that decade, who objected most strongly to Thatcher when she was leader of the opposition because of her supposed lack of forward thinking, accusing her of wanting 'to put the clock back to the 1950s'.

It took one of the best British horror movies of the era to challenge the cosy perception of the '50s. Pete Walker's *Frightmare* (1974) tells the story of a psychopathic cannibal, played by Sheila Keith, who was incarcerated in a psychiatric institution in 1957 for a series of murders, along with her complicit husband (Rupert 'Maigret' Davies, in his last movie role). On their release fifteen years later, supposedly now cured, she suffers what he euphemistically calls 'a very serious relapse' and reverts to her antisocial practices, her murderous style now impressively augmented by the easy availability of power tools. As their daughter – played by the appropriately named Kim Butcher – begins to show signs of having inherited the same tendencies, the film presents a terrible and disturbing portrait of family values gone very wrong indeed. This was a vision of the '50s that was sufficiently out of touch with the public mood that it failed to chime with a mass audience.

Despite the warm glow of affection felt for other eras, however, there was never any real doubt about the nation's finest hour. The Second World War was still very much within living memory for the majority of the population, and its presence loomed large throughout the decade. In a

1973 episode of the BBC sitcom *Are You Being Served?*, the staff of Grace Brothers' department store are caught up in a transport strike and decide to stay the night in the shop, where they set up tents and spend the evening gathered round an ersatz campfire, singing old songs and reminiscing about the war. 'Some people seem to forget,' laments Mr Rumbold (Nicholas Smith), 'that men like Captain Peacock and myself were instrumental in making this a country fit for heroes to live in.' And Mrs Slocombe (Mollie Sugden) can only agree: 'These youngsters seem to forget what we went through.' A couple of years later in *Coronation Street*, Albert Tatlock (Jack Howarth) and Stan Ogden (Bernard Youens) manage to get themselves locked into the cellar of the Rovers Return overnight, and celebrate by getting riotously drunk and rivalling each other with songs from the First and Second World Wars respectively. So ubiquitous did this basic situation become as a dramatic shorthand that it even turned up in an episode of the ITV sitcom *Mind Your Language*, where an evening class of mature foreign students, supposedly being taught English, find themselves locked in the classroom and settle in for the weekend; again they respond with a singsong, starting with Vera Lynn's wartime classic 'We'll Meet Again'. Given that the characters here included a German and an Italian, it's not entirely clear how relevant this supposedly shared culture might really be.

Elsewhere the wartime sitcom *Dad's Army*, which had debuted in 1968, ran for a further six series in the '70s, while even the middle-brow quiz show *Mastermind* originated in creator Bill Wright's experience of being interrogated by the Gestapo during the war: a single, isolating light was trained pitilessly on the contestant as Magnus Magnusson demanded not name, rank and serial number, but name, occupation and specialist subject. And the final show in the original series of Howard Schuman's music drama *Rock Follies* (1976) took the theme to a new height. Arguing that 'the English have been nostalgic for World War II ever since it ended', the episode titled 'The Blitz' sees the launching of a club designed to resemble an air-raid shelter, complete with a ration-book menu, while the Little Ladies (the band whose lack of fortunes we have been following) dress in Andrews Sisters outfits and sing songs like 'Glenn Miller Is Missing' and 'War Brides'.

'World War II has turned from history into myth,' commented Gerald Glaister, the producer of TV series *Colditz* and *Secret Army*. 'It is our last frontier, the English equivalent of the western.' At a time of national unease, with social conflict everywhere in evidence, the appeal of a period when the whole country seemed to be pulling in a single direction was obvious, though such national self-indulgence was also, of course, an invitation to mock. There were sporadic parodies of the obsession with the Second World War, from the *Fawlty Towers* episode 'The Germans' to the down-at-heel detective series *Hazell*, which featured in one storyline Richard 'Stinker' Murdoch, veteran of the wartime hit *Band Waggon*, as a character named Dornford casting a sad eye over modern society: 'Corruption, laziness, cynicism – I often ask myself: if we had to fight the Battle of Britain all over again . . .' he sighs. 'Oh, these long-haired layabouts! When I think of all the top-class chaps dying round me in the desert, a great nation spilling its blood.' The kick is that Dornford is a seedy insurance salesman trying to wheedle his way out of a legitimate debt, a thoroughly unheroic figure who one suspects managed to resist his country's call to arms in 1940.

The most devastating assault on the mythology of the Blitz spirit came in Jack Rosenthal's 1974 TV play *There'll Almost Always Be an England*. Here the inhabitants of a typical suburban road, Quigley Street, are evacuated for the night because of a gas leak, and those who can't get into hotels end up bedding down in the village hall. As jealousies, rivalries and passions are magnified by the enforced proximity, one man rises to the occasion. Bernard Hepton plays Mr Joyce (a name, we are reminded, which he shares with Lord Haw Haw), who sees this as an opportunity to display his natural leadership qualities, and to bring together the community in a re-creation of the old days. But he's fighting an uphill battle; no one else cares about such wallowing in the past, this microcosmic society having long since fractured. When he proposes a spot of community singing in the approved manner ('Bless 'Em All', 'There'll Always Be an England'), Alec Shankly, played by Norman Rossington, finally cracks: 'You're in your bloody element, aren't you?' he explodes. 'The dark days of 1940 were *in* 1940, Mr Joyce. Oppo, TTFN, grin and bear it, stiff upper lip, island sodding race, careless talk costs lives, is your journey really necessary – yours was, wasn't it, eh? You wouldn't have missed this for anything. You're loving it, it's the greatest night of your life. It's better than a George Formby picture at the Regal and a spam sandwich when you got home.'

The ubiquity of wartime imagery was such that when Alec Guinness staged a photo shoot in a West London street, dressed in full uniform and make-up for his title role in *Hitler: The Last Ten Days*, a passing policeman was entirely unfazed, and simply pointed out that Guinness had parked his car on a double yellow line. 'I won't give you a ticket this time,' the officer added wearily. 'I have no desire to spend the rest of my life in a concentration camp.'

Political Establishment: Jeremy Thorpe, Harold Wilson and Edward Heath (above), the leaders of, respectively, the Liberal, Labour and Conservative Parties at the beginning of the decade. Below: James Callaghan (right), the last Labour prime minister for eighteen years, with his deputy leader Michael Foot, later to succeed him as party leader. Getty Images/PA Photos

Tory Rebels: The two tribunes of the right, Sir Keith Joseph and (below) Enoch Powell, who led the fight against Heath's leadership of the Conservative Party and sowed the seeds of the Thatcherite revolution. Though Powell had been sacked from the Tory front bench after his 'rivers of blood' speech in 1968, he retained an intensely loyal and vociferous following.
Getty Images/PA Photos

Labour Rivals: Representing the social democratic and socialist wings of the Labour movement, Roy Jenkins and (right) Tony Benn were the two men most widely tipped as future party leaders, though in the event neither made it. Jenkins was speaking at a 1975 meeting in support of Reg Prentice, under threat of deselection by his local party activists, when he was attacked by a flour-bomb. In the same year, Benn led the 'no' campaign in the referendum on membership of the Common Market. PA Photos

Winters of Discontent: The newspaper headlines from January 1974, read by candlelight, as the Conservative government responded to the Middle Eastern oil crisis and to an industrial dispute with the miners with a three-day working week. Below: rubbish piling up in Leicester Square in the early weeks of 1979 as local authority workers went on strike. Getty Images/PA Photos

Unions I: Two of the leading trade unionists of the decade, Joe Gormley and (below) Jack Jones, the leaders of, respectively, the miners and the transport workers. Jones, identified by the public as the most powerful man in Britain, is pictured in 1979 at a pensioners' rally in Trafalgar Square, shortly after becoming President of the National Pensioners Convention. Getty Images

Screen Icons I: Michael Caine in the title role of the 1971 film *Get Carter*, and (below) John Thaw and Dennis Waterman as DI Jack Regan and DS George Carter in *The Sweeney* (1975–78). Both broke existing standards in their depiction of violence on screen.
Corbis/Fremantle Media

Screen Icons II:
Jon Pertwee as the Doctor, together with the Daleks, and (below) Kenneth Williams and Sid James as W.C. Boggs and Sid Plummer in the 1971 film *Carry On At Your Convenience*. Such was the tenor of the times that even non-political series like *Dr Who* and *Carry On* felt the need to comment directly on the level of industrial strife in the country. Getty Images

Unions II: Arthur Scargill, leader of the Yorkshire miners, pictured in 1977, who became the most famous trade union leader in British history, and (below) a picket line at the Grunwick film-processing plant in North-West London the same year. For several months over that summer, clashes between police and pickets at Grunwick became the focal-point for the conflict between right and left. PA Photos/Phil McCowen, Socialist Worker

Civil Disorder: Football hooligans and (right) troops on patrol in Belfast. The upsurge in football-related violence dented Britain's self-image as a law-abiding country, while the escalation of the Irish war damaged perceptions of the country on an international level.
PA Photos/Getty Images

Moral Crusaders:
Lord Longford and
Malcolm Muggeridge
at the launch of the
former's report on
pornography, and (left)
Cliff Richard and Mary
Whitehouse: four
figures who survived
the Sixties and went
on to lead a rearguard
action against what
they denounced as the
permissive society.
Getty Images/PA Photos

Wild Youth: The cover of Richard Allen's *Skinhead* (NEL, 1970), and Malcolm McDowell as Alex DeLarge in the 1971 film, *A Clockwork Orange*. Perhaps the novel most widely read by the nation's youth, *Skinhead* caused concern with what was seen as a celebration of violence, while the outraged reaction to *A Clockwork Orange* led director Stanley Kubrick to withdraw it from distribution in Britain. PA Photos

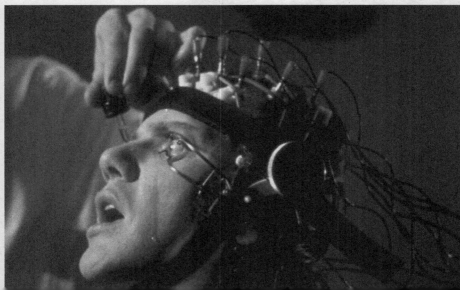

Silver Jubilee: The Queen celebrates the first 25 years of her reign with a walkabout in 1977. The Jubilee was a huge success for the royals, though there were some dissenters, most notably from the punk movement. The Sex Pistols had a #1 hit with 'God Save the Queen' and (left) Adam Ant and Jordan starred in Derek Jarman's film *Jubilee* (1977).
PA Photos/Getty Images

Unlamented: Yootha Joyce and Brian Murphy as the Ropers in *George and Mildred* (1976–79). One of Thames TV's most successful sitcoms, it was a spin-off from *Man About the House*, but is less fondly remembered. Below: The Austin Allegro in its particularly unsuccessful 1500 Super Estate version, launched by British Leyland in 1975; the Allegro range came to symbolize the poor state of British car manufacturing. Fremantle Media/PA Photos

Race on TV: Jack Smethurst, Kate Williams, Nina Baden-Semper and Rudolph Walker in *Love Thy Neighbour* (1972–76). Much criticized for its crude use of racial abuse, the sitcom nonetheless regularly topped the television charts and did at least provide work for black actors. The latter claim could not have been made for the Black and White Minstrels, pictured below with guest star Hughie Green, better known as the host of *Opportunity Knocks*. Fremantle Media (top)

Screen Icons III: John Mills in the title-role of the 1979 revival of *Quatermass*, set in a near-future Britain when social structures have broken down completely and crime has almost tipped into civil war. Right: John Hurt as Quentin Crisp in *The Naked Civil Servant* (1975), perhaps the single most influential portrayal of homosexuality during the decade. Fremantle Media

Matriarchs: Doris Speed as Annie Walker, landlady of the Rovers' Return in *Coronation Street*, flanked by Julie Goodyear (Bet Lynch) and Betty Driver (Betty Turpin). Below: Margaret Thatcher in 1976 with *The Right Approach*, her first policy statement as leader of the Conservative Party, surrounded by Sir Keith Joseph, Angus Maude, Lord Carrington, Geoffrey Howe and Lord Thorneycroft. Getty Images

The memory of the war impacted too on political discourse. Indeed it could scarcely have failed so to do, since so many of the leading politicians in both major parties had themselves served in uniform, including the likes of Major Whitelaw, Captain Joseph, Captain Jenkins and Pilot Officer Benn. And as the sense of crisis worsened, the war was inevitably the image that sprang most readily to mind. Here, for example, is Ronald McIntosh, director-general of the National Economic Development Council, talking of James Callaghan in September 1976: 'one has the feeling that he would be quite a good "peacetime" prime minister but that we are really in a wartime situation now'. And when the left-wing Labour MP Neil Kinnock wanted to denounce the budget that year of Major Healey, he made explicit reference to this tendency: 'In the nostalgic vocabulary so fashionable now, that is not the spirit of Dunkirk, it is the tragedy of Munich.'

Such language was fine for public consumption, but behind the scenes at Whitehall, there was a different mood, a feeling that this constant harping on about the war was not really the done thing in a world where we were supposed to be partners with our former enemies in Europe. In 1975 Sir Arthur Peterson, permanent under-secretary at the Home Office, suggested that, 'as the wars become increasingly distant', it might now be time to abolish the Remembrance Day ceremony at the Cenotaph; a meeting of officials concluded that this was a step too far, but did decide to amend the ceremony to include less contentious civilian services such as the fire brigade and the police.

The hangover from the past that most preoccupied political minds, however, was not the war so much as the years immediately before hostilities. The U-turns of the Heath government had been occasioned by the rapid rise in unemployment, raising the spectre of a return to the Great Depression of the 1930s, a mindset acknowledged and rejected by Keith Joseph in one of his 1974 speeches: 'We talked ourselves into believing that these gaunt, tight-lipped men in caps and mufflers were round the corner, and we tailored our policy to match these imaginary conditions. For imaginary they were.'

No one in the Labour Party could afford be so blasé, for the Depression had impacted so directly on the party itself, halting its forward march and destroying its fragile balance of extra-parliamentary activity and governmental aspirations, that it could never be forgotten. There was no greater hate figure on the left than Ramsay MacDonald, the first Labour prime minister, who, had Dante been a British socialist, would surely have been found in the ninth circle of hell, trapped for all eternity alongside

Judas Iscariot in the jaws of Satan. MacDonald's great crime was that, confronted with the economic catastrophe following the stock market crash of 1929, he had abandoned Labour policies and allowed himself to be talked into heading a National Government in collaboration with Tory and Liberal politicians. He and two of his ministerial colleagues – Philip Snowden and Jimmy Thomas – were promptly expelled from the Labour Party, but by then the damage was done, and in the 1931 election that saw the National Government returned to office, Labour was reduced to a parliamentary rump, crashing from 267 seats to just 52; MacDonald remained prime minister.

The horrors of the ensuing period, when Labour found itself locked out of power and influence during the Depression years and the rise of European fascism, served as a warning to the Labour left and dominated its attitude towards the crises of the 1970s. 'In the '30s, when we last had a slump, the Labour Government broke up and the left disaffiliated and Mosley, the fascist leader, came from the Labour Party,' Tony Benn lectured the Soviet ambassador in 1976. 'The people are determined that it shouldn't happen again. You must understand that is our background, our history, and that is shaping our thinking at this particular moment.' The distrust, even hatred, of Roy Jenkins and other figures on the right of the party, those who flirted with thoughts of coalition, stemmed from the same source: 'The MacDonalds, the Snowdens, the Jimmy Thomases are lurking around,' Jack Jones warned his union conference in 1975, 'their names do not need to be spelt out.' In short, the bogeyman figure of MacDonald was the single most powerful image in Labour demonology right through to the emergence of Tony Blair (during Neil Kinnock's early years as party leader, he was nicknamed 'Ramsay MacKinnock' by the far left). When Joe Haines said that Wilson's only ideology was 'keeping the party together', it was a recognition that he feared being seen as the new MacDonald.

In that ambition, Wilson was largely successful. There were a handful of high-profile departures from the party, but they were isolated cases and the media attention they attracted seemed more concerned with making mischief for Labour than with any serious political analysis. Behind the scenes, however, and away from Westminster, there were signs that splits were developing in the historic alliance that made up the Labour Party. Ever since the threat of fascism in the '30s, and even more since the expansion of the university system in the '60s, intellectual life in Britain had, broadly speaking, been inclined towards left-leaning politics, and this fact had been of increasing significance for Labour, helping to set the terms of the national debate and to shape future developments. Now, prompted by a sense of crisis, there appeared to be the stirrings of a new mood, as Tony Crosland identified in 1974: 'The intelligentsia, always prone to the liberal rhetoric of catastrophe, has adopted an apocalyptic mood, denying (against the facts) that reformist progress can be made and believing in any case that ecological disaster is just over the horizon.' By 1977 Benn was even more convinced that a wing of the party was slipping away. 'I have come to the conclusion that middle-class intellectuals are not attaching themselves to Labour at all,' he wrote in his diary. 'Raymond Williams said to me at Cambridge that the older intellectuals, even those who used to be Labour, were now frightened of the power of the trade unions.'

Two of the most celebrated polemical journalists of the 1960s – Bernard Levin and Paul Johnson – exemplified the trend. Both had initially been seen as radical figures, but espoused increasingly right-wing views as the '70s progressed. Levin was a regular columnist for *The Times* until the industrial dispute that closed the paper for nearly a year from December 1978, pursuing a line dominated by anti-Soviet sentiments; while Johnson, formerly the editor of *New Statesman* magazine, became a high-profile convert to the cause of Margaret Thatcher, who he saw as the only politician prepared to take on the unions. And his distaste for the unions, he argued, stemmed from the fact that for them 'the individual human spirit is a social enemy, to be terrified into subordination to the mass or crushed out of existence'.

The fear of union power was also the central theme in Anthony Burgess's novella *1985*, published in 1978. Inspired by Orwell's totalitarian dystopia, Burgess conjured up a vision of a Britain dominated entirely by the unions, where the closed shop has become compulsory for all citizens and where loss of union membership condemns a worker to a life as a virtual outlaw. There is, though, still work to be done if the revolution is to be completed, as a government official spells out: 'The time's coming, and it won't be long, it may well be before 1990, when every strike will be a general strike. When a toothbrush maker can withdraw his labour in a just demand for a living wage and do so in the confidence that the lights will go off and people will shiver and the trains won't be running and the schools will close. That's what we're moving to, brother.' Meanwhile the massive growth in state ownership of industry has created an economic paradox, whereby workers going on strike are in effect striking against themselves with the result that 'all wage demands are met and inflation flourishes'.

Our hero in this totalitarian bureaucracy is Bev Jones, who rebels against the system after his wife dies because a firemen's strike has allowed the hospital in which she was a patient to burn to the ground. 'Is justice old-fashioned? Is compassion? Is duty?' Jones rages. 'If the modern way approves the burning to death of innocent people with firemen standing by and claiming their workers' rights, then I'm glad to be old-fashioned.' Seeking hope from any quarter, he visits his MP who can only offer him bland assurances that this is the inevitable process of history, adding a warning aimed squarely at the '70s: 'What's happened in Britain has not happened through bloody and wasteful revolution. We've gone our democratic way and not, in the process of changing, seen any violent signs of change. And then one morning we wake up and say: The Rule of the Proletariat is Here.'

A similar portrayal of the same year came in 'Letter From London, 1985', the opening chapter of Robert Moss's *The Collapse of Democracy* (1975), typical of many doom-laden books of the period. In this version of the near-future, the tipping point had come when a Labour prime minister, clearly based on Wilson, allowed himself to be turned into a stooge by the secret machinations of communists. Having engineered a general strike, the communists mobilized their parliamentary support to devastating effect: 'The old weasel's nerve was broken. He was urged to set up a National Government with the Tories, but he was scared of what he described as "doing a Ramsay MacDonald". He accepted our terms . . .' The remainder of the book is a non-fictional discussion of the present trends that will lead to this 'drab Utopia of a minor civil servant, ruled from Moscow', and pays particular attention to 'the growth of trade union power in Britain – and the challenge that it presents to the country's economic and political system'.

Looking further ahead, Prince Philip shared his thoughts on what Britain would look like in the year 2000, in a speech broadcast on independent radio in 1977: 'We can expect to see an increasing bureaucracy,' he warned; 'bureaucratic involvement in almost every aspect of the lives of individual citizens.' And though he just stopped short of an overt denunciation of socialism and militant unions, there was little doubt about his underlying message; it was, Benn commented, 'an absolute party political on behalf of Mrs Thatcher'.

This panic over the alleged march of the proletariat was matched and mirrored by a loss of faith in the artistic avant garde. In the 1960s British musicians and artists had played their part in boldly going where none had gone before, the results of which were satirized by John Summers in his novel *The Rag Parade* (1972), with its description of *Parodia No. 3*, a piece of music by the wonderfully named MacAuley Entwhistle, featuring 'sudden leaps on frantic piano keyboards and the distant foghorning of bassoons'. By the mid-'70s, however, it was becoming clear that this was not a vanguard as such, since there were so few prepared to play follow-my-leader. As the cultural cavalcade paused for breath, it cast a glance back and found, to its horror, that the ranks behind were pitifully thin; furthermore it appeared to be leading its handful of adherents down a blind alley. One response to this painful discovery was shown by the composer Cornelius Cardew, who had become a cutting-edge cult hero in the '60s by following John Cage's experiments with chance, and by developing – as was then de rigueur – a new system of musical notation. In the '70s he abandoned what he had come to see as self-indulgence, denouncing himself as having been 'a servile ideologist of the bourgeoisie' in a book with the splendidly uncompromising title of *Stockhausen Serves Imperialism*. Instead he now buried himself in a group called People's Liberation Music, and wrote a series of explicitly political songs that were aimed at expressing the struggle of the working class, and that reflected his membership of the Revolutionary Communist Party of Britain (Marxist-Leninist). Regrettably, songs such as 'Revolution Is the Main Trend', 'Nothing to Lose But Our Chains' and 'Smash the Social Contract' failed to capture the people's imagination, even amongst those on the left. Nor did a cover version of Paul McCartney's 'Give Ireland Back to the Irish' fare any better.

Other figures on the radical wing of the arts also struggled to be heard. The dramatist Arnold Wesker found that his play *The Journalists*, which had been commissioned by the Royal Shakespeare Company, provoked outright hostility from the actors in the company. Complaining that it had 'no climaxes, emotional relationships, human contact or throughlines', and exercising their rights as workers, they simply refused to stage the piece, and Wesker was ultimately obliged to sue for breach of contract. The days were passing that had produced the kind of playwright parodied in Les Dawson's character Peregrine Gaynor: 'a controversial figure in the arts, his film script based on the book *Maria Monk* had been banned in most English speaking countries, and his modern play, *Queer Times*, includes a scene where two fellows masturbated a bull'. Now much of the trend in radical drama was away from the big-name playwrights of the '50s and '60s and towards performances that were improvised in workshop environments by companies such as the Joint Stock Company and 7:84. The name of this latter referred to the statistic that 7 per cent of the population owned 84 per cent of the nation's wealth, a fact which the company's founder, John McGrath, once explained to a curious petrol pump attendant, who saw the name painted on the side of McGrath's Volvo and asked after it. Having heard the explanation, the attendant looked back at the car and replied with withering contempt, 'No need to show it off though, is there?'

Inevitably, as the politically motivated end of the arts became ever more marginalized, there was a reaction towards the mainstream. In 1973 Laurence Olivier gave his last performance with the National Theatre in the role of a Glaswegian communist, John Tagg, in Trevor Griffiths's play *The Party*, and Kenneth Tynan exulted: 'His long speech at the end of the first act will be the most inspiring call to revolution ever heard on the English stage.' That call, however, was not answered, and by way of symbolic contrast the first critically acclaimed hit of Peter Hall's new regime at the National was a 1975 revival of Ibsen's *John Gabriel Borkman*, which starred that other veteran actor Ralph Richardson as a former bank manager. And the new work that finally provided the National with a massive financial success was Peter Shaffer's decidedly non-political *Amadeus* (1979). Freed from the requirement to see theatre-going as a display of radical commitment, audiences, it appeared, would flock to be entertained and to enjoy themselves.

The last outpost of the avant garde was to be found in the art galleries, which could still whip up a tabloid storm on a quiet news week, as demonstrated by two successive shows at the ICA in London in 1976. The first, Mary Kelly's 'Post-Partum Document', included soiled nappies; the second, 'Prostitution', by the group COUM (out of which would emerge the industrial noise band Throbbing Gristle), featured, amongst other items, extracts from commercial pornography, starring group member Cosey Fanni Tutti, and used tampons. The ensuing press storm mostly centred on the issue of public money for such work at a time of governmental belt-tightening – already Arts Council funding for drama had been frozen – but a somewhat overwrought *Daily Mail* article also found space for Conservative MP Nicholas Fairbairn to denounce COUM as 'the wreckers of civilization', an epithet that they cherished ever after. Elsewhere he was to be found thundering against what he curiously referred to as 'sadistic exhibitions of used Tampax'. (Fairbairn himself, it might be added, was no stranger to giving offence – towards the end of his life, he was reprimanded by the Speaker, and by the chairman of his own party, when he drunkenly interrupted Tony Blair during a Commons debate to express his view that 'putting your penis into another man's arsehole is a perverse act'.)

Those ICA shows became a journalistic shorthand for the monstrosity of modern art, so that when, for example, the *Daily Telegraph* was attempting to defend the Queen against charges of being a philistine, it could ask: 'If she would rather go to Ascot than peer at a lot of dirty nappies in the Institute of Contemporary Arts, what is wrong with that?' But even they paled by comparison with the controversy over 'Equivalent VIII' by the American Carl Andre. This was a 1966 piece of minimalism, comprising 120 firebricks neatly arranged in a long, low cuboid, and it was bought by the Tate Gallery in 1972, a fact which passed without comment at the time. Nearly four years later, a photograph of the work was used in the Business section of the *Sunday Times*, illustrating a story about the gallery's purchasing policy, and within a couple of days the Tate's bricks (as they were now known) were being denounced on all sides, as the media thundered against public funds being thus wasted, and demanded to be told whether this was what now passed for art. It was, in truth, a somewhat tame attempt at being outraged – even when the bricks were attacked with paint – but it did briefly make the piece the most famous work of art in the country. Its only serious rival to emerge in the '70s, in terms of public recognition, was Canadian artist Liz Leyh's group of three Friesian cows and three calves in Milton Keynes. Commonly known as the Concrete Cows (though they were not actually constructed in concrete), the piece was intended to satirize the popular perception of new towns, and to draw attention to the inaccuracy of that perception in regard to Milton Keynes; inevitably it had precisely the opposite effect, particularly after Radio Two disc jockey Terry Wogan began to mock.

Despite the nappies, tampons, bricks and cows, however, and in sharp contrast to the extraordinarily fertile period over the preceding fifteen years that had produced the pop generation, the most – perhaps the only – significant new artists to make their name in Britain in the '70s were Gilbert & George. Their first major work was 'The Singing Sculpture', created in 1970, which saw the two artists, their bodies painted gold, miming to Flanagan and Allen's Depression-era hit 'Underneath the Arches', an early indication perhaps of the mood of nostalgia that was to dominate the culture of the decade.

For this was primarily a time for looking back, even for self-proclaimed iconoclasts. The arrival of punk in 1976 seemed to offer a slash-and-burn alternative to the endless revivals that were consuming rock music, but while much of the style was borrowed from downtown New York, it was overlaid in Britain with a powerful awareness of the past that belied its claim to a Year Zero ideology. The musical debt to mod (the Sex Pistols covering the Small Faces, Generation X hymning Cathy McGowan on 'Ready Steady Go!', the entire output of the Jam) was accompanied by a visual referencing of historical symbols, from the Union Flag to the swastika, even if these were ironically inverted in a spirit of confrontation. The desire to cause 'what shock it is still possible to cause' (in the words of a *Daily Telegraph* leader column) had at least a temporary effect, causing distress to decent-minded folk everywhere, though its long-term impact was more doubtful. The Sex Pistols' biggest hit 'God Save the Queen' provided an alternative perspective for Her Majesty's Silver Jubilee, a rallying point for those opposed to the official festivities, and it was sufficiently challenging that it led to violent assaults in the streets upon band members; it also, however, tied the group so closely to the institution of monarchy they were attacking that come the Golden Jubilee in 2002, they seized the marketing opportunity with glee, playing reunion gigs and releasing a three-CD box set. The long-known ability of the British establishment to assimilate and neutralize its critics was evidently still intact.

The first film to document the career of the Sex Pistols was the posthumously released *The Great Rock 'n' Roll Swindle*, shaped according to the agenda of their manager Malcolm McLaren and purporting to locate the band within a dissident political culture. The movie opened with scenes of the 1780 Gordon Riots (though the connection with punk was never satisfactorily explained), and thus shared with Derek Jarman's earlier film *Jubilee* an evident need to look back to English history. Set in a version of Britain that is at least partially recognizable as the present – an *Evening Standard* news-stand poster is seen with the headline HEALEY'S BUDGET STRATEGY IN RUINS – *Jubilee* featured Elizabeth I transported by the magician John Dee to modern London, and wandering through a post-apocalyptic urban wasteland, where boredom is punctuated by random acts of violence. The soundtrack included versions of 'Rule Britannia' and 'Jerusalem' rendered in collages of mock-operatic singing, new wave guitar riffs and samples of the Nuremberg rallies. 'It's all fucking nostalgia,' reflects Bod (Jenny Runacre, doubling up as Queen Elizabeth). 'It's the only way they can get through the day.'

In both films, it appeared, nihilism was not sufficient in itself; it demanded also to be set against a vision of what Britain had been. To this extent, they – and the punk movement from which they grew – can still be seen as part of a wider post-colonial cultural tradition, juxtaposing the inadequacies of the present with a more heroic past; more violent perhaps than *The Goon Show*'s lampooning of the imperial heritage in stories such as 'The First Albert Memorial to the Moon' (1953), but nonetheless related to it. Even though it held up a distorting mirror to mock the drowning figure of Britannia, as she desperately clutched at the straws of past glories, punk was itself still dependent on that selfsame past if it was to have any meaning. Or, as Johnny Rotten sang: 'God save history, God save your mad parade.'

10
Europe
'This year we're off to sunny Spain'

> It's all these holidays abroad. Too many people go over there these days, bring back Continental ideas – you wait, once we're in the Common Market there'll be revolutions every other Sunday.
> Peter Van Greenaway, *The Man Who Held the Queen to Ransom and Sent Parliament Packing* (1968)

> BASIL FAWLTY: We're all friends now, eh? All in the Market together, old differences forgotten and no need at all to mention the war.
> John Cleese and Connie Booth, *Fawlty Towers* (1975)

> I'd rather live in a socialist Britain than one ruled by a lot of fucking foreigners.
> Alan Clark (1975)

At the turn of the 1970s a group of Scottish musicians, centred on singer Sally Carr, found themselves working in Italy. Formerly Los Caracas, a band specializing in Latin pop songs, they adopted a new name, Middle of the Road, and soon established a successful career backing various local artists – including Sophia Loren – but it took a song by another British expatriate, Lally Stott, to break them on the international market. 'Chirpy Chirpy Cheep Cheep' was a lightweight piece of bubblegum pop that was among the most inane, and insanely catchy, hits of the decade, as the band recognized from the outset. 'We were as disgusted with the thought of recording it as most people were at the thought of buying it,' remembered drummer Ken Andrews. But the song was already doing well in Italy, and the band's record company thought it had a wider potential, so the session went ahead, in a suitably hazy atmosphere: 'We did it our way, with two bottles of bourbon, because we would only record it if we had something inside us. And at the end of the day, we liked it.' The record rapidly became a huge success in Spain and elsewhere in Europe, and in the summer of 1971 it finally entered the British charts, where it spent thirty-four weeks including five at #1, selling 10 million copies worldwide.

The band went on to enjoy a sequence of hits, both at home and more widely in Europe (Agnetha Fältskog recorded a version of their 'Union Silver' before joining Abba, a group whose early work owed much to Middle of the Road's brand of Euro-pop), but their greatest significance was that initial success. For 'Chirpy Chirpy Cheep Cheep' was the first single to break into the charts as a result of British tourists returning home with a record discovered on their travels, and, followed by songs like 'Una Paloma Blanca', 'Mississippi' and 'Y Viva España' (the latter by the inappropriately Swedish singer Sylvia Vrethammer), it offered an early indication that British popular culture might be affected by changing patterns of holiday-making.

In 1970, reported the publication *Social Trends*, some 6 million overseas holidays were enjoyed by Britons and the most popular destination, above Ireland, France and Italy (in that order), was Spain, where many found a sense of order and decency that they felt had been lost in the UK. 'I have recently returned from Spain,' wrote a reader to the *Daily Mirror* that year. 'There were no aggro boys, no vandalism, all the telephone boxes were clean and the phones worked. It was hardly necessary to lock up cars and little children could go anywhere unmolested.' Another reader sought to set the record straight: 'I appreciate that he did not see any aggro boys, but did he notice the armed police, the censored press, the jails crowded with people who merely expressed their dislike of the Franco regime?'

By 1973 the figure for foreign tourism had risen by 50 per cent, with 9 million Britons now holidaying outside the UK. The growth was partially prompted by the relaxation in January 1970 of the limits on taking currency abroad: previously British travellers had been restricted to a maximum allowance of £50 a year to be taken out of the country; now that was amended to £300 in foreign currency and £25 sterling per overseas trip. The resulting explosion in tourism was significant enough to be mocked by the film *Carry On Abroad*, in which the comedy team most closely associated with the British seaside was let loose in a Spanish resort, Elsbels (though the sunbathing scenes were actually filmed in a car park in Pinewood). Here they ridicule the foreigners who cater for the travel industry, and are ridiculed in turn: 'I feel I should point out that we are all British subjects,' explains tour organizer Stuart Farquhar (Kenneth

Williams) to the Spanish police chief who has arrested him and his party; 'You have my deepest sympathy,' he replies gravely. Later variations on the same theme included the movie of *Are You Being Served?* (1977), which saw the staff of Grace Brothers vacationing on the Costa Plonka, and the TV series *Don't Drink the Water* (1974–75), in which Blakey from *On the Buses* retired to Spain ('one of the most excruciatingly poor ITV sitcoms of them all', noted the leading historian of television comedy).

Once the preserve of the wealthy, Europe was now fast becoming a popular destination for the working class, a fact not missed by the comedy series *Monty Python's Flying Circus*, which featured in 1972 a celebrated rant by Eric Idle against the new era of mass travel: 'What's the point of going abroad if you're just another tourist carted around in buses, surrounded by sweaty mindless oafs from Kettering and Coventry in their cloth caps and their cardigans and their transistor radios and their *Sunday Mirror*s, complaining about the tea?' Despite the sneering, however, the trend continued, and 1975 saw the launch of the Union Travel Club, a collaborative venture between the Transport and General Workers' Union and Pickford's Travel, with the approval of Jack Jones himself; prices for the holidays on offer ranged 'from £45 for a May week in Rimini to £119 for a summer fortnight in Malta'. The experience of other countries may have been, as *Monty Python* insisted, heavily coloured by the average Briton's desire to seek home comforts abroad ('fish and chips and Watney's Red Barrel'), but it still marked a major break with the past for a nation whose previous experience of Europe had been restricted to the elite and to those in uniform.

It also brought a less welcome development: the exporting of football hooliganism to the Continent. There had, in fact, been reports of violence abroad involving British teams in the past. As far back as 1908 Manchester United players had been attacked by local fans during a match in Hungary, and more recently the same club saw a 1965 match in Hamburg disrupted by fighting that spilled over from the terraces and onto the pitch. In this latter case, however, the trouble was started by soldiers serving in the British Army on the Rhine, and it wasn't until 1974 that incidents involving travelling fans became major news stories, forming part of a repeated pattern; violence at matches that year between Feyenoord and Tottenham Hotspur and between AS Ostend and (again) Manchester United shifted the focus of media reporting from the domestic to the European stage. Perhaps it was fortunate that the failure to beat Poland ensured that England were absent from the 1974 World Cup, which was staged in easily accessible West Germany, though a 1977 match in

Luxembourg did see the violence step up yet another level to affect an international, rather than simply a club, match. When compared to later events, particularly the 1985 European Cup Final at Heysel that left thirty-nine people dead and English clubs banned from European competitions, and certainly when compared to events in South America, such as the 1964 Peru–Argentina game where 318 were killed in a post-match riot, these incidents from the mid-'70s look like little more than skirmishes, but at the time there was a very real sense of national shame. Football hooligans had been part of the domestic game for some years; for them to appear on European TV coverage was seen as akin to washing one's dirty linen in public.

The hooligan element inevitably captured the headlines, but there were also many tens of thousands of young Britons whose first direct knowledge of Europe was in the context of football, and for whom it was a purely positive experience. There were too those who renewed their acquaintance with the Continent in a more peaceful way. In 1977, for the first time, Liverpool reached the final of the European Cup, which that year was staged in Rome; after they had comfortably defeated Borussia Mönchengladbach, manager Bob Paisley, who had served with the Royal Artillery in the Second World War, pointed out that it was not his first visit to the Eternal City. 'This is the second time I've beaten the Germans here,' he said. 'The first time was in 1944. I drove into Rome on a tank when the city was liberated.'

Such memories of wartime continued to dominate British perceptions of Europe, despite the new-found embrace of foreign climes. Back when Edward Heath was first attempting to negotiate entry into the European Economic Community, the very concept had been dismissed in Frederic Mullally's novel *Split Scene* (1963) in terms that made it clear how deep those memories were: 'What is it going to be a union *for*?' demands the hero of the book. 'What's its morality, its faith, its dialectic? Look whom we're asked to merge our sovereignty with! *Germany*. The most dangerous conglomeration of unrepentant megalomaniacs history has ever known. Make no mistake about *that* lot! *They* have no doubts about who's going to finish up running the European Club.' Nearly a decade later, as the debate over Europe edged its way onto central stage, Kenneth Tynan was even more explicit; the Common Market, he wrote, was 'the greatest historical vulgarity since Hitler's 1,000-year Reich – a capitalist bloc of Germany, Italy, France, Spain, England and the Low Countries, directed against socialism'. The left-wing Labour newspaper *Tribune* employed the same lexicon in its coverage of EEC entry: THE BIGGEST SELL-OUT SINCE MUNICH pronounced one 1971 headline, followed a few weeks later by a simple declaration of anger and sorrow: UNCONDITIONAL SURRENDER.

Those on the other side, those who supported entry into the EEC, drew different lessons from the same memories. 'Personally, my strong support for joining Europe was based more on broad foreign policy than on economic grounds,' wrote William Whitelaw. 'Having lived through the 1939–45 war, I was desperately keen to ensure that no further world wars would start through quarrels in Western Europe.'

The fixation on the past was hardly surprising in a country that so cherished its history and that was in the grip of a nascent nostalgia boom. The end of empire had taken its toll on the nation's self-image, but there was still a legacy in the shape of the Commonwealth, a worldwide voluntary association of former colonies and dominions united by a shared history, such as had never previously been seen in any country's post-imperial experience. The integrity of the Commonwealth, however, was inevitably threatened by Britain's turn towards Europe, and it was perhaps not the most astute political move by the French president Georges Pompidou to challenge too that other great survivor of empire, the English language, when he commented in 1971 that if Britain did join the EEC, it would have to accept French as the official language of the Common Market. Certainly it brought into the lists a new champion in the unlikely form of James Callaghan. 'Millions of people in Britain have been surprised to hear that the language of Chaucer, Shakespeare and Milton must in future be regarded as an American import from which we must protect ourselves if we are to build a new Europe,' he declared in a speech in May of that year. 'If we are to prove our Europeanism by accepting that French is the dominant language in the Community, then the answer is quite clear, and I will say it in French to prevent any misunderstanding: *Non, merci beaucoup.*'

Pompidou's remarks, made in *Le Soir*, may have been prompted by a sense of mischief at having to listen to Heath speak French with what was perhaps the worst accent ever displayed by a British politician. So poor was it that it inspired the writers of the 1980s sitcom *'Allo 'Allo* in their creation of Crabtree, an Englishman posing as a gendarme, whose inability to speak French was conveyed by malapropisms such as his catchphrase greeting 'God moaning'. Heath's linguistic infelicity, however, was not restricted to French. Even as Callaghan was leaping to the defence of Chaucer and Milton, the prime minister was discovering that while an educated person had a vocabulary of 40,000 words, the leading tabloid newspapers used only some 2,000; it was suggested that he might become a more powerful and populist speaker if his writers confined themselves to the same limited verbal palette. As Douglas Hurd once remarked, Heath's ear for music was not matched by a similar gift for language.

Despite this handicap, the relationship Heath struck up with Pompidou was instrumental in overcoming the French hostility, long cherished by Charles de Gaulle, towards British membership of the EEC, thereby realizing Heath's equally long-cherished dream of signing up to the Treaty of Rome. The 1970 Conservative manifesto had stated that 'Our sole commitment is to negotiate; no more, no less.' But few political observers were persuaded that this open-minded approach reflected the totality of Heath's ambitions, and the negotiations that he initiated as prime minister were concluded with remarkable rapidity. By October 1971 a vote was being held in Parliament on the principle of entry, commencing a debate that would last into the next century, that would sporadically break into something close to overt hostility and hatred, and that would ruin more political careers than it made.

From the outset, all the major parties were split on the issue of Europe. The official position of the Labour Party in 1971 was to oppose entry, but sixty-nine MPs ignored the whips and voted with the government (another twenty abstained), while thirty-nine Tories joined Harold Wilson in the opposition lobby. Even the Liberals, who were strongly in favour of membership, saw 16 per cent of their MPs disagree with the party line, in the solitary figure of Emlyn Hooson, who voted against. The resultant government majority of 112 represented what was probably the high point of Heath's premiership; there might have been dissenters in his party (most notably Enoch Powell), but, having decided not to impose a three-line whip, he minimized the damage and ensured that the media's attention was instead drawn to the much more damaging split in the Labour ranks, where the idea of MPs being given a free vote was vigorously if ineffectually opposed. 'Call that democracy!' snorted Tony Benn, when he learnt that Tories were to be trusted to make up their own minds.

Benn himself had previously been a supporter of Europe: 'All the arguments against it are short-term arguments, based on what it looks like now,' he had written earlier that year, 'and omit the possibility that we might make changes when the time comes.' Now, though, he was moving towards the outright opposition that would become his more familiar stance. The unions and the grass roots of the party had long displayed a strong vein of suspicion – even at the time when Harold Wilson was unsuccessfully applying for membership – and the fact that it was Heath now leading the charge did much to strengthen that distrust. If entry was advocated by the Tories and by big business, ran the argument, then it was self-evident that the EEC must be pro-capitalist and against the interests of the working class. More immediately, here was an opportunity to inflict serious, perhaps fatal, damage to Heath, at a time when battle lines were being drawn over the Industrial Relations Act. By uniting with the Tory dissidents, the government's flagship could be blown out of the water.

The actions of the sixty-nine rebel MPs stymied any such strategy. Led by Roy Jenkins, seen by many as the most credible rival to Wilson, their act of defiance outraged many on the left, but had little immediate impact on the balance of forces within the party. Jenkins refused to stand down as deputy leader, despite his open mutiny, and indeed the following month he was re-elected to the job by Labour MPs, comfortably defeating the anti-European Michael Foot; the gap between the national party and its Westminster representatives was becoming ever more apparent. In April 1972 that fragile relationship took a more serious blow when Jenkins finally did resign the post, this time on the much more arcane issue of whether the party should commit itself to holding a referendum of the entire nation to confirm membership. 'It was the moment when the old Labour coalition began to collapse,' reflected Roy Hattersley on the resignation. 'After that day, the Labour Party was never the same again.'

The referendum proposal came from Benn, and was seen by him as a democratic way forward that could bring together the various factions within the party. And though it wasn't initially recognized as such, it did offer Labour a short-term solution to its long-term problems. Wilson, twisting and turning with the tide as he sought to preserve some semblance of unity, claimed that he had been 'wading in shit for three months to allow others to indulge their conscience', and Benn did at least suggest a more honourable alternative. From the outset, though, Jenkins was implacably opposed to the idea, primarily on the grounds that Britain had never before held such a referendum – though he was quick to point out that Hitler had been keen on plebiscites – and that it was dangerous to allow the people to determine individual policy decisions. Acknowledging the truth of the old claim that the political elite was becoming remote from the population, he warned that, once introduced into the British system, referendums would constitute a 'powerful continuing weapon against progressive legislation'. And certainly many of the parliamentary reforms of the 1960s would then have struggled to find majority support in the country, particularly the abolition of the death penalty and the legalization of male homosexuality.

In short, referendums were dangerous waters, a fact of which social democrats of all hues were aware. As Benn recognized, the plan 'went absolutely against the elitist thinking of the right wing of the party and also worried the left, which has a sort of authoritarian flavour about it and is afraid that if you do have a referendum, then the leadership of the trade unions and political leadership of the left will in some way be undermined'. Initially, therefore, he won few supporters for the proposal, and when it first came to the shadow cabinet in early 1972, it was comfortably defeated. Within days, however, the situation was transformed with Pompidou's announcement that France would have a referendum (scheduled, appropriately enough, for St George's Day) to decide whether the UK should be allowed to join, at which point the opposition to Benn's suggestion became unsustainable: if the French could have their say, why should not the British? The shadow cabinet voted again, deciding this time to endorse the measure and to impose a three-line whip. At which point Jenkins resigned as deputy leader.

Effectively that decision marked the end of Jenkins's aspirations to be Labour leader. He was a long way out of touch with the party's members, but retained a high level of support amongst MPs and in the radical sections of the middle class; he was 'the hero of every drawing room', sneered Benn, soon to become the hero of every sixth-form common room. Had Jenkins remained within the shadow cabinet, fighting his corner, or even had he resigned to challenge Wilson outright for the leadership, he could perhaps have shored up his status as the voice of the centre ground. Instead he exiled himself to the backbenches, refused to strike against Wilson, and waited and hoped for a forthcoming Labour defeat at the polls that would give him a way back; as he reflected in his memoirs of this period: 'Every bad by-election strengthened my position, every good one weakened it.'

A House of Commons motion calling for a referendum was defeated, despite the support of twenty-two Tory rebels (including, inevitably, Powell, who had overcome his own distaste for such constitutional irregularities in pursuit of his opposition to Europe), but it was now part of the Labour platform for the next general election, a fact which provoked Powell's apostasy in February 1974.

In theory the Labour policy going into that election was that the terms of EEC membership would be renegotiated, and that only when the government was satisfied that it had got the best possible deal would a referendum be held. Like Heath's 1970 manifesto pledge, however, it was a commitment more honoured in the letter than the spirit. Callaghan, as the foreign secretary in the new Labour government, did engage in discussions with his European counterparts, but beyond a few cosmetic changes, nothing of consequence was gained, save perhaps for a swelling of self-importance. At his first European meeting, Callaghan was told by one of his foreign colleagues that the American secretary of state was interested in him for one reason only: 'You don't think Dr Kissinger would stop off in London on his way to Moscow if Britain were not part of the Common Market, do you?' A neutral observer might think that the UK's position as a nuclear power, and as a permanent member of the UN Security Council, was more significant in the eyes of Washington than an alliance with Belgium and Luxembourg – guns before butter mountains – but the international stage has always lured politicians, and the approval of one's peers is seldom unattractive. In any event, the renegotiation exercise did the job that was asked of it, creating a smokescreen that obscured the issues at stake: opinion polls in late 1974 showed that if the government said it supported a new settlement then a majority against membership could be converted into a vote for, even though few could identify what the negotiations were actually about.

This faith in Britain's leaders to look after the nation's interests was probably the crucial factor when the referendum finally came in June 1975. The forces ranged against each other were massively unbalanced. A majority of the Parliamentary Labour Party rejected the new terms, as did the party beyond, but the cabinet voted in favour, which meant that the pro lobby could count on all three major party leaders – Wilson, Margaret Thatcher and Jeremy Thorpe – as well as other senior figures such as Jenkins and Heath. They had the support of virtually all the media, including the *Sun* (whose owner, Rupert Murdoch, was then pro-Europe) and the *Daily Mirror*. 'This country is no longer strong enough and rich enough to stand alone,' argued the latter. 'Britain can have more sovereignty INSIDE the Market than OUTSIDE.' In the same camp could also be counted the leaders of big business and, some claimed, even the American security forces: 'A dedicated federalist, Cord Meyer Jr, was to become head of the CIA station in London for the duration of the Referendum "to do what it takes" to secure a Yes vote,' wrote the Eurosceptic Tory MP Richard Body.

In the ranks opposite were Benn, Powell, Foot and most of the key union leaders, notably Jack Jones. They were joined by extra-parliamentary parties from both the far right and the far left, a fact to which the pro-Europeans were not slow to draw attention: 'Those who want to come out are deeply divided,' claimed the pamphlet *Why You Should Vote Yes*, happy to impugn by association. 'Some want a Communist Britain – part of the Soviet bloc . . .' The financial backing available to the antis was also considerably less than that of their opponents, partly because, despite the hostile position of the Labour Party, its resources were not permitted to be used in pursuit of the campaign. Benn and Powell commanded substantial followings in their own right, but each could also be counted upon to alienate in equal measure, and their divisive characters enabled the No camp to be too easily painted as the refuge of extremists.

More specifically, and despite the presence of Powell, it was portrayed as almost exclusively harbouring left-wing extremists, with Benn himself becoming very largely the story of the campaign. 'Like all journalists Harry is fascinated by the way Benn has taken over this referendum,' wrote Bernard Donoughue, after meeting Harold Evans, editor of the *Sunday Times*. 'He will lose it, but it has been *his* referendum, from inception to the end.' With the comforting conviction of victory, Wilson could afford to be patronizing; Benn, he said, 'has many of the qualities of a great Old Testament prophet, without a beard, who talks about the new Jerusalem he looks forward to at some future time'. Heath employed the same imagery in his own contribution: 'Before you could say Lord Stansgate, he would be leading us into his vision of the promised land, not flowing with milk and honey but swamped by ration books and state directives,' declared the man who, as prime minister, had been the first since the days of post-war austerity to have ration books distributed. Others were even less courteous. When Benn claimed that the EEC had already cost Britain hundreds of thousands of jobs, Jenkins was withering in his condemnation of his cabinet colleague: 'I find it increasingly difficult to take Mr Benn seriously as an economic minister,' he proclaimed in his most lofty manner. Towards the end of the campaign, Jenkins declared that to leave the EEC would be like entering 'an old people's home for faded nations', and, without mentioning names, made clear his contempt for his opponents: 'I do not think it would be a very comfortable old people's home. I do not like the look of some of the prospective warders.'

The cumulative effect was irresistible. 'My wife and I had agreed that the issue was so important that we ought to watch the long television debate before making up our minds,' remembered the Metropolitan Police chief, Robert Mark; his conclusion at the end of the evening was: 'My God! If that's the lot who want us to come out, let's get up early and go to vote to stay in.' On a relatively high turn-out, the vote was two to one in favour of remaining in the EEC. 'I doubt if ten per cent voted on the merits of the issue or even according to their reaction to the question on the ballot paper,' wrote Hattersley. 'They put a cross against their prejudices and – most important of all – supported the position taken up by the politicians they supported.' Or, as Jenkins put it when the results came in: 'They took the advice of the people they were used to following.'

It was a critical moment in British history. 'There is a swing to the right, which I think one has to accept will continue for the remainder of the 1970s,' reflected Benn, who was removed from his job as industry secretary in the wake of the referendum. 'The 1980s may be different but it is going to be a long hard wait.' There was no doubt that the vote had damaged his political standing, nor that the balance of power had shifted: 'The Labour Party was beaten but the Labour prime minister upheld,' he reflected later. It took the blind faith of the far left to find any comfort in the result. The Revolutionary Workers' Party (Trotskyist), a British group representing the Posadist heresy within worldwide Trotskyism, insisted that those who didn't vote should be counted along with those who opposed the EEC, a calculation which allowed them to claim that in the referendum the working class had expressed its 'rejection of submission to parliament and the need for a consistent policy and programme to throw out capitalism'.

Throughout the campaign, politicians on both sides behaved as though they were merely treading the path of pure principle. The truth was more prosaic. They might not have followed to the letter Terry Collier's description of young British women abroad in *Whatever Happened to the Likely Lads?* – 'once they bridge that strip of English Channel, they drop everything: reserve, manners, morals and knickers' – but even politicians were shaped by their personal experience of Europe. Norman Tebbit, later to become an arch-Eurosceptic, was initially an enthusiast because his job as an airline pilot saw him working alongside colleagues from other European nations whose lives and culture were interchangeable with his own; it was only when he discovered this was not necessarily the case on the shop floor of the average factory that he changed his position. Similarly, the Europhiles in the Labour Party – Jenkins, Hattersley, Shirley Williams, Tony Crosland – tended to be those who felt most comfortable holidaying in France and Italy. This was in sharp contrast to Benn, who, on a working tour of European capitals as energy secretary, adopted the same approach to foreign culture as have millions of British tourists over the years: 'I took my own mug and lots of tea bags.' The former Labour minister Douglas Jay, who was equally opposed to the EEC, went a stage further; he loathed France and its cuisine so much that whenever he was obliged to travel there he made sure that he took a supply of ham sandwiches to sustain him.

Benn's opposition to Europe, once established, was publicly expressed in terms of democracy and loss of parliamentary sovereignty, but underlying these rarefied concepts was a strand of old-fashioned patriotism, manifest in his instinctive defence of the symbols of Britishness. When the long-running saga of the Channel Tunnel returned to the political agenda in 1973 – a bill was passed by the Commons, though it proved to be yet another false start – he insisted that the issue 'has now become inextricably linked with the Common Market'; consequently, 'Peter Shore and Michael Foot are strongly opposed to it, as I am, with Tony Crosland in favour.' Even more painfully, in 1975 the cabinet, of which he was a member, agreed to replace the blue British passport with a new European-styled document: 'This made my stomach turn,' he wrote in his diary. 'I had an absolute gut reaction that this was selling our birthright for a mess of unemployment.' And in cabinet he argued that 'We have got to be careful: like metrication and decimalization, this really strikes at our national identity and I don't like it.'

Earlier that same year, Wilson had evidently come to the same general conclusion, when he initiated a programme called Little Things Mean a Lot. Under this heading he saw, for example, a European proposal to end the selling of beer in pints; this measure would be fought, he explained to his cabinet colleagues, though his argument was, even by his own standards, deeply cynical: 'It is important that we show that we are sensitive to these feelings, especially when doing so does not pre-empt any significant amounts of public expenditure.' The same obsession with symbols, though from the other side, had earlier been displayed by Heath, when he found fault with the design of the new £5 note, depicting the Duke of Wellington and, in the background, what looked like French soldiers in full retreat after the battle of Waterloo; it was an image, Heath felt, that would do little to enhance his rapport with Pompidou.

For most Britons, whichever way they voted in the referendum, there was little confusion over such issues: the pint was sacrosanct, while the offending of French sensibilities was scarcely a cause for widespread concern. For there was still a strong legacy of suspicion aimed at mainland Europe, a reluctance to get too involved. Britain might have been late in joining the EEC, but the same was true also of British football clubs in the European Cup, of the Eurovision Song Contest and even of the slapstick television game show *Jeux Sans Frontières*. This latter grew out of a domestic French series, which de Gaulle himself suggested should be developed into an international tournament to help ease European relations; he calculated that once countries got used to throwing water over each other, whilst dressed as medieval knights and kicking giant beach balls round an obstacle course, the prospect of war would be too absurd to contemplate. When the UK did decide to participate, a couple of years after the start, the show was renamed *It's a Knockout* for domestic consumption, and even when that most internationalist of British rock stars Peter Gabriel had his first top 10 hit in 1980 with a song using the phrase 'Jeux Sans Frontières' as a chorus, the track still had a translated title: 'Games Without Frontiers'.

The residual distrust of Europe was manifest in a revival of one of the recurrent symbols of British isolationism: the rabies scare. The fear of this killer disease, which no human had contracted in Britain since 1902, was a traditional standby for newspaper editors when the flow of real stories was sluggish, but in November 1976 the *Sun* introduced a fresh slant by serializing a novel by David Anne, originally called *Rabid*, but now given the much more sensationalist title *Day of the Mad Dogs*. A TV advert for the serialization was sufficiently shocking that it 'received a record number of complaints and was pulled at 11 p.m. on its first night, provoking huge delight at the *Sun*'. The book itself was published early the following year and was immediately followed by two other entries in the field: Walter Harris's *Saliva* and Jack Ramsay's *The Rage*. The subtext was not hard to find, for although the influence of James Herbert was clearly evident in these tales of killer animals, they were novels that were as much concerned with Europhobia as they were with hydrophobia. In *Saliva* a French civil servant becomes infected by a bite from his dog, and brings the disease to England at a trade conference for European ministers, where he passes it on to one of his mistresses, who happens to be the wife of the British prime minister. *The Rage* has a similar mix of sex and bureaucracy: a British civil servant working with the EEC in Brussels finds that his relationship with a prostitute involves him in a smuggling operation; meanwhile he discovers that his daughter has herself smuggled a stray dog back from France while on a family holiday. The dog is, of course, rabid, and the daughter dies of the disease, sparking an entirely predictable panic.

This trio of rabies novels, all written in 1976 in the aftermath of the referendum, may not have addressed the subtleties of the Common Agricultural Policy, let alone those of economic and monetary union, but they did connect on a visceral level with the fears and anxieties of the British about their neighbours. And as such, they were perfectly in tune with the preceding political arguments, which had similarly avoided detail in favour of broad generalizations. Although, for example, there were those in the Foreign Office discussing amongst themselves 'the creation of a European federal state with a single currency' as early as 1970, little of this reached the general populace. And those who did address such questions in public were not much heeded. 'Last October, without preliminary notice, not to mention debate, Britain was committed to European "economic and monetary union by 1980",' Powell explained in a 1973 speech. '"Economic and monetary union" effectively means unitary government; for when all that concerns economics and money is removed from government, precious little remains. "By 1980" effectively means in the lifetime of one more parliament. Do not laugh or shrug your shoulders. You have been told; it is your fault if you do not listen.' But even those who might have been expected to listen were not doing so, as Thatcher apologetically made clear in her memoirs: 'It then seemed to me, as it did to my colleagues, that the arguments about sovereignty which were advanced by Enoch Powell and others were theoretical points used as rhetorical devices.'

One of the very few on the pro-European side who was prepared to discuss such issues was Jenkins, who cheerfully conceded that ever closer economic integration would necessitate what he called 'a quite substantial pooling of sovereignty'. But such voices were seldom to be heard during the referendum campaign that could and should have addressed the issues. Instead the prime minister, departing for once from his football metaphors, offered instead an even more homely cricketing image: Britain couldn't survive, said Wilson, 'by taking our bat home and sinking into an offshore mentality'. This simplistic account of the fait accompli that was Britain's membership of the EEC was ultimately the one endorsed by the electorate. It was not entirely surprising that in later years there were many who felt they had been cheated.

PART THREE

SENSE OF DOUBT
1976–1979

The great British mistake was looking for a way out,
Was getting complacent, not noticing the pulse was racing.
The mistake was fighting the change, was staying the same.
It couldn't adapt so it couldn't survive.
The Adverts, 'The Great British Mistake' (1978)

AMYL: Life in England these days is inflationary. But we're carrying on regardless, coping with misgovernment and idiocy on every side.
Derek Jarman, *Jubilee* (1977)

If I didn't laugh at people like Thatcher and Callaghan, I'd want to blow my brains out.
Terry-Thomas (1977)

11

The Callaghan Years
'Falling apart at the seams'

> Let us put behind us the unnecessary disputes, the scrimshank-
> ing and the sloppy management. Let future historians look
> back on 1977 as a pendulum year in our history – the year when
> the people of Britain found themselves and began to climb
> back.
>
> James Callaghan, New Year's message (1977)

> Friends, let us take – yes, take, not borrow – this year of 1977. Let
> it be our year. To lift up our heads and resolve that this time
> next year, we can say: We did it! And it cost nothing but
> determination, hard work, freedom from strikes, better
> management, and from all of us: guts! Lest without these
> virtues, we lose our freedom for ever.
>
> Hughie Green, 'Stand Up and Be Counted' (1976)

> Rigsby: I can see 1977 hasn't been your year. But cheer up –
> things are bound to get better.
>
> Eric Chappell, *Rising Damp* (1977)

It was probably the most upmarket soap ever broadcast. The BBC's 1976 adaptation of Robert Graves's *I, Claudius* novels depicted a Roman empire wallowing in corruption and depravity, as it told the story of the five emperors of the Julio–Claudian dynasty, a family whose members seemed to spend less time ruling than they did squabbling, scheming and murdering their way to the imperial throne. And behind the lashings of sex and violence was a lurking fear that this society was inherently unstable, that it might yet slip back into conflict and anarchy. 'Only a single hand at the helm will keep this ship on course,' insists Livia (Siân Phillips), a matriarch with a predilection for poison. 'The only question is:

whose hand will it be? If there is any doubt, the rivalry will plunge us into civil war again.'

Earlier that year Britain had enjoyed a bloodless dry run of the same internecine struggle, with the battle to succeed Harold Wilson as leader of the Labour Party and therefore as prime minister. Labour too was in fear of open warfare, riven as it was by splits, both between left and right, and then again within each of those groupings. From the outside, it was a confusing spectacle, particularly since the terms of the debate were uncertain, with the clear red water between socialists and social democrats now muddied by the European question, so that, for example, Peter Shore – essentially on the right of the party in terms of workers' control in industry – was seen as a left-winger because of his opposition to EEC membership, even though he always phrased his arguments in terms of patriotism. 'I can't conceive of us ever having the kind of revival of morale and effort and achievement,' he explained, 'except within the concept of being the British nation.'

The three principal candidates of the right in the election were Roy Jenkins, Denis Healey and Anthony Crosland, who had respectively voted for, voted against and abstained in the crucial 1971 Commons debate on entry into Europe. The rivalry between them ensured that there was no single figure around whom the right could comfortably coalesce, though the election did go some way towards resolving the issue for the future. In the first ballot Crosland was decisively beaten into last place with barely 5 per cent of the 314 votes cast by Labour MPs (who then made up the entire constituency), and was therefore automatically knocked out. Jenkins came third in a field of six but, distraught at having got only fifty-six votes, withdrew from the race, to the undisguised glee of his arch-enemy: 'When I think of the fantastic press that man has had, year in year out, and all the banging I've had, it is gratifying that he should have only got eighteen votes more than me,' exulted Tony Benn, who had already announced his own withdrawal. It was indeed a disastrous performance by Jenkins; ninety Labour MPs were considered at the time to be strongly pro-European and yet the man who had risked his career by defying the party whip on the issue, and should therefore by rights have been the leader of that group, attracted little more than half of them.

Healey, however, coming second to last, with a paltry thirty votes to his name, refused even to consider withdrawing, and thereby enhanced his position for the future. Where Jenkins looked like a beaten man, Healey was revealed as a born fighter, determined to stay in the ring until forcibly ejected from it – next time round, it was clear, he would be the champion of the right and would probably be the favourite to win. Crosland's analysis of the contest summed up the shifting fortunes of the also-rans: it was, he said, 'A year too soon for Denis. Four years too late for Roy. Five years too soon for Tony. Two years and one job too soon for me.'

The left was also split, despite the performance of Michael Foot. He came top in the first ballot, getting three times as many votes as Benn, but Benn was able to take comfort from a *Sunday Times* poll that showed him as the second-placed candidate among Labour voters, clearly ahead of Foot. Amongst Labour activists it was to be assumed that his support was stronger still, such was the growing gap between the old left in Parliament and the younger, more radical factions in the party outside, who looked to Benn as their tribune. Foot had only joined the front bench in 1974, after many years on the backbenches, and though he brought with him a history as the conscience of the left and as the passionate defender of the memory of the sainted Nye Bevan, whose constituency he had inherited, he was starting to seem like something of a relic, a platform orator in a world shaped by the mass media. Moreover he was a man whose fierce loyalty to the party ensured that he would always side with the leadership in moments of crisis, a fact that was anathema to the idealist Jerusalem-builders two generations below him. For it wasn't just the attitudes that were looking elderly; now approaching his sixty-third birthday, Foot was older than Wilson himself. Even so, he was still younger than the man who beat him in the third and final ballot. (Healey had been knocked out in the interim round, gaining just one vote more than Benn had on the first ballot, which again gave the latter 'great pleasure'.)

James Callaghan, the ultimate victor in the contest, was in many ways – like Claudius himself, the self-proclaimed Old King Log – an outsider in the race, overcoming the handicaps of birth and circumstance. 'Prime minister, and I never even went to university,' he marvelled in his moment of triumph, revelling in his defeat of five Oxford graduates. He had succeeded largely by remaining outside the fray; aligned with the factions of neither left nor right, but instead establishing himself as the master of the party machine, he carried no ideological baggage, just a reputation as a safe, if unadventurous, pair of hands. By these means he had already occupied the other three great offices of state – chancellor, home secretary and foreign secretary – before ascending to the highest position of all. As Claudius put it, when he finally became emperor and was accused of being half-witted: 'I have survived to middle age with half my wits, while thousands have died with all theirs intact. Evidently quality of wits is more important than quantity.'

Son of a Catholic named James Garoghan, who had changed his surname to adjust to British society, Callaghan left school at sixteen to become a clerk and then a union official, later serving in the Royal Navy during the war. He was elected as a Cardiff MP in 1945, and became a junior member of the Attlee government, with an appointment as parliamentary secretary to the ministry of transport; it was in this capacity that he made what have turned out to be his most durable contributions to the everyday life of Britain: the introduction of cats-eyes and of zebra crossings to the country's roads. He was far from a conspicuous success in any of his subsequent political posts, but he proved himself an articulate spokesman for an innately conservative section of the working class, an attribute that became of ever greater significance as the 1960s cabinet lost one by one its trade union representatives (Frank Cousins, Douglas Houghton, George Brown, Ray Gunter). A lone working-class voice in a room full of intellectuals, he was unrepentantly isolated on most of the fashionable issues of the day; as far back as 1961 he had shuddered at television's depiction of 'the morals of the farmyard and the violence of the jungle', pre-dating even Mary Whitehouse's outrage. Also in doubt was his attitude towards questions of race and immigration. 'If you ever want to engage Jim's interest,' commented one of his friends, 'talk about the problems of the poor – he's far more interested in them than he is, say, in black people.' When confronted by Benn over the position of the Kenyan Asians in 1970, he had summed up his position as being simply: 'We don't want any more blacks in Britain.' And when, as prime minister, he removed Jim Lyons from the Home Office, Lyons, who had campaigned for anti-racist causes, claimed that 'I have paid the price of trying to get justice for the blacks in this country. Jim has never had much time for those who espoused that cause.'

By the time of his election as leader, however, Callaghan had, by virtue of his longevity, experience and shrewd positioning, assumed a role as, in Bernard Donoughue's words, 'very much the conservative elder statesman'. Or, as Benn saw him, he was 'the party fixer with the block vote and the praetorian guard of the trade unions behind him'.

He was an unexpectedly tall man, whose slight stoop and kindly face gave him an avuncular appeal; he looked as though he were likely at any moment to press 50p in your hand and tell you to buy some sweets, but not to tell your mum. (Ted Heath, of course, had been another kind of uncle altogether, the one who meant well but got it slightly wrong, putting a 50p postal order in your birthday card.) Revelling in the popular nicknames of 'Sunny Jim' and 'Farmer Jim', he made conscious play of his age, continually referring to his colleagues as young men with great futures in front of them, to their great irritation: 'The truth is that, at fifty-two, I was not so young!' fumed Eric Heffer of one such patronizing reference, while Benn, on another occasion, tried to point out the same truth to him: 'I'm not a young man. I'm fifty-one. I've been here twenty-six years.' However annoying such a habit was to its victims, it reflected an impression of solid seniority that played well with the public; after what was seen as the evasive, manipulative style of Wilson, the genial and seemingly unflappable Callaghan seemed a more straightforward, dependable man of the people. 'A socialist government must lead,' he wrote reassuringly in his memoirs, 'but if those marching in the vanguard are so far ahead of their followers that they are out of sight, then the general body of the army will lose touch and stray off in different directions.'

The strength of the field of candidates to succeed Wilson suggested that a level of continuity and experience could be expected from Callaghan's administration. Events, however, conspired against such an outcome. His first actions were to remove Barbara Castle from the cabinet, and to appoint Crosland to take over from himself as foreign secretary. This latter decision was to the great frustration of Jenkins, who had also wanted the job; he responded by shaking the dust of British politics from his hand-crafted sandals and exiling himself in the promised land, as president of the European Commission, where his nouveau patrician manner earned him the nickname 'Le Roi Jean Quinze'. Within months there was a further, more terrible loss when Crosland died suddenly, the victim of a cerebral haemorrhage. The two great heroes of the right were now gone from government for ever, and the future of the Labour Party shifted accordingly. 'One day it may be resurrected,' wrote Roy Hattersley of the untimely death of Crosland, 'but British egalitarian socialism died with him.' (Jenkins, incidentally, was later to write the entry for Crosland in the *Oxford Dictionary of National Biography*, where he noted – wrongly – that he 'ran fifth of five candidates' in the election to become leader. Who, some wondered, was the sixth candidate that Jenkins was writing out of history? Was it his own dismal result that he sought to erase?)

Despite the changes in personnel, one thing that remained constant was the appeal to the nation to tighten its collective belt. In August 1975 Wilson had made a television broadcast urging the public to 'give a year for Britain' in the battle against inflation and unemployment; 'harder work' and 'national self-discipline' were apparently required if that battle was to be won. In Callaghan's first New Year message to the country, he made much the same call in the passage quoted at the head of this chapter, though the inclusion of the fine old naval word 'scrimshanking' at least indicated a change of style. Meanwhile, Jack Jones was also getting in on the act, suggesting that 1977 should be 'the year of the beaver', a phrase which disappointingly turned out to refer yet again to the need for hard work. All these appeals were reminiscent of the 1960s 'I'm Backing Britain' campaign, now recast in a grimmer, less celebratory shape, and without the benefit of a cash-in single by Bruce Forsyth. And like that movement, they failed to achieve their objective, and were regarded with outright hostility by those who resented what were seen as spurious appeals to patriotism; the London dockers' leader Jack Dash contemptuously dismissed such campaigns as being fit 'only for the proles, well-meaning office-girls and misguided factory workers'.

Perhaps more authoritative than these pleas from politicians and union leaders was the call to the nation issued in 1975 by Donald Coggan, the newly enthroned Archbishop of Canterbury. Speaking of a 'drift towards chaos', he insisted that 'each man and woman counts', and revived the recruiting slogan of the Great War: 'Your country needs you'. He denounced materialism and the worship of money, and rather than seeing denial and discipline as temporary evils, he celebrated them as part of a well-ordered society. 'A bit of hardship hurts none of us,' he declared from the comfort of Lambeth Palace. 'We're growing soft.' For a brief moment Coggan managed to spark a debate on the spiritual health of the country, with the most spectacular contribution coming from Mervyn Stockwood, the Bishop of Southwark, a man whose love of publicity and espousal of faux radicalism made him an enduring, if not always endearing, part of British life for two decades. Writing in the *Morning Star*, the newspaper of the Communist Party of Great Britain, Stockwood paraded himself as a revolutionary: 'I have no intention of shoring up a society which, because of its basic injustice, is at last crumbling in ruins.' And he drew hope from the rigours of the Soviet Union: 'If a communist government were to be established in Britain,' he wrote, 'the ugly features of our permissive society would be changed in a matter of days.'

If the appeals to the populace to get a moral grip on itself were not noticeably successful, the Callaghan government could at least claim to be making progress in its dealings with the unions. Wilson had returned to office trumpeting the 'social contract', a somewhat nebulous pact struck with union leaders which would ensure a fair deal for workers (primarily the repeal of Heath's Industrial Relations Act) in exchange for what turned out to be a negotiated pay policy, intended to combat inflation. In 1975 this resulted in a flat increase in wages of £6 per week, and the following year Healey's first budget under Callaghan's premiership produced a new proposal, a package that, if accepted (as it subsequently was), would see pay rises restricted in return for tax breaks that would improve on those increases. Healey later wrote of the TUC that 'they were stunned by being made formally responsible for the level of income tax in this way', but they were not alone; the idea that the chancellor of the exchequer would make his budgetary decisions for the nation dependent on the wishes of union leaders reinforced the views of those who believed that power no longer resided in an elected parliament, and that the system of government was itself under threat. And the critics were not all on the right: 'I think that parliamentary democracy is in danger,' said John Cousins, son of the former TGWU general secretary Frank Cousins. 'Quietly and methodically we are burying our democracy, and trade union members – ordinary working men and women – have more reason than anyone else to fear this loss.' Elsewhere, the left (like the Tory right) was beginning to move against the very idea of a pay policy. 'We were not elected to nurse an unjust and inefficient system through yet another crisis,' argued Benn. 'We are not just here to manage capitalism but to change society and define its finer values.' Neil Kinnock put his objection in more personal terms in response to the 1976 package: 'This budget codifies the beliefs of the most selfish and short-sighted saloon-bar loudmouth that income tax is the source of all evil and stagnation.'

The crisis of which Benn spoke was not long in coming. In mid-1976, with sterling falling rapidly on the international markets, Healey arranged a five-billion-dollar credit agreement with the USA and other central banks, and imposed a series of cuts in public expenditure, but neither was sufficient to stabilize confidence in the British economy, and more serious measures appeared to be called for. At that year's party conference, in September, Callaghan made perhaps his most famous speech, reading the funeral rites for the Keynesian era. 'We used to think that you could spend your way out of a recession and increase employment by cutting taxes and boosting government spending. I tell you in all candour that that option no longer exists,' he warned the delegates. 'For too long, perhaps ever since the war, we postponed facing up to fundamental choices and fundamental changes in our society and in our economy. This is what I mean when I say we have been living on borrowed time.' And he pointed out what most of the country had already noticed: 'The cosy world we were told would go on for ever, where full employment would be guaranteed by a stroke of the chancellor's pen, cutting taxes, deficit spending – that cosy world is gone . . .'

Even as he spoke, Healey was opening the negotiations that would lead to the granting of what was then the largest loan ever approved by the International Monetary Fund, a loan that would bail Britain out of its immediate difficulties in return for a further set of cuts in spending. The deal was of a kind more normally associated with Third World countries, allowing domestic policy to be determined by international bankers, and it provoked anguish and anger amongst many in the Labour Party. Callaghan allowed his colleagues prolonged discussion in a series of cabinet meetings and then, having given everyone the chance to air their opinions, threw his weight behind the IMF agreement. Ironically, he had rebelled against his own government in 1945 over the very establishment of the IMF (as had Foot, his deputy prime minister), but the precarious position of sterling also carried more powerful, personal echoes: as chancellor in the '60s, he had been forced by the markets to devalue the currency, and he had no desire to repeat that humiliating experience.

The objections that were raised during those cabinet meetings came from two quarters. Benn and the left prepared what became known as the alternative economic strategy, which amounted to a siege economy buttressed by import controls, an attitude that had been mocked as 'socialism in one country' by Jenkins a few years earlier: 'That is not a policy, it's just a slogan.' Meanwhile Crosland, in his last great fight, advocated a more daring approach; arguing that the situation was nowhere near as catastrophic as was being painted, he suggested simply facing down the IMF. Divided amongst themselves, the dissidents proved no match for Callaghan and Healey, and by the end of the year, in the words of the former, 'The cabinet had reached a decision and, unlike 1931, would stay together.' The ghostly memory of Ramsay MacDonald had been exorcised again.

Crosland's analysis was, by any objective measure, perfectly sound, as was demonstrated posthumously when it became clear that the government was not going to have to draw on the totality of the IMF funds that had been made available. The economic crisis was indeed not as acute as was believed in those traumatic months at the end of 1976. But international finance, like politics, is not merely a matter of economics, nor is it objective. 'The markets wanted blood,' commented Gavyn Davies, later chairman of the BBC but then an economic adviser to Callaghan. 'We didn't understand that in No. 10 at the time, we didn't know that what they wanted was humiliation. Trying to avoid the humiliation was a waste of time.'

Humiliation was certainly how it was perceived in the country at large. The expression 'going cap-in-hand to the IMF' became part of the lexicon of the right, to indicate just how shamefully far Britain had fallen. 'In your farewell to 1976, did you see Britain old and worn, on the brink of ruin, bankrupt in all but heritage and hope, and even those were in pawn?' challenged Hughie Green on *Opportunity Knocks*, on the eve of the new year, almost as though he were the British incarnation of Howard Beale in *Network*, mad as hell and not prepared to take it any more. And he appropriated Callaghan's conference phrase 'borrowed time' to twist the knife. 'Where do we go from here if time – bought with borrowed money – is lost through lack of conscience?'

The sense of lost prestige and self-respect was palpable in the early months of 1977, and the tightening of the economy added to the atmosphere not necessarily of crisis as such, but certainly of exhaustion. 'Every time the housewife went to shop, she found the prices were still rising fast, mainly because the measures the government had taken had not had time to slow down the inflation rate,' admitted Callaghan in his memoirs. 'Another source of discontent was that the flat-rate pay increases of earlier years were compressing the skilled workers' differentials.' But ultimately 'the most important cause of discontent was a fall in real take-home pay of as much as five per cent during the preceding twelve months'. And the underlying problems remained, despite the social contract and despite the IMF deal: in 1977 some 10 million days were lost in industrial disputes, nowhere near as bad as in the last days of Heath, but still four times higher than in France and not even remotely comparable to the situation in West Germany, where just 86,000 days were lost. The national mood – in danger of becoming chronic – was one of depression and resignation. 'I believe in the final good sense of the British people,' wrote Peter Hall in his diary, 'but by Christ they have to be in trouble before they wake up. I feel the country isn't yet in trouble enough.'

Things weren't getting any better but, for a moment at least, they weren't quite in a state of acute crisis. The resulting fatalism was exemplified at its most extreme by the Christmas episode of *The Goodies* in 1977. Eschewing the slapstick and the special effects for which the series was best known, 'Earthanasia' instead observed the classical unities of drama, set in a single room in real time, starting with a radio announcement at 11.30 p.m. on Christmas Eve: 'World leaders have been meeting in Washington over the past week to consider the ever worsening problems of inflation, overpopulation, racism, pollution – you name it, they've considered it. They have come to the conclusion there is no point in going on. It is their unanimous decision that at 12 o'clock tonight, in a final act of unprecedented international military cooperation, the world will be blown up.' The episode ended with a blinding white flash and the sound of an explosion, abruptly cutting to the then current BBC1 logo – a revolving globe in blue and yellow – before that too exploded. It was one of the team's best shows, but it didn't exactly ring out with seasonal good cheer.

Symbolic of the hollowness at the core of the country was the performance of British athletics' great white hope, David Jenkins. An ex-public schoolboy who had studied chemical engineering at Edinburgh University, Jenkins was the very epitome of sporting amateurism. He won the European 400 metres title in 1971 at the age of just nineteen, took silver as part of the 4 × 400 m relay team at the 1972 Olympics and went into the 1976 Olympics as the world's number one at the distance. A nation's hopes were dashed, however, when he not only failed to win the gold medal in Montreal, but could manage only a meagre seventh place, leaving his many fans deeply disappointed. (Brendan Foster's bronze in the 10,000 metres turned out to be Britain's only track and field medal that year.) The disillusion would have been greater still had those fans realized that Jenkins's underperformance was drug-assisted. 'I started taking steroids at the end of 1975,' he confessed later. 'It was all about the insecurity of going to the 1976 Olympics with such expectation on me. I wasn't caught. But it changes you. From the moment you take the first pill, it starts to change you – and I don't mean chemically. You become a liar.' A decade after that Olympic appearance, he was arrested smuggling steroids into the US from Mexico and given a seven-year jail sentence.

Even more characteristic of the times was the chronic under-performance of the country's largest car manufacturer, British Leyland. Formed in 1968 by the merger of British Motor Corporation and Leyland Motors, with all the blessings and goodwill that the Wilson government could bestow, British Leyland brought together a number of major brand names under its umbrella: the Mini, Jaguar, Rover and Triumph. The very size of the company, however, carried its own dangers and it soon acquired a reputation for industrial action, particularly at its largest plant in Longbridge, Birmingham, where the chief convener of the shop stewards was the communist Dick Etheridge. On his retirement in 1974, he was followed by the most famous shop steward of them all, Derek Robinson, rapidly known to the tabloids as 'Red Robbo'. He too was a communist – he had unsuccessfully stood as a parliamentary candidate for the party on four occasions – and he came to symbolize for the right-wing media all that they loathed about the trade unions. 'Between 1978 and 1979,' according to one account, he 'was credited with causing 523 walk-outs at Longbridge, costing an estimated £200m in lost production.'

In 1975 the firm found itself in such severe financial difficulty that the government, desperate to save the hundreds of thousands of jobs involved, felt obliged to step in and to nationalize British Leyland. Robinson was clear where the blame lay – 'Sheer mismanagement is responsible for the mess we are in' – though even Benn could see that there was an alternative explanation: 'If there were no industrial disputes, you would be making hundreds of millions of pounds a year and wouldn't have any financial troubles at all,' he told the Leyland board, arguing that this meant there should be greater union involvement in the new state-run company. But despite its reincarnation, and the billions of pounds of taxpayers' money consumed, the problems remained, and 1977 proved to be particularly disastrous for the industry, with production of 400,000 cars lost through industrial disputes, a quarter of the expected output for the year; of that total, Leyland accounted for 250,000 lost vehicles. To complete the *annus horribilis*, in October 1977 Tariq Ali, editor of the newspaper *Socialist Challenge*, obtained and published a tape of the company's chairman, Sir Richard Dobson, making a speech at a private dinner, in which he said that those who accused BL of holding a slush fund were doing no more than to point to the 'perfectly respectable fact that it was bribing wogs'. He also expressed his view that 'trade unions are bastards', but complained that there was such a level of hypocrisy in public discourse that 'I cannot say anything like that.' He was correct in this latter assumption and he was obliged to resign, to be replaced by Michael Edwardes, who had two years earlier been named Young Businessman of the Year by the *Guardian*.

There was, though, one hopeful sign for the ailing firm in September of 1977 when the workforce rejected yet another strike proposed by Robinson and his fellow shop stewards in pursuance of a 47 per cent pay rise. 'I'm old-fashioned. I believe in home, in Britain, in work,' one worker, Ron Hill, was quoted as saying. 'Strikes are nothing more than bloody stupid. Nobody wins. Well, I'm not allowing someone who lacks my values to run my life.' It may have seemed desperate to see this as a straw in the wind, but so it proved to be: in 1979 Robinson was sacked and there was little support amongst Leyland's employees for a strike call intended to have him reinstated.

Behind the industrial strife was the stark commercial reality that British Leyland was simply unable to match the products of its competitors, particularly at Ford, whose Escort and Cortina models were setting new standards and which remain icons of the era. By way of contrast, a 2004 study named two of Leyland's models from the 1970s – the much ridiculed Austin Allegro and Morris Marina – in the top five worst cars of all time, ahead of their nearest Lada rival. Sadly, they were not isolated examples: the Leyland Princess and the Triumph Stag also failed to win much of an enthusiastic following. And even beyond the design faults, there was a singular lack of build quality with which to contend; frustrated motorists became accustomed to the expression 'Friday afternoon car', referring to those vehicles produced hurriedly on the last shift of the week at Longbridge and elsewhere. In 1979 the company was officially renamed BL, and many were convinced that the dropping of the national reference was out of embarrassment at the standards of British workmanship.

Against this background of simmering disenchantment came a week of respite with the Silver Jubilee in 1977. In the twenty-five years since Queen Elizabeth II had inherited the crown from her father, the nation had undergone some drastic adjustments, both to its everyday life and to its psychology, but there were still constants, and the nuclear royal family was very definitely among them: the Queen remained a unifying figure, Prince Philip was then mostly considered a man of blunt common sense, and their children had only one marriage and no divorces between them, Princess Anne being, as far as anyone could judge, blissfully happy with her equally horsey husband.

The jubilee was marked with enormous enthusiasm, both official and spontaneous, starting with a hymn from the poet laureate, Sir John Betjeman, that was described by Tory MP Nicholas Fairbairn as 'poetic plonk':

> In days of disillusion,
> However low we've been,
> To fire us and inspire us
> God gave to us our Queen.

Elsewhere, the London buses on the 25 route – which fortuitously went past Buckingham Palace – were painted silver in celebration, a new London Underground line was renamed the Jubilee Line from the originally proposed Fleet Line (though it didn't actually open for another two years), the Queen embarked upon a three-month tour of the country, beacons were lit and thousands of street parties and other festivities were staged throughout the country. At Wimbledon, which was itself celebrating the centenary of its tennis championships, the Queen made a rare appearance to watch Virginia Wade win the singles title, the last time a British player of either gender would do so in the twentieth century. It was, however briefly, a time of rejoicing, of celebrating the monarchy as the symbol of a British identity that rose above the impoverished political standards of the day. And it was, against all the pessimistic predictions, a huge success.

It was also, though, a time of taking stock, of measuring the decline of the nation. The most watched TV programme in jubilee week itself was an episode of *Coronation Street* in which the Rovers Return prepared a float on the theme of Britain Thro' the Ages for the Weatherfield parade, with the regulars dressed as historical and mythical characters: Ena Sharples as Queen Victoria, and Bet Lynch as Britannia, amongst others. Unfortunately, Stan Ogden left the lorry's headlights on overnight and ran the battery flat, so that it didn't start on the day, and the project had to be abandoned. And as a crestfallen Annie Walker sits in her parlour, still incongruously wearing her costume as Elizabeth I, she berates Ken Barlow, the Street's resident liberal, when he suggests that the float probably wasn't missed: 'I'm sorry, I can't see it in that easygoing, don't-care attitude. I'm surprised to hear it from you. That's one of the things that's wrong with the country today.' He attempts to defend his position, and she dismisses his arguments with yet more despair: 'Nobody tries hard enough any more, and when things go wrong, nobody seems to care any more.' The pathetic spectacle of this stately figure, the closest thing that television had to an embodiment of Old England, stranded out of context, sunk in the depths of regal hopelessness, was reminiscent of William Hogarth's *Election* engraving 'The Polling', some two centuries earlier, with its depiction of Britannia trapped in a broken-down coach.

The clash between ancient and modern was reflective of the times. Despite the genuine enthusiasm generated by the jubilee, and its massive endorsement by the media, the coverage of cheering crowds at the Queen's walkabouts could not conceal the continuing unrest in the country. 'The place gets more schizophrenic every day,' wrote film director Lindsay Anderson in his diary, 'with this example of unruffled and smiling traditionalism on one page, and on the other, generally facing, strikes and inflation of prices, and corruption in the police, and violent conflict on the picket lines. Which is the real Britain? I wish I knew!'

For the summer of 1977 was far from peaceful. The week of the jubilee was also the forty-fourth week of the increasingly bitter and violent dispute at the Grunwick film processing plant in North London, perhaps the most controversial employment struggle of the Callaghan years and a key factor in strengthening anti-union feeling. The conflict was initially between Grunwick's boss, George Ward, and some of his employees – mainly British Asian women – who wished to join the union APEX and whom he promptly sacked. None of this endeared Ward to many people, but he was entirely within the law, even as constituted under a Labour government, and he saw no reason to compromise, even less so when the dispute broadened. Several cabinet ministers made an appearance on the picket lines (including Shirley Williams), the far left became involved, and other unions sent down members to try to close down the plant, so that at times there were upwards of ten thousand present. And the policing got much heavier, and the conflicts much more violent: 'I was at Saltley Gate,' commented one shaken miner, 'and it was a children's Sunday picnic by the side of this.' The length of the struggle, and the fact that it was played out on the streets of London ensured that it was a huge media event. When, that is, the media were able to report it – there were, on occasion, blank pages in the newspapers that summer, when the print unions decided not to print pieces that were supportive of management. 'The country gets more and more like Germany in the twenties,' bemoaned Peter Hall. 'And there's clearly a jolly band of extremist brothers on picket outings at Grunwick to see that it does.'

Two months after the jubilee celebrations, as Grunwick continued to rumble on, the battle of Lewisham saw the biggest street confrontation between fascists and anti-fascists since Cable Street in 1936, while punks and Teddy boys were busy fighting in the King's Road over the spoils of youth culture. And a few weeks later the Notting Hill Carnival again saw clashes between police and black youths, even if not on the same scale as in the previous year. When TV producer Brian Clemens was challenged about the level of violence in his new series, *The Professionals*, he shrugged: 'You can't portray 1977 realistically without violence being somewhere.'

The soundtrack to this summer of discontent was likewise a disturbing juxtaposition. 1977 was supposed to be the year of punk, and certainly the music industry believed it to be so, dropping entire rosters of semi-established acts and signing every guitar group who had the foresight to get a short haircut on their way to the Oxfam shop for a second-hand suit. Despite fevered media coverage, however, and the appropriate expressions of concern at the decline of Western civilization (the *Daily Telegraph* sternly pointed out that 'capitalism, to survive, must have respect for values not its own'), there were few financial returns to be made from the movement: only the Sex Pistols and the Stranglers could truly be said to have looked like a serious investment at this stage, though the Jam and the Clash went on to greater success. Instead the charts continued to be dominated by British bands from the early years of the decade – the likes of 10cc, the Electric Light Orchestra, Hot Chocolate – and by the other new sound on the block, disco. In November a milestone of sorts was reached when *Never Mind the Bollocks, Here's the Sex Pistols* replaced Cliff Richard's *40 Golden Greats* at #1 in the album charts, but in truth the record-buying public was not noticeably receptive to innovation; this was, after all, the year that started with clean-cut actor David Soul, from the US cop show *Starsky & Hutch*, at #1 in the singles charts with 'Don't Give Up on Us', and that ended with the country's first 2-million-selling single, 'Mull of Kintyre' by Paul McCartney's band, Wings. Meanwhile David Bowie's Berlin romance 'Heroes' – which became one of his best-known and most celebrated songs – couldn't even make the top 20.

The conservative tastes of the public were largely shaped by the BBC, whose two pop radio stations were then obliged to share airtime, so that the David Hamilton Show occupied three hours every weekday afternoon on both Radio One and Radio Two; it was seldom noted for its adventurous choice of music, nor for an enthusiastic espousal of punk. The BBC's television shows – *Top of the Pops* and *The Old Grey Whistle Test* – were similarly disinclined to take risks, and even when in 1977 the BBC launched a new series, *Sight & Sound in Concert*, broadcast on BBC2 and in simultaneous stereo on Radio One, it opened with a performance by Renaissance, a band whose blend of progressive rock and folk was hardly on the cutting edge of modern culture. Subsequent programmes were devoted to the worthy, if conventional, sounds of the Jess Roden Band, Santana and Rory Gallagher.

In both music and politics there was a dislocation between what was happening on the streets and what was acceptable in the centres of power. It was a tendency noted by Liberal MP Cyril Smith, who was increasingly frustrated by his own party. 'We were a bit too *respectable*, a trifle too *smooth*,' he wrote in 1977. 'The image went down well in the suburbs among the young-marrieds, but had made no inroads on the council estates and the terraced streets of the great industrial areas. We needed, I thought, to be more *abrasive*.' Nonetheless this was the year in which the Liberals took their first serious stride towards power since the days of Lloyd George, by forming a parliamentary alliance with the Labour Party.

The Lib–Lab pact was the lawful union of two parliamentary parties to the exclusion of all others. It was, however, something of a shotgun wedding. Its primary, indeed its only, cause was the parlous state of the Labour Party, whose three-seat majority in the Commons, established in October 1974, was soon whittled away in by-election defeats, meaning that additional lobby fodder was desperately needed in order to remain in office. And the catalyst for the agreement was the vote in March 1977 on the spending cuts that had been demanded by the IMF; fearful that backbench rebels would side with the Tories, the government chose to abstain in the vote and was immediately faced with a no-confidence motion from the opposition. It was in order to defeat this motion that Callaghan came to an understanding with the Liberal leader, David Steel, that the latter would henceforth ensure his MPs voted with Labour in exchange for consultations over future legislation.

As an example of coalition government, the pact offered few tangible benefits to the junior partner, but Steel was an ambitious young leader who took a long-term view that the Liberals would never make serious progress until they were seen to be active at the highest level; this was their best chance to establish some credibility and maybe thereby break through the restrictions of the electoral system. Even if proportional representation, or even a cabinet seat, were not on offer, he believed there was still mileage to be got out of the arrangement. Come the start of the new parliamentary term, Steel was already claiming that under the pact 'we have removed the extremist sting from Labour; it has governed under our influence in the national interest as opposed to party interest'. And, he suggested, the Liberals were 'the militants for the reasonable man'. This fear of extremism – epitomized, as ever, by Benn – was also at the heart of Smith's endorsement of the coalition, which he saw as a chance 'to wound the sectional interest which, to me, represents the greatest single threat to the future stability of this country, the Labour left wing'.

In the short term, though, the pact was an electoral disaster for the Liberals, particularly since it didn't allow for electoral candidates from either party to stand down in favour of the other. The May 1977 local election results made dreadful reading for Steel, with only 8 per cent in the GLC elections (compared to 5 per cent for the National Front), and there was a string of poor by-elections, including being beaten by the NF in two Birmingham constituencies that year. 'So far it has done us more harm than good,' admitted Liberal MP David Penhaligon after the local elections, adding hopefully: 'But I believe it will start to pay off in six to nine months.' A year later the party was still being beaten into fourth place by the NF in the parliamentary by-election for Lambeth Central. Tainted by association with an unpopular government, the Liberals were no match for a Conservative Party that was beginning to find some confidence and which could at least claim to be in opposition.

For these were days of steady, if unspectacular, achievement by the Tories, and a concomitant decline for Labour. Some of Labour's lost seats were unavoidable – the departure of Jenkins for Europe, for example, led to a resounding Conservative victory in the Birmingham Stechford constituency – but there were also some elementary political errors on Callaghan's part. In November 1976 three by-elections were called by the government on the same day, when Callaghan decided to promote long-standing MPs Fred Peart and Ted Short to the Lords, resulting in the loss of two safe Labour seats to the Tories. The third seat contested that day, the only one outside the government's control, was formerly occupied by John Stonehouse, and had been left vacant when he was convicted on various charges of fraud.

The case was one of the more bizarre episodes in the politics of the time. As a Labour MP, Stonehouse had spent nearly two decades in Parliament without quite reaching the front rank of politics, though he had been postmaster general in Wilson's 1960s government, and had displayed an especial interest in post-colonial Africa and Asia. In the early 1970s his various business interests began to go seriously wrong, and in November 1974 a pile of his clothes was found on a beach in Miami; it was assumed that he had committed suicide by swimming out to sea and drowning himself. But when he was subsequently discovered in Australia, living as Joseph Markham (a dead man from his own constituency, in whose name he had obtained a passport), that assumption changed and it was generally believed that he had faked his own death in order to evade his creditors. His own version of events, however, gave an alternative explanation, that he had suffered a breakdown and committed 'psychiatric suicide'. This he attributed to the pressures of being a decent man in a corrupt world: 'The collapse and destruction of the original man,' he wrote (he had developed a tendency to refer to himself in the third person), 'came about because his idealism in his political life had been utterly frustrated and finally destroyed by the pattern of events, beyond his control, which had finally overwhelmed him.' He was, in short, a victim of Britain's political crisis.

At his trial, once he had finally been extradited back to Britain, he insisted – with some justification – that none of his actions were in and of themselves criminal; they only became so if one accepted that he had deliberately, consciously staged the supposed suicide: the acquisition of someone else's birth certificate and thence a passport in their name was, for example, then perfectly legal. If one believed his version, then he had acted just about within the letter of the law. And he pointed to the fact that he had already been making appearances in London as Markham even before the disappearance: would a sane man do such a thing, given the risk of discovery? Whatever truth there might have been in his claims, however, he made the fundamental mistake of defending himself in court, and of doing so at colossal length; his opening statement took up six whole days, and the jury might reasonably have thought they had been trapped in a corner by the world's greatest-ever pub bore, even though he himself seemed to find the experience something of a healing process: 'It was marvellous to have that court as my captive audience – it was so attentive – and to know that my time was not limited as it would have been in any other forum.' The therapy session ended when the jury returned guilty verdicts and he was sentenced to seven years in jail.

Purely by coincidence, Stonehouse's pseudo-suicide was mirrored in fiction. David Nobbs's novel *The Death of Reginald Perrin* told the story of a man in middle management having a nervous breakdown, feeling that he 'was going mad and sane at the same time', and attempting to escape the rat race by faking his suicide in Lyme Bay in exactly the same manner, with discarded clothes left on the beach. Written before the moment of madness in Miami, though not published until 1975, it actually had no causal connection with Stonehouse in either direction (the only link with politics was Perrin's first name, taken from Nobbs's local MP, Reginald Maudling), but it undoubtedly benefited from the coincidence. Its continuing success, though, stemmed more from the way that it chimed with the national mood, particularly when televised as *The Fall and Rise of Reginald Perrin* with Leonard Rossiter in the title role. Here was a decent man who loved his wife but felt that his life was utterly pointless, a middle-aged, middle-class rebel without any prospect of a cause and overwhelmed by a loss of self-confidence. 'I believe in nihilism,' he proclaims, 'in the sense that I believe in the absence of ism. I know that I don't know and I believe in not believing.' However much he flounders in his absence of meaning, he instinctively recognizes that his doubt is more hopeful than the self-deluding certainties that the world venerates: 'How many wars would be fought, how many men would have been tortured in this world, if nobody had believed in anything?' And in a final rhetorical flourish, he encapsulates the anarchy, the insecurity and the warmth that lie at the heart of the best British comedy: 'Would the sun shine less brightly if there was no purpose in life? Would the nightingale sing less sweetly? Would we love each other less deeply? Man's the only species neurotic enough to need a purpose in life.'

Reggie's only son, Mark, is a struggling actor, the kind whose c.v. includes playing a hat-stand in a twelve-minute play, 'Can Egbert Poltergeist Defeat the Great Plague of Walking Sticks and Reach True Maturity?', in 'a new experimental tea-time theatre in Kentish Town'. He is also prone to wearing, both in the novel and in the TV adaptation, a T-shirt with the slogan 'Wedgwood Benn For King'. But Benn himself was also struggling in the Callaghan era. The Labour government, now locked into the partnership with Steel, was displaying a lack of vision that made Reggie Perrin look positively decisive, and Benn was drifting ever further from the centre of power. 'The whole Labour leadership now is totally demoralised,' he wrote, on returning from a depressing evening with Michael Foot, Peter Shore and the economist Lord Balogh in January 1978. 'This is the death of the Labour Party. It believes in nothing any more, except staying in power.'

Indeed it was becoming legitimate to ask what the purpose of the Labour Party now was. What was its point? In its previous periods of majority government, in the 1940s and '60s, it had been driven by a reforming zeal. In the first instance it had created the modern welfare state, with groundbreaking reforms of social security, health and education, and had nationalized great swaths of British industry in pursuit of social justice and efficiency. Even in the '60s, despite the distractions and difficulties of the economy, it had succeeded in profoundly changing the relationship between the state and the individual, creating what was intended to be a more tolerant and civilized society. And it had found, in comprehensive schooling, a new cause, as identified by Crosland in *The Future of Socialism*: 'Education, not nationalization, was to be the main engine in the creation of a more just society.' In the summer of 1974, however, Crosland reviewed his own performance in his first six months as environment secretary and concluded: 'Perhaps main thing is having presided over vast and politically sensitive department and avoided cock-ups.' By the standards of previous aspirations, it wasn't much, but it was a fair summary of the entire government, at least in its early years.

There were, of course, some achievements to be chalked up. Comprehensive schools might have had a bad press, but there was public support for the project, as seen in the 1977 local elections: Labour was trounced in the GLC, losing thirty of its fifty-eight seats, but still managed to retain control of the parallel administration of ILEA, suggesting that it continued to be trusted on education. Jenkins, in his second spell at the

Home Office, continued the reforms of the previous decade with the 1975 Sex Discrimination Act and the 1976 Race Relations Act (the latter building on the 1968 Act, whose introduction had provoked Enoch Powell's 'rivers of blood' speech). And Foot was to claim a much wider range of successes: 'industrial relations, public ownership, the rescue of many industries large and small, the extension of social services and the fulfilment of long-standing promises on such items as child benefit, comprehensive education, the abolition of the tied cottage'. Allowing for the scale of the crisis they took over in 1974, and for the precariousness of the government's majority, he wrote, 'here was a situation which a democratic socialist could honourably defend'.

He was right to point to the extenuating circumstances. The situation left by the Tories was the worst inherited by any incoming government in the post-war years, and the erosion of the slim majority was a crucial factor in restricting the government's freedom of manoeuvre. In the words of Austin Mitchell, who had followed Crosland as MP for Grimsby in a rare Labour by-election victory: 'We were skating on thin ice. And we carried on skating long after the ice had melted.' Even so, there were few prepared to join in Foot's celebration of accomplishments. From a left perspective, the '70s Labour government was responsible for having saved capitalism from its own crisis; it had begun to get inflation under control, but only at the price of higher unemployment and of a doubling of the numbers living in poverty in the two years to 1976. 'We don't think of full employment now,' bemoaned Benn. 'We have actually dropped it as an objective.' So bad was the situation becoming that Jan Hildreth, director-general of the Institute of Directors, was predicting a jobless total of 10 million within a few years.

For many voters, the chief intention in electing a Labour government had been to restore some stability to the country; after Heath's running battles with the unions had brought Britain to the brink of industrial civil war, Wilson and Callaghan were expected to adopt a less confrontational approach. For a while they succeeded in so doing, much to the annoyance of Arthur Scargill: 'The one thing that annoys me about the trade union movement,' he fumed, 'is that we've got one set of standards when we've got a Tory government and a completely different set of standards when we've got a Labour government.' Despite his distaste, pay deals were agreed and strike levels were reduced, but there were still rumblings from every quarter. In late 1975 the hospital doctors – not a group of workers normally associated with militant industrial action – staged an overtime ban, a dispute that had the unexpected consequence of reducing the death rate by 3 per cent. And by 1977 there were indications that industrial peace could not be depended upon, as power cuts made a brief return, blacking out TV coverage of the state opening of Parliament in jubilee year, and as the Grunwick dispute was followed by a firemen's strike.

This was the first time that the members of the Fire Brigades Union had staged a national strike, though there had been an unofficial stoppage in Glasgow in 1973, with troops being deployed to provide essential cover. That same year had also seen the first time that ambulance workers anywhere in Britain had gone on strike, with a dispute in Durham – despite calls from the union, however, the Army was not sent in on this occasion, with services instead being provided by 300 volunteers, including the likes of Arthur Winn, who had driven ambulances in Tunisia in the Second World War. The use of troops to do the work of strikers, even in the emergency services, was thus a matter of extreme political sensitivity, particularly within the Labour movement, but when the 32,000 FBU members walked out in November 1977, there was little choice, and a total of 18,000 soldiers were immediately deployed, manning a thousand Green Goddess fire engines.

These vehicles had been built in the 1950s for civil defence purposes and, though they were not entirely safe (two soldiers were killed in Manchester when their engine overturned on the way to a fire), they briefly became a symbol of the nation's grim determination when it felt it had its collective back to the wall. On the other side, the firemen themselves attracted a higher level of public support than had been evident for some time in a strike, largely because of their easily perceived value to the community, and because it was assumed that the provocation must have been great indeed to have precipitated a vote for industrial action, particularly since their own union executive had advised against it. The dispute even resulted in the resignation of Gordon Honeycombe – recently voted the sexiest newsreader on television – from ITN, after he publicly supported the action. Nonetheless the two-month strike was unsuccessful, resulting in a 10 per cent pay rise, well below the 30 per cent that had been demanded, and within the government's wages policy. The price, however, had been high; despite the Army's best efforts, the cost of fire damage to property that December was twice the level of the corresponding month in 1976 and, perhaps more importantly, the strike saw a Labour government in conflict with one of the most venerated sections of the working class. 'A civilized democracy like Britain is finished,' warned the *Sun*, 'if groups of essential workers are prepared to risk the lives and limbs of ordinary citizens in pursuit of their claims.' The entire episode added to an atmosphere of things going wrong.

The same impression would have been gleaned from the television schedules in the period. In 1975 a new BBC series, *Survivors*, was launched, created by Terry Nation, who had previously written for Tony Hancock and was best known as the man who had given us the Daleks in *Doctor Who*. Here a virus escapes from a laboratory and wipes out virtually the entire human population, leaving behind only a scattered handful of survivors, some of whose fortunes were followed over the course of three series. Inspired by John Seymour's books on self-sufficiency (as was *The Good Life*), the story began with a rumination on the fragility of modern civilization. 'I never thought what happens to a city if it all breaks down, all at the same time,' reflects Abby Grant (Carolyn Seymour), the heroine of the first series, as she cooks her husband's supper in their stockbroker-belt home. 'There's no power, there's no lighting or cooking. And food, even if you get it into the city, you can't distribute it. Then there's water, sewage, ugh! Things like that. The city's like a great big pampered baby, with thousands of people feeding it and cleaning it and making sure it's all right.'

Once the virus had done its job, though, the focus turned to the proto-societies tentatively being founded by the remnants of humanity. The first such that Abby encounters, as she roams the home counties, is run by Arthur Wormley (George Baker), a dictator in the making, who sets up a rudimentary administration based on martial law. Revelling in the unfettered power he now enjoys and enforcing his decrees at the point of a gun, he was, we discover, the president of a trade union prior to the plague, in stark contrast to the white middle-class survivors who have gathered around Abby. The language of their encounters is highly charged; she accuses him of behaving like a feudal baron, using the familiar tabloid title for union leaders, while one of his henchmen brags, 'We're the authorities now,' in a deliberate allusion to Hartley Shawcross's 1946 misquote: 'We are the masters now.'

In the second season, the two themes of city vs nature and of nascent autocracy were brought together with a visit to London, where some 500 survivors have formed a community centred on the Oval cricket ground. They have electricity, radio and hot water, but life is far from idyllic: an electric fence is needed to keep out the rats that have taken over much of the city, and the group is afflicted with a new disease, known as the London Sickness. Manny (Sydney Tafler), the seemingly benevolent ruler of this fiefdom, ends his radio broadcasts with the catchphrase 'TTFN' from the wartime comedy show *ITMA*, a practice which, combined with the use of Tube tunnel locations and a virtual blackout, carries heavy echoes of Britain's finest hour. But Manny too turns out to be a ruthless and violent power-hungry despot, and the regular characters soon flee back to the purer world outside the city.

By this stage, Nation had abandoned the programme, unhappy at the way that his original post-apocalyptic vision was being corrupted by too sanguine a view of survival. He re-emerged in 1978 with a new series, *Blake's 7*, that offered a much less rosy image of the future. Centred on a small group of characters on board an advanced spaceship, in a galaxy run by the Federation, it was to some extent a riposte to *Star Trek*; where that series had reflected American optimism in the confident days of the 1960s, *Blake's 7* was very definitely a product of late-'70s Britain. This Federation is a quasi-fascist state, which uses drugs in the water supply to control its population and which crushes all opposition without compunction, while the only opposition comes from the rebels brought together by Roj Blake (Gareth Thomas), a collection of criminals engaged on a doomed campaign of terrorism. The key reference point is clearly the myth of Robin Hood, but this is a far bleaker proposition; there is no rightful king over the water here, no prospect of ultimate success, just the faint hope of doing some temporary damage to the Federation, a personal, Orwellian rebellion that achieves little beyond asserting that there are still those who choose life in a universe of brainwashed automata. And even that is a tenuous thread, for, unusually in a populist TV series, all the characters are ultimately expendable, killed off as required by the dictates of the plotlines. As critic Shaun Usher pointed out, it depicted 'the future as being much the same as the present, Lord help us, only worse'.

The fact that the key figure in the Federation was Servalan (Jacqueline Pearce), beautiful but utterly merciless, undoubtedly helped the popularity of *Blake's 7* as Britain edged towards its first-ever female prime minister, and it remains one of the most cherished science fiction series in British TV, rivalled only by *Doctor Who* and by Nigel Kneale's *Quatermass*. This latter made a slightly unexpected return to the screen in 1979 for a fourth series, twenty years on from its last television appearance. This time John Mills took the title role, playing the now retired scientist Professor Bernard Quatermass, who travels from Scotland to London to try to find his lost granddaughter. The city he finds is in the grip of nigh on civil war, torn between the violent thugs of the Badder-Mindoff gangs and the Blue Brigades, made up of even more violent vigilantes; meanwhile the Pay Cops – the privatized police force recruited predominantly from the South African security forces – stand to one side, unless one slips them some money to keep the nightmare at bay. As Quatermass escapes to the country, he encounters a District Commissioner and comments that her title is reminiscent of the days of empire and of putting down the natives. 'Yes,' she replies. 'That's what we were for: putting down the natives. Our own.' The authority she once represented has now failed utterly, leaving behind nothing but shadows of social structures. And beyond the warring factions are the Planet People, the missing link between hippies and new age travellers, who have turned their back on modern society and on the scientific faith that Quatermass represents. 'Stop trying to know things,' one of them tells him.

The first draft of this *Quatermass* had been written in 1972, having been commissioned by the BBC, but the piece did not emerge until it was finally made by Euston Films for ITV and broadcast in November 1979, by which time it seemed even more potent, even more cataclysmic than it would have done a few years earlier. The voice-over at the start of the first episode seemed to capture perfectly the current mood of confused despair. 'In that last quarter of the twentieth century the whole world seemed to sicken. Civilized institutions, whether old or new, fell as if some primal disorder was reasserting itself. And men asked themselves: Why should this be?'

12

Race

'I was born here just like you'

> The conception that in Britain everyone is fair-minded, toler-
> ant and free from colour prejudice is such obvious nonsense
> that the most remarkable feature of this change in our way of
> life is that it has not fulfilled the blood-curdling predictions of
> Enoch Powell. That in itself is a tribute to the innate decency of
> the British people rather than to the wisdom of their rulers.
> Robert Mark, *In the Office of Constable* (1978)

> LONDON TAXI DRIVER: Oh, it's changed all right. Chinese, sooties,
> towel-heads, Yanks, Eyeties, bubbles – there won't be a
> Londoner left in the smoke soon.
> Trevor Preston, *Out* (1978)

> The National Front are fascists;
> We don't hate the black kids.
> The National Front are fascists;
> Ain't nothing wrong with the black kids – no way.
> The Pigs, 'National Front' (1977)

In January 1970 a character named Melanie Harper, played by black actress Cleo Sylvestre, walked into the Crossroads Motel and asked the receptionist, 'Could I speak to Mrs Richardson, please?' She added, 'Tell her it's her daughter, Melanie.' And as Tony Hatch's theme tune struck up, and the credits rolled, millions of soap viewers felt the earth move under their feet. For matriarch Meg Richardson was the fans' favourite, and the idea that she had a daughter of whom we had not previously been aware was shock enough; that she might have a black daughter was positively seismic. In the following episode it emerged that Melanie was in fact adopted, but the impact of the character was nonetheless significant, particularly in the West Midlands where the series was set and made. 'It did a tremendous amount of good just having an ordinary character in there who happened to be black,' Sylvestre commented later. 'It is important to remember this happened around the time Enoch Powell was making all those terrible "rivers of blood" speeches, and British television audiences needed to see someone like Melanie every week. She was someone they could identify with.'

Crossroads went on to be the first British soap to feature a black family – the James family in 1974 – and to have, in the mechanic Mac (Carl Andrews), a black character as a long-term regular, with eight years' service. Its chief rival *Coronation Street* was much more timid, fearful that the mere presence of black people on the screen would somehow raise 'issues' that would be incompatible with the domestic dramas of Weatherfield. The limited horizons of its production team were apparent when Janice Stubbs (Angela Bruce) appeared in a 1978 storyline that saw her having an affair with Ray Langton, the first of Deirdre's many husbands; on the wall of her bedsit was a poster for the group Boney M, an entirely implausible choice for the character, even if the band members were black.

The paucity of these roles was an indication of how few opportunities there were for black actors on TV, though they were still a considerable improvement on previous decades. Elsewhere, a handful of entertainers emerged from *The Comedians* (Charlie Williams, Jos White) and from the talent show *New Faces*, which made stars of Patti Boulaye, Gary Wilmot and Lenny Henry, then a sixteen-year-old specializing in not very good impressions of the standard targets of the day – Tommy Cooper, Frank Spencer from *Some Mothers Do 'Ave 'Em* – but winning over the audience by cheerfully admitting: 'You've seen them before, but not in colour.' He went on to star in the first black British sitcom, *The Fosters*, produced by LWT in 1976. The same company later gave us *Mixed Blessings*, a comedy about a newly-wed white man and black woman, while Thames TV's children's series *The Tomorrow People* featured a racially mixed cast.

What is notable is that these were all ITV productions. The BBC – allegedly the home of dangerous subversives and revolutionaries – showed little enthusiasm for putting black faces on television, a fact which didn't escape attention at the time: 'You've never seen a coloured comedian on the BBC, have you?' joked black stand-up Sammy Thomas. 'BBC – it stands for Ban Black Comics.' The contrast between the channels could be seen most glaringly in the BBC's *Till Death Us Do Part* and in ITV's derivative *Love Thy Neighbour*. The latter, with its continual stream of racist abuse from Eddie Booth towards his next-door neighbours, never won any critical plaudits and was regarded in polite circles as being well beyond the pale, but it did at least provide work for the actors Rudolph Walker and Nina Baden-Semper. *Till Death*, on the other hand, was still featuring Spike Milligan made up as an Indian as late as the 1974 episode 'Paki-Paddy'. In the same way Michael Bates continued to black up for *It Ain't Half Hot Mum* (also on the BBC) right up until his death in 1978, all the while keeping up a humorous banter about 'we British' as opposed to 'these damn natives', and amusingly mangling the English language: 'Shut your cakey hole!'

Nor were Milligan and Bates alone. *The Goodies* had a fondness for donning blackface, as in a storyline that saw them making a promotional film for apartheid with Tim Brooke-Taylor blacked up. 'We thought it was funny,' he said in retrospect, 'but we upset a lot of people, and were in trouble with the BBC.' It was just possible to offer a defence that there was a political point being made here, however muddled, but the same was hardly true of a subsequent show when Bill Oddie turned up wearing shoe polish and claiming to have joined the Black Muslims, having changed his name to Rastus Watermelon. In both instances, an absurd parody of a black American accent was affected.

And behind these examples was the extraordinary twenty-year success of the BBC's light entertainment series *The Black and White Minstrel Show*, which finally came off air in 1978 (though it continued on stage, with Lenny Henry appearing for three seasons as the resident comedian). Descended from the minstrel troupes that had sprung up in America in the mid-nineteenth century, and had played to packed houses in Britain whenever they toured, the show featured white singers, wearing curly wigs and with their faces covered in black greasepaint save for exaggerated white mouths and eyes, as they ran through medleys of singalong numbers in heavily choreographed routines. Initially the blackface make-up was worn by all the singers, but early on it was decided to restrict it to the men only, presenting the culturally curious spectacle of white women dancing with caricatures of black men, as though such a depiction might inoculate the nation against the possibility of miscegenation. The result was a show that won both the Golden and Silver Rose at the first Montreux television festival in 1961, and which the BBC's director of television, Kenneth Adam, said was proof 'that the popular song need not be vulgar, ruin public taste or symbolize degeneracy'. It was, in short, the antidote to the mixed-race messages of rock & roll. The series was hugely successful, and though audiences declined a little in later years, the 1976 Christmas special was still amongst the top five most watched programmes that week. It was also increasingly controversial at a time when sensitivities were becoming slightly more attuned. Indeed as far back as 1963, at the height of the civil rights movement in America, *That Was the Week That Was* had drawn attention to the incongruity of its existence, with a parody of the Minstrels singing merrily about lynchings in Mississippi.

By the time the Minstrels were finally pulled from the schedules, doubts were being raised over the entire nature of television's treatment of minorities. At the Edinburgh Television Festival in 1978, a series of speakers denounced the stereotyping that had become a stock part of entertainment, not merely in relation to black people but also the Irish, with the writer Brian Phelan arguing that the comedian's caricature of the Irishman as being 'lazy, ignorant and incredibly stupid was the media's way of telling mothers of soldiers killed in Northern Ireland that their sons were being killed by savages'. Less emotively, Howard Schuman, writer of *Rock Follies*, spelt out what was to become the new agenda for humour: 'Comedy that diminishes the already powerless I find despicable and increasingly obscene.' And Trevor Griffiths explored the same territory in his 1975 play *Comedians*, in which a music hall veteran, Eddie Waters – played by Jimmy Jewel in the original production, and by Bill Fraser in the subsequent BBC adaptation – teaches a class of aspiring comedians the tricks of the trade. Or rather, he teaches them to ignore accepted commercial wisdom and to pursue comedy as truth, beyond stereotypes. 'A joke that feeds on ignorance starves its audience,' he insists. 'Most comics *feed* prejudice and fear and blinkered vision, but the best ones, the best ones illuminate them, make them clearer to see, easier to deal with.'

These new images of comedy were to become a powerful force by the end of the decade, but there was a high degree of resistance from established comics and their audiences, those who agreed with Bernard Manning's maxim 'You never take a joke seriously; it's a joke.' Indeed Manning himself came to epitomize for many the unacceptable face of comedy, a man who continued to tell jokes about race long after they had been deemed inappropriate for television, though there was little in the '70s to indicate that he would become such a symbolically charged figure.

Like many other comics from the Northern clubs, he made his TV debut on *The Comedians*, a series that had no pretensions to being anything but a succession of gags, cutting from one performer to another as soon as each joke was finished. Frank Carson, Jim Bowen, Tom O'Connor and Mike Reid were amongst those who made their names on the show, but the most accomplished was undoubtedly Manning; while the other comics would telegraph their wisecracks and be the first to laugh at their own jokes, Manning's delivery was casual to the point of contempt – virtually motionless, and with a Mancunian monotone, he would throw away his punchlines as though he didn't much care either for them or for his audience. Technically he was head and shoulders above his rivals, with a unique sense of timing and a commanding stage presence. His material, however, was not particularly racist by the standards of the time, and when a spin-off series, *The Wheeltappers and Shunters Social Club*, set in a fictitious Northern club, was launched in 1974, he was the obvious choice to be the host compère. It was not until the 1980s, when television came to regard certain subjects as being off-limits, that Manning acquired his reputation as the king of politically incorrect comedy, since he – unusually amongst his contemporaries – refused to adapt his material. Indeed, it almost seemed as though he deliberately emphasized jokes about race in a defiant response to the new orthodoxy, revelling in his new role as the most controversial comic in the country, even if he was seldom seen on TV any more and had clearly lost the ideological battle.

Similar arguments were also heard in other fields, particularly in education. Earlier Bridget Harris of the pressure group Teachers Against Racism had called for the book *Little Black Sambo* and its sequels to be removed from schools and libraries, because they 'have become both dangerous and obsolete in the multi-racial Britain of 1972 where people of good will are trying to foster *respect* for black people among white children, in order to avoid the kind of terrible race tension and separatism which has occurred in the United States'. As was to be expected, such statements provoked an outcry amongst some commentators, who denounced what was seen as censorship, and who defended staunchly the charm of Helen Bannerman's books. But the Children's Rights Workshop (Book Project) broadened the scope of the attack on the canon of childhood literature: 'Where is the rest of the world in children's bookland? Where are the working class, black people, the handicapped, travelling people, the children with one parent or none?'

These disputes were to become very familiar over the coming years, with the positions on both sides entrenched at a fairly early stage. Camden Council in London became in 1978 one of the first to introduce the concept of positive discrimination in its employment policies. 'If two people of equal ability apply for a job and one of them is Indian, Pakistani or West Indian, then I would appoint from the second group,' explained Alan Evans, chairman of the council's staff committee, in defence of the new practice. 'Are there any real racial differences?' pondered *Daily Telegraph* columnist Robin Page, from the other side of the political spectrum.

'Anybody who asks the question honestly, or who suggests that race is more than a matter of skin pigmentation, is immediately accused of being a "racist".'

More serious was the warning from the Nobel Prize-winning bio-physicist Sir Andrew Huxley in 1977 that scientific research was being hampered by political pressure, particularly in the study of whether intelligence was hereditary. Professor Hans Eysenck, a leading figure in the field, unsurprisingly agreed, having had a resolution passed against him by the National Union of Students, and having been physically assaulted when trying to deliver a talk at the London School of Economics in 1973. His opponents, he claimed, were enemies of both free speech and of science, using 'every power within their means – breaking up scientific meetings or lectures, beating up opponents, boycotting their public appearances, threatening arson and violence to booksellers who dare to stock books of which they disapprove'.

Eysenck's experience inspired a key plotline in *The History Man*, Malcolm Bradbury's 1975 satire of pseudo-revolutionary politics in a red-brick university. As the freewheeling protests of the '60s are supplanted by the attritional class war of the Heath years, the left-leaning members of the faculty find themselves floundering in a world where intellectuals appear increasingly irrelevant, and none more so than sociologist Howard Kirk. He comforts himself by alternately bullying and sleeping with his students, and by manufacturing a confrontation with a visiting geneticist named Mangel, of whom he and his colleagues disapprove. 'It's all been exposed by the radical press,' explains one of them, as though further argument were neither necessary nor possible. 'Jensen, Eysenck, Mangel. It's all been shown to be racist.' Regrettably Mangel dies on the eve of his visit, but the demonstration goes ahead regardless, an unsympathetic lecturer is hospitalized and Howard declares it a 'famous victory'. The TV adaptation, screened in 1981, ended with a mischievous caption pointing out that Howard voted for the Conservatives in the 1979 election.

In the face of such controversies, even the BBC was catching up with the idea of a multiracial culture. In 1978 it launched *Empire Road*, a drama series set in Handsworth, which lasted for two seasons, with a black and Asian cast and with a black writer and producer (Michael Abbensetts and Peter Ansorge). More enduring, in critical terms, was the earlier *Gangsters*, which had begun as a film in the *Play for Today* slot before spinning off into its own series. Also set in Birmingham, it featured all the usual locales and themes of underworld thrillers – strip club, snooker hall, drug dealing, protection rackets – but added new elements, not merely in its depiction of the city's wide ethnic diversity, but in having a racially mixed partnership at its centre. Mr Khan (Ahmed Khalil) is an undercover security agent seeking to deal with corruption in 'positions of power in the established worlds of business, politics and the law', a task for which he needs to recruit ex-SAS man John Kline (Maurice Colbourne), who's just been released from jail, having served time on a manslaughter charge. For once the denunciations of modern Britain are articulated by a non-white face. 'Corruption is a cancer that has spread through the Midlands,' explains Khan. 'It needs a surgeon to cut it out. I require the anaesthetist.' And Kline, the white man, shrugs his reply: 'The problems of the National Health don't concern me.'

Beyond drama and comedy, the situation in popular culture was much the same: few opportunities for anyone not possessing the requisite shade of skin. Black music, for example, where one might have expected a degree of visibility, was fine when it was imported – and a brace of British singer-songwriters, Labi Siffre and Joan Armatrading, thrived away from the public spotlight – but when it came to home-grown soul and rock, the British record industry was out of its depth.

Eddy Amoo, for example, started his career with Liverpool doo-wop band the Chants, whose first gig saw them singing at the Cavern Club with musical accompaniment by the Beatles. But even this high-level endorsement counted for nothing when they did finally get a record deal: 'In that era,' remembered Amoo, 'most black bands in this country, those that were ever recorded, were recorded like white bands, and they *sounded* like white bands.' The Chants, despite some fine releases, never realized their potential, but among those who did have hits were the Foundations and the multiracial London band the Equals, the latter featuring the songwriting talent of Eddy Grant. With a series of bubblegum pop singles behind them, the Equals adopted a much more militant approach on their 1970 funk classic 'Black Skinned Blue Eyed Boys' (they 'ain't gonna fight no doggone wars'), which was inspired by witnessing a fight at one of their gigs between a white man and a black man; when a police officer attempted to break it up, they both turned on him instead. To mark their newer, angrier incarnation, Grant announced that he'd burnt the white wig he had been sporting, 'because black musicians are people to be respected'. The single was the band's best work, but it was also their last hit, and Grant left the following year, to launch a solo career in which he would be beholden to no one: he wrote, performed and produced his records, which were issued on his own label and even manufactured at his own pressing plant. Eddy Amoo also finally made it big when he joined his brother Chris in the Real Thing, recording a #1 disco-pop single in 'You to Me Are Everything' (1976) and a groundbreaking album, *Four from Eight* (1977), which was the closest that Britain got to the ethereal polemics of Curtis Mayfield.

The biggest of the black British pop stars was Errol Brown, singer with Hot Chocolate, a group that defied all trends to have hits in every year of the decade. They were the living proof of Amoo's analysis of record companies, an R&B band converted into mainstream white pop by producer Mickie Most. When, on a tour of America, Most suggested that they should concentrate on black audiences, guitarist Harvey Hinsley had to point out that it was a bit late in the day to be changing his mind: 'We don't play for black people in England, you don't see any black people at the gigs,' he explained patiently. 'We're *not* black music.' At the same time, however, black American music – from Motown to Philly to disco – was being lapped up by a British audience that was considerably more open-minded than the industry that served it.

In sport, too, there was a discrepancy between the imported and the domestic stars. By 1971 every football fan knew that perhaps the two greatest-ever players of the game were Pelé and Eusebio, but still an English FA official who specialized in schoolboy football was able to claim that it would be more difficult for black players in Britain, because 'a lot of them don't like to play when it's cold or wet'. Such myths were to linger for years to come. At the same time, however, future England manager Ron Greenwood, who had signed Clyde Best and Nigerian Ade Coker to West Ham, pointed out that 'Negro players have a suppleness and natural ability rare in whites'. Greenwood also predicted that 'within ten years there might be four or five playing at the top end of the game'. Actually by the end of the '70s there were around fifty black professional footballers in England (out of perhaps two thousand), enough for the testimonial game for Len Cantello at Ron Atkinson's West Bromwich Albion to have the novelty of an all-white team playing an all-black team, an event that caused disquiet even at the time. 'Politics should be left to the politicians,' said Garth Crooks defensively, when challenged about his participation in the match. 'This is just a game of football played for a fellow professional.'

Meanwhile, in the 1970–71 season, Ben Odeje had become the first black footballer to play at schoolboy level for England, to be followed by Cliff Marshall, and in 1978 Viv Anderson of Nottingham Forest became the first to do so at full international level. (The time lapse between the two was partly accounted for by the FIFA regulations of the time, which allowed schoolboys to play for the country in which they were being educated, while an adult could only play for the country in which he or his father had been born, thus making ineligible any immigrant players.)

Perhaps the one genuine exception to the white dominance of televised sport was professional wrestling, which became a Saturday teatime ritual, a regular appointment in homes right across the social spectrum. Mum looked on admiringly at real men like Vic Faulkner, as dad – nervously fingering his pools coupons in anticipation of the football results – rolled his eyes and muttered about how it wasn't real and it was all fixed, and gran screamed blue murder at the screen whenever Mick McManus delivered yet another illegal punch to yet another blue-eye hero on the blind side of the ref, but in full view of the cameras. Meanwhile the kids revelled in the fabulous fantasy figures: Massambula, the African witch doctor, Billy Two Rivers, the Native American chief who sported a Mohican haircut years before punk and delivered tomahawk chops, and Kendo Nagasaki, the masked oriental (played by Peter Thornley from Staffordshire; his speciality was the kamikaze roll, and he had his portrait painted by Peter Blake). Like the American TV detectives of the era, every wrestler had to have his own gimmick, whether it was the temper tantrums of 'Crybaby' Jim Breaks, the jodhpurs of 'Tally Ho' Kaye or the deafness of Alan Kirby. This latter was a good guy, but he couldn't hear the ref, so he'd frequently get a public warning for not breaking a hold on command, and the audience would share his anguish. But that was part of the attraction – the whole ritual was drenched in ersatz emotion and a cosy kind of catharsis.

More than that, though, it was a wonderfully accommodating world; all popular culture was here. There was room for glitter pop (the Hell's Angels tag team of 'Exotic' Adrian Street and 'Bad' Bobby Barnes), for a British take on blaxploitation (the bowler-hat-wearing 'Soulman' Dave Bond) and for shameless TV rip-offs: Kung Fu and Catweasel took their names from contemporary series, bringing to the grapple game the latest fads in martial arts and medieval wizardry. There was also space for image-driven stars from other fields: show-jumper Harvey Smith and Radio One DJ Jimmy Savile both pursued wrestling careers. Even *Coronation Street* had its own wrestler for a while, when Stan Ogden tried his hand at the forearm smash and the straight-finger jab. This was sport – or at least a member nation of the *World of Sport* – as all-inclusive family entertainment. And then came Big Daddy.

Shirley Crabtree, who had earlier been a heel billed as the Blond Adonis and as Mr Universe, reinvented himself as Big Daddy, the biggest of all the blue-eyes, in 1976 when he was already in his mid-40s. The name he chose carried an odd set of associations; essentially a friendly identity, with hints of Burl Ives in the 1958 movie *Cat on a Hot Tin Roof*, it had also an immediate context: the name Big Daddy in a tabloid headline of the time invariably referred to Idi Amin. The wrestling incarnation of this dubious heritage wore a Union Flag leotard, loved little kiddies and ended every bout with his speciality, the splash, in which he belly-flopped on the head and torso of a prostrate opponent. No one got up after a Big Daddy splash.

And he had the same effect on wrestling itself. Despite the arrival of even bigger bad boys in the unappealing shapes of Giant Haystacks and the forty-two-stone Fatty Thomas, the course and outcome of every Big Daddy bout was crashingly obvious. And what had been a diverse and multicultural tradition was crushed by twenty-five stones of sentimentality, patriotism and predictability. It was noticeable that the rise of Big Daddy coincided with the rise of Margaret Thatcher, and that she was on record as saying that he was her favourite wrestler.

If, despite music, football and the wrestling, black Britons were largely invisible in entertainment and sport, the same was even more true of positions of power within the establishment. Writing in 1987, James Callaghan reflected on the famous claim that 'in fifteen or twenty years' time the black man will have the whip hand over the white man', as reported by Enoch Powell in 1968. 'That period has now elapsed,' he commented, 'and I note that there is not yet a single black member of Parliament, that they are absent from the higher ranks of the law, the civil service, the police and the armed forces, and that the election of a black mayor is still regarded as newsworthy.' There were, in short, very few role models available to suggest to black people that this society offered much hope of advancement.

From the perspective of the white population, the depiction of ethnic minorities in the media was a particularly crucial issue in the 1970s, since for many people the only black faces they were likely to encounter came on the television screen. Britain was certainly becoming multiracial, but it was a patchy phenomenon, and the contrast between the ethnic composition of the major cities and that of the country beyond was striking: official figures showed that one child in every fourteen born in Britain in 1976 had an immigrant mother; in London it was one in three and in some boroughs – Westminster, Kensington and Chelsea, Brent, Haringey and Ealing – the figure rose to one in two.

In the context of such a disparity, it was perhaps inevitable that the spectre of overt political racism should arise, though the boundaries between Nazi, nationalist and racist were to remain awkwardly blurred. In

1967 a collection of far-right groups – the League of Empire Loyalists, the British National Party, and members of the Racial Preservation Society and the Greater Britain Movement – came together to form the National Front, which rapidly emerged as the most powerful such party since the days of Oswald Mosley in the 1930s. Although an uneasy alliance from the outset (its first chairman A.K. Chesterton, a veteran of Mosley's movement, resigned within months of the launch), it drew strength from Powell's newly raised profile for its own anti-immigration stance and fielded ten candidates in the 1970 general election, averaging over a thousand votes apiece. In 1974, as the recession began to make more acute the accusations of 'coming over here and taking our jobs', the number of candidates rose to fifty-four, enough to warrant a five-minute TV broadcast, and then to ninety, and although the average vote was less than 1,500 per constituency, the cumulative total of over 100,000 people prepared to register their support for a racist party was beginning to cause a certain level of concern amongst mainstream politicians. And, of course, for any non-white residents in one of the targeted constituencies, the concern was somewhat more pressing.

A major factor in the NF's progress was the announcement in August 1972 by Idi Amin that all those resident in Uganda of Asian origin and with British passports would be expelled from the country as part of a process of Africanization. At a time when the British government was pledged to ensure there would be 'no further large-scale immigration', this presented a problem for Heath, but, despite a crowd-pleasing speech by Powell at that year's Tory conference, he insisted that Britain would honour its obligations to the victims of Amin's racism. When, in due course, some 28,000 Ugandan Asians arrived in Britain, their long-term impact proved to be entirely beneficial, but in the interim period, fears of immigration returned to the top of the political agenda, Powell reached his peak popularity, with 'one quarter of the electorate wanting to see him as prime minister', and Martin Webster of the National Front got nearly 5,000 votes in the West Bromwich by-election that saw Labour's Betty Boothroyd returned as an MP.

But the NF was, for black and Asian Britons, only the more explicit manifestation of a racism that was felt in society more generally, as evidenced by a justice system that did not appear to reflect the new complexion of the country. This was perceived to be the case at every level, most visibly in a police force that was disproportionately white. In November 1970 the press reported that there were now 'ten coloured policemen in London' and, though 'five had joined in the past three weeks', it could hardly be called even a token presence. And the rate of progress was painfully slow, despite Robert Mark launching a campaign to recruit ethnic minorities into the Met: the 1976 figures showed seventy such officers in a force of over 22,000. In such a situation, it was hardly surprising that there were accusations of a low-lying prejudice against blacks from police officers, expressed in daily harassment on the streets. Such claims, however, went largely unreported, which meant that the occasional explosion of conflict appeared without context, as though it were a force of nature.

The violence that flared at the 1976 Notting Hill Carnival came at the end both of the hottest, driest summer of the century, and of several months' worth of warnings from community leaders and police chiefs alike that tensions were getting close to breaking point. In the absence of any political response, the resentments did indeed boil over and the riot that ensued was Britain's worst racial conflict since the war, with hundreds injured, many of them policemen who had been ill-equipped to deal with the running battles of that bank holiday weekend; the following year, the Home Office authorized the introduction of riot shields so that officers might not again have to resort to using dustbin lids to defend themselves. 'It was like nothing so much as a return to the sordid celebrations attending the hangings at Tyburn Tree,' wrote Mark of the 1976 Carnival. 'Blatant disregard of liquor and other laws, hooliganism, drunkenness, vandalism and most of all, pocket picking and robbery all occurred on a large scale.' From another perspective, Robert Elms recalled attending the Carnival and being greeted on arrival by a policeman asking 'why I wanted to be here with "all the niggers"'.

The courts too were suspected by many of a racial bias. This was particularly the case with magistrates' courts, though the most controversial trial was that heard at the Old Bailey in January 1978. John Kingsley Read, a former member of the Conservative Party and an ex-chairman of the NF, had made a speech some eighteen months earlier in which he had spoken of 'niggers, wogs and coons' and, in reference to the murder of an Asian man in Southall, had commented: 'One down, a million to go.' He had consequently been prosecuted for incitement to racial hatred.

In his summing-up to the jury, Judge Neil McKinnon argued that the latter statement was an insult to the dead man, but that that was not in itself an offence. He also took issue with the notion that the word 'nigger' was itself offensive, citing rhymes such as 'Ten Little Niggers', 'Eenie Meenie Minie Mo' and 'Nigger, nigger, pull the trigger' and asking: 'All these old jokey nursery rhymes, have they become criminal offences

suddenly because of the multiracial society into which we have moved?'
More speculatively, he ruminated on the issue of immigration itself,
claiming that 'the black man wanted to follow the white man to England'
because of the 'affection engendered' by British colonists in the days of
empire. While this influx was understandable, he said, it had to be
controlled: 'Goodness knows, we have one and a half million unemployed
already and all immigrants are going to do is to occupy jobs that are
needed by the local population.' And it wasn't just jobs they would take: 'It
will be said that immigrants will occupy homes which are needed by
ordinary English folk in this country.' And, in a final bizarre twist, he
lapsed into personal reminiscence, saying that when he was at school in
Australia he had once sung a hymn in an Aboriginal language, and had
himself been nicknamed 'Nigger'; the implication was that it had done
him no harm, and he could see no reason why anyone else would take
exception.

Unsurprisingly in the light of such comments, the jury – which
happened to contain only white people – took just ten minutes to acquit
Read. At which stage a storm broke over what *The Times* discreetly
described as McKinnon's 'eccentric summing up'. Twenty black barristers
announced that they would refuse to appear in cases before him, at his
next court appearance demonstrators had to be removed from the public
gallery, and 133 MPs signed a Commons motion calling for him to be de-
wigged. Of these responses, it was the MPs' action that provoked the most
hostile comment; even if, it was argued, one accepted that McKinnon
would have been wiser not to wish Read 'good luck' as he dismissed him
without a stain on his character, still the historical separation of the
powers of the legislature and the judiciary made any such protest by
politicians dangerously unconstitutional. Amidst the heat of the debate –
and there were plenty prepared to support McKinnon's defence of free
speech – it was not always borne in mind that the alleged offence had
taken place just days before the 1976 Race Relations Act had come into
force. Read was therefore tried under the 1965 Act, which had the added
hurdle for the prosecution of having to prove intent to incite racial hatred;
the new law removed the concept of 'intent' and it is doubtful whether,
had he been prosecuted under its provisions, he would have been
acquitted.

If the police force and the courts were considered to be sometimes
discriminatory on grounds of race, the third leg of the judicial system was
even less trusted. The prison service was widely considered to be – in an
expression from a later era – institutionally racist, and few were comforted

by the knowledge that the NF was actively recruiting prison officers. 'This evening a friendly warder gave me a game of chess,' wrote John Stonehouse while on remand in Brixton jail in 1976, 'as well as confiding to me that he used to be active in the Young Conservatives. It seems that most of the warders support the National Front, so he must be an exception.' The following year, it was reported that the chaplain at the same jail, the Reverend Terry Spong, who had recently returned from Rhodesia, was himself a member of the Front. 'I am appalled to see what has happened in Britain, the country of my birth,' he was quoted as saying. 'There are many other churchmen who do not agree with the left wing point of view, but I have had the courage to say so.' Even before this, Brixton had a bad enough reputation to warrant a mention in the sitcom *Porridge*; in a 1975 episode Napper Wainwright (Peter Jeffrey), an officer transferred to the fictional Slade prison from Brixton, tells a black inmate: 'I'm not just prejudiced against your lot. Oh no! I'm prejudiced against liberals, longhairs, pillheads, winos, queens, slags, squealers, pikeys and greaseballs.'

The extent of racial prejudice in Britain was both hotly disputed and frequently hidden for many years, even within the Labour movement. 'Every year the head office gets a lot of resolutions for the union's annual conference from branches all over the country which are strongly colour prejudiced,' commented a former official of the Transport and General Workers' Union back in 1968. 'The senior officers see to it that none of them comes up in debate.' A decade later Tony Benn noted in his diary a meeting with John Boyd, general secretary of the engineers' union, at which he was told that: 'Our people are very worried. There is no doubt the Labour Party in the Commons hasn't got its feet on the ground. We have *got* to limit the number of immigrants, partly because of employment and partly because of colour.' Similar expressions were to be found too in fiction, as in Frederic Raphael's novel *The Glittering Prizes*, where a shop steward spells it out: 'The lads've got nothing against blacks as such, I'm not saying that, I'm not having anyone say it, but we don't want 'em in here, taking jobs from local people.' And again, in the sitcom *Sykes*, a shop steward played by George A. Cooper explains his men's position to the boss: 'We have no racial prejudice. You can employ as many coloureds as you like,' he says. 'Once we get another canteen.'

The canteen reference is revealing, for food was of course one of the most visible signs of difference in multicultural Britain. In 1977 the Union of Muslim Organizations wrote to the home secretary requesting that there be a statutory requirement to provide halal food in schools and works canteens where there was a significant number of Muslims. Other demands included prayer time for employees and the adoption of elements of Islamic law for the million Muslims then resident in the country, particularly where it concerned inheritance of property.

More widely, the issue of eating in company was central to Britain's gradual readjustment to its new multi-ethnic nature. By the start of the decade there were reckoned to be some two thousand Indian restaurants in Britain and twice that number of Chinese restaurants (the latter seen by Alf Garnett as being a communist front: 'hotbeds of fifth-column activity, they are'), and for millions of white Britons, this was their first encounter with an alien culture. Elements even began to creep into home cooking, so that in the late '60s Heinz introduced a new range of baked beans in a curried sauce with added sultanas, a product which proved sufficiently popular that by 1971 Hilda Ogden was seen serving it to her husband Stan in *Coronation Street* ('bit of a funny colour', he notes), while in P.D. James's novel *Death of an Expert Witness* a couple dine on 'curry made with tinned beef, together with rice and tinned peas'. It was a development ridiculed by comedian Jeremy Hardy some years later in his description of his mother's attempts at making curry: 'a great amount of fruit seems to creep into the scenario: apples, sultanas and bananas; hundreds and thousands on the top; sponge fingers on the bottom'. There were, though, limits; in an early episode of *Love Thy Neighbour* the two wives decide to swap traditional vegetables for their husbands' dinners, leading to the plaintive cry from Eddie Booth: 'I don't want yams, I want King Edwards!' Next door, Bill Reynolds is trying to come to terms with 'a typical English vegetable', which turns out to be Smash instant potato.

Behind the mockery, there was a multiculturalism of sorts at work here, the seeds of a more open-minded future. As the decade wore on, however, the very concept of multiculturalism itself came under attack on two fronts. From the right there was the entrenched complaint, articulated by Enoch Powell in 1968, that the Race Relations Acts in fact discriminated against the white majority, a position which extended into a belief that basic freedoms were being denied. The Race Relations Board became the butt of bitter jokes and the source of some resentment, though the statistics showed that its power was hardly draconian. Between its inception in 1966 and 1972, the Board investigated 2,967 complaints, of which just seven resulted in court cases, and of the five where verdicts had then been reached, two had been lost; a conviction rate of 0.1 per cent did not suggest that too many civil liberties had been lost for ever. Of those cases which never reached the courts, there were both anomalies – Abdul Goni of Smethwick was told his advert for an English lodger was illegal, even though his intention was to find someone to help his five children improve their English – and instances that revealed distressing levels of hardcore racism: three women won a case against a Coventry pub that had barred them 'because they spoke to a group of West Indian men'.

At the same time there were some on the left who were also beginning to challenge the multicultural approach, arguing that the mere celebration of differences was not a sufficiently radical position. Previously multiculturalism had been seen as a progressive development, replacing the old assimilationist model of immigration with a frank acknowledgement that the country had been irrevocably changed by the migration from the West Indies and the Indian subcontinent. Now this was considered to be inadequate, particularly in educational circles where multiculturalism was scorned as having added little to schools beyond what became derisively known as the Three Ss: saris, samosas and steel bands. A more direct tackling of the issues of racism was urged, locating the problem within the white culture and seeking a common front of the dispossessed. From this emerged the anti-racist approach of the 1980s, though its first and finest flowering came at the end of the '70s, when rock & roll began to address racism.

The radicalization of race as a political issue in Britain was primarily the result of the growing strength of the National Front and the increasing levels of street violence; in the five years from 1976, there were some thirty-one racist murders of non-whites, primarily in East London and the Midlands. Chief amongst the responses to this horrific situation was the Anti-Nazi League, launched at a press conference in the Commons hosted by Neil Kinnock, and with a list of celebrity supporters that included Brian Clough, Warren Mitchell and Arnold Wesker, though the driving force was – and remained – the Socialist Workers Party. Over the next two years, it was claimed, some 9 million leaflets were distributed by the ANL and three-quarters of a million badges sold. Its work in continually staging counter-demonstrations every time the NF tried to mobilize did much to bring that party into disrepute.

Even more influential was the ANL's sister organization, Rock Against Racism, launched in response to two incidents in 1976. The first was David Bowie's increasingly wayward behaviour, fuelled by a cocaine addiction that exaggerated his long-standing interest in the occult and in Nietzschean theories of the superman. 'I'd be an excellent dictator,' he told *Rolling Stone* that year, adding in a subsequent interview with *Playboy*: 'I believe very strongly in fascism.' When asked to explain these remarks, he did little to improve the situation: 'As I see it, I am the only alternative for the premier in England. I believe Britain could benefit from a fascist leader.' The fact that he then came to Britain for a series of gigs whose staging owed a great deal to Albert Speer – and was photographed arriving at Victoria Station wearing a black shirt, standing in an open-top Mercedes-Benz and giving what certainly looked like a Nazi salute – didn't help either. What was strikingly absent from the episode, however, though the point was lost in the furore that followed, was any hint of racism. Nor did Bowie's flirtation with fascism have any point of contact with the far right as it then existed in Britain; it is hard to imagine that a single person from his legions of fans decided to enlist in the National Front as a result of his comments, or that he would have wished them so to do. None of which stopped RAR producing a photomontage of him in profile with Powell and Adolf Hitler.

The second incident, and the one that was directly responsible for the launch of RAR, was an Eric Clapton concert in Birmingham later that year. Since the gig was not recorded, accounts vary of the exact words used, but during the performance a clearly drunk Clapton began rambling about foreigners and immigration, and suggested that the audience should support Enoch Powell. His attempts to explain himself afterwards were unambiguous: 'I think Enoch is a prophet,' he declared. And he added, seemingly unaware of the irony: 'His diplomacy is wrong and he's got no idea how to present things.' Nearly a decade later, he filled in some of the background to his outburst, explaining that in the Churchill Hotel in London his partner, Pattie Boyd, had been insulted by an Arab: 'I was incensed when I looked round and saw all these Arabs and all the signs in Arabic. I began thinking: what the hell is happening to this country?' It was not the most savoury episode in Clapton's career and his endorse-ment of Powell, delivered in Powell's own heartland, had an immediacy and a political context that went far beyond Bowie's fantasies of the *Homo superior*.

Clapton was neither the first nor the last musician to reference Powell. In the aftermath of the 'rivers of blood' speech, the Beatles had toyed with the idea of a satirical piece, 'The Commonwealth Song', elements of which found their way into the early incarnations of 'Get Back' with its lyrics: 'Meanwhile back at home there's nineteen Pakistanis living in a council flat.' The Jamaican-born singer Millie Small, best known for her hit version of 'My Boy Lollipop', released a single called simply 'Enoch Powell', and Manfred Mann included an instrumental track on their *Chapter Three, Vol. 1* album with a title intended to be read backwards: 'Konekuf'. The continuing potency of the man's myth was evidenced in later years by artists as diverse as Mensi, singer with punk band the Angelic Upstarts, and Genesis star Phil Collins. 'He was probably the most underestimated politician of all time,' said the former. 'I think he should have been prime minister.' Collins added: 'You could sense that there was a bit of magic there, that here was a great man.'

By the time of Clapton's drunken rant, Powell was, by any conventional standards of politics, a strictly peripheral figure, an MP for a minor regional party, the Ulster Unionists, who could never hope to occupy high office again, particularly now that the Tories had a leader cast in his own image. No one, wrote Margaret Thatcher's first biographer in 1975, 'could regard Enoch Powell even as a remote rival to her, while under Edward Heath he remained a very definite possible contender'. Meanwhile, the press was claiming that 'his hot-eyed supporters have already disappeared in the direction of the National Front'. And yet he remained a hugely influential, populist presence, still capable of generating front-page stories and leader columns in a way that other politicians could only envy. 'Whether you detest him or admire him,' pointed out the *Daily Express*, just a few days before Clapton's gig, 'you have to accept that Mr Powell is still a very powerful political figure.' And the launch of Rock Against Racism confirmed this analysis – Clapton's approbation of such a controversial symbol was too incendiary to be ignored.

Powell thus inspired, albeit indirectly, the movement that did more than anything else to ensure racism was to become unacceptable in Britain. Over the next couple of years RAR staged a series of gigs and one-day festivals that had a more direct and immediate effect on the political culture of the country than music had ever previously achieved.

The arrival of punk, with its refusal to address the traditional pop subject matter of teen love, had politicized rock to an unprecedented degree, whether it was Chelsea demanding that they had a 'Right to Work', Menace denouncing the 'GLC' ('You're full of shit!') or the Clash querying the very existence of MPs:

> Who needs the Parliament sitting making laws all day?
> They're all fat and old, queuing up for the House of Lords.

Such sloganeering attracted some ridicule for its simplicity, but even at this level there was some truth in their analysis: the cabinet at the time was headed by the future Baron Callaghan and included the future Barons Hattersley, Healey, Lever, Merlyn-Rees, Mason, Morris, Mulley, Orme, Rodgers, Shore and Baroness Williams; also members were the already ennobled Baron Elwyn-Jones and Baron Peart and, of course, the former 2nd Viscount Stansgate.

Elsewhere punk brought the issue of Northern Ireland back into play with songs like 'Ulster' by Sham 69 and 'Suspect Device', the debut record by Belfast band Stiff Little Fingers. (Though the most successful single of the period to address the troubles was actually 'Belfast', which gave the German-based disco band Boney M a top 10 hit in 1977.) The broadening of the lyrical lexicon also opened up space for more sophisticated artists, including Tom Robinson, Linton Kwesi Johnson and, particularly, Elvis Costello, whose 1977 debut, 'Less Than Zero', spoke of Oswald Mosley, and whose first top 10 single was 'Oliver's Army' (1979), attacking the effects of the armed forces on British society.

RAR drew on this new element in rock & roll, promoting the more politically engaged punk and new wave acts, as well as the newly emerging British reggae bands such as Steel Pulse, Aswad and Misty in Roots, and putting them on a much larger stage than they would otherwise have commanded. By 1979 there was nothing more unfashionable among the nation's youth than racism and fascism. 'There were tens of thousands of young people,' enthused Tony Benn after attending a Hyde Park rally organized by the ANL and RAR. 'The average age was about twenty to twenty-five, and there were banners and badges and punk rockers, just a tremendous gathering. It was certainly the biggest meeting that I had ever attended in this country. Multiracial rock music has given the movement leadership and it is a tragedy that the Labour Party can't give a firmer lead, but it has never done so.'

The worthiness of RAR was sometimes ridiculed – Terry Hall, of the multiracial ska band the Specials, used to mock that 'Tonight we're rocking against bacon and eggs', while Wolfie in *Citizen Smith* once staged a Snooker Against Racism tournament in his local pub – but its intervention was crucial in ensuring that the National Front failed to make the breakthrough that it had been threatening. At a time of growing youth unemployment and with a sense of alienation in the air, the NF had lowered its minimum age of membership from sixteen to fourteen in 1977, and begun targeting schoolchildren with a campaign against 'red teachers'. The RAR counter-offensive staunched the potential flow of recruits to the Front, and grounded the next generation of opinion-formers in the basics of anti-discrimination, rendering obsolete at least the worst excrescences of the casual racism so evident in earlier popular culture. And at the heart of its campaigning was a simple but devasta-tingly effective slogan: 'The National Front is a Nazi Front.'

Had Dennis Potter's 1976 play *Brimstone and Treacle* been screened by the BBC as scheduled, the same message would have been heard earlier. Here Denholm Elliott played Tom Bates, a middle-aged, slightly bewildered member of the lower middle class who has recently joined the National Front. 'Drugs, violence, indiscipline,' he laments, 'strikes, subversion, pornography . . . If you ask me, what this country needs is a new sense of direction and a clearer sense of values.' And he goes on to articulate the fatigue felt by many at the endless changes in society: 'All I want is the England I used to know, the England I remembered as a younger man. I don't want anybody to be hurt, but so many things seem to have gone wrong. I just want things to be like they used to be when there were no bombs and not so much sniggering, and you knew where you were, and old ladies could feel safe in the street and, well yes, I do want the blacks to go.' His young house guest Martin (Michael Kitchen), who may or may not be the Devil incarnate, excitedly develops his call for repatriation into an imagined panoply of cattle trucks, concentration camps and all the associated images of Nazism, at which point Bates recoils in horror and abandons his support for the Front. The invocation of the war against fascism, with memories still so strong in the '70s, was sufficient to brand the NF as being inherently unBritish and therefore unacceptable.

The other crucial factor in the marginalization of the National Front as the decade came to its end was a single television interview given by Margaret Thatcher to *World in Action* in January 1978. 'We are a British nation with British characteristics,' she argued. 'Every country can take some small minorities and in many ways they add to the richness and variety of this country. The moment the minority threatens to become a big one, people get frightened.' And, in the most significant statement uttered on immigration since the 'rivers of blood', she added: 'People are really rather afraid that this country might be rather swamped by people with a different culture.' The effects of the interview, and particularly of that one word 'swamped', were instantaneous. She received five thousand letters in a week (way above her average of fifty a day), surveys showed increased support for the proposition that there were too many immigrants, up from 9 to 21 per cent, and the Tories enjoyed a surge in popularity. In Thatcher's own words: 'Before my interview, the opinion polls showed us level-pegging with Labour. Afterwards they showed the Conservatives with an eleven-point lead.'

The remark didn't quite sit with previous unscripted comments. A year earlier she had been asked at the Young Conservatives' annual conference what should be done about Conservative clubs that operated a colour bar, and had been booed when she suggested that such practices should be discontinued. 'Look, what are you trying to do?' she snapped. 'I think we are trying to get rid of discrimination wherever it occurs.' That remark received far less coverage than the 'swamped' reference, however, and although Thatcher didn't develop the anti-immigration theme in the way that Powell had, the *World in Action* interview was to linger long in the public memory. It was reinforced two months later when Sir Keith Joseph spoke during the by-election campaign in Ilford North, a Labour-held seat that was expected to see a substantial showing by the National Front. 'There is a limit to the number of people from different cultures that this country can digest,' he said. And in an unusually direct appeal to the Jewish vote (he was himself Jewish), he added: 'Therefore I say that the electors of Ilford North, including the Jews – who are just like everyone else, as the saying goes, only more so – have good reason for supporting Margaret Thatcher and the Conservative Party on immigration.' The Tory candidate was successful, defeating Labour's Tessa Jowell, and the Front was contained in fourth place, but the whole incident left a nasty taste in some mouths: 'The party is depressed at the apparent success of Thatcher's exploitation of the race issue,' noted Benn glumly.

Race and immigration were not overtly at the centre of the Conservative Party's subsequent campaigns leading up to the 1979 general election, but the message had by then been sent and clearly understood. The National Front fielded over three hundred candidates in that election, but faced a substantial reduction in their average vote per constituency and lost their deposits in every case, virtually bankrupting the party. They had passed their moment of potential breakthrough and were never again serious players even on the fringes of British politics. The image of Thatcher, however, remained associated with a right-wing anti-immigration stance. During the conference season that followed her victory at the polls, Rowan Atkinson appeared in a sketch on *Not The Nine O'Clock News* as a speaker at the Tory gathering: 'A lot of immigrants are Indians and Pakistanis, and I like curry, I do,' he explained, an eminently rational man, slightly pained by his conclusions. 'But, now that we've got the recipe . . .'

13

Fringes

'It's coming some time, so maybe . . .'

> BENNY LEWIS: I had hoped that the younger members of the
> proletariat might have made a few changes. They seem to have
> given up though.
> Leslie Duxbury, *Coronation Street* (1972)

> ALAN: Look, the workers and the students must unite, right? We
> must link arms against the common enemy.
> RIGSBY: They won't be linking arms with you. Not in those
> trousers.
> Eric Chappell, *Rising Damp* (1974)

> She had all the trendy ideas, men were destructive, society was
> polluting itself to death, our food was poisoned, war was
> coming in two minutes and our only hope was to kneel in front
> of hairy gurus from caves in India and find inner harmony.
> P.B. Yuill, *Hazell and the Menacing Jester* (1976)

For the two big parties the rise of the National Front provided a worrying indication of how far their own support had slipped over recent years. In 1951 Labour and the Conservatives had between them been able to attract nearly 80 per cent of the electorate; by February 1974 this had fallen to a mere 55 per cent, hardly a ringing endorsement of the Westminster orthodoxy, and the establishment was beginning to get anxious. 'A people drilled, dragooned and distracted into believing that there is no choice, that they are denied any real power to choose, can find themselves drifting into a target for extremists,' warned Harold Wilson in a 1973 speech. 'This is the danger, as democrats, that we could face in Britain, that we could see a lurch into fascism.'

As the threat from the NF grew, and particularly as the party began occasionally to outperform the Liberals in by-elections, so the nervousness increased. In 1977 Nesta Wyn Ellis, a former Liberal candidate, wrote that Britain was displaying the preconditions necessary for fascism: 'breakdown of traditional values, a militant working class/trade union caucus opposed to the capitalist status quo, monopoly capitalism (both state and private), economic crisis, high unemployment, state of war and therefore of emergency in relation to Ulster, the existence of the immigrant scapegoat, increasing powers of central government'. Such a society, she argued, 'is especially threatening to a seemingly bewildered bourgeoisie of small shopkeepers, business people and professionals whose status and security are thus at risk'. And she concluded that a fascist movement might yet make serious headway, though for now the generalized disillusion 'has taken the form of voting Liberal in England, SNP in Scotland and Plaid Cymru in Wales with increasing intensity in succeeding elections since 1955'.

With a collapse in confidence in the mainstream, the 1970s did indeed prove fertile ground for fringe groups, both in politics and beyond. Some such began to transcend their position as fringe organizations in the period, as with the Liberals gaining nearly 20 per cent of the vote in February 1974, and the Scottish National Party later the same year topping 30 per cent in Scotland, though neither succeeded in overturning the iniquities of the first-past-the-post electoral system. Others, including the National Front and the Campaign for Social Democracy (founded by Dick Taverne, after he was deselected as a Labour MP), flourished but briefly and then disappeared, their place taken by others of a similar inclination. What they had in common, at least from a traditional perspective, was their appeal to that 'bewildered bourgeoisie' identified by Ellis. Jimmy Jack, secretary of Scottish TUC, was reported as saying in 1974 that 'there was very little support for the Scottish National Party among the working class of Scotland; its adherents were mostly professional people, shopkeepers and small businessmen'. And, as home secretary Merlyn Rees saw it: 'Welsh nationalism shows many of the traits of fascism.'

Such comments reflected the establishment fear that nationalism could become a powerful threat to the Tory–Labour duopoly, and might ultimately lead to the break-up of the United Kingdom. These fears were not entirely groundless. A Scottish opinion poll in 1977 showed the SNP in the lead, with a clear margin over the Tories and Labour, and the following year the press became even more excited by the prospect of Scotland's football team giving the cause of devolution a boost.

Having qualified for the 1978 World Cup (unlike England), Scotland were drawn in what looked like a straightforward group from which they were considered sure to qualify, along with Holland, at the expense of Peru and Iran. And after that, with a team that included the likes of Kenny Dalglish, Joe Jordan and Archie Gemmill, who knew what might happen? The manager, Ally MacLeod, had promised to come home from Argentina with the trophy, and there were plenty who believed he might just do it, including the tens of thousands who put the official single, 'Ole Ola' by Rod Stewart, into the top 10. If they did win, warned the *Daily Mail* in a leader column whose jocular tone could not conceal a very real unease, 'Scottish pride would be like distilled firewater. Hooched up on that, the nationalists could rampage to victory up there in any general election that followed.' (The imagery of 'rampaging' was a veiled reference to the match played in the summer of 1977 at Wembley, when Scotland beat England 2–1 to win the Home Championship, and their fans celebrated by invading the pitch, ripping up large chunks of the turf and breaking the crossbar of one of the goals by swinging from it.) 'With their lips Jim and Maggie may be shouting for Scotland,' added the *Mail*. 'But in their political hearts they'll be rooting for those bonny outsiders from Peru and Iran.' If so, then they were not to be let down, unlike the high expectations of Scottish fans which suffered a shattering blow; a loss to Peru and a draw with Iran meant that not even a 3–2 victory over Holland was enough for Scotland to progress beyond the group stages of the tournament.

Even so, the issue of devolution dominated the last period of the Callaghan administration. Support for some form of separate legislatures in Scotland and Wales was by now running too high for the Labour government to ignore, while there was pressure too from its parliamentary partners in the Liberal Party, who were long-standing supporters: 'Unlike the other two parties,' Jeremy Thorpe had pledged in the 1970 election campaign, 'I would see that Scotland and Wales had their own parliaments, running all domestic affairs.' Even the Conservatives, while opposing devolution, were wary of sensibilities north of the border. Back in 1973, in the days of Heath, a proposed set of stamps commemorating great Britons had been amended at the last minute to remove Edward I ('the Hammer of the Scots') and to replace him with Henry V; to be on the safe side, Robert the Bruce was also included. And behind the scenes was the fear of another Ulster if some sort of concession were not made. 'I don't want them to turn to violence, of course,' said Michael Foot, 'but I think it's quite likely.'

And so the Scotland Act and the Wales Act of 1978 were passed, allowing for the creation of assemblies in Edinburgh and Cardiff that would take over the functions of the appropriate Whitehall departments, but only when and if referendums in the territories concerned showed a clear majority in favour. And, controversially, that was defined as entailing not simply a majority of those voting, but also the expressed support of 40 per cent of the entire electorate.

This requirement, this one final hurdle for the nationalists to overcome, was not of the government's making. Desperate to stay in office, Callaghan was keen to appease the MPs of the SNP and Plaid Cymru and to see the devolution proposals through with as few quibbles as possible, but there was considerable disquiet amongst his own backbenchers. In Wales Neil Kinnock, a rising star of Labour, became known for his vociferous denunciations of nationalism, even claiming that there was a 'linguistic racism' operating in the principality against non-Welsh-speaking children. Since the language question was of paramount importance to Plaid – the party's first manifesto, written in 1925 by John Saunders Lewis, had insisted 'We can aim at nothing less than to do away with the English language in Wales' – it was not surprising that he became the target of nationalist attacks, including a 1977 pamphlet titled 'Neil Kinnock and the Anti-Taffy League'. A more subtle approach to linguistic sensitivity was displayed in 1974 when Selwyn Lloyd, as speaker of the House of Commons, allowed the two Plaid MPs to swear their oaths of allegiance in Welsh, so long as they also did so in English: 'I thought that the two members concerned were slightly disappointed that I had deprived them of the chance of a public protest on behalf of the Welsh language,' he chuckled.

Also opposed to devolution was Tam Dalyell, who, as Labour MP for West Lothian, raised what Enoch Powell promptly dubbed the West Lothian Question: How could it be right to propose that Scottish, Welsh and Northern Irish MPs sitting in a Westminster Parliament should be able to pass laws affecting the population of England but not their own constituents? And, as a corollary, what was the point of him representing a Scottish constituency if he couldn't have any influence over domestic affairs there?

When therefore an amendment was placed before Parliament calling for a mandate of 40 per cent of the electorate, there were many Labour MPs inclined to support the idea, seeing it as a reasonable prerequisite for such a major constitutional change, as well as being a way of snatching victory from the jaws of the nationalists. Thirty-four joined the Conservatives in the voting lobbies and ensured that the requirement was passed into law, despite the opposition of their own government. It was to prove a crucial decision in determining the subsequent fate of the

Callaghan premiership, though the assumption was still that some form of devolution was probably inevitable and even perhaps, in some quarters, desirable. 'Thank God they're going independent,' reflected Regan in *The Sweeney*. 'We'll be able to put that wall up again.'

There was no equivalent to Plaid or the SNP in England, in terms either of philosophy – the National Front could hardly claim to be opposing a foreign ruling class – or of the cross-class alliances that the nationalists were beginning to build. For, despite the jibes of the political mainstream, the Welsh and Scottish parties were not simply the vehicles for a sup-posedly quasi-fascist petit bourgeoisie, but could draw on broad coalitions of support in the way that any successful party in an electoral democracy must. The same could not have been said of the NF; unlike Oswald Mosley's movement forty years earlier, no intellectuals were attracted to its cause, no plausible leader emerged from within, and it never broke out from its heartlands in isolated sections of the working class and lower middle class.

Precisely the opposite was sometimes alleged of their rivals on the far left, where intellectuals were said to be thicker on the ground than workers.

The story of the British extra-parliamentary left in the '70s was essentially that of the rise of Trotskyism and the associated decline of the Communist Party of Great Britain, the long-standing voice of the far left, but now seen as being tainted by its allegiance to Moscow, particularly after the Soviet Union crushed the liberalizing Czech regime in 1968. Inspired by the anti-Vietnam campaigns and by events in France in May of the same year – when student demonstrations briefly spread into a general strike, before normal service was resumed and Charles de Gaulle won a resounding election victory – a series of small Trotskyist factions began to see their profile raised in Britain, attracting a new generation of activists, most of them the children of working-class families, many of them beneficiaries of the expansion of tertiary education. When Ruth Rendell's fictional detective Chief Inspector Wexford encounters a youth talking about revolution, he reflects that he 'hadn't actually heard anyone speak seriously of the promised revolution as a foreseeable thing since he was himself a teenager in the early '30s'.

The first to benefit from the new mood was the International Marxist Group, a relatively recent creation that was principally associated in the public mind with Tariq Ali: the former president of the Oxford Union edited the party newspapers *Black Dwarf* and *Red Mole*, and his con-nections with the likes of John Lennon and Mick Jagger ensured that he was always good copy. Coming up fast behind, however, and soon to overtake, were a trio of veteran Trotskyists – Ted Grant, Tony Cliff and Gerry Healy – who had in the 1940s been comrades in the Revolutionary Communist Party, but who had by now each founded his own organization, respectively Militant, the Socialist Workers Party and the Workers Revolutionary Party. (These were their best-known incarnations, though all three groups had passed through other names en route.) These were the factions that would inherit the media's red scares from the traditional Communists, though the numbers involved were less impressive than the coverage they received. One assessment claimed that in 1970 the orthodox communists outnumbered Trotskyists by around twelve to one, and that by the end of the decade this lead had shrunk to two to one, while the Institute for the Study of Conflict estimated there were 15,000 members of the various Trotskyist groups. Though it was certainly an overstatement, this was more than in any other Western nation but still a far cry from any kind of mass movement. And even if accepted, these figures were, in terms of total membership of the Marxist left, no real advance on where the CPGB had been in the late '40s. Nor was it clear that the public at large was following the heated debates on the far left about whether, for example, the Soviet Union was a workers' state, a degenerated workers' state or a form of state capitalism, or that it cared either one way or the other.

If it did care, then it would have been hard to tell. For as far as the media coverage was concerned, Trotskyism introduced just one major new element to British politics: the tactic of entryism, whereby the members of a revolutionary group would join the Labour Party for the purposes of gaining recruits and of promoting their message on a wider scale than would otherwise be available to them. All three of the major Trotskyist factions engaged in the practice at one time or other, but the most successful by far was Militant, the only major grouping still within Labour in the '70s.

Recruiting a predominantly young membership, often without family or even employment commitments, Militant made some headway in moribund party branches of the Labour Party, where meetings of the general management committee (GMC) of a constituency could be turned into ideological workshops to the exclusion of all others. 'Making the GMC a place you wouldn't go to unless you were a fanatic became a very commonplace thing,' reflected Shirley Williams. 'Resolutions going on until one o'clock in the morning. Voting down standing orders.' Even Tony Benn, who devoted virtually all his waking hours to politics, had similar experiences of being bored to within an inch of his life. 'The GMC went on for three hours and was entirely dominated by Bryan Beckingham, Pete Hammond and others from the Militant Tendency,' he wrote wearily in his diary. 'They moved endless resolutions. Their arguments are sensible and they make perfectly good radical points but they do go on interminably in their speeches. They have a certain pleading manner which just infuriates the others.'

The more public attitude of Benn and the non-Marxist left towards Trotskyist groups did nothing to reassure those on the right who regarded all of them as being virtually synonymous. When a report on Militant's infiltration of the party was produced in 1977, a subcommittee of the national executive committee, including Michael Foot and Eric Heffer, was appointed to decide upon a course of action. 'The NEC has declared against witch hunts,' it concluded. 'It is because of our principles of democratic socialism that the NEC urges tolerance and believes that Trotskyist views cannot be beaten by disciplinary action.' For those who remembered the bitterness of past expulsions, including that of Foot himself, there was a logic here; for others there was simply bafflement: if a witch hunt uncovered genuine witches, then why not prosecute? And Militant members were undeniably witches, their allegiance resting not with the Labour Party but with their own leadership, as Benn admitted: 'people thought Militant was a piggy-back operation, riding on the back of the party and building up its own organization – which is true'. He too, however, opposed the expulsion of Militant members from Labour.

The perspective from the far left saw Benn as a potentially useful figure. He recorded a speech by Militant founder Ted Grant in which 'He paid tribute to me for the work I had done in trying to introduce more democracy into the Labour Party. He said the spirit of democracy and discussion was a great tradition and the Militant Tendency could only gain from it.' But Benn also argued that he was democracy's best chance against such extremists. 'The reason I am bitterly attacked by the ultra-left is because they know I am really the only guy who might save the parliamentary system by making the necessary reforms.' This was probably a fair assessment. The Trotskyist groups may have grown during the second half of the '70s, but to nowhere near the same degree as did the Labour left in the same period, when it looked possible, perhaps even probable, that Benn would inherit the party. In the 1930s the fear of fascism had been so great that any idealistic young person, from Denis Healey to Alfred Sherman, was likely to join the Communist Party, but now it was Labour that attracted the future generation of leaders; Charles Clarke, later to become home secretary in Tony Blair's government, was elected president of the National Union of Students in 1975, and though he described himself as 'a Marxist to the left of Tony Benn' he was still well within the Labour fold.

The chief problem that the Trotskyist left faced was its ultimate unattractiveness. It enjoyed limited success recruiting amongst students, some of whom found talk of permanent revolution and transitional demands intellectually stimulating, but its ability to build sustainable structures on the shop floor was less impressive. And a key element in that failure was the left's lack of cultural connection with the working class. 'Come off it,' says the hero of Anthony Burgess's *1985* to a socialist intellectual. 'You don't like the majority. You don't like beer, football pools, darts.' The reality could be even more dour. As the actor Corin Redgrave became increasingly fixated on his membership of the WRP, and began cutting down on his non-party socializing, his wife protested that she liked mixing with people who made her laugh. 'Humour,' he retorted, apparently with a straight face, 'is the last bastion of the bourgeoisie.' There was some truth in a *Sunday Telegraph* report on the far left that concluded it would never make much headway in Britain because here 'people are intensely suspicious of intellectualized social theory'. This was, it claimed, why the mainstream parties relied on 'good old British commonsense', a tendency described as 'the most antirevolutionary instinct in history'.

Indeed, what is perhaps most surprising in 1970s politics is the lack of progress made by parties on the fringes, despite their proliferation. The nationalists only became genuinely popular to the extent that they began to look like orthodox parties (Plaid Cymru blamed their temporary setback in 1970, losing their one parliamentary seat, on the violent activities of the Free Wales Army and the Mudiad Amddiffyn Cymru), while in England neither the far right nor the far left managed to win a seat on a local council, let alone in the Commons. However impressive the SWP's organizing skills proved to be in the Anti-Nazi League and Rock Against Racism, however real the achievements of those organizations, the party itself never looked like being a rival to Labour in the political world, nor to the CPGB in the unions. And however much noise Militant made, it had no chance of becoming the dominant force within Labour, still less of staging the revolution about which it dared to dream.

The same was true of the WRP, which was for a while the largest and best known of the Trotskyist groups, partly because of the membership of Corin and, particularly, Vanessa Redgrave. Frances de la Tour, famous as

Miss Jones in *Rising Damp*, was also a supporter. 'The proportion of our members involved in ultra-left activities is greater than in most unions,' Peter Plouviez, general secretary of Equity, commented wryly. 'I think it appeals psychologically to some of them. There is an air of drama to a life based on a belief in imminent revolution.' As the decade progressed, however, the numbers in the WRP began to fall, some members unable to cope with the workload demanded by the party, others splitting to form their own groups (both of which were common conditions on the far left), but it still felt able to field more than fifty candidates in the 1979 election. Their performance was even less impressive than that of the National Front. In fact the best result by a non-nationalist fringe party that year, measured in terms of votes per candidate, was that of the Ecology Party, forerunners of the Greens.

The contribution of these groups to the future shape of society came primarily in the heightening of the sense of crisis. A belief that a collapse of capitalism was on the cards was not unreasonable at a time of stagflation – the new term coined to describe the unthinkable combination of rising unemployment and inflation – and Marxists had been predicting such a catastrophe for over a century. Now that the reality was believed to be almost upon us, the rhetoric became positively millennial in some quarters: 'The stage is set in Britain for a general strike and a civil war, whoever wins the coming general election,' declared the WRP's newspaper in April 1979, wrongly. The apocalyptic imagery was a regular feature of industrial disputes, which became occasions for frenzied attempts at recruitment, with every sign of militancy cheered to the rafters and every step towards compromise denounced as a sell-out of the working class (or 'the class' as it was known more simply). No strike could any longer be seen simply as a fight for better pay and conditions; now it was a proto-revolutionary struggle that would raise the class consciousness of the workers involved, building for the glorious day that was just around the corner. And, paradoxically, it was often the unsuccessful campaigns that brought the greatest benefits – as when Militant supporter, Joe Marino, became general secretary of the Bakers' Union in 1979, following a failed strike – since they allowed revolutionaries the opportunity to scourge the failings of moderation. And, as Stan Ogden once observed, 'Moderation's another word for misery.'

Perhaps because few save the far left themselves actually believed that a revolution was really very likely, there were some prepared to argue that the fringe parties were inadvertently beneficial to liberal democracy. 'I do not think they present a serious threat to this country,' wrote Robert Mark of both the National Front and the Trotskyists. 'In fact, in a curious way, their very existence offers a reasonable assurance of continued moderation because each offers a frightening glimpse of the possible.' Others, particularly those whose authority had previously been paramount within the Labour Party, were less forgiving. 'They are as bad as the Nazis in Germany during the '30s. There is nothing to choose between them and the National Front,' declared a shaken Joe Gormley, after an unpleasant encounter at the TUC Congress with SWP-inspired demonstrators, who had jostled him and even spat in his face. 'This is democracy gone mad. The time has come to clamp down on the freedom allowed to this kind of people to abuse our society.' Or, in the words of Inspector Regan of *The Sweeney*: 'When one bunch of people tries to force its opinions on another, I don't give a damn whether they're commies against the rest, anarchists, Irish, they're all in the wrong as far as I'm concerned. We may not think much of the present modern system – and I don't, for a start – but it's all we've got.'

Political extremism was not, however, the only facet of the '70s fondness for fringe movements. Reginald Hill's novel *An Advancement of Learning*, the second volume to feature the detectives Dalziel and Pascoe, is set in a college of higher education and much of the story revolves around two key students. One is Stuart Cockshut, a member of the fictional International Action Group, who sees a bright future for himself: 'There was a career in protest these days for the dedicated true-believer, which is what he was.' The other is the equally archetypal Franny Roote, an amused dabbler in what Cockshut calls a 'mumbo-jumbo of séances and magic rituals', a charismatic figure with a desire to break on through to the other side, aided by sex and drugs and ouija boards. Dalziel, magnificently grumpy as ever, is not impressed by either. 'My generation, most of 'em, worked bloody hard, and accepted deprivation, and fought a bloody war, and put our trust in politicians, so our kids could have the right to come to places like this,' he grumbles. 'And after a few days here, I wonder if it was bloody worth it.'

Despite his complaints, the 'mumbo-jumbo' found fertile ground, flowering into a thousand blooms. First to show themselves were the alternative theories that had been hawked around for decades, normally involving the Pyramids, the lost civilization of Atlantis, and the possibility that the planet might actually be hollow at its core. Given a new impetus by the mystically inclined end of the hippy era, each found a willing body of new disciples. So too did newcomers like Erich von Däniken, who sold millions of copies of his pseudo-scientific books, starting with *Chariots of the Gods*, which explained how extra-terrestrial beings had genetically engineered humanity in prehistoric times, and had run up Stonehenge, the Easter Island statues and – of course – the Pyramids while they were here. Strangely, even the fact that the second of these books, *Gods from Outer Space*, was written while he was in a Swiss jail, convicted of forgery, did nothing to dent his popularity. But then this was a strange decade, a time when a young Israeli conjurer named Uri Geller could convince TV audiences that his spoon-bending tricks were proof of the paranormal powers latent in each one of us, when every rock star worth his salt name-checked the sex magic guru Aleister Crowley, and when biorhythms could become an overnight craze.

One of the few fringe theories that was apparently unacceptable was fundamentalist Christianity, as religious education teacher David Watson found when he was sacked by Hertfordshire County Council for refusing to accept the truth of evolution, and for teaching instead the Genesis creation myth. A former missionary in India, Watson was a man of some conviction and he stuck to his guns, later becoming the director of the Midwest Center of the Institute for Creation Research, based in Chicago, an indication that America was even more receptive to minority faith than was Britain. Indeed many of the more peculiar religious manifestations had their origins in the States and were imported to the UK, including cults such as the Church of Scientology, the Children of God and the Unification Church (commonly known as the Moonies), all of which were regular subjects of scare stories about converts allegedly being brain-washed. Whether or not the tales were true, recruits to these and other cults often had the same experience as some members of the far-left sects, finding a social, almost a familial, network that was essentially inward-looking, that allowed no room for doubt and that was psychologically difficult to leave. 'The danger of seeing only members of your own group,' pointed out Tony Crosland, 'is you begin to think more people are likeminded than is the case, think your convictions are the only authentic convictions.' He was actually referring to the disciples of Roy Jenkins, but his analysis had a wider application.

From America too came the sensationalist, though theologically ortho-dox, movie *The Exorcist*, based on William Peter Blatty's best-selling novel, which resuscitated a ritual normally associated with the middle ages, and dragged it blinking and cursing into the modern world. Although this was the first that many had heard of exorcism, the normally staid Church of England had already started the process of rehabilitating the practice, with a commission under the Bishop of Exeter recommending that every diocese should have its own exorcist; demand rose substantially for their services in the aftermath of the movie. And in the wake of exorcism, other New Testament traditions began to receive a more favourable press than might have been anticipated, so that, for example, the Anglican clergyman Reginald East enjoyed considerable success with his book *Heal the Sick*, calling on Christians to take up faith healing.

But Christianity remained very much on the back foot, besieged by a host of rival challengers seeking to satisfy the nation's spiritual needs. Some of these, such as Satanism or the prophecies of Nostradamus, were familiar follies from centuries past; others were of more recent origin, including the Rastafari movement and the UFO obsession; and others still were simply cults built around charismatic leaders, from the Rolls-Royce-driving Bhagwan Shree Rajneesh to the Afro-haired Sathya Sai Baba. What they had in common was the boost they received as the idealism of the 1960s dissipated in the face of a right-wing revival, turning many away from social and political goals to purely personal concerns. And as the long period of economic growth in the West went into reverse, and post-war consumerism began to look ever more fragile, so too the desire to find meaning elsewhere increased.

For those not committed to a single group or guru, the '70s offered a finger buffet of faith, from which any combination of magi and messages could be taken. Frequently this produced little more than garbled confusion, a pantheistic mishmash that looked as though it was designed to validate G.K. Chesterton's (misquoted) epigram: 'When a man stops believing in God, he doesn't then believe in nothing, he believes anything.' But at its best it allowed for a work such as Colin Wilson's *The Occult*, a massive volume that proved to be his most influential book since his 1956 debut, *The Outsider*, and that rounded up everyone from William Blake to Madame Blavatsky, from Casanova to Crowley, and from Dostoevsky to Dr John Dee (as played by Richard O'Brien in *Jubilee*). All were brought together, along with evidence from contemporary science, to produce a coherent attempt at restoring significance to human life in the modern world, even if the boast on the cover of the paperback – 'The ultimate book for those who would walk with the Gods' – did seem a trifle ambitious.

The relationship between the traditional churches and the new approach to religion was played out in the 1973 film *The Wicker Man*. Here a God-fearing police officer, Sergeant Howie of the West Highland Police (Edward Woodward), follows a trail to a remote Scottish island in pursuit of a missing girl, and encounters a pagan community in complete opposition to what he insists 'is still in theory a law-abiding, Christian country, however unfashionable that may seem'. Presiding over this world is his charming but sinister host, Lord Summerisle (Christopher Lee), who tells him: 'Here, the old gods aren't dead.' Deeply shocked, Howie demands, 'What of the true God, to whose glory churches and monasteries have been built on these islands for generations past?' And Summerisle shrugs: 'He's dead. He can't complain. He had his chance and, in modern parlance, He blew it.'

As it turns out, this is a trifle disingenuous, for the old gods certainly had been dead until they were resurrected by Summerisle's grandfather. Attracted by the combination of the Gulf Stream and a fertile volcanic soil, this 'distinguished Victorian scientist, agronomist, freethinker' had chosen the island as the site of his experimental fruit-growing business, and added the religious element simply as a means of motivating the local workforce; he sought 'to rouse the people from their apathy by giving them back their joyous old gods'. This is not then, as first it seems, the blissful survival of a pre-Christian religion, but a cynical exploitation of credulous folk by capitalism. As such, it was perhaps an apt metaphor for the new religious movements that sometimes seemed like nothing more than disreputable traders in half-truths, fleecing customers by flogging them second-hand furniture as though it were antique, whilst charging them modern prices.

In common with the political sects of the left, much of the new spirituality spoke in millennial imagery, prophesying the imminent collapse of the world that we knew. Even so, no one expected the shock of the Jonestown massacre in 1978. Established in Guyana by Rev. Jim Jones, founder and leader of the People's Temple, Jonestown was a settlement of around a thousand people, predominantly black Americans from California, who had fallen for what Jones called his message of 'apostolic socialism'. When a delegation led by a US congressman visited the community to investigate claims of abuse, it came under small-arms fire as it tried to leave, and the entire membership of the cult then proceeded – perhaps under duress – to kill themselves, most of them by consuming a soft drink laced with cyanide, in an act that was intended to be seen as revolutionary suicide. Over nine hundred died that day, including Jones, and the incident cast something of a shadow over newly founded religious groups.

Nothing of even vaguely comparable impact occurred in Britain, nor was it conceivable that it might, for somehow the British versions of fervour and disciplined organization in spiritual matters never quite convinced. A congregation at an evangelical church in England was a very different proposition from its equivalent in the southern states of America: more reserved, less inclined to indulge in overt displays of possession by the Holy Spirit, reluctant to tithe what was left of their wages after taxation to the glory of their pastor. Nor was Britain blessed with any great preachers to rival their American counterparts in terms of charisma, chutzpah or political influence. Indeed churches in Britain – even an avowedly anti-communist group like the Moonies – tended not to engage in politics to any great extent. Certainly there was nothing to match the great anti-communist crusade of Pastor Richard Wurmbrand, who had been jailed for his faith for many years in Romania, and relocated to America when he was exiled from his own country. His revelations about the treatment of Christians in Eastern Europe were amongst the most important witnesses of the late twentieth century, though they were sometimes undermined by wild flights of fancy, as in his book *Was Karl Marx a Satanist?* 'I do not claim to have provided undisputed proof that Marx was a member of a sect of devil-worshippers,' admitted Wurmbrand reluctantly, 'but I believe that there are sufficient leads to imply this.'

For such hardcore fringe thinking, Britain had to look abroad, as it did to find the authentic voice of blue-skies socialism. Juan Posadas was an Argentinian revolutionary who had split with the Fourth International, the mainstream of world Trotskyism, over the issue of nuclear war (the majority disapproved, while he welcomed the prospect as a step towards the dictatorship of the proletariat), and who had subsequently founded his own, slightly self-aggrandizing, organization: the Fourth International (Posadist). By the '70s he was to be found arguing for UFOs to be accepted as a socialist presence in the world, with a logic based on a straightforward socialist syllogism. First, communism was, following established Marxist theory, the inevitable final stage of an advanced society; second, any alien race that had achieved interplanetary travel was by definition an advanced society; thirdly, therefore, the crew of a UFO must be communists. A small band of his followers, never more than a few dozen, kept the faith alive in Britain under the banner of the Revolutionary Workers' Party (Trotskyist). Where Leon Trotsky had argued that Stalin was wrong to advocate socialism in one country, Posadas refused even to accept socialism on one planet.

Largely eschewing devil-worshipping revolutionaries and communists from outer space, the British fringe produced instead Roger Protz. The first editor of *Militant* and later the editor of *Socialist Worker*, Protz could thus claim to have been a leading member of the two most significant Trotskyist groups in Britain, as well as helping to launch a rival faction, the

Workers League. More influentially, however, he also became a leading light in the Campaign for Real Ale, founded in 1971. He edited that organization's annual publication *Good Beer Guide*, and was the recipient of the first-ever Lifetime Achievement Award from the British Guild of Beer. His contribution wasn't as spectacular as the imported ideologies, but it did, one suspects, have a more lasting impact on British society than ever they managed.

14
Sexualities
'The buggers are legal now'

> Bob: Another well known fact: anybody who's always putting
> queer people down and being aggressively masculine like you,
> is only masking their own latent tendencies.
> Dick Clement and Ian La Frenais,
> *Whatever Happened to the Likely Lads?* (1973)

> The main reason we want the age of consent lowered to 14 is
> that, with the exception of rape and assault, and very young
> girls, we believe that the law has no place in the bedroom. The
> present law does not stop young people going to bed together.
> It does stop them getting contraception.
> Patricia Hewitt (1977)

> Rigsby: In my day, it meant prison.
> Alan: We live in more enlightened times, Rigsby. Parliament's
> made it legal.
> Rigsby: I'm not surprised, with that lot. We're lucky they didn't
> make it compulsory.
> Eric Chappell, *Rising Damp* (1977)

At the beginning of 1978 the Tom Robinson Band, having reached the top five with their debut single '2-4-6-8 Motorway', issued their second release, a four-track EP titled *Rising Free*. It was a record that had been long awaited, for it included the already famous anthem 'Glad to Be Gay', an overtly polemical account of homosexuals under attack from the police, the press and queer-bashers. With a singalong chorus and a tone of weary irony in the lyrics, it came on like the great lost Kinks song:

> Lie to your workmates, lie to your folks,
> Put down the queens and tell anti-queer jokes.
> Gay Lib's ridiculous, join their laughter:
> 'The buggers are legal now, what more are they after?'

Unsurprisingly, Radio One declined to play the song, even though it was clearly the primary selling point of the record, and instead opted for another track, 'Don't Take No for an Answer', which duly became the officially approved incarnation of the release. Indeed, according to the *Guinness Book of British Hit Singles*, the self-proclaimed 'Bible of Pop', that was the hit song (making #18 in the charts), and it was listed as such with no indication that it came from an EP, nor what the other tracks were, despite this being standard practice elsewhere in the book. Like 'God Save the Queen', which many high-street retailers refused even to list in their charts, leaving instead a gap where it should have been, and which was announced in the *Top of the Pops* chart rundown as being 'a record by a band calling themselves the Sex Pistols', 'Glad to Be Gay' was the hit that dare not speak its name.

Such treatment was probably inevitable in the context of a BBC establishment that fought shy of any explicit sexual references in pop music. In 1979 the Gang of Four were invited onto *Top of the Pops* to perform their single 'At Home He's a Tourist' but were told they'd have to change a line about 'Rubbers you hide in your top left pocket'; when they declined to accept the proposed alternative ('Rubbish you hide . . .'), they were dropped from the show. (The following year, however, the Vapours were happily allowed to perform their million-selling hit 'Turning Japanese', presumably because no one spotted that it was celebrating masturbation.) In such a world 'Glad to Be Gay' clearly went too far in its espousal of sexual politics, and particularly in its allegations of police violence, but eighteen months earlier an explicit tale of queer-bashing had received BBC approval and had reached #2.

Rod Stewart's self-penned 'The Killing of Georgie' was, he was later to claim, the record that had given him the most satisfaction in his career: 'I'm very proud of this,' he said, 'because it was a subject that no one had ever tackled.' Actually he was wrong; by coincidence, it was released almost simultaneously with 'Under One Roof' by the Rubettes, a group still primarily associated with a bubblegum take on pre-Beatles pop. For this single, however, they created an authentic Nashville country sound that would have been perfectly at home on a Don Williams album, save for the fact that – like 'Georgie' – the lyrics told the tale of a man being beaten to death because of his sexuality. And, raising the stakes a little, it's the man's father doing the killing. Evidently this was one gay song too many, and it was largely ignored by the media, barely making the top 40; had Stewart's record not come out at the same time, it might perhaps have received wider coverage and been better remembered. (It did, however, do much better in Europe, reaching #3 in Germany, whilst a cover version, 'Raymond und Freund' made it to #1 there and in Switzerland.)

These records were rare occurrences. Homosexuals, even more than black people, were virtually invisible in the mainstream of 1970s Britain. The Sexual Offences Act of 1967 had made male homosexual acts legal in England and Wales (Scotland followed in 1980, with a parliamentary bill proposed by Labour MP Robin Cook, and Northern Ireland in 1982), so long as they were between consenting adults over the age of twenty-one and were conducted in private, which was interpreted to mean in a domestic setting, that there were only two people in the house, not merely in the room. Even with this limited dispensation, there was no rush on the part of gay men to make their presence known. David Bowie announced that he was bisexual just before he became famous, and Elton John followed suit in 1976, though in his case it was something of a compromise: he acknowledged later that he was exclusively homosexual. Until the emergence of Robinson, who, as the least flamboyant of rock stars, did much to challenge social perceptions of gay men, that was as far as British rock music got.

Even so, it was progress at a level that was difficult to find elsewhere. The only major British sports star to come out in the decade was the ice-skater John Curry, who won Olympic gold in 1976 and was promptly voted BBC Sports Personality of the Year by a viewing public too enthralled by his extraordinary ability to care about his sex life. The fact that he had a two-year affair with the actor Alan Bates was a secret only because the latter concealed his bisexual proclivities. Bates had also had a long relationship with *Jason King* star Peter Wyngarde, which again was concealed, though Wyngarde's career later suffered when he was prosecuted in 1975 for gross indecency in the lavatory of Gloucester bus station. The same hesitancy was to be found elsewhere in the acting profession. Ian McKellen, for example, starred in the première of Martin Sherman's play *Bent* in 1979, but despite the subject matter – the treatment of gay men in the Third Reich – he had not then come out as homosexual, and did not do so until 1988. For though the theatre was widely known to be a tolerant world for gays, it was seldom acknowledged in public: John Gielgud was fined in 1953 for importuning, yet his sexuality was never mentioned in his later press coverage.

This was also the case in the world of light entertainment, where camp had long been established, while its roots in homosexuality remained unspoken. Larry Grayson got his big break on television in 1972 with appearances on ATV's *Saturday Night Variety* that made him an overnight star at the age of nearly fifty, and that led on to his own series, *Shut That Door!*, and ultimately to replacing Bruce Forsyth as the host of *The Generation Game*. But despite his anecdotes about dubiously named friends like Everard, Slack Alice and Pop-It-In Pete, and despite his catch-phrases 'What a gay day' and 'Seems like a nice boy', Grayson was keen to distance himself from the suggestion that any of it might be personal. 'I'm not really a queer or a homosexual,' he told the press. 'I'm just behaving like one. That's the big difference.'

It was, of course, untrue. He was gay, as was John Inman, who became a huge family favourite as the ultra-camp Mr Humphries in *Are You Being Served?*, though in public Inman denied even that the character was homosexual. Both were the '70s inheritors of a tradition that had pre-viously produced the likes of Frankie Howerd, Charles Hawtrey and Kenneth Williams, none of whom were out, but who brought elements of gay culture to a mass audience happy to connive at the pretence that it was all play-acting. The mainstream public didn't really believe their public disavowals of homosexuality, but chose not to ask too many questions, largely because their talent was irresistible, whilst for many young gay men 'they were a light in the dark', in the words of Matthew Parris. 'If our oh-so-modern, who-gives-a-damn, 21st-century gays, of whom I am one,' he wrote on the death of Inman, 'suppose that these men were not brave, that they were not trail-blazers, not part of the struggle, then we don't know the half of it.'

The one major field that bucked the trend of apologetic self-denial was that of the visual arts, where Francis Bacon, David Hockney and Gilbert & George made no attempt to conceal their sexuality, perhaps benefiting from the lack of interest that the popular media took in their work. But if there was a single person who stood out as an exception, a man who became famous primarily *because* he was homosexual, it was Quentin Crisp. Born Dennis Pratt in 1908, Crisp became a familiar figure in the demi-monde of gay London in the 1930s, but it was not until he was sixty that he reached a wider audience with the publication of his auto-biography, *The Naked Civil Servant*. And even then the book sold just 3,500 copies until it was adapted for television by Philip Mackie. Rejected by the BBC, the play was picked up by Thames Television and, with John Hurt ('my representative on earth') in a BAFTA-winning performance as Crisp, it became one of the most talked about programmes of 1975.

Here, for the first time, was a depiction of a gay man that made no concessions to orthodox sensibilities, that refused to countenance apology. Crisp was an effeminate homosexual and he had never made any bones about the fact. He knew that he was not the first, that this was a recurring and eternal part of humanity, and he had the courage to present himself as such throughout his life, whether enduring hostility and violence on the London streets of the 1930s, or celebrating his position as 'one of the stately homos of England' in 1975, a time when 'The symbols I adopted forty years ago to express my sexual type have become the uniform of all young people.' This was not a performance that asked the viewers to accept a gay man as being cosily the same as a heterosexual, but rather one that celebrated the diversity of human nature and faced down its detractors, that imposed dignity and decency on pure camp. As Julian and Sandy would have said in *Round the Horne*, it was bold, very bold. And when the sales of the original book were boosted by the TV adaptation, tens of thousands of readers discovered that Crisp was also amongst the most original and challenging thinkers of the time, as well as being a gifted epigrammist in the manner of Oscar Wilde and Joe Orton; the one line that was cut from the play shortly before transmission was his comment that 'sexual intercourse is a poor substitute for masturbation', curiously one of the few jokes that was not specifically gay.

Tom Robinson and Quentin Crisp represented, in their very different ways, the most unabashed, open face of homosexuality in the '70s, pointing the way forward to a less censorious world. A more depressingly familiar image surfaced in 1976 when Norman Scott, universally described as 'a former male model', alleged in court that he had been the lover of Jeremy Thorpe, the leader of the Liberal Party. It was a story that was to rumble on for over three years, and that had its roots way back in the early 1960s. Scott was then working as a stable boy whilst Thorpe was an unmarried backbench MP with, it was claimed, an active gay sex life; the physical relationship, it was said, had been brief, but Scott had continued to call on favours to a point where he was considered a threat to Thorpe's exalted public position. The alleged affair pre-dated legalization (though both men were at the time over twenty-one) and if there had been a relationship, it was certainly over by 1967 when, shortly before the passing of the Sexual Offences Act, Thorpe was elected to succeed Jo Grimond as party leader, but only after rumours concerning his private life had been firmly denied. No word of the story reached the press, which instead celebrated the arrival of this youthful, colourful figure on centre stage: 'Politics and the Liberal Party will be gayer for his leadership,' declared the *Daily Mirror*.

The eruption of Scott into national prominence came in 1975 when he was walking a friend's Great Dane on Exmoor and encountered an armed man named Andrew Newton, who shot the dog and threatened Scott. The gun, however, failed to fire a second time, and Newton was subsequently tracked down by the police, prosecuted and sentenced to two years in jail for having an automatic pistol with intent to endanger life. It was at his trial, in March 1976, that Scott first made public his allegations about Thorpe, insisting that the attempt on his life was made in order to silence him, that Newton was a hit man hired by the Liberal leader and his inner circle. The case revealed much about the existing stereotypes of gay men. They had 'a terrifying propensity for malice', said Newton's defence counsel. 'Were you taken in by him? It was a little Uriah Heep act, and at the crucial moment there came the tears. Were they real or crocodile?' he asked the jury in reference to Scott's appearance in the witness box, and he concluded: 'This type of man is dangerous.'

Though Thorpe was not directly involved in the trial, the accusation was crippling, however much colleagues such as Cyril Smith tried to laugh it off in what must have been the most tiresome fashion: '"Shot any dogs, lately?" I would say when I saw Jeremy, hoping that a ribbing might help him throw off a mood of quiet desperation that seemed to have settled on him.' The story was so sensational that it filled the papers and by May, his position having become untenable, Thorpe resigned as leader.

Was this 'the action of a politically motivated Fleet Street, aware and afraid that Jeremy Thorpe was leading a party which was threatening the cosy, if ineffectual, two-party system?' wondered Smith. 'Furthermore had they realized that the success of the Tory Party could be achieved by destroying the Liberal Party – a cause for which a few newspaper proprietors would prostitute the British press.' He was not alone in drawing such conclusions. 'Nobody in the Tory press has pointed out the clear political advantage the Tory party stands to gain from the collapse of the Liberals, who have always taken more votes from the Tories than from Labour,' noted Kenneth Tynan in his diary. And Tony Benn shared the same sentiment: 'I think the press have decided to destroy the Liberal Party because it is now an embarrassment to the cause of building up Mrs Thatcher.'

Whether it did do any lasting damage to the Liberals is unclear, particularly since the party elected David Steel to be the new leader, its one figure who looked like a professional politician rather than a misfit without a home in either of the major parties. But certainly Thorpe was finished. When Newton was released from jail a year later, the stories began again, and in 1978 Thorpe, along with three others, was formally charged with conspiring to murder Scott. The case was scheduled to be heard at the Old Bailey the week after the 1979 general election and, though Thorpe was of course considered innocent until proved guilty, in the grand tradition of British justice, he was duly removed from Parliament by the voters in his Devon constituency, amidst widespread sniggering. 'What's the similarity between Jeremy Thorpe and William the Conqueror?' ran a contemporary joke, recorded by Michael Palin. 'They're both fucking Normans.'

The trial was notable primarily for the performance of the judge, Mr Justice Cantley, whose grip on modern mores was not renowned; in a 1970 case where a man was suing for damages, having suffered injuries that adversely affected his sex life, Cantley was plainly baffled, arguing that, since the plaintiff was not married, 'I can't see how it affects his sex life.' His summing-up in the Thorpe trial was equally eccentric and was instantly celebrated as a master class in establishment bias. 'He is a fraud. He is a sponger. He is a whiner. He is a parasite,' he said of Scott, before shrugging: 'But, of course, he could still be telling the truth. It is a question of belief.' Or, in the words of Peter Cook's famous parody, he was 'a scrounger, parasite, pervert, a worm, a self-confessed player of the pink oboe, a man or woman who by his or her own admission chews pillows'. It required some effort to remember that Scott was the injured party here, the man who had come within a whisker of being shot dead. Even with the judge's words ringing in their ears, it took the jury fifteen hours to come up with a verdict of not guilty on all the defendants. For Thorpe, however, it was a pyrrhic victory; thereafter doors were politely but firmly shut in his face, as the ranks of society closed against him. At the age of just fifty, a man who should have had a glittering political career was effectively destroyed.

Thorpe himself denied not only the charge of conspiracy but also the allegation that he had ever had a sexual relationship with Scott. If the tales of this and other relationships were indeed true, however, he would hardly have been the only MP to engage in gay sex, nor the only one to conceal it. It was an open secret in Westminster, for example, that Tom Driberg, who died shortly after he retired from Parliament as a Labour MP in 1974, was particularly promiscuous, but not even he was out; it took the posthumous publication of his autobiography, *Ruling Passions*, to put his previously private life into the public domain. There was, in fact, just one openly acknowledged homosexual in the 1970s House of Commons, and that was Maureen Colquhoun.

Elected in 1974 as the Labour member for a Northampton constituency, Colquhoun was on the left of the party and attracted little media attention until, in 1976, it was revealed that she had left her husband of twenty-six years and moved in with another woman. Soon thereafter she committed a further sin in the eyes of Labour activists by suggesting that Enoch Powell was not necessarily a barking-mad racist. It was that supposed support of Powell, as it was portrayed, that became the primary charge laid against her when her constituency party began the process of deselecting her as their candidate for the next election. 'It is increasingly difficult to talk intelligently about the race issue within the Labour Party,' she commented. 'They prefer to attack Powell rather than attack the real problems of racial conflict.' She was convinced, however, that this, and the other charges laid at her door, were little more than convenient covers for those who objected to her living arrangements, and she remained unrepentant. 'I am gay and proud of it. I am glad that in my private life I have love and care from someone,' she declared. 'This is an underlying issue here and I am astounded by the hypocrisy and prejudice of my opponents. My sexuality has nothing to do with my ability to do my job as an MP.' The protests were in vain, and delegates to the Liberal Party assembly, acutely sensitive to anti-gay sentiment, sent her a message of condolence when she lost the support of her local party, 'apparently because you are open and honest about being a lesbian'.

The moves against Colquhoun coincided with the rise of a politically active lesbian culture that grew out of feminism, that was to become much stronger in the following decade, and that was capable of scaring the life out of both the right and the left. Lesbianism had historically received much less attention than male homosexuality, but in 1978 it was to be found occupying large areas of the news pages, when it was revealed that a London doctor was providing an artificial insemination service for lesbian couples wishing to have children. The response was predictable, with press denunciations in every quarter and with right-wing MPs in full cry. Sir George Young demanded that such techniques be made 'available only to married couples', Rhodes Boyson called it 'a sickness of society', and Jill Knight, later to introduce the notorious Section 28 to the Local Government Act of 1986, explained, with her characteristically curious turn of phrase, that 'I cannot imagine it is in the interest of children to be born in lesbian circumstances.' Less expected was the response of the militant lesbians who occupied the offices of the *Evening News* in London, the newspaper that had first broken the story, in protest at the tone of the coverage. The advent of lesbian activists was a new element in British society, and it did little to reassure those who already believed standards had slipped appallingly, perhaps for ever. It was a small movement, but it augured ill for traditionalists.

If, for the most part, homosexuals were notable for their low visibility in public life, so too were their fictional counterparts on screen. Camp there was in abundance, but few depictions of gay men and women, save where they were essential to the plotline, where indeed the story centred on homosexuality. So, for example, the movie *Sunday, Bloody Sunday* saw Glenda Jackson and Peter Finch each having an affair with the very beautiful Murray Head. Directed by John Schlesinger, who had previously made *Midnight Cowboy* about male prostitution in New York, and who was himself gay, *Sunday, Bloody Sunday* became briefly controversial for its portrayal of two men kissing, but was mostly celebrated simply for being one of the best films of its era, nominated for four Oscars and winning five BAFTAs.

Less worthy, and certainly less acclaimed, was *Girl Stroke Boy*, also released in 1971, in which a young middle-class man, Laurie (Clive Francis), brings his new partner, Jo, home to meet his parents. Played by the even more beautiful Peter Straker – credited here simply as Straker – Jo is so androgynous that his gender is never determined, though Laurie's mother, Lettice (Joan Greenwood), is outraged by 'a relationship that is as godless as it is fashionable'. Perhaps the lack of critical plaudits stemmed from the fact that the movie was directed by Bob Kellett and produced by Ned Sherrin, the team who also gave us *Up Pompeii* and *Up the Chastity Belt* the same year, or perhaps it was simply that *Girl Stroke Boy* refused to take itself seriously, and didn't treat its subject matter with any degree of agonizing or melodrama. Laurie's father, George (Michael Hordern), isn't quite sure what all the fuss is about anyway: 'If he is nightly in the arms of a young man – which, pray God, he isn't – does it matter?' To which Lettice retorts: 'You'll have to resign from the golf club.'

With the exception of *The Naked Civil Servant*, popular television was even less inclined to venture beyond camp, though it did have its moments. Peter Bowles's character Hilary in *Rising Damp* inverted the conventions of the genre; playing an actor who had supposedly appeared in *I, Claudius* in an orgy scene (though you couldn't recognize him because he was wearing a stag's head), his performance was an exercise in limp-wristed cliché, but he ended by demonstrating his heterosexuality to Miss Jones's complete satisfaction. Not all, it transpired, was what it seemed, even in sitcoms.

The same was true of ITV's version of the *Raffles* stories, adapted – as was Crisp's life – by Philip Mackie. Written by E.W. Hornung, the stories were set in Victorian London and chronicled the disparity between the public and private worlds of the amateur cricketer Raffles, whose social status conceals his true nature as a burglar, and of Bunny, his former fag from school and now his partner in crime. In the TV adaptation, with Anthony Valentine and Christopher Strauli, the idea that their secret double life might actually be little more than a metaphor bubbled mischievously under the surface, with double entendres about batting and bowling, and lines that, taken out of context, had an entirely different meaning. 'Gentlemen are always open to corruption,' purrs yet another aristocratic crook, Lord Ernest Belville (Robert Hardy), to Bunny. 'Come into the bedroom . . .'

In one memorable scene, the two men return, somewhat symbolically, to Bunny's childhood home to steal some diamonds. Confronted by a locked green-baize door, Raffles cuts a hole through the baize, and inserts his hand to turn the key from the other side, only to find his wrist gripped fast by the householder. Fortunately the amateur cracksman never ventures out without a small flask of oil, which he gets Bunny to pour down his arm. And, as the camera shot switches to the other side of the door, we see a man's disembodied fist, slippery with grease, twisting and turning in the grasp of another man, and finally sliding free. It was hard not to see a subtext, particularly since the scene didn't come from the source material, but was newly created for TV.

Other variations on human sexuality also surfaced on occasion in the television of the era. *I, Claudius* could claim historical authenticity, of course, but still it made the most of moments such as Nero going to bed with his mother, Agrippinilla (Christopher Biggins and Barbara Young), or Caligula (John Hurt) groping the breasts of his great-grandmother, Livia. The excesses of Tiberius, however, were, perhaps fortunately, rather played down.

The series was rivalled in its depiction of confused family relationships only by *A Bouquet of Barbed Wire*, adapted by Andrea Newman from her own novel. Here a wealthy London publisher, Peter Manson (Frank Finlay), has an incestuous obsession with his married daughter, Prue (Susan Penhaligon), a fact of which she, in her sulky, pouting innocence, is perfectly well aware. Unable physically to realize his lust – even publishers, apparently, had some moral standards in those days – he instead starts an affair with his new secretary, who is young enough to be his daughter, sleeping with her in the flat he has given Prue, while she and her husband, Gavin, are away on holiday. And then the revelations start. Manson is shocked to discover that Gavin has been beating Prue up, and that she rather enjoys a bit of violence; even more shocked when his wife reveals that she too has the same inclinations: 'Most women like a man to be masterful. Maybe even a little bit rough. You only have to push this a stage further and you've got real pain, real violence. The problem is where to stop it.' Having nurtured his own dark desires for so long, he is horrified that others too might have their secrets. 'I'm too old-fashioned to appreciate the finer points of sadism,' he snaps at his now estranged wife, happily unaware that she has meanwhile started an affair with Gavin, her son-in-law, while Prue is recovering in hospital from a particularly savage beating.

What was most surprising about the series was that every nuance of the novel was reproduced faithfully on mainstream TV, going out at 9 o'clock on a Friday evening to huge public enthusiasm and some critical confusion. Manson and Prue had 'the most extravagant father–daughter relationship since Herod and Salome', wrote Philip Purser, but actually it was Manson who ultimately seemed the most straightforward of the four principal characters, a confused man adrift in a world of melodramatic passion over which he had no control. Such subject matter was far from common on British television, but the fact that it figured at all was startling, both at the time and perhaps even more so in retrospect.

In literature variations on the theme of relationships were becoming familiar. *Together*, a novel by Ingeborg Pertwee (whose husband, Jon, was then starring as Doctor Who), was billed as being about 'a man's need for two women – a mother and a daughter'. But it was in crime fiction that alternative sexualities were really played out, within a familiar environment where the reader could confidently expect normality to be restored by the end of the story. In P.D. James's *An Unsuitable Job for a Woman* a male student is discovered hanging from a rafter by his belt: 'He was dressed like a woman,' confides a witness, 'in a black bra and black lace panties. Nothing else. And his face! He had painted his lips . . .' (The image of what is assumed to be an act of auto-erotic asphyxiation gone horribly wrong also occurs in Kingsley Amis's *Jake's Thing*. Meanwhile, however, the man who would later become Britain's most famous victim of such practices, *Economist* journalist Stephen Milligan – as a Tory MP, he died in similar circumstances in 1994 – was concentrating on the more orthodox concern of trade union power in his book *The New Barons*.)

Elsewhere, Ruth Rendell's *A Guilty Thing Surprised* featured a sympathetic treatment of a long-standing incestuous relationship. Julian Symons's *The Players and the Game* centred on a series of sadistic *folie à deux* murders, but also found room for a man paying to be humiliated by a prostitute and her maid, and for another man molesting a thirteen-year-old girl. (Neither of them are the killers.) And in Colin Wilson's *The*

Schoolgirl Murder Case there is likewise a relaxed attitude to sex with underage girls. When it is discovered that another schoolgirl has been the victim of the so-called North Circular rapist, one police officer asks, 'Was she hurt?' 'Not badly,' replies his colleague. 'A few scratches. But she was raped.'

The casual tone was not untypical, for it was in the 1970s that questions over the age of consent and of paedophilia really came to the fore, despite some earlier rumblings. Back in the mid-'60s the Swedish doctor Lars Ullerstam – speaking, according to his American publisher, with 'the authentic voice of the boldest of Europe's young generation' – had called for the new tolerance being shown towards homosexuals to be extended to other 'sexual eccentrics', including paedophiles. Not, he hastened to add, that he thought 'all grown men ought to be allowed to manipulate children's genitals', but rather that understanding should replace criminalization until a better solution could be found: 'The sexual deprivation of the "dirty old men" is a problem to be solved by tomorrow's humanely oriented society.'

It wasn't solved, of course, but there was at least a brief period when the general culture acknowledged that the lines of what was permissible were on occasion blurred. 'Sometimes, I'm the new master at a girls' high school,' says Terry in *Whatever Happened to the Likely Lads?*, reflecting on his sexual fantasies. 'That one seems to come back more and more.' And Bob knows precisely what he's talking about: 'Yes, gymslips. I've been worried about that. I think the sexiest programme on television is *Top of the Form* not *Top of the Pops*.'

Politically, the issue began to gather at least a small head of steam in 1976 when home secretary Roy Jenkins asked the Criminal Law Revision Committee to look into the age of consent. The following year a series of widely reported court cases suggested that attitudes might be shifting, not in relation to pre-pubescent children but to those in their early teens. First came twenty-one-year-old Gary Lea who had been given a six-month sentence for having consensual sex with a thirteen-year-old girl after a party; the sentence was quashed on appeal, with Lord Justice Scarman saying: 'It was not only too severe, but was quite wrong in principle.' In the wake of this judgment, and in very short order, an eighteen-year-old man was given a £20 fine for having sex with a thirteen-year-old, a thirty-nine-year-old was put on probation for having sex with his son's fifteen-year-old girlfriend, and a nineteen-year-old was given a two-year conditional discharge for getting a thirteen-year-old pregnant, the judge admonishing him to 'behave sensibly in future and keep away from young girls'. All of these cases – and there were others – concerned older men and younger girls and received relatively sympathetic treatment; when the roles were reversed and when, for example, a twenty-six-year-old female teacher was accused of molesting an eleven-year-old boy, the press coverage reverted to its more normal approach of salacious reporting, even though the accused woman was acquitted.

This spate of judgments provoked the *Sun* to run a week-long series of articles by Jeremy Sandford on the vexed issue of the age of consent. And he found many prepared to suggest that the time had come for it to be reconsidered. Labour MP Colin Phipps called for it to be abolished, while the likes of John Robinson, dean of Trinity College, Cambridge, suggested it be lowered to fourteen, as did Patricia Hewitt, then with the National Council for Civil Liberties and later to become health secretary under Tony Blair. Michael Schofield, a psychologist, claimed that one in six girls and one in four boys were having sex underage. Later in 1977 the *News of the World*, which would later become the self-proclaimed scourge of paedophilia, gave space to the Catholic priest and child psychologist Father Michael Ingram, who had studied a number of cases of men having sexual relations with boys under the age of fourteen, and who was due to report his findings to the British Psychological Society. 'If a child has been deprived of love, he can get a lot more good than harm from a relationship with a man,' Ingram claimed. 'I'm not saying it is right or wrong from a moral point of view – I'm speaking purely from the psychological standpoint. The real harm to a child can come not from a sex act but from the reaction of other adults afterwards.'

And then there was a perceptible turning of the tide. The Paedophile Information Exchange, the principal campaigning group for those who sought reform of the laws concerning sex with children, received increasingly hostile treatment by the press, much of it centred on its most prominent figure, Tom O'Carroll, then a press liaison officer at the Open University. The first public meeting of PIE was held in Conway Hall, London – the traditional home of alternative thought – and the few attendees were attacked both by the National Front and by a bussed-in mob of two hundred women, armed, in the words of one of them, with 'stinkbombs, rotten eggs, tomatoes, apples and peaches'. Ingram was invited to attend but had to send his apologies, having been instructed not to do so by the Catholic Church, presumably fearful for its public image. The previous month, on the other hand, a conference of the Campaign for Homosexual Equality had condemned the media treatment of PIE and called for 'objective rational discussion of paedophilia and child sexuality'.

Instead the focus of debate was shifted sideways towards the question of child pornography. The law at that stage meant that it was not illegal to take photographs of naked children nor to sell them, so long as no sexual assault had taken place. And there was, so it was claimed, a massive and sudden increase in the number of publications exploiting this situation. 'It is this furtive network of amateur photographers now cashing in on child-sex that is our biggest headache,' a senior Scotland Yard officer was quoted as saying, and Mary Whitehouse, who swiftly made the cause her own, had no doubt about the scale of the problem: 'We know that 200,000 children are involved in the "kiddie porn" industry in the United States,' she declared, though the evidence to back up such a startling assertion was not forthcoming.

Margaret Thatcher, alert to the prospects of a populist cause, met with Whitehouse to discuss this latest outrage against public decency, and emerged with the perfect soundbite for the occasion; child porn, she said, was 'a crime against innocence'. Meanwhile Tory MP Cyril Townsend was busy launching a private member's bill, which Whitehouse urged politicians to support, though she couldn't resist slipping in a dig at those on the left who opposed racism: 'It is a matter of great regret,' she said, 'that our government, which takes such notice of black exploitation in South Africa, takes little notice of child exploitation in Britain.' In the face of overwhelming media opinion, Jim Callaghan ensured that parliamentary time was made for the passage of the bill, which duly became the Protection of Children Act 1978. At which point all discussion of reform to the age of consent ceased.

It was not Whitehouse's first success. Following her failed attempt to invoke the Vagrancy Act in the suppression of *Blow Out*, she discovered an even more archaic law in 1976 with which to attack the publication *Gay News*. In a June issue of the magazine, its editor, Denis Lemon, had published a poem titled 'The Love That Dares to Speak Its Name' by James Kirkup, being the fantasy of a Roman centurion lifting Christ off the cross and having sex with him. It was not a great work by any means, but it had an impish vitality with its *Carry On* puns about 'my spear' and being 'well hung', and it did have some genuinely transgressive images ('that great cock, the instrument of our salvation') and thoughts: Jesus, the poem suggests, had already had sex with – *inter alia* – Pontius Pilate, John the Baptist and Judas Iscariot ('a great kisser'), and His first thought on His resurrection was to continue where He had left off. This, Whitehouse decided, was all a bit strong and, exhuming the long-neglected law of blasphemous libel, she launched a private prosecution against the magazine and against Lemon himself.

The judge, Alan King-Hamilton, refused to allow any expert testimony as to the literary or sociological value of the piece, but his own thoughts were unequivocal once the jury had found the defendants guilty as charged. 'This poem is quite appalling,' he shuddered, pronouncing himself horrified by its 'scurrilous profanity'. He fined both *Gay News* and Lemon, with a suspended sentence of two years for the latter, adding that it was 'touch and go' whether he should be sent to prison immediately. On appeal, the suspended sentence was quashed but the fines, and the legal costs, stood.

The case attracted widespread coverage. The journalist Bernard Levin and the novelist Margaret Drabble went into the witness box to testify to *Gay News*'s character, while Enoch Powell, amongst others, saw it as an opportunity to celebrate the counter-charge against 'the movement which started about the middle-'60s and swept around the world like an epidemic, taking a multitude of forms but always with essentially the same end and aim: The destruction of organized society, not for the sake of replacing it with a different and supposedly better one, but for the sake of destruction itself.' This movement, he insisted, employed 'the deliberate use of obscenity of every kind as a battering-ram – or rather one of the battering-rams – to break down the walls of civilized society'. Whitehouse would undoubtedly have agreed, and was herself jubilant: 'I did what I did,' she said, echoing the thoughts of the fictional centurion, 'out of love for the Lord.'

Tom Robinson, meanwhile, had an alternative perspective:

> Pictures of naked young women are fun
> In *Titbits* and *Playboy*, page three of the *Sun*.
> There are no nudes in *Gay News*, our one magazine,
> But they still find excuses to call it obscene.

Crisis

'Sending out an S.O.S.'

> Rape and murder throughout the land,
> and they tell me that you're still a free man.
> Well, if this is freedom I don't understand
> cause it seems like madness to me.
> The Jam, '"A" Bomb in Wardour Street' (1978)

> By all accounts, the working class is busy creating a sort of hell
> on earth for itself: rubbish lies uncollected in the street, old-age
> pensioners are mercilessly raped whenever they venture out
> after dark, dying like flies in any case and their corpses left
> unburied, everybody in work is on strike and the rest are
> unemployed.
> Auberon Waugh (1979)

> We'll beat the bastards yet.
> Margaret Thatcher (1978)

By 1978 it appeared as though perhaps the worst had passed for James Callaghan's minority administration. The rate of inflation, while not exactly impressive, was down sufficiently for the government to claim that it was coming under control, industrial disputes were nowhere near the levels of the Heath years, and the opinion polls were looking more favourable. The early enthusiasm for Margaret Thatcher was falling away a little, and it was widely assumed that an election that year could produce another Labour victory.

Underneath, however, there were still disturbing indications of instability. Structurally British industry remained fragile. In the period 1968–73, British productivity had grown at 3 per cent per year, much slower than its competitors; following the international oil crisis, both France and West Germany fell below that level in 1973–79, but Britain fell still further and averaged just 1.3 per cent, less than half the growth rate of those countries. For the Labour Party, an even more damaging fact was that the underlying unemployment levels were rising, largely because of the government's own policies. And then there was the certain knowledge that the pay restraint deals agreed between the TUC and the government were losing support among ordinary trade unionists. The first unmistakable warning of this trend had come at the TGWU conference in July 1977 when Jack Jones, soon to retire as general secretary, lost a vote for the first time; despite his passionate speech urging delegates to accept a further round of a wages policy in order to sustain the Labour Party in office, the conference voted instead for 'a return to unfettered collective bargaining'. A new, much looser, agreement was cobbled together, but the 'humiliating snub' to Jones was a shot across the government's bows. As Denis Healey pointed out, 'The union leaders are completely out of touch with the rank and file.'

Labour's lead in the polls could not, therefore, be relied upon. 'Jim's good news basket is a very small one and all the signs are that the present drop in inflation (now down to 7.8 per cent) and unemployment figures cannot be maintained,' noted Michael Palin in 1978. 'Still,' he added, 'I'm better disposed to letting the present Labour government run my country for me than any other group – apart, perhaps, from Pan's People.' It was a lovely image, but sadly one from a fast-vanishing age. For the five-woman dance troupe Pan's People had recently retired, after ten years of providing visual relief for dads obliged by their children to watch *Top of the Pops*. They were replaced by the short-lived and barely remembered Ruby Flipper, whose mixed-gender line-up failed to console a bereaved audience.

And still the major source of discontent in the nation remained. A poll by MORI in September 1978 showed that 82 per cent of the electorate thought that the unions were 'too powerful'. Nearly three-quarters of trade unionists themselves agreed with the proposition. For a Labour Party that was seen, and that saw itself, as the political wing of the unions, these were worrying figures. And it had nothing in its policy locker that might address the issue.

Over half the working population were members of unions, putting Britain somewhere around the middle of the league table of industrialized nations in terms of unionization, but that still left many millions outside, resenting the fall in living standards caused by the wages policies, yet fearful of a free-for-all that would surely benefit others at their expense. Symptomatic of their plight was the tragic story of Ernest Bishop, as enacted by Stephen Hancock in *Coronation Street*.

For its first decade or more, the soap's most articulate spokesman for the upwardly mobile working class had been Ken Barlow (William Roach), a college graduate who had been briefly jailed in the militant student days of the 1960s, but who had settled down to become a repository of reason and liberalism. When, for example, a gang of skinheads rampaged down Rosamund Street in 1971 and put a brick through the window of Ernie Bishop's shop, it was Ken who tried to understand, comparing their motivation to that of George Mallory's famous comment on climbing Mount Everest: 'You ask these skinheads, they'll probably give you the same sort of reason why they destroyed a tree or carved up a train: because it's there. To the chap who climbed Everest, it was big and it was frightening so he had to show who was boss. The kids today find the world big and incomprehensible and they want to show who's boss.'

But as the decade wore on, and the gloss came off the radical dream, Ernie – a grammar school boy who had studied photography at the local polytechnic – emerged as a counterbalancing voice of lower-middle-class morality and respectability, unwilling any longer to play second fiddle to Ken's rosy optimism. 'Does the victim of a mugging care about democracy?' he stormed on one occasion. 'Or a child blown up by a terrorist bomb? Or the soldier with a bullet in his back? Any one of those things happening to a single person, and democracy has failed in my book.'

By 1976 his photographic business was struggling, as were those of many of the self-employed, and his generalized complaints about society were becoming intensely personal. 'Why, if you're ordinary and honest and you slave away, why does life just become more and more impossible every day? And don't tell me it's not the government. They don't care. If the TUC barks, they throw them a bone. And where does the bone come from? From the skeletons of all the rest of us. Labour, Conservative, they're all the same, they've all got their nests nicely feathered. And I defy Jim Callaghan to come in here and tell me any different. Sometimes, it just feels like a great conspiracy.' The shop duly collapsed, and the forty-six-year-old Ernie had to endure what he – and many others of his generation – perceived as the ultimate humiliation of being out of work and dependent on his wife's income. And then things took a turn for the better. He found a new job as the wages clerk in Mike Baldwin's denim factory, and by January 1978 he was able to feel some hope for the future for the first time in years. 'It's a funny thing, you know,' he reflected, 'if you asked me to choose the best time of my life, I think I'd say now.'

Those were among his last words. Later in the same episode he was shot during a bungled wages raid on the factory, and he subsequently died of his wounds in hospital. The nation was horrified – 'It mustn't happen,' gasped Sir John Betjeman on learning that Ernie was to be killed off – but the sacrifice of this decent man, a lay preacher who played the piano in a Congregationalist chapel, seemed somehow appropriate for the era.

The theme of the middle classes being squeezed between the rival power blocks of big business and the unions was becoming increasingly common, with the latter being the target of most attacks. In *Fawlty Towers*, Basil is never happier than when ranting about the state of the working class. 'Another car strike. Marvellous, isn't it? Taxpayers pay millions each year, they get the money, go on strike. It's called socialism,' he spits, before launching into a fantasy about 'the British Leyland Concerto in four movements, all of them slow with a four-hour tea-break in between'. Similarly Mike Leigh's play *Abigail's Party*, which transferred from stage to screen in 1977, focused on an *arriviste* couple, existing in a state of jittery desperation, who stage a small drinks party. The early discussion – when conversation is still tolerably social – centres on whether the men present have got 'a good job', not in any spirit of solidarity but rather of a suspicion that will later break into overt hostility. The play leavened its melodrama by ridiculing the cultural pretensions of those it clearly felt should have resisted the call to social mobility, and who were destined always to be looking over their shoulder. And the cultural snobbery made the piece a huge success amongst those who could claim to be at least second-generation bourgeois: 'The audience was frightful,' wrote Kenneth Williams in his diary, after attending the original production. 'Hampstead sophisticates knowingly laughing at all the bad taste lines "Oh! A bottle of Beaujolais! How lovely! I'll just pop it in the fridge . . ." and they fell about, loving their superiority.'

Such was the pinch being felt by the middle classes that in 1977 Surrey County Council announced that it was re-examining its supply of free school meals to those in need, now taking into consideration not simply income but the income that was left after essentials including mortgage, rates, insurance and travel costs. And the belief spread that such concerns were simply not understood by the government. That year Thatcher used her speech to the Conservative Party conference to make great play of being a product of a grammar school, as compared to Tony Benn's privileged public school background. It was, as the *News of the World* pointed out, a somewhat disingenuous comparison, since Labour MPs from grammar schools outnumbered those in the Tory ranks by three to one, while there was only one public school Labour MP to every seven amongst Conservatives, but nonetheless the attack struck home: 'It was a very subtle argument,' conceded Benn. She continued to push hard on the theme: 'The only difference between the Marxists and the social democrats in the Labour Party,' she mocked in 1978, 'is that the Marxists want to see the socialist millennium tomorrow whereas the social democrats wish it to be deferred until their children have completed their private education.'

Much of this chimed with Ernie Bishop's talk about politicians feathering their own nests. Another *Coronation Street* character, the mild-mannered Mavis Riley, had a similar feeling, suggesting that come the next election she wanted to speak to the local Labour candidate: 'I shall ask him why, if he believes in everybody being equal, he's got two homes.' In real life, the same question about ministers purchasing country houses was being asked by Jack Jones: it 'did not endear me to everyone', he reflected, 'but the lesson had to be driven home'. It was a reputation that did the party's leadership no good, and that swiftly affected public perceptions. When the fictional private eye James Hazell finds himself in a Chelsea mews where you couldn't buy a house 'for much less than fifty thou', he comments cynically: 'Be a strong Labour ward then.' Again parallels could be found in the ancient Rome of *I, Claudius*. His nephew Caligula having been murdered, Claudius is chosen by the Praetorian Guard to become the new emperor. He insists that he doesn't want the job, that – like his late brother Germanicus – he doesn't believe in emperors and wants to see a republic. And a centurion has to put him straight: 'It's all very well for you, sir. Being members of the imperial family, you can afford the luxury of republican sentiments. I can't. I rose through the ranks.'

All of this was grist to Thatcher's mill, as she increasingly portrayed herself as the humble grocer's daughter, untainted by such implied venality. Even though such an image was not entirely candid – her marriage to a millionaire businessman was seldom emphasized – she had found a vulnerable point in Labour's class armour and, like a professional wrestler discovering that his opponent had a weak right shoulder, she worked on it, particularly in terms of what was seen as a lack of opportunity in comprehensive schooling. As a former education secretary, albeit one who oversaw the closure of large numbers of grammar schools, she was here on familiar territory where she could claim some expertise.

And education was becoming a key battleground, with London being singled out as the prime example of what would one day become known in the right-wing press as the 'loony left' and then as 'political correctness'. 'A mother in North London,' reported the *News of the World*, 'complains that on sports day at her daughter's primary school, pupils were told they were only allowed to win one race.' Meanwhile the *Daily Mail* was denouncing ILEA, who 'want to encourage teachers to ditch textbooks that show boys in too dominant a role. They want to prod schools into wooing more girls into taking up mathematics.' And Robert Mark claimed that there was a drain of police officers from the capital to other parts of the country 'where the grass is greener, where living conditions were pleasanter and, in particular, where their children would not have to attend the schools of Inner London'. The spirit of non-competitive education was part of the new orthodoxy, as shown when Charles Curran, the director-general of the BBC, had decreed that success in the eleven-plus should not be mentioned as a reason for requests being played on Ed 'Stewpot' Stewart's *Junior Choice* programme on Radio One, for fear that it might upset those who had failed. 'We should be sorry if mention of the examination caused distress to some of the children,' explained the ex-grammar school boy.

Most powerful of all was the critique offered by Rhodes Boyson, himself a headmaster, attacking teachers who 'do not aim to teach but to "liberate" their pupils, which means leaving them trapped in their ignorance so they grow up illiterate and anti-social as unemployed and unemployable juveniles with a genuine grievance against society'. He cited the extraordinary case of one who 'actually refused to teach decimals because it was used in the form of accounting which accompanied the capitalist system'.

Partially in response to this barrage against what were seen as leftist attitudes to teaching, Callaghan launched his one great policy initiative, a debate on the future of education, in a 1976 speech at Ruskin College, Oxford: 'The essential tools are basic literacy and numeracy; the understanding of how to live and work together; respect for others; and respect for the individual.' The goal of education is 'to equip children to the best of their ability for a lively constructive place in society and also to fit them to do a job of work', he argued, 'not one or the other, but both'. It was an intelligent and honourable venture, but not one – given the economic crises he was facing – that he was able to follow through satisfactorily. It was to take another decade, and another government, to implement the national curriculum and the parental choice for which he called, and to challenge the 'informal methods of teaching' that he criticized. He was destined to receive little of the credit.

The education system, alongside taxation and a general feeling that there was a lack of opportunity in Britain, was one of the key reasons cited by those who were emigrating from the country. And there were plenty who did so. The peak year was 1974, when it seemed as though the trade unions had acquired the power to make or break governments, and when 269,000 left the country (compared to 184,000 coming in), but it was hardly a new phenomenon, with the expression 'the brain drain' having been coined in the 1960s. Nor was it short-lived. In 1970 Boyson had warned that state interference in everyday life had reached intolerable proportions: 'Little wonder that tens of thousands of our most enterprising vigorous people now emigrate every year to Australia, Canada, New Zealand, South Africa and Rhodesia where they have more chance of fulfilling themselves and shaping their lives to their own choice.' By the mid-'70s South Africa had overtaken even Australia as the destination of choice, with the press reporting that 29,000 men from the managerial class had chosen to relocate there in 1975, with numbers rising still further in 1976, the year of the Soweto uprising.

Most newsworthy of the émigrés were the rock musicians, including the Rolling Stones, who fled to the south of France and whose 1972 album *Exile on Main Street* had a title indicating their status as refugees from taxation. 'I owed the Inland Revenue a fortune,' admitted Bill Wyman, before dismissing his homeland: 'All the ambitious people leave.' Under Callaghan – the man who, as chancellor of the exchequer, had inspired George Harrison's song 'Taxman' for the Beatles – the situation grew worse, in quantity if not quality. Amongst those who left later, less celebrated than the Stones, was the Australian-born producer Mike Chapman, who had given us acts such as the Sweet, Mud and Suzi Quatro, and who departed Britain for LA: 'Los Angeles is a more receptive city for music than London is,' he explained. 'And the tax system in Britain is pretty bad.' He went on to produce a series of #1 hits in America for the likes of Blondie, Exile and the Knack.

Even record-producer Biddu, who had hitchhiked from India in order to move to Britain and who had gone on to help invent disco, with #1 hits for Carl Douglas ('Kung Fu Fighting' in 1974) and Tina Charles ('I Love to Love' in 1976), was losing faith in his adopted country. 'I was getting very disillusioned with the scene over here, because punk had come in and I can't stand people swearing and cussing,' he remembered. 'My wife and I even thought about emigrating, we just thought the country was going downhill, morally and in everything else. I was very disillusioned at that time.'

And then, in 1977, came the most spectacular departure of all when the England football manager, Don Revie, flew out of the country, leaving behind a letter of resignation addressed to the FA. He had secretly accepted a post as coach to the United Arab Emirates, a job whose remuneration – allowing for the absence of tax – equated to a salary of £2 million a year in Britain, compared to the £25,000 he was getting as England manager.

Given those figures, it might be thought that few could blame him, but pretty much everybody did, for rats who choose to leave sinking ships are seldom honoured by the passengers obliged to remain, and Revie had precious little in the way of reputation to win over his detractors. He had already ensured England's failure to qualify for the 1978 World Cup, and had seen the nation's team comprehensively destroyed at Wembley by Johann Cruyff's Holland. 'There is no point in kidding ourselves,' Revie admitted after that defeat, as though commenting on Britain's economic position relative to its rivals. 'We just couldn't cope.'

Nor, by the winter of 1978–79, could the government, which was busily paddling itself into the most dangerous of waters. It was taken as read that Callaghan would call an election for the autumn of 1978, when most commentators felt that he had a fair chance of winning. He chose not to do so, having made his own calculations which suggested the outcome would be a hung parliament with the Tories having the largest number of seats. 'Why run the risk of a very doubtful election result in October 1978 if we could convert it into a more convincing majority in 1979?' he reflected. 'Moreover, the polls showed that as the country began to understand what we were trying to do, an increasing number liked what they saw.'

In retrospect, it was a miscalculation even greater than that of Edward Heath when he called an unnecessary election in 1974. And it was compounded by the decision to go for another year of a wages policy. The selected figure this time was a maximum 5 per cent pay rise across the board, an arbitrary and unachievable target that enjoyed no support whatsoever within the union movement and had not been agreed by the TUC. Even as Callaghan was arguing for the new proposal at the Labour Party conference that autumn, workers at Ford were striking for 30 per cent. Buoyed by the company's declared profits of £246m in 1977 for the British arm of its operations, Ford's management were inclined to negotiate a deal, and after a nine-week strike did precisely that, settling for 17 per cent. The policy having thus been blown out of the water almost before it was launched, the government was clearly in for a stormy winter. Just how stormy did not become clear until the following year.

It was, to start with, bitterly cold, the coldest January since 1963. Weeks of frost, freezing fog, hailstorms, sleet and snow were followed in early February by a combination of a sudden thaw and heavy rain that produced widespread flooding. And then came yet more blizzards. In Scotland there were reports of beer freezing in pub cellars and of frozen waves in Oban harbour as the temperature plunged to −25° Celsius, while the whole country's transport system struggled to cope. Heath had at least been lucky with the weather in 1973–74; Callaghan was not. 'Let those who possess industrial muscle or monopoly power resolve not to abuse their great strength,' he had pleaded in his New Year's message. 'Individual greed and disregard for the well-being of others can undermine and divide our society.' His call fell on deaf ears and the New Year started instead with strikes by the drivers of oil tankers and lorries. A series of one-day stoppages by rail workers and even by short-haul British Airways pilots added to the problems.

Within days there was a fuel shortage, with just one petrol station reported open in Liverpool and with prices inflating daily from the existing 75p a gallon up to £2 and even £3 in some places. The AA warned drivers not to undertake long journeys: 'They probably won't be able to get back, because the situation is grim in many areas.' Flying pickets sealed off the ports to lorries coming from abroad and fears of imminent food shortages sparked a wave of panic buying, many taking advantage of the deep-freezes that had become part of every middle-class household over the previous few years. Two million workers were threatened with being laid off if the strikes continued, pigs were reported to be resorting to cannibalism as food supplies to farms ran low, supermarkets began rationing essentials such as butter and sugar, and newspapers shrank in size as supplies of newsprint dwindled.

Callaghan missed the onset of all this, being out of the country on a six-day trip to a summit meeting of Western leaders, a meeting which – to add insult to injury – was being held on the agreeably warm Caribbean island of Guadeloupe. His absence was duly noted, generally with an appropriately British reference to the weather. 'Britain could well be on the brink of a disaster that will make Ted's three-day week seem like a golden age,' raged the *Sun*. 'Meanwhile Jim yawns lazily on his tropic isle.'

He returned on 10 January to be met at the airport by journalists demanding to hear his comments on the mounting chaos in the country. Adopting the reassuring, emollient attitude that had served him so well over the years, he dismissed such concerns as being parochial in their vision: 'I don't think that other people in the world would share the view that there is mounting chaos,' he said cheerily. For once he got it completely and stupidly wrong, misjudging the mood of a freezing, fed-up nation with catastrophic consequences.

CRISIS? WHAT CRISIS? mocked the headline in the *Sun* the next day, with withering scorn; 'Sun-tanned premier Jim Callaghan breezed back into Britain yesterday and asked: Crisis? What Crisis?' And, although Callaghan had not uttered the phrase, had not even used the word 'crisis', the expression attached itself to him instantly and came to symbolize his premiership in the popular memory, his apparent dislocation from reality, in much the same way as Marie Antoinette will for ever be remembered as saying 'Let them eat cake.' (She, of course, was also misquoted.) For several days the *Sun* ran a ticker tape across the top of its news pages with the words WHAT CRISIS? repeated over and over again, and it passed into other newspapers so that within a couple of weeks it had become the accepted shorthand to refer to the alleged indifference of the Labour movement to the people's suffering. The formulation also became the key to Mike Yarwood's impression of Callaghan: 'I portrayed him as permanently believing that everything in the garden was lovely – "Strike? What strike?"'

The phrase, however, was not new. It had been used as a newspaper headline as far back as December 1973 when the *Daily Mail* had run a pair of linked articles by the humorists Frank Muir and Benny Green, trying to have some fun in a previous winter of industrial disruption. Even the *Sun* itself had used the same headline in a 1974 article, trailing a television programme in which David Dimbleby looked at American portrayals of contemporary Britain. And since then it had turned up as the title of the fourth album by the progressive-pop band Supertramp, which reached the top 20 in late 1975. The cover showed a man wearing bathing trunks and sitting in a deckchair under a sunshade, while behind him sprawled a bleak, grey industrial landscape.

In fact, the phrase derived ultimately from Kenneth Ross's screenplay for the 1973 movie adaptation of Frederick Forsyth's novel *The Day of the Jackal*. The terrorist group who are planning to assassinate Charles de Gaulle allocate to a female member the task of becoming the mistress of a senior official, so that they may keep track of the government's movements. He stumbles into her apartment one evening, muttering his apologies for being late. 'I didn't go out,' she says, 'I just sat waiting for you to call.' 'It was impossible,' he replies, 'there was a crisis on.' At which stage she utters the immortal words: 'Crisis? What crisis?' 'Never mind,' he answers, as though he can expunge the phrase from the record. But she continues to ask as she begins her seduction of him.

If 'Crisis? What crisis?' had already been common currency back in the final throes of the Heath government, what of the other phrase that became indelibly associated with those early months of 1979: the winter of discontent? Since it came from Shakespeare (the opening line of *Richard III*), the expression was already part of the language, so that, for example, Roy Jenkins could employ it as an image in a 1973 speech bemoaning the

Labour Party's poor performance in by-elections: 'There is something very wrong indeed with an opposition party which in mid-term and in the winter of the government's discontent cannot do better than this.' In terms of Fleet Street and industrial disputes, however, it too came to prominence during Heath's darkest days: THE WINTER OF OUR DISCONTENT read the headline in London's *Evening Standard* in February 1974, shortly before the election that saw the Conservatives removed from office. Again, though, it was the *Sun* that revived and popularized the expression in early 1979, and from then on it became the standard expression for Callaghan's last winter.

Thus did 1978–79 adopt the linguistic imagery – and eclipse the memory – of 1973–74, so that the Labour Party became associated with all the ills of 1970s Britain, as though the pre-Thatcher Tories had never really existed, or rather as though they had been closet socialists all along. In future years the phrase 'the winter of discontent' would frequently prompt confused memories of the three-day week, alongside the genuine events of the Callaghan era.

Those events were to take a turn for the worse as January 1979 wore on. The transport strikes seemed like a return to the bad old days of all-powerful union leaders, especially when the lorry drivers' dispute was made official by the TGWU, a fact that was damaging enough to a Labour government whose perceived job was to work in partnership with the unions, but there was more to come. The campaigns for pay rises of up to 40 per cent in private industry emboldened those in the public sector. Strikes by the low-paid employees of local authorities began to kick in by the end of the month, and suddenly it became not merely a grim acceptance of food and petrol shortages but something much more personal and emotive. 'It was a nightmare,' recalled Labour cabinet minister Peter Shore. 'No one, in their wildest dreams, could have predicted such collective barbarity.' Rubbish again began piling up in public places, schools closed for weeks on end for want of a caretaker, and hospitals found themselves at the mercy of picket lines composed of porters and cleaning staff.

This latter was not entirely new. The previous year Tory MP Norman Tebbit had found, to his fury, that his wife was refused treatment at their local hospital because 'some NHS maintenance workers were in dispute and were refusing to allow the admission of new "non-urgent" cases. It was their clinical judgement which over-rode that of my wife's doctors.' Now such stories became commonplace. So extreme did the disputes over medical care become that one orthopaedic consultant, Patrick Chesterman – sick of seeing patients turned away by pickets – staged a one-day protest of his own, refusing to treat trade unionists.

But still it became worse, with London's ambulance staff staging a work-to-rule. Even those who regarded themselves as sympathetic to Labour were feeling desperate. 'The piles of uncollected rubbish are now being blown apart by the wind and central Soho looks like a tip from which buildings emerge,' wrote Michael Palin in his diary, while Peter Hall went further: 'We are a society of greed and anarchy: no honour, no responsibility, no pride. I sound like an old reactionary, which I'm not, but what we have now isn't socialism, it's fascism with those who have power injuring those who do not.'

And then came the image that, above all others, was to dominate the folk memory of that winter. THEY WON'T EVEN LET US BURY OUR DEAD shuddered the front page of the *Daily Mail* in disbelief. The story concerned the gravediggers and crematorium workers employed by Liverpool City Council, who as members of NUPE were on strike with their colleagues. The consequence, it was reported, was that some two hundred corpses had had to be embalmed and were waiting in a temporary mortuary in a disused factory, while the area medical officer suggested that burial at sea might yet become an option. The absolute anger that the story provoked was sufficient to convince the strikers to return to work, while in Sedgefield, it was reported, a similar dispute also ended when the bereaved members of two families themselves dug graves for their deceased relatives. Thereafter, no account of the period was complete without reference to the story. 'Our society was sick – morally, socially and economically,' commented Thatcher in 1981. 'Children were locked out of school; patients were prevented from having hospital treatment; the old were left unattended in their wheelchairs; the dead were not buried; and flying pickets patrolled the motorways.'

But even without the gravediggers, the events of January and February 1979 were a disaster for Callaghan. 'The sheer viciousness and nastiness of unions such as NUPE in the hospital service was displayed day after day on every TV screen in the land,' wrote Tebbit in his memoirs, 'as the sick, the old and little children were kicked around in a dirty fight between the government and the trades union wings of the Labour Party.' For the first time, since these were disputes in services rather than manufacturing, it was the most vulnerable in society who could be reported as being hurt by industrial militancy – this was viewed not as a class but a moral issue. A Gallup poll found that the unions had reached a level of unpopularity unknown since such surveys had first started forty years earlier; 44 per cent even thought the very existence of unions was a bad thing. In the opinion polls, meanwhile, the Tories had opened up a nineteen-point lead over Labour, overturning the three-point lead Labour had held as recently as December.

For the one person who had a good winter of discontent was Margaret Thatcher. She had been preaching about the follies of governmental pay policies – the immediate cause of the current disruption – and against the abuse of trade union powers for some time, and now it appeared as though her stance was vindicated. MORI found that 91 per cent of trade unionists supported her view that any strike should be preceded by a compulsory postal ballot of union members. Although her own employment spokesman, Jim Prior, and many other Heathite Tories disagreed with her entire stance, she had some support from her future chancellor Geoffrey Howe, who argued that union reform was essential to ensure that 'it is much less easy for so many of their leaders to continue the pursuit of socialism, regardless of the wishes of their members'. She pressed on, calling for social security benefits for strikers to be abolished. The tougher she sounded, the more public support she got. 'If someone is confronting our essential liberties and inflicting injury and hardship on the sick, the elderly and children,' she declared defiantly, 'then, by God, I will confront them.'

A year earlier Peter Shore had warned that she was a serious threat, capable of connecting with the public on a gut level: 'Mrs Thatcher is beginning to reflect a genuine English nationalist feeling, a deep feeling about the English and how they see themselves in terms of their own history.' And Tony Benn had agreed: 'What she is doing is long-range shelling deep behind our lines, attacking things we had assumed were already part of the consensus. There is a danger she will be political and we will be managerial.' Now she was indeed responding politically, and Labour didn't look capable even of being managerial. The 5 per cent pay policy was being revised upwards almost daily, and no matter what figure was arrived at, no one believed any more that it stood a chance of sticking. Freed from the restraints of the previous three years, there was a stampede of millions who had seen their wages fall behind prices and were determined to remedy the situation, heedless – it appeared – of political, personal and social consequence. In the ten months that led up to the general election of May 1979, some 13.5 million days were lost to strikes, more than in any single year of any Labour government, and comparable to the rates of industrial action in the early days of Heath. Now it was genuinely becoming a commonplace question: What was the point of a Labour government? 'We've stumbled,' admitted Callaghan in a TV interview, and if that hardly did justice to the situation, it was at least a franker admission of the situation than that offered by many on the left, who insisted that the crisis was largely the creation of a hostile media. 'If anything was ever talked up,' commented Dennis Skinner, years later, 'it was that so-called winter of discontent.' Benn had much the same perspective, noting in his diary: 'We are in an atmosphere of siege and crisis which the media are continuing to play up.'

If trade union militancy was the backdrop to the coming election, the immediate cause was the return of the nationalist question. The referendums on devolved government that had been promised in the Scotland Act and the Wales Act were held on 1 March 1979 with mixed results. In Wales the proposal was simply thrown out, by a majority of four to one of those voting, while in Scotland a narrow majority (51.6 per cent) voted in favour of devolution. This was not, however, anywhere near enough to meet the requirement that 40 per cent of the entire electoral roll should support the move, and both Acts were subsequently repealed by Parliament, provoking fury amongst nationalist MPs and precipitating the downfall of the Callaghan administration.

The Conservative Party tabled a motion of no confidence in the government, hoping that all the minor parties would now rally to their side. And on 28 March, a packed House of Commons heard Michael Foot wind up the debate in one of the great parliamentary speeches, made all the more memorable for being also heard by the nation, full radio broadcasts of the House having commenced the previous year. Mocking both Thatcher and David Steel (the Lib-Lab pact had come to an end), he described her 'leading her troops into battle snugly concealed behind a Scottish nationalist shield, with the boy David holding her hand', and he warned the nationalists that they would suffer at the polls should they side against the government. It was all in vain, for the opposition parties held firm. By a single vote the Commons declared that they had no confidence in the government, and a general election was duly called, to be held on 3 May 1979, the only time in the century that an administration had fallen on such a vote.

Going into that election, some on the Labour side took comfort from the fact that Callaghan was still far ahead of Thatcher in the polls when it came to individual popularity, forgetting perhaps that incumbent prime ministers, being familiar figures, generally do have the edge over untried leaders of the opposition. Others, most notably Tony Benn, were outraged by the way that Callaghan exercised a personal veto over the contents of the manifesto, striking out – in particular – any commitment to the abolition of the House of Lords. And even then, he 'never mentioned the manifesto at all', instead concentrating on his own personal appeal. Here was another crime to be added to the charge sheet being compiled by those who felt that the party lacked internal democracy. But even if the Lords commitment had been included, it is hard to see how it could have swung over sufficient votes.

For the truth was that it was Thatcher's moment. Callaghan and his colleagues looked tired and ineffectual, entirely lacking in ideas for the future, while the Tory leadership was reinvigorated and had the supreme value of looking new. Whatever else she might have been, Thatcher was very clearly a different proposition from Heath, Wilson or Callaghan, and to a nation wearily accustomed to settling for second-best, she at least talked of aspiration and achievement. And she bristled with challenges to the orthodoxy that had held the nation in its grasp for a quarter of a century, even if her own party did not realize it. 'We do not pretend to be the repositories of doctrines or principles which are absolutely true and have to be carried to their logical conclusion,' Conservative MP Julian Amery had written in the early days of Thatcher's leadership, but he was wrong: her party was doctrinaire in a way that none had been since Labour in 1945.

Whether that message was fully understood is doubtful, for this was primarily a case of a government losing an election rather than the opposition having to win one. But the Conservatives made the most of their brief, and their success came in the context of fighting Labour on its own ground. Just as the phraseology of 'Crisis? What crisis?' and 'the winter of discontent' had been appropriated from the Heath years, so the Tories borrowed the clothes of left-radical politics from a decade earlier, arguing for individual liberty and freedom from the state (though the state was here defined to include the TUC). Their poster campaign, prepared by the newly founded advertising firm Saatchi & Saatchi, focused on the key Labour issues of health, education and unemployment, with the slogans 'Britain isn't getting any better', 'Educashun isn't working' and – most famously – 'Labour isn't working'. The last of these featured a depiction of a dole queue snaking away into the distance, to reflect the fact that there were then 1.3 million unemployed in the country, though the people in the photograph were actually members of Hendon Young Conservatives. But the slogan that expressed the national mood most effectively was the more general 'Cheer up, they can't last for ever'.

The chaos of January and February played heavily in the election, reviving all the fears of rampant trade unionism that had dominated popular perceptions of politics for the previous decade or more. In the words of Shirley Williams: 'The crisis had changed from "Who governs?" to "Who can control the unions?"' And the answer was: not Labour. Thatcher not only articulated anti-union sentiments (even winning over a substantial number of union members), but brought them together with a deeper underlying sense that things had been going wrong ever since the 1960s. Those who were uncomfortable with permissiveness, with pornography, with anti-police propaganda, with rising levels of violence, with immigration and with multiculturalism found in Thatcher a party leader in whom they could place their trust, a semi-domesticated Enoch Powell crossed with a less cranky Mary Whitehouse. The fact that she also shared with Powell a faith in the obscure doctrine of monetarism meant little one way or the other; what was important was that she seemed to have tapped into the nostalgia that permeated the '70s, harking back to better, more peaceful times.

In James Herbert's 1978 novel *The Spear*, an MI5 agent who is part of a neo-Nazi plot to take over Britain had denied that he and his comrades were revolutionaries: 'What we're talking about is *counter*-revolution. The revolution is already taking place. We intend to oppose it.' Benn was unconsciously to echo the thought, arguing that Thatcherism 'was a counter-revolution against democracy'.

The result of the election was unequivocal. The Conservatives won sixty-two more seats than did Labour, and became the first party to secure a comfortable government majority since Heath in 1970, while the Liberals and the nationalists suffered, just as Foot had predicted they would. As she stood on the steps of 10 Downing Street, Thatcher turned to the assembled media and shared with the nation a prayer by St Francis of Assisi: 'Where there is discord, may we bring harmony. Where there is error, may we bring truth. Where there is doubt, may we bring faith. And where there is despair, may we bring hope.' It was, snorted Jim Prior, 'the most awful humbug'. Worse than that, it turned out that it wasn't even a genuine work by St Francis at all, but rather a nineteenth-century imitation.

Perhaps that fraudulent note is the appropriate place to leave the politics of the 1970s, as the nation entered its new, Thatcherite era. Or perhaps one should end with the last-ever episode of *Fawlty Towers*, which should have been broadcast during the election campaign but which, rather appropriately, was delayed for seven months by industrial action at the BBC. In 'Basil the Rat', Manuel's pet rodent, which he's convinced is a Siberian hamster, escapes and runs wild in the hotel. In what was virtually the final shot of the series we see a health inspector confronted by the sight of the rat in a tin of cheese biscuits, the great symbol of '70s urban decay having finally broken into the most domestic of settings.

Better still, leaving the decade where it began, one should look to the England football team. In November 1979 Don Revie, having returned from the Middle East, initiated a court case in an attempt to overturn the ten-year ban on management that had been handed down by the FA in retaliation for his moonlight flit. For eighteen days the bloated, decaying corpse of the English football administration was dissected and pored over in the high courts, bringing nothing but shame and embarrassment to all concerned. And at the end of it all, the judge found in favour of Revie, even though his sympathies clearly lay with the FA; he rescinded the ban, while denouncing Revie's actions as 'a sensational and notorious example of disloyalty, breach of duty, discourtesy and selfishness'.

Despite the judgment, Revie never managed a club in Britain again. But on the field of play the England team ended the decade on something of a high, qualifying in style for their first major tournament since 1970. In their first game of the 1980 European Championship, staged in Italy, they played Belgium and drew 1–1, but the match was marred when English fans turned violent, attacking Italian spectators who had the audacity to cheer the Belgian equalizer. Play had to be suspended as the riot police waded into the crowd and as England's goalkeeper, Ray Clemence, collapsed under the influence of the tear gas drifting out from the stands and onto the pitch. It was not an auspicious start for the return to international competition. And England, of course, failed to progress in the tournament. Some things, it seemed, had not changed.

Outro
Farewell
'It's cold outside'

In Margaret Thatcher's first major television interview after her election as prime minister, with Brian Walden on *Weekend World*, she offered her own, slightly unorthodox, interpretation of Jesus' best-known parable. 'No one would remember the Good Samaritan if he'd only had good intentions,' she remarked; 'he had money as well.' And this, she said, confirmed her vision of the society she wished to build, a society that eschewed the socialist dream of egalitarianism and offered instead the natural elitism of a meritocracy. 'If opportunity and talent is unequally distributed, then allowing people to exercise that talent and opportunity means more inequality, but it also means you drag up the poor people, because there are the resources to do so.'

She was not the only one to draw lessons from the parable. In his memoirs, the veteran left-winger Ian Mikardo celebrated the frequently derided figure of the political activist, as opposed to the much-vaunted silent majority. The latter he characterized as: 'the people who stay silent, who don't utter a word of protest against the fruits of social injustice and deprivation; or against the system which hoards mountains of food in cold stores in rich countries whilst millions starve in the waste-lands; or against the erosion for company profit of the world's natural resources, and the pollution of its air and its rivers and its oceans; or against the slide towards nuclear war and nuclear winter and nuclear holocaust'. He concluded: 'The Good Samaritan was an activist: those who passed by on the other side were members of the silent majority.'

There was yet another interpretation of the Good Samaritan, this time from the one serious student of the New Testament in the House of Commons. Enoch Powell insisted the story had to be understood in the historical context of those who heard it first, an audience who would have understood the racial relationship between the Jews and the Samaritans: 'If the parable has a "moral", it is that Jews and Samaritans should remember that they are not merely neighbours (literally) but kinsmen.'

As ever, Powell's was something of a maverick position. But the gap between Thatcher and Mikardo – each claiming the Good Samaritan as, variously, a man of property or a radical activist – symbolised the split in British politics as it entered the new decade. And that split was about to grow ever wider.

The divisions that resulted and were manifest in social and cultural, as well as political terms are chronicled in another book, *Rejoice! Rejoice!*, which covers the period of Thatcher's premiership. So powerful a grip did she exert on the public consciousness of Britain during her time in office, both at home and abroad, that in retrospect perceptions of the 1970s have been changed. Where once the era was seen as a bitter comedown from the heady excitement of the Swinging Sixties, it has since been recast by some as being simply a prelude to the traumatic upheavals of the subsequent decade, a disruptive moment that created the conditions for the necessary changes to come. In either event, it emerges merely as a transition phase; if not quite a bridge, then perhaps an ill-lit, graffitied underpass between two bigger, brasher, more self-advertising eras. Some decades are louder than others, and the voice of the 1970s is frequently drowned out by its noisy neighbours. Elsewhere, depictions of the popular culture of the time have sometimes seemed rooted in an ironic celebration of Space Hoppers, Spangles and Smash.

There is some truth in these perceptions, but they tell only a part of the story. Culturally, the 1970s was indeed seen at the time as amounting to little more than the leftovers from the previous decade. Many of the era's rock stars, for example – most notably David Bowie, Marc Bolan and Rod Stewart – had been releasing records unsuccessfully for almost as long as the Beatles and the Rolling Stones and were much the same age; each of those three singers had released four albums before finally breaking into the top ten. 'The ones who got into glam were the losers of our generation,' was pop producer Jonathan King's perception; 'they used to tag along.' But the music that emerged has proved remarkably durable, not simply glam but also heavy metal and punk. Even if the sales of records were incomparable, nearly four decades later there were more bands in the world drawing from the work of Black Sabbath and the Sex Pistols than from that of either the Beatles or the Stones. The pattern was repeated elsewhere. *Monty Python's Flying Circus*, the members of which had likewise failed to become household names in the 1960s, still exerts a powerful influence over sketch comedy in Britain. And stand-up comedy continues to build to the blueprint drawn by Billy Connolly and Jasper Carrott, veterans of the folk-club circuit, part of the same generation as the rock stars and both in their thirties by the time they became successful.

A parallel process could be found in politics. The forward march of liberalism had been halted by the counter-revolution of 1968, manifest in such diverse events as the crushing of the Prague Spring by the Soviet Union, the assassinations of Martin Luther King and Robert Kennedy, the overwhelming electoral victory of the Gaullists in France and Richard Nixon in America, and the popular response to Enoch Powell's 'Rivers of Blood' speech in Britain. As the self-proclaimed forces of progress splintered, the resultant pieces were generally considered to be marginal to the mainstream of political activity. The launch in 1972 of the magazines *Spare Rib* and *Gay News* didn't make much of a stir at the time; the repercussions, however, were profound and transformed both the country and its politics, such that, forty years on, a Conservative-led coalition government announced legislation to permit same-sex marriages. From Britain's perspective the biggest political event of the decade – the entry into the European Community, confirmed by the subsequent referendum – was also an issue left hanging from the 1960s. The effects of that decision too continued to reverberate.

In short, much of what was then seen as being a postscript to the 1960s turned out to be the foundation of modern Britain. The 1970s was a period not of transition but of transformation.

Nor was it the case that the decade was just a protracted setting of the scene for the advent of Margaret Thatcher, though that has become orthodoxy in some quarters. With the ending of Empire, the 1970s saw modern Britain's fondness for bemoaning the state of the nation come to fruition, and a note of gloomy declinism became a familiar part of the national identity. There were plenty of commentators – then and subsequently – eager to echo the perspective of Airey Neave, the Conservative MP who helmed Thatcher's challenge for the party leadership: 'The country is on the verge of revolution,' he wrote in his diary of October 1974. Thatcher herself was less apocalyptic but equally gloomy: 'This is the twilight of the middle class,' she observed around the same time.

The truth was a little more prosaic and a little more positive. For most of the country, for most of the decade, times were really quite good. In retrospect, the 1970s can look like a period of comparative calm and stability. It was still possible for an average working-class family to live on a single wage, very few were required to work anti-social hours, and housing was affordable for most. Many of the problems that were identified – unemployment, the balance of trade, youth violence, unassimilated immigration, environmental degradation, pornography, drugs – appeared dramatic then, but were to become far worse in subsequent decades.

There were two key exceptions to this in the public sphere. First, the widespread phenomenon of industrial conflict was never again to reach the same levels as it did in the 1970s, once the Thatcher government introduced the restrictions on trade union activity previously attempted by Harold Wilson and Edward Heath. This came, however, at a price; an active union movement had ensured that pay and conditions improved for most of the workforce during the 1970s, as well as helping to provide a level of job security that was soon to disappear entirely.

And second, inflation had also peaked; the problem was not easily solved but by the mid-1990s, it had finally been brought under control. Even here, though, the picture had been painted too starkly. The conditions bequeathed by Edward Heath's government had seen historically high levels of inflation, but the situation was nowhere near catastrophic enough to warrant the rhetoric employed by some. 'Unchecked inflation could destroy the mature democracies in the contemporary world as it did the Weimar Republic between the wars,' warned Conservative MP Norman St John-Stevas in 1974, and the Liberal John Pardoe was one of many who shared the same fears, suggesting 'the smell of the Weimar Republic is in the air'.

Such comments were themselves absurdly inflated, and one can discern if not quite a note of scaremongering, then at least a relish in talking up what was seen as social disintegration. And perhaps this was only to be expected, for among those who felt most threatened by the unions were the two groups who specialized in generating comment and opinion: politicians, who feared a rival power-base, and journalists, who worked in an industry plagued by restrictive practices and union militancy. The two groups had a mutual interest in seeing the worst. Herein lay the roots of the belief that drastic action needed to be taken if Britain was to survive as a democracy, that the country was sliding into anarchy until the intervention of Margaret Thatcher, and that she thus became – to use a phrase much bandied about after her death in 2013 – 'the woman who saved Britain'.

But the Thatcherite revolution was neither obvious nor inevitable. Had James Callaghan called a general election in the autumn of 1978, as was widely expected, he would probably have been returned to power. And the Conservative Party would have been extremely unlikely to have given Thatcher the kind of leeway accorded to Edward Heath when he lost elections in 1966 and 1974; the chances are that she would have been removed and replaced by a more emollient figure such as William Whitelaw or Peter Walker, her leadership to be remembered as a bizarre, dead-end episode in Tory history.

In terms of economic performance, the consequences would have turned out much the same: Britain, despite following the monetarist path embarked upon by Callaghan in 1976, would still have continued its slow slide down the international league tables, just as it actually did under the long Tory government. And even in the short-term, although there might have been a difference in degree, the early years of the 1980s would still have seen a major recession and a rapid growth in unemployment, since these were largely the product of a global slump and the arrival in the workforce of a huge wave of school-leavers. But without Thatcher's constant railing against the reality of national decline, the tone and culture of the country would have been very different.

In a celebrated sketch on the BBC's *Not the Nine O'Clock News* in 1979, Rowan Atkinson parodied the Thatcherite approach: 'If it doesn't work, then we'll be more than prepared to revert to the old, liberal, wishy-washy, nigger-loving, red, left-wing, homosexual commie ways of the recent past. But please, let's have a chance . . .' That the chance existed was primarily due to Callaghan's miscalculation the previous year. Without it, the polarization of politics and culture would have been far less marked.

Which is not to say that the divisions were caused by one side alone. At the opening of the new Parliament in 1979, Tony Benn shared an ice-war moment with Heath, inadvertently borrowing one of the adjectives from that list of Atkinson's Tory: 'I said I had some sympathy with Thatcher – with her dislike of the wishy-washy centre of British politics. He gave me such a frosty look that I daresay I had touched a raw nerve.'

The question of what would have happened to the Labour Party had Callaghan been re-elected in 1978 is less clear than the impact on the other side. In reality, the growing anger among activists exploded in the wake of the actual election defeat, plunging the party into a bout of fratricidal blood-letting without parallel in modern times, and ultimately leading to a split on the left with the creation of the Social Democratic Party. How much of that anger might have been contained had Labour remained in office is debatable, but it would surely have erupted at some point.

Meanwhile, the huge wave of public support for the SDP on its launch in 1981 suggested much of the country had a yearning for the old 'wishy-washy centre' after all. Asked to choose between, on the one hand, a right-wing government that was presiding over an appallingly deep recession and, on the other, a left-wing opposition widely perceived to be more extreme than any that had gone before – between Margaret Thatcher and Michael Foot – more than half the respondents in opinion polls opted instead for the calm reassurance offered by Roy Jenkins, in alliance with the youthful, non-aligned enthusiasm of David Steel. There were many, on both left and right, who wanted to believe that 1979 was Britain's Year Zero; that the future could not be built on the scorched earth of the centre ground. The electorate, however, begged to differ. Already there was a sense that change was happening too quickly; the country was leaving its comfort zone, and the dogmatic assertions of neither side were winning much favour. Social democracy, however unfashionable in Westminster and Fleet Street, still had an attraction.

That highpoint of SDP support lasted barely a year, culminating in the return to Parliament of Jenkins, elected as MP for Glasgow Hillhead in a by-election of March 1982. A week later, the military dictatorship of Argentina staged an invasion of the Falkland Islands, and normal politics was temporarily suspended as British armed forces attempted to recapture the territory.

In terms of the country as a whole, the Falklands War was of little lasting significance. Public support for the action was overwhelming but interest proved short-lived and, although the retaking of the islands was an impressive and swift military operation, the fact remained that more British servicemen had been killed in Northern Ireland in the 1970s than died in the Falklands. The conflict did, however, allow the prime minister to tap into one of the great cultural themes of recent years: nostalgia for the certainties of the Second World War, a celebration of the myths surrounding 1940. Draping herself in Churchillian colours, Thatcher argued that victory in the South Pacific was a harbinger of the great days that still lay ahead for Britain, that the nation had rediscovered its soul and its historic mission. For just long enough, sufficient numbers of former Conservative voters were convinced by the rhetoric of the past, tempted back into the fold to defeat a divided left. And the hopes for a return to consensual, centrist politics were deflated.

That outcome was not a foregone conclusion. On 20 May 1982, the night before the British troops landed on East Falkland, Enoch Powell and Tony Benn – the two men who had embodied the long struggle against the consensus, who had fought to imprint their own separate visions on the country and who had faced all the consequent desolation and dejection – met once more, this time in a lavatory in the House of Commons. 'As we stood side by side,' recorded Benn, 'I said: "Well, Enoch, we may disagree about what we should do but our analysis is the same – they are selling out."'

References

Note: References taken from personal communication are indicated here by the letters 'pc'.

Title page
p. v **We're living** – Leslie Bricusse & Anthony Newley, Rondor Music, 1972; **Howard turns** – Bradbury, *The History Man* p. 18; *Titanic* – Chappell, *Rising Damp*, 'The Good Samaritans' 1977

Intro: Seventies
p. x **New Economics Foundation** – www.neweconomics.org/gen/news_mdp.aspx; **as I might** – Cato, *Crash Course for the Ravers* p. 125
p. xi **well chuffed** – ibid. p. 19; **cigarette butts** – author's memory; **consumed arts** – *Daily Mail* 7 January 1978; **18.6 hours** – ibid. 1 December 1971; **22 hours** – ibid. 4 January 1978; **over 95 per cent** – Adonis & Pollard, *A Class Act* p. 223
p. xii **until 1977** – Butler & Sloman, *British Political Facts 1900–1979* p. 462; **always impartial** – Brian Whitaker, *News Limited* p. 20
p. xiii **trivialization** – *Daily Mail* 12 November 1971; **staggering** – Powell, *No Easy Answers* p. 84

Part One: Hang On To Yourself: 1970–74
p. 1 **our difficulties** – Benn, *Office Without Power* p. 232; **Affluence** – Pawley, *The Private Future* p. 13; **Tory saying** – Tony Marsh, *The Sweeney*, 'Jackpot'

1: The Heath Years
p. 3 **master plan** – Sullivan, *Citizen Smith*, 'Spanish Fly' 1979; **swinging London** – *Sunday Times* 20 January 1974; **'70s** – Pete Townshend, *Melody Maker*, 12 December 1970; **Huddersfield Town** – Wilson, *Memoirs* p. 9
p. 4 **date for the election** – Benn, *Office Without Power* p. 249; **cup final** – Boyson (ed.), *Right Turn* p. 89
p. 5 **international incident** – Hunt, *World Cup Stories* p. 126; **the beginning** – ibid. p. 143; **political effect** – Benn op. cit. p. 289
p. 6 **strange reversals** – *Times* 18 June 1970; **haunting feeling** – Castle, *Diaries 1964–70* p. 805; **explaining** – *Daily Mirror* 19 June 1970; **voted Labour** – *Sun* 20 June 1970; **union movement** – Heffer, *Never A Yes Man* p. 135
p. 7 **City of London** – Dennis Skinner (pc); **fed up** – Stewart, *Protest or Power?* p. 14; **two evils** – *Sun* 23 April 1970; **In an era** – *Daily Mirror* 1 June 1970; **a pipe** – *Daily Mail* 17 June 1970; **Selsdon Man** – Pimlott, *Harold Wilson* p. 553

p. 8 **populism** – Thatcher, *The Path to Power* p. 160; **campaign poster** – Campbell, *Edward Heath* p. 274; **Edgar Broughton Band** – Peter Jenner (pc); **people say** – *Daily Telegraph* 1 October 1970; **hidden wish** – Campbell op. cit. p. 295; **visited the set** – *Daily Mirror* 13 January 1978

p. 9 **decadent people** – Campbell op. cit. p. 254; **feared** – Hennessy, *The Prime Minister* p. 342; **malice** – *Times*, 1 December 1973; **achievement** – Yarwood, *And This Is Me!* p. 157

p. 10 **Millions of gallons** – *Daily Telegraph* 5 October 1970; **Downing Street** – *Times* 2 November 1970

p. 11 **non-inflationary** – *Times* 6 November 1970; **Driving home** – Tebbit, *Upwardly Mobile* p. 102; **unofficial** – Coates, *The Crisis of Labour* p. 63; **a crime** – Gormley, *Battered Cherub* p. 93

p. 12 **seven-thirty** – Steve Jones (pc); **conviction could mean** – *Daily Telegraph* 14 February 1972; **potential gravity** – ibid. 15 February 1972

p. 13 **remaining source** – ibid. 11 February 1972; **living proof** – Routledge, *Scargill* p. 73; **battlefield** – Clarke, *The Shadow of a Nation* p. 107; **victory for violence** – Thatcher op. cit. p. 218; **power cut** – Prior, *A Balance of Power* p. 73

p. 14 **national strike** – Gormley op. cit. p. 95; **great strikes** – Rigelsford, *The Doctors* p. 96; **one of the leaders** – Dicks, *Doctor Who and the Monster of Peladon* p. 20; **I believe** – Gormley op. cit. p. 89

p. 15 **absolutely sick** – Benn op. cit. p. 239; **boat is sunk** – Benn op. cit. p. 301; **use the crisis** – Benn, *Against the Tide* p. 66; **not much good** – Campbell, *Roy Jenkins* p. 152

p. 16 **One estimate** – *Times* 2 May 1972; **The nation** – Stewart op. cit. p. 17; ***The Grocer*** – *Daily Mirror* 7 January 1972

p. 17 **street numbering** – *Sunday Express* 7 June 1970; **six weeks** – James Herbert (pc)

p. 18 **I would like** – Tebbit op. cit. p. 114; **a captain** – Van Greenaway, *The Man Who Held the Queen to Ransom* p. 88; **ashamed** – *Daily Mirror* 21 January 1971; **U-turn** – Benn, *Office Without Power* p. 417

p. 19 **It is fatal** – *Times* 8 November 1972; **rallied reluctantly** – Tebbit op. cit. p. 128; **in the mind** – ibid. p. 126; **cold-shouldered** – Thatcher op. cit. p. 225; **socialist country** – Childs, *Britain Since 1945* p. 235; **Israel's intransigence** – ibid. p. 236; **Arab Oil** – *Daily Telegraph* 19 November 1973

p. 20 **world underdog** – *Daily Mail* 6 December 1973; **the principle** – *Sun* 14 January 1974; **fingers crossed** – *Times* 19 December 1973

p. 21 **three-day spirit** – *Sunday Times* 20 January 1974; **switch on** – *Daily Telegraph* 17 February 1972; **SOS** – *Sun* 18 January 1974; **one room** – *Daily Mail* 28 December 1973; **The suggestion** – *Sun* 19 January 1974; **help the government** – *Daily Mail* 19 December 1973

p. 22 **Bad news** – Hall, *Diaries* p. 70; **sales of wines** – *Daily Mail* 13 December 1973; **disastrous period** – Holder, *Who's Crazee Now?* p. 190; **moved to England** – Russell Mael (pc)

p. 23 **economic crisis** – *Times* 1 January 2005; **colonial masters** – *Times* 31 December 1973

p. 24 **same course** – Weight, *Patriots* p. 537; **early days** – Benn op. cit. p. 247; **Bernard Levin** – *Times* 25 October 1977

Bowie lyrics published Mainman/Chrysalis, 1972–74

2: Rivals

p. 26 **wilder fringes** – *Daily Mirror* 3 January 1975; **hope** – Hall, *Diaries* p. 170; **noteworthy contenders** – Amis, *Memoirs* p. 198; **a politician** – *Sun* 21 May 1970

p. 27 **Press Association** – Shepherd, *Enoch Powell* p. 392; **on the country** – Crosland, *Tony Crosland* p. 210; **millions** – Wise, *Who Killed Enoch Powell?* p. 30; **the pattern** – ibid. p. 42

p. 28 **His vision** – ibid. pp. 121–2; **Frightening** – *Morning Telegraph*, quoted in blurb of Wise, *Who Killed Enoch Powell?*; **Order and Authority** – Roth, *Enoch Powell: Tory Tribune* p. 123

p. 29 **official policy** – Powell, *Freedom and Reality* pp. 213–19

p. 30 **racialist** – Shepherd, *Enoch Powell* p. 352; **overwhelming majority** – Powell op. cit. p. 227; **Gallup poll** – Smithies & Fiddick, *Enoch Powell on Immigration* p. 13; **Television programmes** – Hiro, *Black British, White British* p. 288; **clever people** – Powell op. cit. p. 230; **intellectuals** – Wise op. cit. p. 10; **once-bisexual** – Parris, *Chance Witness* p. 259; **can't do** – *Times* 1 December 1973

p. 31 **threat of division** – Shepherd op. cit. p. 393; **bit slow** – Muller, *The Lost Diaries of Albert Smith* p. 205; **excellent speaker** – ibid. p. 33; **We are lucky** – ibid. p. 264

p. 32 **without purpose** – Van Greenaway, *The Man Who Held the Queen to Ransom* p. 81; **impotent** – Barlow, *The Burden of Proof* p. 54; **They talked** – Palin, *Diaries* p. 63; **I hope** – *Times* 2 June 1970; **Bolts** – *Daily Mirror* 2 June 1970

p. 33 AMAZING ATTACK – *Sun* 4 June 1970; ENOCH PERIL – *Daily Mirror* 5 June 1970; BELSEN FLAG – *Daily Telegraph* 4 June 1970; **evil feature** – *Daily Mirror* 5 June 1970; **whole emphasis** – *Daily Telegraph* 5 June 1970; **Union Jack** – Wharton, *The Stretchford Chronicles* pp. 159–60; **grotesque exaggeration** – *Sun* 4 June 1970; **savage** – *Daily Mirror* 5 June 1970; **silly** – *Sun* 5 June 1970; **In 1939** – Shepherd op. cit. p. 395; **talks about money** – *Sun* 5 June 1970; **nonsense** – *Daily Mail* 15 June 1970

p. 34 **biggest mistake** – Shepherd op. cit. p. 401; **he is saying** – *Daily Express* 15 June 1970; DOUBLES HIS MAJORITY – *Sun* 19 June 1970; **would not say** – Clark, *Diaries* p. 19; **Commons** – Benn, *Against the Tide* p. 76

p. 35 **straight as a die** – Balham, *The Human Pipeline* p. 41; **Not their fault** – Yuill, *Hazell and the Menacing Jester* p. 62; **great energy** – Lenny Henry blog 10 September 2006: www.lennyhenry.com/home/blog_archive.aspx?id=84; **sounds daft** – Williams, *Ee, I've Had Some Laughs* p. 94; **Powell went** – Onyeama, *Book of Black Man's Humour* p. 29

p. 36 **seen crying** – ibid. p. 29; **weighty** – Williams-Ellis, *England and the Octopus* p. 9; **left-wing answer** – Crosland op. cit. p. 210; **insuperably difficult** – Powell, *No Easy Answers* p. 111

p. 37 **thoughtful lectures** – Benn, *Against the Tide* p. 486; **ambition** – Gilmour & Garnett, *Whatever Happened to the Tories*; **the motive** – Mitchell, *Four Years in the Death of the Labour Party* p. 30; **Tony fell out** – Foot, *Loyalists and Loners* p. 117; **way forward** – Benn, *Office Without Power* p. 285

p. 38 **significant development** – Benn, *Against the Tide* p. 61; **upper reaches** – Stewart, *Protest or Power?* p. 98; **come from below** – *Times* 1 June 1970; **Women's Lib** – Stewart op. cit. p. 100; **aristocratic disdain** – Chapple, *Sparks Fly!* p. 144; **profound contempt** – ibid. p. 145; **curious way** – Benn, *Against the Tide* p. 482; **upper-class** – Mitchell op. cit. p. 30; **weakness** – Ashton, *Red Rose Blues* p. 203

p. 39 **was transformed** – Foot op. cit. p. 110; **I had the idea** – Benn, *Office Without*

Power p. 443; **his background** – *Who's Who* (A&C Black, London, 1968–83); **older Tories** – Norman Tebbit (pc)

p. 40 **dangerous figure** – *Evening Standard* 27 February 1974; **Llew Gardner** – Benn, *Office Without Power* p. 443; **resort to anarchy** – *Times* 1 May 1972; **I think** – Benn, *Against the Tide* p. 148

p. 41 **immatures with age** – Powell, *Tony Benn* p. 121; **tasteless self-parody** – *Sunday Times* 6 January 1974; **genuine fear** – Benn, *Against the Tide* p. 486

p. 42 **spoken up** – Wise op. cit. p. 134

3: Environment

p. 43 **elil** – Adams, *Watership Down* p. 159; **Vicar** – Kneale, *The Stone Tape*; **pollution** – Clement & La Frenais, *Whatever Happened to the Likely Lads?*, 'Moving On' 1973; **rat population** – *Daily Telegraph* 6 October 1970

p. 44 **rotting garbage** – *Daily Mail* 11 March 1975; **biggest hazard** – *Sun* 9 April 1975; **dim shadows** – Herbert, *The Rats* p. 15; **invisible** – James Herbert (pc)

p. 45 **councils** – Herbert op. cit. p. 59

p. 46 **puppies** – *Times* 15 January 1975

p. 47 **fashionable** – ibid. 24 November 1978; **much the same** – ibid. 19 March 1975; **relative safety** – *Daily Mail* 7 November 1973; **offers smokers** – *News of the World* 10 July 1977; **disgusting insult** – Pawley, *The Private Future* p. 148

p. 48 **Gold Award** – *Daily Telegraph* 3 January 1977; **British smokers** – *Sun* 3 April 1975; **New Inn** – *Daily Mail* 10 November 1971; **the biggest** – *Times* 3 February 1968; **Brentford Nylons** – *Daily Telegraph* 30 November 2006; **£3.3 million** – *Times* 27 February 1976; **Lonrho directors** – ibid. 12 February 1982

p. 49 **The kids** – Rhodes & Knight, *The Art of Zandra Rhodes* p. 174; **a skirt** – *Daily Mirror* 3 January 1978; **temporary craze** – Prince Charles, speech in Cardiff 18 February 1970

p. 50 **sudden fad** – Schumacher, *Small Is Beautiful* p. 14; **overpopulation** – Prince Philip, foreword to Loraine, *The Death of Tomorrow*; **real challenge** – Benn, *Office Without Power* p. 399; **anti-democratic** – Crosland, *Tony Crosland* p. 257; **technological** – Chapple, *Sparks Fly!* p. 158

p. 51 **capital items** – Schumacher op. cit. p. 12; **great rhythms** – ibid. p. 186

p. 52 **rabbits** – Adams, *Watership Down* p. 261; *lingua franca* – ibid. p. 153; **Doomsday Disney** – *Daily Mail* 22 September 1977; **the good** – Adams, *The Plague Dogs* p. 27

p. 53 **no cruelty** – *Times* 3 April 1975; **William Molloy** – *Guardian* 7 March 1975; **Lady Parker** – *Times* 5 February 1975; **flood of letters** – *Sun* 3 April 1975; **volleyed** – Oakes, *Experiment at Proto* p. 97; **the chimpanzee** – ibid. p. 112; **oil companies** – Bryers, *Hollow Target* p. 174

p. 54 **Nature abhors** – Harris, *The Fifth Horseman* p. 48; **barrier project** – Doyle, *Deluge* p. 40

p. 55 **very ingenious** – Chris Spedding (pc); **one director** – Mike Batt (pc)

p. 56 **isolated store** – quoted *Daily Telegraph* 16 February 1972; **local authority** – *Times* 11 December 1972; **go-ahead** – *Daily Mail* 19 November 1971; **initial period** – *Times* 23 September 1972; **power** – *Daily Telegraph* 16 February 1972

p. 57 **alarm** – ibid. 3 October 1970; **modern methods** – *Times* 1 January 2001; **My dad** – Yuill, *Hazell and the Menacing Jester* p. 8; **petrol prices** – Michie & Hoggart, *The Pact* p. 105; **natural resources** – *Daily Mail* 22 November 1971

4: Violence

p. 59 **assumed** – *Times* 18 February 1971; **bimbos** – Wodehouse, *Aunts Aren't Gentlemen* p. 10; **boots** – Lee Hazlewood, 'These Boots Are Made for Walkin'' (Mecalico, 1966)

p. 60 **unique** – Barlow, *The Burden of Proof* p. 192

p. 61 **Power** – Newman, *Sir, You Bastard* pp. 38–9; **more villains** – Cox, Shirley & Short, *The Fall of Scotland Yard* p. 15; **general acceptance** – Mark, *In the Office of Constable* p. 129

p. 62 **Four-letter words** – Alvarado & Stewart, *Made for Television* p. 61; **opinion poll** – *Sun* 2 February 1977; **What are we for** – Everett, *You'll Never Be 16 Again* p. 104

p. 63 **single group** – Pete Fowler, 'Skins Rule' in Gillett (ed.), *Rock File* p. 15; **exploited** – Daniel & McGuire (ed.), *The Paint House* p. 79; **restaurants** – Fowler op. cit. p. 20; **blacks in China** – Daniel & McGuire op. cit. p. 81; **long-haired** – *Daily Mirror* 4 June 1970; **also be possible** – *Times* 27 May 1970; *Mashriq* – Hiro, *Black British, White British* p. 311

p. 64 **policeman's job** – *Times* 7 February 1970; **schoolboy** – Elms, *The Way We Wore* p. 63; **36 hours** – *Daily Mirror* 12 January 1972; **disillusioned** – Allen, *Skinhead* p. 6; **violence** – ibid. p. 127

p. 65 **swarmed** – ibid. p. 95; **dictator** – ibid. p. 97; **permissive society** – Allen, *Suedehead* p. 5; **1968 survey** – *Daily Mail* 27 November 1971

p. 66 **aim of the Act** – *Times* 13 January 1976; **vandalism** – ibid. 21 January 1976; **survey of teachers** – *Daily Mail* 5 September 1977; **caretakers** – *Times* 19 November 1970; **James of England** – *Daily Mail* 12 January 1978

p. 67 **teacher training** – ibid. 5 March 1975; **London swing** – *Daily Telegraph* 16 April 1965; **Garbo!** – Steven Thomas (pc); **Biba weekend** – Bradbury, *The History Man* p. 76; **macabre tribute** – *Guardian* 19 July 1975

p. 68 **busy being born** – *The Angry Brigade* p. 31; **dubious claim** – Craig Austin (pc); **call for Ireland** – Andrews, 'Soldier' (Essex International, 1972); **on the brink** – *Sunday Times, Ulster* p. 96; **bloody awful** – McKittrick & McVea, *Making Sense of the Troubles* p. 63

p. 69 **Other possibilities** – *Times* 1 January 2002; **blind man** – Reed, *Ireland* p. 162; **2,000 explosions** – McKittrick & McVea op. cit. p. 83; **the dead dog** – Hill (ed.), *Tribune* 40 p. 188; **politicians' failure** – *Daily Express* 5 January 1974; **Jack and Jill** – *The Regimental Journal of 15th/19th the King's Royal Hussars*, vol. 3 no. 4, May 1972, p. 924

p. 70 **blackened** – *Daily Telegraph* 3 February 1972; **Let us remember** – ibid.; **turmoil** – Whitelaw, *The Whitelaw Memoirs* p. 84; **rival slogans** – *Sunday Telegraph* 2 January 1977; **1969 survey** – Target, *Unholy Smoke* p. 14

p. 71 **hate the IRA** – Denim, 'The Osmonds' (Lawrence, Boys Own Recordings, 1992); **you are tremendous** – Wings, 'Give Ireland Back to the Irish' (McCartney Music Ltd/ATV Music Ltd, 1972); **propaganda** – *Times* 1 December 1971

p. 72 **values** – Schlesinger, Murdock & Elliott, *Televising 'Terrorism'* p. 122; **two communities** – Quicke, *Tomorrow's Television* p. 194; **Two UDA men** – *Guardian* 1 March 1975; **getting boring** – Williams, *Big Morning Blues* p. 133

p. 73 **it is known** – *Daily Mirror* 20 June 1970; **must not compromise** – *Sun* 20 June 1970; **RTB** – Leslie, *The Extremists* p. 10; **concern myself** – Freeborn, *Good Luck Mister Cain* p. 86; **I don't know** – ibid. p. 102; **sudden anger** – Lord, *The Spider and the Fly* p. 33

p. 74 **political implications** – *Evening Standard* 29 January 1972; **very good novel** – Burgess, *1985* p. 91

p. 75 **Buckinghamshire** – *Uncut* 35, April 2000; **rape scene** – *Motion Picture Guild Encyclopedia* review, cited on DVD (2004)
p. 76 **penchant** – *On Location* documentary, included on DVD (2004)

5: Unions
p. 77 **one thing** – Gormley, *Battered Cherub* p. 140; **Union Leader** – Shipway, *The Chilian Club*, paperback blurb; **Russian gold** – Chappell, *Rising Damp*, 'Stand Up and Be Counted' 1974; **coal strike** – Hain, *Political Strikes* p. 12; **Shrewsbury** – Mark, *In the Office of Constable* p. 160
p. 78 **very embarrassed** – Ross, *The Carry On Companion* p. 99; *The Classic Carry On Film Collection* 6 p. 12
p. 79 **unexpurgated copy** – Gormley op. cit. p. 81; **300,000** – Milligan, *The New Barons* p. 82; **Heath's misguided view** – Norman Tebbit (pc)
p. 80 **trade unionist** – Childs, *Britain Since 1945* p. 224; **Tolpuddle** – Milligan op. cit. p. 72; **electricity** – Dennis Skinner (pc); **protests** – Heffer, *Never A Yes Man* p. 141
p. 81 **Barons aren't elected** – Tony Benn (pc); **most popular** – Muir, *A Kentish Lad* p. 266; **below the surface** – Ferris, *The New Militants* p. 20
p. 82 **funeral** – *Daily Mail* 8 November 1971; **Billy White** – Alan Price, 'The Jarrow Song' (Jarrow Music, 1974); **working man** – John Ford & Richard Hudson, 'Part of the Union' (1973)
p. 83 **Kinnock** – Drower, *Neil Kinnock* p. 34; **no records** – Don Smith (pc); **MU guy** – Chris Redburn (pc)
p. 84 **You weren't even** – Visconti, *Bowie, Bolan and the Brooklyn Boy* p. 120; **Vanessa Redgrave** – McCann, *Morecambe & Wise* p. 249; **protective practices** – Dash, *Good Morning, Brothers!* p. 143; **outrageously high** – Chippindale & Horrie, *Stick It Up Your Punter!* p. 52
p. 85 **Wilson himself** – see Leigh, *The Wilson Plot*; **communist menace** – Crozier (ed.), *'We Will Bury You'* p. 141; **change society** – Stewart, *Protest or Power?* p. 60
p. 86 **Tiny in numbers** – *Daily Express* 8 February 1974; **his country** – Clarke, *The Shadow of a Nation* p. 168; **three drugs** – ibid. p. 174; **no good compromising** – Routledge, *Scargill* p. 261; **In 1953** – Socialist Labour Party website
p. 87 **a Lenin** – Freeman, *The Benn Heresy* p. 43; **£3.3 million** – Milligan op. cit. p. 13; **Eight workers** – Benn, *Conflicts of Interest* p. 19
p. 88 **overt violence** – McKittrick & McVea, *Making Sense of the Troubles* p. 103; **the first time** – Reed, *Ireland* p. 207; **spend their lives** – McKittrick & McVea op. cit. p. 105
p. 89 **strong government** – Campbell, *Edward Heath* p. 595; **4 million workers** – *Sun* 7 February 1974; **outbreak of war** – *Evening Standard* 6 February 1974; **four-day week** – *Sun* 18 January 1974; **two-day week** – Money, *Margaret Thatcher* p. 13

Part Two: Golden Years: 1974–1976
p. 91 **While everything** – Lessing, *The Memoirs of a Survivor* pp. 19–20; **this country** – Clement & Le Frenais, *Porridge*, 'Disturbing The Peace' 1975; **Goodbye** – *Sun* 1 May 1975

6: The Wilson Years
p. 93 **Labour government** – Lord, *The Spider and the Fly* p. 178; **tired** – Bryers, *Hollow Target* pp. 105–6; **Democracy** – *Sunday Telegraph* 5 May 1974; **Hurrah!** – *Sunday Times* 3 March 1974; **Sick Man** – ibid.
p. 94 **south of England** – Leys, *Politics in Britain* p. 204; **the government** – McIntosh,

Challenge to Democracy p. 23; **political dispute** – Gormley, *Battered Cherub* p. 141; **brought himself down** – ibid. p. 144; **ungovernable** – Hain, *Political Strikes* p. 115; **William Hill** – *Sun* 15 January 1974; **Joe Coral** – *Daily Express* 9 February 1974; VOTE LABOUR – *Daily Mirror* 28 February 1974; **support Heath** – *Sun* 27 February 1974

p. 95 **must point out** – *Daily Mirror* 1 March 1974; **someone else** – Auden, 'Musée des Beaux Arts', *Selected Poems* p. 28; **great shock** – Benn, *Against the Tide* p. 75; I QUIT – *Sun* 8 February 1974

p. 96 **Judas was paid** – Shepherd, *Enoch Powell* p. 405; **in the loo** – Pimlott, *Harold Wilson* p. 611; **national swing** – Shepherd op. cit. p. 449; **little doubt** – Johnson & Schoen, 'The "Powell effect"' p. 170

p. 97 **put him in** – Shepherd op. cit. p. 499; **one's children** – Michie & Hoggart, *The Pact* p. 43; **off the fence** – Smith, *Big Cyril* p. 150

p. 98 **unsatisfactory** – Williams, *Diaries* p. 468; **every position** – Pimlott op. cit. p. 617; **score the goals** – Donoughue, *Downing Street Diary* p. 100

p. 99 **bloody job** – Corbett, *England Expects* pp. 291–2; **the dirtiest** – Clough, *The Autobiography* p. 139; **real bastard** – Corbett op. cit. p. 312; **trying to bribe** – see Stott, *Dogs and Lampposts* pp. 173–81; **opinion poll** – *Daily Express* 25 February 1974

p. 100 **Augean stables** – Healey, *The Time of My Life* p. 392; **howls of anguish** – ibid. p. 396; **didn't vote** – Clark, *Diaries* p. 38

p. 101 **national will** – Holden, *Of Presidents, Prime Ministers & Princes* pp. 158–9; **authoritarian government** – McIntosh op. cit. p. 172; **17 per cent** – Bullock Report figures in 1975; **electricity board** – *Times* 4 April 1975

p. 102 **£1,500 a year** – Hall, *Diaries* p. 209; **Wedgie's nightclub** – Steven Thomas (pc); **a tape** – Strong, *Diaries* p. 140; **hallowed Mecca** – *Melody Maker* 11 October 1975

p. 103 **glam party** – Mick Rock (pc); **desperate hope** – *Daily Mirror* 11 January 1975; **the pools** – ibid. 13 January 1975; **6 million** – *Sun* 3 February 1977; **Alcohol** – *Daily Mail* 9 September 1977

p. 104 **cataclysm** – ibid. 14 March 1975; **Crisis Deepens** – *Sunday Times* 8 September 1974; **bewailed** – Hall op. cit. p. 188; **All over** – Drabble, *The Ice Age* p. 65; **sliding, sinking** – ibid. p. 97

p. 105 **most damaging** – Radice, *Friends & Rivals* p. 193; **a miserable sight** – Donoughue, op. cit. p. 503; **party's over** – Crosland, *Tony Crosland* p. 295

p. 106 **cultivate our gardens** – Donoughue op. cit. p. 503; **my defeat** – *Daily Mirror* 20 June 1970

p. 107 **It wasn't** – Hall op. cit. p. 434; **Labour to win** – ibid. p. 123; **emasculated** – Heffer, *Labour's Future* p. 12

p. 108 **outside left** – Sampson, *The Changing Anatomy of Britain* p. 79; **maiden aunt** – Mikardo, *Back-Bencher* p. 198; **The laws** – Shipway, *The Chilian Club* p. 86; **rule industry** – ibid. p. 27

p. 109 **It worked** – King (ed.), *Why Is Britain Becoming Harder to Govern?* p. 76; **cricket pitch** – ibid. p. 79; **£60,000** – Freeman, *The Benn Heresy* p. 70; **Lord Watkinson** – *Sun* 8 May 1975; **refuse** – Freeman op. cit. p. 64

p. 110 **go to prison** – McIntosh op. cit. p. 201; **We regret** – Benn op. cit. p. 378; SACK BENN! – *Sun* 9 May 1975; BYE BYE – *Sunday Mirror* 11 May 1975; **It is obvious** – Benn op. cit. p. 375; **you are doing** – ibid. p. 394; **undemocratic situation** – Mikardo op. cit. pp. 195–6; **needed a man** – Jones, *Union Man* p. 281

p. 111 **bringing peace** – Benn op. cit. p. 536; **sharp shysters** – ibid. p. 571; **defeated** –

Hennessy, *The Prime Minister* p. 359; **old boxer** – Donoughue op. cit. p. 700; **No regrets** – ibid. p. 719; **saw Harold** – Benn op. cit. p. 557

7: Opposition
p. 112 **day of the woman** – Esmonde & Larbey, *The Good Life*, 'The Happy Event' 1976; **Once upon a time** – Mortimer & Cooke, *George and Mildred*, 'The Right Way to Travel' 1977; **Keith Joseph** – John Cooper Clarke, 'Beasley Street' (April Music Ltd/Split Beans, 1980); **Ivy Williams** – *Daily Mirror* 5 June 1970; **40 per cent** – *Social Trends* figures for 1970, quoted in *Daily Mail* 1 December 1971; **It only dawned** – Wells, *Jane* p. 118
p. 113 **all cleavage** – Strong, *Diaries* p. 103; **Wimpy** – *Forum* vol. 4 no. 11, January 1972; *Female Eunuch* – Spender, *For the Record* p. 50; **it was women** – Ashton, *Red Rose Blues* p. 133
p. 114 **every decent** – Harman, *W*I*T*C*H* p. 122
p. 115 **naively assumed** – Tebbit, *Upwardly Mobile* p. 94; **We believe** – Boyson (ed.), *Right Turn* p. 1; **completed our work** – ibid. p. 2; **business-friendly** – *Daily Telegraph* 16 December 1998
p. 116 **rethinking** – *Sunday Times* 17 March 1974; **In the eyes** – *Daily Express* 6 January 1975; **Mr Heath** – *Sunday Telegraph* 5 May 1974; **Inflation** – Thatcher, *The Path to Power* p. 255; **death-bed** – Shepherd, *Enoch Powell* p. 460; **never focused** – Halcrow, *Keith Joseph* p. 67; **Compare our position** – ibid. p. 70
p. 117 **never goes abroad** – Donoughue, *Downing Street Diary* p. 503; **Your analysis** – Baker, *The Turbulent Years* p. 42; **path to Benn** – Russel, *The Tory Party* p. 16; **John the Baptist** – *Times* 19 January 1976; **small group** – Benn, *Office Without Power* p. 345; **a coalition** – McIntosh, *Challenge to Democracy* p. 184
p. 118 **Different people** – *Times* 1 January 2004; **November 1976** – Smith, *Big Cyril* p. 223; **last three years** – ibid. p. 230
p. 119 **high and rising** – Halcrow op. cit. p. 83; **it is not those** – *Times* 22 October 1974; **The trouble was** – Thatcher op. cit. pp. 262–3
p. 120 **It's great fun** – Halcrow op. cit. p. 85; **Ever since** – Thatcher op. cit. p. 266; **votes Labour** – Alvarado & Stewart, *Made for Television* p. 94; **wealth-creating** – Halcrow op. cit. pp. 99–100; **someone who represents** – Thatcher op. cit. p. 266
p. 121 **barriers** – Williams, *Diaries* p. 417; **rather pretentious** – *Sunday Telegraph* 16 January 1972; **her plummy voice** – *Daily Mirror* 24 January 1975; **those hats** – *Times* 11 September 1974; **middle-aged lady** – Cosgrave, *Margaret Thatcher* p. 14; **very pleased** – *Daily Mail* 12 February 1975; **male-dominated party** – Castle, *Diaries 1974–76* p. 309
p. 122 **opinion poll** – *Sun* 18 January 1977; **only man** – *Daily Mail* 5 February 1975; **Suddenly** – *Daily Mirror* 5 February 1975; **majority** – *Daily Mail* 12 February 1975
p. 123 **man's right** – *Times* 11 October 1975; **straightforward provincial** – Sampson, *The Changing Anatomy of Britain* p. 41; **It hurts** – Steven Thomas (pc)
p. 124 **Crikey** – *Times* 12 February 2006; **the opposition** – Pete Fowler, 'Skins Rule' in Gillett (ed.), *Rock File* p. 22; **Italian bastards** – Clough, *The Autobiography* p. 95
p. 125 **Regan is contemptuous** – Alvarado & Stewart op. cit. pp. 62–3
p. 127 **I certainly do notice** – Benn, *Against the Tide* p. 430; **naked propaganda** – Tynan, *Diaries* p. 68
p. 128 **volunteers** – *Times* 7 April 1975; **steady encroachment** – *Guardian* August 1974, quoted Powell, *Tony Benn* p. 125; **Two years ago** – *Sun* 22 January 1977; **anarchy** – Nobbs, *I Didn't Get Where I Am Today* pp. 293–4

p. 129 **puzzled** – Tynan op. cit. p. 237; **a calculated call** – *Times* 13 October 1975; **The economy** – Thatcher op. cit. pp. 305–6; **half the population** – *Sun* 4 January 1977
p. 130 **lurching** – Thatcher op. cit. p. 309

8: Obscenity
p. 131 **moral standards** – Clement & Le Frenais, *Porridge*, 'Heartbreak Hotel' 1975; **Every night** – Ramsay, *The Rage* p. 57; **Last night I saw** – Reg Presley, 'Strange Movies' (Pye Records, 1973); **football hooligans** – *Daily Mail* 7 September 1977
p. 132 **positions of influence** – Thatcher, *The Path to Power* p. 160; **ugly child** – *Times* 22 April 1971; **Powellite** – Caulfield, *Mary Whitehouse* p. 18
p. 133 **irreverence** – ibid. p. 112; **played havoc** – *The Late Show*, BBC2, 1994; **Freedom dies** – ibid.; **The 1960s** – Deedes, *Dear Bill* pp. 228–9
p. 135 **shocking film** – *Daily Mail* 28 December 1973; **dangerous woman** – *Times* 2 December 1971; **sheer noise** – Caulfield op. cit. p. 127
p. 136 **likely to outrage** – Carpenter, *Dennis Potter* p. 324; **brilliant playwright** – ibid. p. 371; **Book of Daniel** – Caulfield op. cit. p. 2; **They've infiltrated** – ibid. p. 140; **the sympathies** – *Times* 10 November 1971; **polarization** – *Evening Standard* 6 February 1974
p. 137 **first step** – Carvel, *Citizen Ken* p. 53; **the Council** – Wistrich, *'I Don't Mind the Sex, It's the Violence'* p. 58; **People go** – *Times* 22 April 1971; **revolting film** – *Daily Mirror* 28 December 1973; **dashed off** – Caulfield op. cit. p. 155
p. 138 **vicious spiral** – *Times* 19 January 1975; **cesspools of iniquity** – Wistrich op. cit. p. 71; **Enid Wistrichs** – Caulfield op. cit. p. 168; **voted for abolition** – Wistrich op. cit. p. 73; **It is as serious** – Ferris, *Sex and the British* p. 234
p. 139 **I first read** – Marcus, *A Taste for Pain* p. 207; **Sorry, mate** – Freeman, *The Undergrowth of Literature* p. 79
p. 140 **most profitable** – Sweet, *Shepperton Babylon* p. 293; **Taxi Driver** – ibid. p. 307
p. 141 **Shirley Temple** – *Daily Mail* 5 March 1975; **Future historians** – ibid. 10 March 1975; **solemn and formal** – ibid. 7 November 1973; **means of tackling** – Longford, *Pornography* p. 12; **one in five** – *Sun* 10 January 1977
p. 142 *Till Death* – Caulfield op. cit. p. 99; **never thought** – Holden, *Makers and Manners* p. 214; **young woman** – Stanford, *The Outcasts' Outcast* p. 324; **pervasive and corrupting** – Caulfield op. cit. p. 96; **heated amateurism** – Levin, *Taking Sides* p. 189; **the prefects** – Longford op. cit. p. 109; **chamois leather** – Tynan, *Diaries* p. 233
p. 143 **single issue** – *Forum* vol. 3 no. 10, 1970; *Observer* – Cox, Shirley & Short, *The Fall of Scotland Yard* p. 160; **I was offered** – ibid. p. 165; **real fear** – Mark, *In the Office of Constable* p. 174
p. 144 **suitable guest** – Cox, Shirley & Short op. cit. p. 175; **going too far** – *Times* 2 June 1977; **sales of porn magazines** – *News of the World* 11 September 1977; **He realizes** – Dexter, *Last Bus to Woodstock* p. 71
p. 145 **He's sick** – ibid. p. 188; **What worries me** – Michie & Hoggart, *The Pact* p. 89; **shining example** – Halcrow, *Keith Joseph* p. 82
p. 146 **the Cross** – Caulfield op. cit. p. 98; **There will always** – Ferris op. cit. p. 250; **birching** – Thatcher op. cit. p. 116; **men really pay** – Strong, *Diaries* p. 169

9: Nostalgia
p. 147 **opened in 1974** – Schuman, *Rock Follies*, 'The Blitz' 1976; **simply want** – Potter,

Brimstone and Treacle; **really learned** – Bickerton/Waddington, 'I Can Do It' (Chelsea Music, 1975)

p. 148 **pound sterling** – *Women's Wear Daily* 15 December 1967; **never get better** – Hare, *Teeth 'n' Smiles* p. 52

p. 149 **Brian Wilson** – Tony Burrows (pc)

p. 150 *Good Old Days* – *Sun* 24 February 1977; **second-order emotion** – Carpenter, *Dennis Potter* p. 353

p. 151 **daring originality** – Mark Eastment, 'Portmeirion Pottery' in Turner (ed.), *Portmeirion* p. 144; **shops find it** – *Daily Telegraph* 6 January 1977; **truly subversive** – Tynan, *Diaries* p. 273; **gnaw away** – *Times* 11 October 1975

p. 152 **the last moment** – Forster, *Maurice* p. 221; **put the clock back** – McIntosh, *Challenge to Democracy* p. 347

p. 153 **World War II** – *Daily Mail* 3 September 1977

p. 154 **a ticket** – *Times* 5 October 1977

p. 155 **has the feeling** – McIntosh op. cit. p. 301; **nostalgic vocabulary** – Drower, *Neil Kinnock* p. 54; **increasingly distant** – *Daily Telegraph* 29 December 2005; **talked ourselves** – Halcrow, *Keith Joseph* p. 72

p. 156 **the '30s** – Benn, *Against the Tide* p. 512; **The MacDonalds** – Pimlott, *Harold Wilson* p. 663; **keeping the party** – Donoughue, *Downing Street Diary* p. 34

p. 157 **intelligentsia** – Crosland, *Tony Crosland* p. 263; **the conclusion** – Benn, *Conflicts of Interest* p. 277; **individual human spirit** – *Times* 12 November 1976; **time's coming** – Burgess, *1985* p. 117; **all wage demands** – ibid. p. 136

p. 158 **old-fashioned** – ibid. p. 123; **What's happened** – ibid. p. 129; **weasel's nerve** – Moss, *The Collapse of Democracy* p. 26; **drab Utopia** – ibid. p. 34; **trade union power** – ibid. p. 97; **We can expect** – *Times* 28 October 1977; **party political** – Benn op. cit. p. 236

p. 159 **sudden leaps** – Summers, *The Rag Parade* p. 70; **servile ideologist** – Cardew, *Stockhausen Serves Imperialism* p. 79; **no climaxes** – Leeming, *Wesker the Playwright* p. 96; **controversial figure** – Dawson, *A Card for the Clubs* p. 85

p. 160 **No need** – *Sunday Herald* 5 March 2006; **long speech** – Tynan op. cit. p. 160; **wreckers** – *Daily Mail* 19 October 1976; **sadistic exhibitions** – *Daily Telegraph* 19 October 1976; **your penis** – D'Arcy (ed.), *Order! Order!* p. 297

p. 161 **go to Ascot** – *Daily Telegraph* 5 February 1977

p. 162 **what shock** – ibid. 8 January 1977

10: Europe

p. 164 **holidays abroad** – Van Greenaway, *The Man Who Held the Queen to Ransom* p. 57; **We're all friends** – Cleese & Booth, *Fawlty Towers*, 'The Germans' 1975; **socialist Britain** – Clark, *Diaries* p. 64; **disgusted** – Ken Andrews (pc)

p. 165 **six million** – quoted *Daily Mail* 1 December 1971; **recently returned** – *Daily Mirror* 1 June 1970; **I appreciate** – ibid. 5 June 1970; **9 million** – *Daily Mail* 28 November 1973

p. 166 **excruciatingly poor** – Lewisohn, *Radio Times Guide to TV Comedy* p. 203; **from £45** – *Daily Mirror* 16 January 1975; **football hooliganism** – see Williams, Dunning & Murphy, *Hooligans Abroad*

p. 167 **What is it** – Mullally, *Split Scene* p. 92; **historical vulgarity** – Tynan, *Diaries* p. 49; SELL-OUT – Hill (ed.), *Tribune 40* p. 182

p. 168 **strong support** – Whitelaw, *The Whitelaw Memoirs* p. 74; **Millions of people** – Kellner & Hitchens, *Callaghan* p. 116; **40,000 words** – Clark, *The Tories* p. 445

p. 169 **Douglas Hurd** – Hennessy, *The Prime Minister* p. 354; **Call that democracy!** – Rose, *Backbencher's Dilemma* p. 6; **All the arguments** – Benn, *Office Without Power* p. 346

p. 170 **the moment** – Hattersley, *Who Goes Home?* p. 109; **continuing weapon** – Childs, *Britain Since 1945* p. 234

p. 171 **elitist thinking** – Benn op. cit. p. 425; **drawing room** – ibid. p. 449; **bad by-election** – Jenkins, *A Life at the Centre* p. 351

p. 172 **Dr Kissinger** – Kellner & Hitchens op. cit. p. 154; **This country** – *Daily Mirror* 7 January 1975; **dedicated federalist** – Body, *England for the English* p. 118; **Those who want** – Elliott & Atkinson, *The Age of Insecurity* p. 181

p. 173 **all journalists** – Donoughue, *Downing Street Diary* p. 392; **the qualities** – *Sun* 12 May 1975; **Lord Stansgate** – Powell, *Tony Benn* p. 154; **increasingly difficult** – ibid. p. 155; **old people's home** – Campbell, *Roy Jenkins* p. 173; **My wife and I** – Mark, *In the Office of Constable* p. 234; **ten per cent** – Hattersley op. cit. p. 158

p. 174 **took the advice** – Tynan, *Diaries* p. 248; **swing to the right** – Benn, *Against the Tide* p. 386; **Labour Party** – Freeman, *The Benn Heresy* p. 72; **rejection of submission** – *Red Flag* 11 July 1975; **airline pilot** – Norman Tebbit (pc); **my own mug** – Benn, *Conflicts of Interest* p. 9; **ham sandwiches** – Shirley Williams (pc)

p. 175 **inextricably linked** – Benn, *Against the Tide* p. 73; **my stomach turn** – ibid. p. 473; **to be careful** – ibid. p. 474; **It is important** – *Daily Telegraph* 29 December 2005; **£5 note** – *Times* 1 January 2002; **de Gaulle himself** – *Independent* 24 June 2003

p. 176 **a record number** – Chippindale & Horrie, *Stick It Up Your Punter!* p. 34

p. 177 **European federal state** – *Times* 1 January 2001; **Last October** – ibid. 9 June 1973; **It then seemed** – Thatcher, *The Path to Power* p. 210; **taking our bat** – Pimlott, *Harold Wilson* p. 659

Part Three: Sense of Doubt: 1976–1979

p. 179 **British mistake** – TV Smith, 'The Great British Mistake' (Twist & Shout Music, 1978); **Life in England** – Jarman, *Jubilee*; **If I didn't laugh** – *News of the World* 9 October 1977

11: The Callaghan Years

p. 181 **unnecessary disputes** – *Sunday Telegraph* 2 January 1977; **let us take** – Sharples/Drummond, 'Stand Up and Be Counted' (Chappell & Co, 1977); **I can see** – Chappell, *Rising Damp*, 'The Good Samaritans' 1977

p. 182 **I can't conceive** – Sampson, *The Changing Anatomy of Britain* p. 91; **When I think** – Benn, *Against the Tide* p. 546

p. 183 **year too soon** – Jefferys, *Anthony Crosland* pp. 194–5; **great pleasure** – Benn, op. cit. p. 549; **Prime minister** – Powell, *Tony Benn* p. 70

p. 184 **farmyard** – Michie & Hoggart, *The Pact* p. 88; **Jim's interest** – ibid. p. 84; **We don't want** – Benn, *Office Without Power* p. 320; **paid the price** – *Times* 15 April 1976; **elder statesman** – Donoughue, *Downing Street Diary* p. 694; **party fixer** – Benn, *Against the Tide* p. 553

p. 185 **fifty-two** – Heffer, *Never A Yes Man* p. 153; **a young man** – Benn, op. cit. pp. 561–2; **socialist government** – Callaghan, *Time and Chance* p. 269; **One day** – Hattersley, *Who Goes Home?* p. 189; **fifth of five** – www.oxforddnb.com/view/article/30985; **year for Britain** – *Times* 21 August 1975

p. 186 **proles** – Dash, *Good Morning, Brothers!* p. 138; **drift towards chaos** – Lean, *Rebirth of a Nation?* pp. 15–16; **no intention** – ibid. pp. 25–6

p. 187 **stunned** – Healey, *The Time of My Life* p. 397; **parliamentary democracy** – *Daily Telegraph* 8 January 1977; **We were not elected** – Freeman, *The Benn Heresy* p. 78; **This budget** – Drower, *Neil Kinnock* p. 54; **used to think** – Callaghan op. cit. pp. 425–6

p. 188 **socialism in one country** – Campbell, *Roy Jenkins* p. 141; **The markets** – Radice, *Friends & Rivals* p. 254

p. 189 **the housewife** – Callaghan op. cit. p. 447; **10 million** – Clutterbuck & Crainer, *The Decline and Rise of British Industry* p. 24; **final good sense** – Hall, *Diaries* p. 312

p. 190 **taking steroids** – *Independent* 14 December 1998; **Between 1978** – news.bbc.co.uk/1/hi/uk_politics/4294709.stm

p. 191 **mismanagement** – *Times* 24 April 1975; **industrial disputes** – Benn, op. cit. p. 287; **perfectly respectable** – *Times* 20 October 1977; **old-fashioned** – *Daily Mail* 7 September 1977

p. 192 **Leyland's models** – Richard Porter, *Crap Cars* (BBC Books, London, 2004); **poetic plonk** – *Sun* 7 February 1977; **days of disillusion** – *Sunday Telegraph* 6 February 1977

p. 193 **more schizophrenic** – Anderson, *The Diaries* p. 341

p. 194 **Saltley Gate** – Routledge, *Scargill* p. 102; **blank pages** – see, for example, *Sun* 1 July 1977; **more like Germany** – Hall op. cit. p. 303; **can't portray** – *Daily Mail* 7 September 1977; **respect for values** – *Daily Telegraph* 8 January 1977

p. 195 **We were a bit** – Smith, *Big Cyril* pp. 172–3

p. 196 **we have removed** – *News of the World* 2 October 1977; **to wound** – Smith op. cit. p. 216; **more harm** – *Sun* 5 May 1977

p. 197 **psychiatric suicide** – Stonehouse, *My Trial* p. 179; **collapse** – ibid. p. 75

p. 198 **marvellous** – ibid. p. 202; **mad and sane** – Nobbs, *The Death of Reginald Perrin* p. 169; **Maudling** – Nobbs, *I Didn't Get Where I Am Today* p. 272; **nihilism** – Nobbs, *Perrin* p. 154

p. 199 **Egbert Poltergeist** – ibid. p. 264; **Labour leadership** – Benn, *Conflicts of Interest* p. 270; **Education** – Crosland, *Tony Crosland* p. 69; **main thing** – ibid. p. 278

p. 200 **industrial relations** – Foot, *Loyalists and Loners* p. 113; **here was a situation** – ibid. p. 115; **skating** – Austin Mitchell (pc); **full employment** – Benn, *Conflicts of Interest* p. 227; **Jan Hildreth** – *Sun* 4 January 1977; **annoys me** – Clarke, *The Shadow of a Nation* p. 176; **the death rate** – *Daily Telegraph* 2 February 1977

p. 201 **Arthur Winn** – *Daily Mail* 13 November 1973; **civilized democracy** – *Sun* 7 November 1977

p. 203 **the future** – *Daily Mail* 10 January 1978

12: Race

p. 205 **The conception** – Mark, *In the Office of Constable* p. 302; **changed all right** – Preston, *Out*, 'It Must Be The Suit' 1978; **National Front** – Kit Gould, 'National Front' (New Bristol Music, 1977)

p. 206 **tremendous amount** – Bourne, *Black in the British Frame* pp. 175–6; **You've never seen** – Onyeama, *The Book of Black Man's Humour* p. 33

p. 207 **it was funny** – *Sun* 1 November 1977; **popular song** – *The Black and White Minstrel Show* p. 2

p. 208 **lazy, ignorant** – *Times* 30 August 1978; **feeds on ignorance** – Griffiths, *Comedians* p. 23

p. 209 **dangerous and obsolete** – *Times* 24 April 1972; **rest of the world** – Wharton, *The Stretchford Chronicles* p. 215; **two people** – *Daily Mirror* 28 January 1978; **racial differences** – *Daily Telegraph* 3 February 1977

p. 210 **Andrew Huxley** – *Daily Mail* 1 September 1977; **every power** – ibid. 2 September 1977; **all been exposed** – Bradbury, *The History Man* p. 158; **famous victory** – ibid. p. 235

p. 211 **black bands** – Eddie Amoo (pc); **black musicians** – *Melody Maker* 14 November 1970

p. 212 **We don't play** – Harvey Hinsley (pc); **a lot of them** – *Daily Mail* 11 November 1971; **ten years** – Garland & Rowe, *Racism and Anti-Racism in Football* p. 39; **Politics should be left** – *Guardian* 26 January 1979

p. 214 **That period** – Callaghan, *Time and Chance* p. 269; **official figures** – *News of the World* 6 November 1977

p. 215 **immigration** – Thatcher, *The Path to Power* p. 212; **one quarter** – Johnson & Schoen, 'The "Powell effect"' p. 170; **coloured policemen** – *Times* 19 November 1970

p. 216 **1976 figures** – *Daily Telegraph* 7 January 1977; **sordid celebrations** – Mark op. cit. p. 234; **niggers** – Elms, *The Way We Wore* p. 156; **nursery rhymes** – *Times* 7 January 1978

p. 217 **eccentric** – ibid. 9 January 1978

p. 218 **This evening** – Stonehouse, *My Trial* p. 180; **appalled** – *News of the World* 16 October 1977; **Every year** – Hiro, *Black British, White British* p. 290; **Our people** – Benn, *Against the Tide* pp. 587–8; **nothing against blacks** – Raphael, *The Glittering Prizes* p. 245; **Union of Muslim Organizations** – *Daily Mail* 6 September 1977

p. 219 **start of the decade** – Winder, *Bloody Foreigners* pp. 298, 305; **fifth-column** – Speight, *Till Death Us Do Part*, 'Dock Pilfering' 1972; **tinned beef** – James, *Death of an Expert Witness* p. 129; **great amount** – Hardy, *Jeremy Hardy Speaks to the Nation* p. 23; **2,967 complaints** – Hiro op. cit. p. 221; **Abdul Goni** – *Sun* 5 May 1970

p. 220 **because they spoke** – *Times* 2 December 1971; **dictator** – Gillman & Gillman, *Alias David Bowie* pp. 426–7

p. 221 **photomontage** – Widgery, *Beating Time* p. 60; **I think Enoch** – Coleman, *Survivor* pp. 218–19

p. 222 **He was probably** – *Rising Free Fanzine* no. 3, c.1981; **You could sense** – *Q* November 1996; **remote rival** – Money, *Margaret Thatcher* p. 120; **hot-eyed supporters** – *Sun* 24 January 1977; **Whether you detest** – *Daily Express* 7 August 1976; **Who needs the Parliament** – Jones/Strummer, 'Remote Control' (Nineden, 1977)

p. 223 **tens of thousands** – Benn, *Conflicts of Interest* p. 345

p. 224 **five thousand** – Parris, *Chance Witness* p. 192; **surveys showed** – Winder op. cit. p. 307; **Before my interview** – Thatcher, op. cit. p. 408

p. 225 **trying to do** – *Times* 14 February 1977; **a limit** – Halcrow, *Keith Joseph* p. 121; **party is depressed** – Benn op. cit. p. 287

13: Fringes

p. 226 **I had hoped** – Leslie Duxbury, *Coronation Street* 29 November 1972; **workers** – Chappell, *Rising Damp*, 'Stand Up and Be Counted' 1974; **trendy ideas** – Yuill, *Hazell and the Menacing Jester* p. 41; **In 1951** – Leys, *Politics in Britain* p. 66; **A people drilled** – Stewart, *Protest or Power?* p. 119

p. 227 **traditional values** – *Times* 1 June 1977; **little support** – McIntosh, *Challenge to*

Democracy p. 138; **nationalism** – Weight, *Patriots* p. 416; **opinion poll** – *Daily Telegraph* 2 February 1977

p. 228 **Scottish pride** – *Daily Mail* 16 January 1978; **two parties** – *Daily Mirror* 15 June 1970; **stamps** – *Times* 1 January 2004; **I don't want** – Drower, *Neil Kinnock* p. 50

p. 229 **linguistic racism** – ibid. p. 51; **We can aim** – Ellis, *The Celtic Revolution* p. 84; **Anti-Taffy** – Drower op. cit. p. 51; **two members** – Lloyd, *Mr Speaker, Sir* p. 152

p. 230 **hadn't actually heard** – Rendell, *Some Lie and Some Die* p. 29

p. 231 **One assessment** – Tomlinson, *Left, Right* p. 67; **15,000 members** – *Sun* 16 April 1977; **Making the GMC** – Kogan & Kogan, *The Battle for the Labour Party* p. 74

p. 232 **The GMC** – Benn, *Conflicts of Interest* p. 565; **witch hunts** – Heffer, *Never A Yes Man* p. 181; **piggy-back** – Benn op. cit. p. 566; **paid tribute** – Benn, *Against the Tide* p. 21; **bitterly attacked** – ibid. p. 96

p. 233 **Marxist** – *Times* 9 April 1975; **last bastion** – Redgrave, *To Be a Redgrave* p. 200; **intensely suspicious** – *Sunday Telegraph* 6 April 1972; **Plaid Cymru** – Ellis op. cit. p. 91

p. 234 **stage is set** – *News Line* 7 April 1979; **Joe Marino** – Crick, *Militant* p. 167; **serious threat** – Mark, *In the Office of Constable* p. 299

p. 235 **as bad** – *Daily Mail* 6 September 1977; **one bunch** – Balham, *Regan and the Bent Stripper* p. 28; **career in protest** – Hill, *An Advancement of Learning* p. 155; **My generation** – ibid. p. 183

p. 236 **David Watson** – *Daily Telegraph* 7 February 1977; **The danger** – Crosland, *Tony Crosland* p. 229; **Bishop of Exeter** – *Times* 20 April 1972

p. 239 **do not claim** – Wurmbrand, *Was Karl Marx a Satanist?* p. 76

14: Sexualities

p. 241 **fact** – Clement & La Frenais, *Whatever Happened to the Likely Lads?*, 'No Hiding Place' 1973; **main reason** – *Sun* 15 February 1977; **prison** – Chappell, *Rising Damp*, 'Stage Struck' 1977; **workmates** – Tom Robinson, 'Glad to Be Gay' (EMI Music Publishing, 1978)

p. 242 **Bible** – Roberts (ed.), *Guinness Book of British Hit Singles* p. 381; **very proud** – *Q* January 2007

p. 244 **I'm not really** – *Daily Mirror* 8 January 1972; **light in the dark** – *Times* 10 March 2007

p. 245 **gayer** – Freeman & Penrose, *Rinkagate* p. 119

p. 246 **terrifying propensity** – ibid. p. 238; **Were you taken in** – *Times* 19 March 1976; **Shot any dogs** – Smith, *Big Cyril* p. 186; **Fleet Street** – ibid. p. 211; **the Tory press** – Tynan, *Diaries* p. 327; **the press** – Benn, *Against the Tide* p. 533

p. 247 **What's the similarity** – Palin, *Diaries* p. 520; **I can't see** – Freeman & Penrose op. cit. p. 351; **a fraud** – Chester, Linklater & May, *Jeremy Thorpe* p. 359; **a scrounger** – Cook, *Tragically I was an Only Twin* p. 275

p. 248 **increasingly difficult** – *Times* 22 August 1977; **I am gay** – ibid. 28 September 1977; **you are open** – ibid. 1 October 1977; **married couples** – *Daily Mail* 10 January 1978; **sickness of society** – ibid. 14 January 1978; **I cannot imagine** – *Daily Mirror* 7 January 1978

p. 250 **Most women** – Newman, *A Bouquet of Barbed Wire* p. 212

p. 251 **old-fashioned** – ibid. p. 226; **most extravagant** – *Sunday Telegraph* 6 February 1977; **a man's need** – Pertwee, *Together*, paperback blurb; **He was dressed** – James, *An Unsuitable Job for a Woman* p. 136

p. 252 **all grown men** – Ullerstam, *The Erotic Minorities* p. 69; **sexual deprivation** –

ibid. p. 74; **too severe** – *Sun* 9 February 1977; **eighteen-year-old man** – ibid. 11 February 1977; **thirty-nine-year-old** – ibid. 12 February 1977; **behave sensibly** – ibid. 17 February 1977

p. 253 **female teacher** – *Daily Mail* 1 September 1977; **Jeremy Sandford** – *Sun* 15 February 1977; **If a child** – *News of the World* 4 September 1977; **stinkbombs** – *Daily Mail* 20 September 1977; **rational discussion** – *Times* 30 August 1977

p. 254 **furtive network** – *Sun* 11 November 1977; **We know** – *Times* 10 October 1977; **crime against innocence** – *Daily Mail* 6 September 1977; **matter of great regret** – *Daily Mirror* 5 January 1978

p. 255 **This poem** – *Guardian* 11 July 2002; **the movement** – *News of the World* 17 July 1977; **I did what I did** – *The Late Show*, BBC2, 1994

15: Crisis

p. 256 **Rape and murder** – Paul Weller, '"A" Bomb in Wardour Street' (And Son Music, 1978); **By all accounts** – Waugh, *Another Voice* p. 50; **beat the bastards** – Tebbit, *Upwardly Mobile* p. 157; **productivity** – Clutterbuck & Crainer, *The Decline and Rise of British Industry* p. 25

p. 257 **humiliating** – *Times* 7 July 1977; **union leaders** – Benn, *Against the Tide* p. 674; **good news** – Palin, *Diaries* p. 469; **poll by MORI** – Hain, *Political Strikes* p. 87

p. 258 **It mustn't happen** – *Daily Mirror* 14 January 1978

p. 259 **audience was frightful** – Williams, *Diaries* p. 541; **Surrey** – *Sun* 2 November 1977; **disingenuous** – *News of the World* 16 October 1977; **subtle argument** – Benn, *Conflicts of Interest* p. 230

p. 260 **only difference** – *Daily Mail* 10 January 1978; **did not endear** – Jones, *Union Man* p. 328; **fifty thou** – Yuill, *Hazell and the Menacing Jester* p. 120; **North London** – *News of the World* 7 August 1977; **want to encourage** – *Daily Mail* 4 March 1975

p. 261 **grass is greener** – Mark, *In the Office of Constable* p. 147; **should be sorry** – *Daily Mail* 21 November 1973; **aim to teach** – *News of the World* 14 August 1977; **essential tools** – Callaghan, *Time and Chance* p. 411; **peak year** – *Daily Mirror* 17 January 1978

p. 262 **29,000 men** – *Daily Express* 6 August 1976; **Inland Revenue** – Paytress, *The Rolling Stones Off the Record* p. 196; **more receptive** – *Daily Mail* 5 March 1975; **disillusioned** – Biddu (pc)

p. 263 **no point** – Corbett, *England Expects* p. 306; **run the risk** – Callaghan op. cit. p. 516; **beer freezing** – *Daily Telegraph* 15 January 1979

p. 264 **Individual greed** – ibid. 2 January 1979; **able to get back** – ibid. 9 January 1979; **cannibalism** – ibid. 12 January 1979; **brink of a disaster** – *Sun* 9 January 1979; **Sun-tanned** – ibid. 11 January 1979

p. 265 **portrayed him** – Yarwood, *Impressions of My Life* p. 140; **Frank Muir** – *Daily Mail* 24 December 1973; **Dimbleby** – *Sun* 25 January 1974; **very wrong** – Stewart, *Protest or Power?* p. 19

p. 266 OUR DISCONTENT – *Evening Standard* 6 February 1974; **nightmare** – Shore, *Leading the Left* p. 118; **maintenance workers** – Tebbit op. cit. p. 159; **Patrick Chesterman** – *Daily Telegraph* 7 February 1979

p. 267 **uncollected rubbish** – Palin op. cit. p. 533; **greed and anarchy** – Hall, *Diaries* p. 407; BURY OUR DEAD – *Daily Mail* 1 February 1979; **Sedgefield** – *Daily Telegraph* 2 February 1979; **Our society** – Sampson, *The Changing Anatomy of Britain* pp. 44–5; **sheer viciousness** – Tebbit op. cit. p. 161; **Gallup poll** – *Daily Mail* 12 February 1979; **opinion polls** – *Daily Telegraph* 1 February 1979

p. 268 **MORI found** – *Daily Express* 6 February 1979; **less easy** – *Times* 7 January 1978; **essential liberties** – *Daily Telegraph* 1 February 1979; **Thatcher** – Benn op. cit. p. 282; **We've stumbled** – *Daily Mail* 9 February 1979

p. 269 **If anything** – Dennis Skinner (pc); **siege** – Benn op. cit. p. 449; **her troops** – D'Arcy (ed.), *Order! Order!* p. 47; **the manifesto** – Benn op. cit. p. 492

p. 270 **do not pretend** – *Times* 5 April 1975; **1.3 million** – Coates, *The Crisis of Labour* p. 71; **Hendon** – Clarke, *The Shadow of a Nation* p. 106

p. 271 **crisis had changed** – Shirley Williams (pc); **we're talking about** – Herbert, *The Spear* p. 174; **counter-revolution** – Tony Benn (pc); **humbug** – Gilmour & Garnett, *Whatever Happened to the Tories*

p. 272 **sensational** – Corbett op. cit. p. 316

Outro: Farewell

p. 273 **No one** – margaretthatcher.org; **stay silent** – Mikardo, *Back-Bencher* p. 220; **parable** – Powell, *No Easy Answers* p. 110

p. 274 **got into glam** – Jonathan King (pc)

p. 275 **on the verge** – Moore, *Margaret Thatcher* p. 267; **This is the twilight** – ibid. p. 272

p. 276 **Unchecked inflation** – *Times* 14 September 1974; **the smell of the Weimar Republic** – *Guardian* 27 June 1972; **saved Britain** – *Daily Mail* 9 April 2013

p. 277 **some sympathy** – Benn, *Conflicts of Interest* p. 505

p. 278 **side by side** – ibid. p. 224

Bibliography

Much of the material included in this book, as will be apparent from the references, is drawn from the newspapers of the time. The following works have also been consulted.

Non-Fiction
Note: Where a paperback or revised edition is shown, it indicates that any page references cited are to that edition.

Andrew Adonis & Stephen Pollard, *A Class Act: The Myth of Britain's Classless Society* (Hamish Hamilton, London, 1997 – pbk edn: Penguin, London, 1998)

Manuel Alvarado & John Stewart, *Made for Television: Euston Films Limited* (BFI, London, 1985)

Kingsley Amis, *Memoirs* (Hutchinson, London, 1991)

Lindsay Anderson (ed. Paul Sutton), *The Diaries* (Methuen, London, 2004)

The Angry Brigade 1967–1984: Documents and Chronology (Elephant Editions, London, 1985)

Joe Ashton, *Red Rose Blues: The Story of a Good Labour Man* (Macmillan, London, 2000)

Kenneth Baker, *The Turbulent Years: My Life in Politics* (Faber & Faber, London, 1993)

Tony Benn (ed. Ruth Winstone), *Office Without Power: Diaries 1968–72* (Hutchinson, London, 1988 – pbk edn: Arrow, London, 1989)

Tony Benn (ed. Ruth Winstone), *Against the Tide: Diaries 1973–76* (Hutchinson, London, 1989 – pbk edn: Arrow, London, 1990)

Tony Benn (ed. Ruth Winstone), *Conflicts of Interest: Diaries 1977–80* (Hutchinson, London, 1990 – pbk edn: Arrow, London, 1991)

Tony Benn (ed. Ruth Winstone), *The End of an Era: Diaries 1980–90* (Hutchinson, London, 1992 – pbk edn: Arrow, London, 1994)

The Black and White Minstrel Show (BBC, London, n.d. c.1965)

Richard Body, *England for the English* (New European Publications, London, 2001)

Stephen Bourne, *Black in the British Frame: The Black Experience in British Film and Television* (Continuum, London, 2001)

Rhodes Boyson (ed.), *Right Turn: A symposium on the need to end the 'progressive' consensus in British thinking and policy* (Churchill Press, London, 1970)

David Butler & Anne Sloman, *British Political Facts 1900–1979* (Macmillan, London, 1980 – fifth edition)

James Callaghan, *Time and Chance* (William Collins, London, 1987)

John Campbell, *Edward Heath: A Biography* (Jonathan Cape, London, 1993 – pbk edn: Pimlico, London, 1993)

John Campbell, *Roy Jenkins: A Biography* (Weidenfeld & Nicolson, London, 1983)

Cornelius Cardew, *Stockhausen Serves Imperialism* (Latimer New Dimensions, London, 1974 – reprinted UbuClassics, 2004, available ubu.com)

Humphrey Carpenter, *Dennis Potter: The Authorized Biography* (Faber & Faber, London, 1998)

John Carvel, *Citizen Ken* (Chatto & Windus/The Hogarth Press, London, 1984)

Barbara Castle, *The Castle Diaries 1964–70* (Weidenfeld & Nicolson, 1984)

Barbara Castle, *The Castle Diaries 1974–76* (Weidenfeld & Nicolson, 1980)

Philip Cato, *Crash Course for the Ravers: A Glam Odyssey* (ST Publishing, Lockerbie, 1997)

Max Caulfield, *Mary Whitehouse* (Mowbrays, Oxford, 1975)

Frank Chapple, *Sparks Fly! A Trade Union Life* (Michael Joseph, London, 1984)

Dominic Chellard, *British Theatre Since the War* (Yale University Press, New Haven, 1999)

Lewis Chester, Magnus Linklater & David May, *Jeremy Thorpe: A Secret Life* (André Deutsch, London, 1979)

David Childs, *Britain Since 1945: A Political History* (University Paperbacks, London, 1986 – second edition)

Peter Chippindale & Chris Horrie, *Stick It Up Your Punter! The Rise and Fall of the Sun* (William Heinemann, London, 1990 – pbk edn: Mandarin, London, 1992)

Alan Clark, *The Tories: Conservatives and the Nation State 1922–1997* (Weidenfeld & Nicolson, London, 1998 – pbk edn: Phoenix, London, 1999)

Alan Clark, *Diaries: Into Politics 1972–82* (Weidenfeld & Nicolson, London, 2000 – pbk edn: Phoenix, London, 2001)

Ossie Clark (ed. Lady Henrietta Rous), *The Ossie Clark Diaries* (Bloomsbury, London, 1998)

Nick Clarke, *The Shadow of a Nation: The Changing Face of Britain* (Weidenfeld & Nicolson, London, 2003)

The Classic Carry On Film Collection (partwork – De Agostini, London, 2003–2005)

Martin Cloonan, *Banned! Censorship of Popular Music in Britain: 1967–92* (Arena, Aldershot, 1996)

Brian Clough & John Saddler, *The Autobiography* (Partridge, London, 1994 – pbk edn: Corgi, London, 1995)

David Clutterbuck & Stuart Crainer, *The Decline and Rise of British Industry* (Mercury, London, 1988)

David Coates, *The Crisis of Labour: Industrial Relations & the State in Contemporary Britain* (Philip Allan, Oxford, 1989)

Ken Coates, *The Crisis of British Socialism: Essays on the Rise of Harold Wilson and the Fall of the Labour Party* (Spokesman, London, 1971)

Michael Cocks, *Labour and the Benn Factor* (Macdonald & Co, London, 1989)

Ray Coleman, *Survivor: The Authorized Biography of Eric Clapton* (Sidgwick & Jackson, London, 1985 – pbk edn: Futura, London, 1986)

James Corbett, *England Expects: A History of the England Football Team* (Aurum, London, 2006)

Patrick Cosgrave, *Margaret Thatcher: A Tory and Her Party* (Hutchinson, London, 1978 – revised pbk edn: *Margaret Thatcher: Prime Minister*, Arrow, London, 1979)

Barry Cox, John Shirley & Martin Short, *The Fall of Scotland Yard* (Penguin, Harmondsworth, 1977)

Michael Crick, *Militant* (Faber & Faber, London, 1984)

Roger Crimlis & Alwyn W Turner, *Cult Rock Posters 1972–1982* (Aurum, London, 2006)

Susan Crosland, *Tony Crosland* (Jonathan Cape, London, 1982)

Brian Crozier (ed.), *'We Will Bury You': A Study of Left-Wing Subversion Today* (Tom Stacey, London, 1970)

Susie Daniel & Pete McGuire (ed.), *The Paint House: Words from an East End Gang* (Penguin, Harmondsworth, 1972)

Mark D'Arcy (ed.), *Order! Order! – 60 Years of Today In Parliament* (Politico's, 2005)

Jack Dash, *Good Morning, Brothers!* (Lawrence & Wishart, London, 1969 – pbk edn: Mayflower, London, 1970)

W.F. Deedes, *Dear Bill: W.F. Deedes Reports* (Macmillan, London, 1997)

Bernard Donoughue, *Downing Street Diary: With Harold Wilson in No. 10* (Jonathan Cape, London, 2005)

G.M.F. Drower, *Neil Kinnock: The Path to Leadership* (Weidenfeld & Nicolson, London, 1984)

Reginald East, *Heal the Sick* (Hodder & Stoughton, London, 1977)

The Ecologist, *A Blueprint for Survival* (Penguin, Harmondsworth, 1972)

Larry Elliott & Dan Atkinson, *The Age of Insecurity* (Verso, London, 1998)

Peter Berresford Ellis, *The Celtic Revolution: A Study in Anti-Imperialism* (Y Lolfa Cyf, Talybont, Ceredigion, 1985)

Robert Elms, *The Way We Wore: A Life in Threads* (Picador, London, 2005 – pbk edn: Picador, London, 2006)

Jeff Evans, *The Penguin TV Companion* (Penguin, London, 2001)

Peter Everett, *You'll Never Be 16 Again: An Illustrated History of the British Teenager* (BBC, London, 1986)

Paul Ferris, *The New Militants: Crisis in the Trade Unions* (Penguin, Harmondsworth, 1972)

Paul Ferris, *Sex and the British: A Twentieth-Century History* (Michael Joseph, London, 1993)

Michael Foot, *Loyalists and Loners* (Collins, London, 1986)

Simon Ford, *The Wreckers of Civilisation: The Story of COUM Transmissions and Throbbing Gristle* (Black Dog, London, 1999)

Alan Freeman, *The Benn Heresy* (Pluto, London, 1982)

Gillian Freeman, *The Undergrowth of Literature* (Thomas Nelson & Sons, London, 1967 – pbk edn: Panther, London, 1969)

Simon Freeman with Barrie Penrose, *Rinkagate: The Rise and Fall of Jeremy Thorpe* (Bloomsbury, London, 1996)

Jon Garland & Michael Rowe, *Racism and Anti-Racism in Football* (Palgrave, Basingstoke, 2001)

Charlie Gillett (ed.), *Rock File* (New English Library, London, 1972)

Peter & Leni Gillman, *Alias David Bowie* (Hodder & Stoughton, London, 1986)

Ian Gilmour & Mark Garnett, *Whatever Happened to the Tories: The Conservatives since 1945* (Fourth Estate, London, 1997)

Edward Goldsmith (ed.), *Can Britain Survive?* (Tom Stacey, London, 1971 – pbk edn: Sphere, London, 1972)

Geoffrey Goodman, *From Bevan to Blair: Fifty Years' Reporting from the Political Front Line* (Pluto, London, 2003)

Joe Gormley, *Battered Cherub* (Hamish Hamilton, London, 1982)

Germaine Greer, *The Female Eunuch* (MacGibbon & Kee, London, 1970)

Germaine Greer, *The Madwoman's Underclothes: Essays & Occasional Writings 1968–1985* (Picador, London, 1986)

Peter Hain, *Political Strikes: The State and Trade Unionism in Britain* (Viking, London, 1986 – pbk edn: Penguin, Harmondsworth, 1986)

Morrison Halcrow, *Keith Joseph: A Single Mind* (Macmillan, London, 1989)

Peter Hall (ed. John Goodwin), *Peter Hall's Diaries: The Story of a Dramatic Battle* (Hamish Hamilton, London, 1983 – pbk edn: 1984)

Roy Hattersley, *Who Goes Home?: Scenes from a Political Life* (Little, Brown, London, 1995)

Denis Healey, *The Time of My Life* (Michael Joseph, London, 1989 – pbk edn: Penguin, London, 1990)

Edward Heath, *The Course of My Life* (Hodder & Stoughton, London, 1998)

Eric Heffer, *Labour's Future: Socialist or SDP Mark 2?* (Verso, London, 1986)

Eric Heffer, *Never A Yes Man: The Life and Politics of an Adopted Liverpudlian* (Verso, London, 1991)

Peter Hennessy, *The Prime Minister: The Office and Its Holders since 1945* (Penguin, London, 2001)

Douglas Hill (ed.), *Tribune 40: The First Forty Years of a Socialist Newspaper* (Quartet, London, 1977)

Dilip Hiro, *Black British, White British* (Eyre & Spottiswoode, London, 1971 – revised edn: Pelican Books, Harmondsworth, 1973)

Andrew Holden, *Makers and Manners: Politics and Morality in Post-War Britain* (Politico's, London, 2004)

Anthony Holden, *Of Presidents, Prime Ministers & Princes: A Decade in Fleet Street* (Weidenfeld & Nicolson, London, 1984)

Noddy Holder, *Who's Crazee Now? My Autobiography* (Random House, London, 1999 – pbk edn: Ebury, London, 2000)

Lord Home, *The Way the Wind Blows: An Autobiography* (Collins, London, 1976)

Chris Hunt, *World Cup Stories: The History of the FIFA World Cup* (Interact, Ware, 2006)

Kevin Jefferys, *Anthony Crosland* (Richard Cohen, London, 1999)

Roy Jenkins, *A Life at the Centre* (Macmillan, London, 1991)

R.W. Johnson & Douglas Schoen, 'The "Powell effect": or how one man can win' (*New Society*, 22 July 1976)

Jack Jones, *Union Man: An Autobiography* (William Collins, London, 1986)

Peter Kellner & Christopher Hitchens, *Callaghan: The Road to Number Ten* (Cassell & Co, London, 1976)

Anthony King (ed.), *Why Is Britain Becoming Harder to Govern?* (BBC, London, 1976)

David Kogan & Maurice Kogan, *The Battle for the Labour Party* (Kogan Page, London, 1982 – 2nd revised edn: 1983)

Garth Lean, *Rebirth of a Nation?* (Blandford Press, Poole, 1976)

Glenda Leeming, *Wesker the Playwright* (Methuen, London, 1983)

David Leigh, *The Wilson Plot: The Intelligence Services and the Discrediting of a Prime Minister* (William Heinemann, London, 1988)

Bernard Levin, *Taking Sides* (Jonathan Cape, London, 1979 – pbk edn: Pan, London, 1980)

Bernard Levin, *Speaking Up: More of the Best of His Journalism* (Jonathan Cape, London, 1982)

Mark Lewisohn, *Radio Times Guide to TV Comedy* (BBC Worldwide, London, 1998)

Colin Leys, *Politics in Britain: An Introduction* (Heinemann, London, 1983)

Selwyn Lloyd, *Mr Speaker, Sir* (Jonathan Cape, London, 1976)

Lord Longford, *Pornography: The Longford Report* (Coronet, London, 1972)

John A. Loraine, *The Death of Tomorrow* (Heinemann, London, 1972)

Graham McCann, *Morecambe & Wise* (Fourth Estate, London, 1998 – pbk edn: 1998)

Ronald McIntosh, *Challenge to Democracy: Politics, Trade Union Power and Economic Failure in the 1970s* (Politico's, London, 2006)

David McKittrick & David McVea, *Making Sense of the Troubles* (Blackstaff Press, Belfast, 2000 – revised edn: Penguin, London, 2001)

Maria Marcus (trans. Joan Tate), *A Taste for Pain: On Masochism and Female Sexuality* (Souvenir, London, 1981)

Robert Mark, *In the Office of Constable* (William Collins, London, 1978 – pbk edn: Fontana, London, 1979)

Alistair Michie & Simon Hoggart, *The Pact: The Inside Story of the Lib–Lab Government, 1977–8* (Quartet, London, 1978)

Ian Mikardo, *Back-Bencher* (Weidenfeld & Nicolson, London, 1988)

Stephen Milligan, *The New Barons: Union Power in the 1970s* (Maurice Temple Smith, London, 1976)

Austin Mitchell, *Four Years in the Death of the Labour Party* (Methuen, London, 1983)

Ernle Money, *Margaret Thatcher: First Lady of the House* (Leslie Frewin, London, 1975)

Robert Moss, *The Collapse of Democracy* (Maurice Temple Smith, London, 1975)

Frank Muir, *A Kentish Lad: His Autobiography* (Bantam, London, 1997 – pbk edn: Corgi, London, 1998)

David Nobbs, *I Didn't Get Where I Am Today* (William Heinemann, London, 2003 – pbk edn: Arrow, London, 2004)

Michael Palin, *Diaries 1969–1979: The Python Years* (Weidenfeld & Nicolson, London, 2006)

Matthew Parris, *Chance Witness: An Outsider's Life in Politics* (Penguin, London, 2003)

Martin Pawley, *The Private Future: Causes and consequences of community collapse in the West* (Thames & Hudson, London, 1973)

Mark Paytress, *The Rolling Stones Off The Record: Outrageous Opinions & Unrehearsed Interviews* (Omnibus, London, 2003)

Mike Phillips & Trevor Phillips, *Windrush: The Irresistible Rise of Multi-Racial Britain* (HarperCollins, London, 1998)

Ben Pimlott, *Harold Wilson* (HarperCollins, London, 1992 – pbk edn: HarperCollins, London, 1993)

Ben Pimlott, *The Queen: A Biography of Elizabeth II* (HarperCollins, London, 1996 – pbk edn: John Wiley & Sons, New York, 1997)

David Powell, *Tony Benn: A Political Life* (Continuum, London, 2001)

Enoch Powell, *Freedom and Reality* (B.T. Batsford, London, 1969)

Enoch Powell, *No Easy Answers* (Sheldon, London, 1973)

Jim Prior, *A Balance of Power* (Hamish Hamilton, London, 1986)

Andrew Quicke, *Tomorrow's Television* (Lion, Berkhamstead, 1976)

Giles Radice, *Friends & Rivals: Crosland, Jenkins and Healey* (Little, Brown, London, 2002 – pbk edn: Abacus, London, 2003)

Deirdre Redgrave with Danae Brook, *To Be a Redgrave: The Inside Story of a Marriage* (Robson Books, London, 1983)

David Reed, *Ireland: The Key to the British Revolution* (Larkin, London, 1984)

David Renton, *This Rough Game: Fascism and Anti-Fascism* (Sutton, Stroud, 2001)

Zandra Rhodes & Anne Knight, *The Art of Zandra Rhodes* (Michael O'Mara Books, London, 1984)

Adrian Rigelsford, *The Doctors: 30 Years of Time Travel* (Boxtree, London, 1994)

Penny Rimbaud (aka J.J. Ratter), *Shibboleth: My Revolting Life* (AK Press, Edinburgh, 1998)

David Roberts (ed.), *The Guinness Book of British Hit Singles* (1977 – 14th edition: Guinness World Records, London, 2001)

Paul Rose, *Backbencher's Dilemma* (Frederick Muller, London, 1981)

Robert Ross, *The Carry On Companion* (1996 – revised pbk edn: B.T. Batsford, London, 2002)

Andrew Roth, *Enoch Powell: Tory Tribune* (Macdonald, London, 1970)

Paul Routledge, *Scargill: The Unauthorized Biography* (HarperCollins, London, 1993)

Trevor Russel, *The Tory Party: Its Policies, Divisions and Future* (Penguin, Harmondsworth, 1978)

Anthony Sampson, *The Changing Anatomy of Britain* (Hodder & Stoughton, London, 1982)

Philip Schlesinger, Graham Murdock & Philip Elliott, *Televising 'Terrorism': Political Violence in Popular Culture* (Comedia, London, 1983)

E.F. Schumacher, *Small Is Beautiful: A Study of Economics as if People Mattered* (Blond & Briggs, London, 1973 – pbk edn: Abacus, London, 1974)

Dominic Shellard, *British Theatre Since the War* (Yale University Press, New Haven, 1999)

Robert Shepherd, *Enoch Powell: A Biography* (Hutchinson, London, 1996 – pbk edn: Pimlico, London, 1997)

Manny Shinwell, *Lead with the Left: My First Ninety-Six Years* (Cassell, London, 1981)

Peter Shore, *Leading the Left* (Weidenfeld & Nicolson, London, 1993)

Alan Sked & Chris Cook, *Post-War Britain: A Political History* (2nd edn: Penguin, Harmondsworth, 1984)

Cyril Smith, *Big Cyril: The Autobiography of Cyril Smith* (W.H. Allen, London, 1977 – pbk edn: Star, London, 1978)

Bill Smithies & Peter Fiddick, *Enoch Powell on Immigration: An Analysis* (Sphere, London, 1969)

The Socialist Party, *Socialism or Your Money Back: articles from the Socialist Standard 1904–2004* (SPGB, London, 2004)

Dale Spender, *For the Record: The Making and Meaning of Feminist Knowledge* (The Women's Press, London, 1985)

Peter Stanford, *The Outcasts' Outcast: A Biography of Lord Longford* (Sutton, Gloucestershire, 2003)

Margaret Stewart, *Protest or Power? A Study of the Labour Party* (George Allen & Unwin, London, 1974)

John Stonehouse, *My Trial* (Star, London, 1976)

Richard Stott, *Dogs and Lampposts* (Metro, London, 2002)

Roy Strong, *The Roy Strong Diaries 1967–1987* (Weidenfeld & Nicolson, London, 1997 – pbk edn: Orion, London, 1998)

Sunday Times Insight Team, *Ulster* (Penguin, Harmondsworth, 1972)

John Sutherland, *Bestsellers: Popular Fiction of the 1970s* (Routledge & Kegan Paul, London, 1981)

John Sutherland, *Reading the Decades: Fifty Years of the Nation's Bestselling Books* (BBC Worldwide, London, 2002)

Matthew Sweet, *Shepperton Babylon: The Lost Worlds of British Cinema* (Faber & Faber, London, 2005 – pbk edn: 2006)

G.W. Target, *Unholy Smoke* (Hodder & Stoughton, London, 1969)

Norman Tebbit, *Upwardly Mobile* (Weidenfeld & Nicolson, London, 1988)

Margaret Thatcher, *The Path to Power* (HarperCollins, London, 1995)

John Tomlinson, *Left, Right: The March of Political Extremism in Britain* (John Calder, London, 1981)

Alwyn W Turner, *The Biba Experience* (Antique Collectors Club, Woodbridge, 2004)

Alwyn W Turner (ed.), *Portmeirion* (Antique Collectors Club, Woodbridge, 2006)

Gordon Turner & Alwyn W Turner, *The History of British Military Bands Volume One: Cavalry & Corps* (Spellmount, Staplehurst, 1994)

Kenneth Tynan (ed. John Lahr), *The Diaries of Kenneth Tynan* (Bloomsbury, London, 2001)

Lars Ullerstam, *The Erotic Minorities* (Zindermans förlag, Sweden, 1964 – English language edn, trans. Anselm Hollo: Grove Press, New York, 1966)

Tony Visconti, *Bowie, Bolan and the Brooklyn Boy* (HarperCollins, London, 2007)

William Waldegrave, *The Binding of Leviathan: Conservatism and the Future* (Hamish Hamilton, London, 1978)

Christine Wallace, *Germaine Greer: Untamed Shrew* (Richard Cohen Books, London, 1997)

Auberon Waugh, *Another Voice: An Alternative Anatomy of Britain* (Sidgwick & Jackson, London, 1986 – pbk edn: Fontana, London,1986)

Richard Webber, *A Celebration of The Good Life* (Orion, London, 2000)

Richard Weight, *Patriots: National Identity in Britain 1940–2000* (Macmillan, London, 2002 – pbk edn: Pan, London, 2003)

Michael Wharton, *The Stretchford Chronicles: 25 Years of Peter Simple* (Papermac, London, 1981)

Brian Whitaker, *News Limited: Why You Can't Read All About It* (Minority Press Group, London, 1981)

William Whitelaw, *The Whitelaw Memoirs* (Aurum, London, 1989)

David Widgery, *Beating Time: Riot 'n' Race 'n' Rock 'n' Roll* (Chatto & Windus, London, 1986)

Charlie Williams, *Ee – I've Had Some Laughs* (Wolfe Publishing Ltd, London, 1973)

John Williams, Eric Dunning & Patrick Murphy, *Hooligans Abroad: The Behaviour and Control of English Fans in Continental Europe* (Routledge & Kegan Paul, London, 1984)

Kenneth Williams (ed. Russell Davies), *The Kenneth Williams Diaries* (HarperCollins, London, 1993)

Clough Williams-Ellis, *England and the Octopus* (originally published 1928 – new edn: Golden Dragon, Portmeirion, 1975)

Colin Wilson, *The Occult* (Hodder & Stoughton, London, 1971 – pbk edn: Granada, St Albans, 1979)

Harold Wilson, *Memoirs: The Making of a Prime Minister 1916–64* (Weidenfeld & Nicolson, London, 1986)

Robert Winder, *Bloody Foreigners: The Story of Immigration to Britain* (Little, Brown, London, 2004)

David Winner, *Those Feet: A Sensual History of English Football* (Bloomsbury, London, 2005)

Enid Wistrich, *'I Don't Mind the Sex, It's the Violence'* – Film Censorship Explored (Marion Boyars, London, 1978)

Richard Wurmbrand, *Was Karl Marx a Satanist?* (Diane Books, USA, 1979)

Mike Yarwood, *And This Is Me!* (Jupiter, London, 1974)

Mike Yarwood, *Impressions of My Life* (Willow, London, 1986)

Fiction

Note: Where a paperback edition is shown, it indicates that any page references cited are to that edition.

Richard Adams, *Watership Down* (Rex Collings, London, 1972 – pbk edn: Puffin, Harmondsworth, 1973)

Richard Adams, *The Plague Dogs* (Allen Lane, London, 1977 – pbk edn: Penguin, Harmondsworth, 1978)

Richard Allen, *Skinhead* (New English Library, London, 1970)

Richard Allen, *Suedehead* (New English Library, London, 1971)

Kingsley Amis, *Jake's Thing* (Hutchinson, London, 1978 – pbk edn: Penguin, Harmondsworth, 1979)

David Anne, *Day of the Mad Dogs* (W.H. Allen, London, 1977)

W.H. Auden, *Selected Poems* (Faber & Faber, London, 1968)

Joe Balham, *The Sweeney: The Human Pipeline* (Futura, London, 1977)

Joe Balham, *The Sweeney: Regan and the Bent Stripper* (Futura, London, 1977)

James Barlow, *The Burden of Proof* (Hamish Hamilton, London, 1968 – pbk edn: *Villain*, Pan, London, 1970)

Eddie Braben, *The Best of Morecambe and Wise* (Woburn Press, London, 1974)

Malcolm Bradbury, *The History Man* (Secker & Warburg, 1975 – pbk edn: Picador, London, 2000)

Paul Bryers, *Hollow Target* (André Deutsch, London, 1976 – pbk edn: Coronet, London, 1978)

Anthony Burgess, *1985* (Hutchinson, London, 1978 – pbk edn: Arrow, London, 1980)

Peter Cook, *Tragically I was an Only Twin* (Century, London, 2002)

Robin Cook, *A State of Denmark* (Hutchinson, London, 1970 – pbk edn: Panther, London, 1973)

Edmund Cooper, *Five to Twelve* (Hodder, London, 1968)

Edmund Cooper, *Who Needs Men?* (Hodder & Stoughton, London, 1972 – pbk edn: Coronet, London, 1974)

Richard Cowper, *Clone* (Victor Gollancz, London, 1972 – pbk edn: Quartet, London, 1974)

Les Dawson, *A Card for the Clubs* (Sphere, London, 1974)

Colin Dexter, *Last Bus to Woodstock* (Macmillan, London, 1975 – pbk edn: Pan, London, 1977)

Terrance Dicks, *Doctor Who and the Monster of Peladon* (Target, London, 1980)

Richard Doyle, *Deluge* (Arlington Books, London, 1976 – pbk edn: Pan, London, 1978)

Margaret Drabble, *The Ice Age* (Weidenfeld & Nicolson, London, 1977)

Constantine Fitzgibbon, *When the Kissing Had to Stop* (Cassell & Co., London, 1960)

E.M. Forster, *Maurice* (Edward Arnold, London, 1971 – pbk edn: Penguin, Harmondsworth, 1972)

Anthony Fowles, *Pastime* (W.H. Allen, London, 1974 – pbk edn: Star, London, 1974)

Brian Freeborn, *Good Luck Mister Cain* (Secker & Warburg, London, 1976)

Gillian Freeman, *The Leader* (Anthony Blond, London, 1965)

Trevor Griffiths, *Comedians* (Faber & Faber, London, 1976 – revised 1979)

William Haggard, *The Doubtful Disciple* (Cassell & Co., London, 1969 – pbk edn: Corgi, London, 1971)

William Haggard, *The Hardliners* (Cassell & Co., London, 1970 – pbk edn: Corgi, London, 1972)

Jeremy Hardy, *Jeremy Hardy Speaks to the Nation* (Methuen, London, 1993)

David Hare, *Teeth 'n' Smiles* (Faber & Faber, London, 1976)

Jane Harman, *W*I*T*C*H* (New English Library, London, 1971)

Walter Harris, *The Mistress of Downing Street* (Michael Joseph, London, 1972)

Walter Harris, *The Fifth Horseman* (Panther, London, 1976)

Walter Harris, *Saliva* (Star, London, 1977)

James Herbert, *The Rats* (New English Library, London, 1974)

James Herbert, *The Spear* (New English Library, London, 1978)

Reginald Hill, *An Advancement of Learning* (William Collins, London, 1971 – pbk edn: Fontana, London, 1974)

P.D. James, *An Unsuitable Job for a Woman* (Faber & Faber, London, 1972 – pbk edn: Penguin, London, 1974)

P.D. James, *Death of an Expert Witness* (Faber & Faber, London, 1977 – pbk edn: Penguin, London, 1978)

Pamela Kettle, *The Day of the Women* (Leslie Frewin, London, 1969 – pbk edn: New English Library, London, 1970)

Timothy Lea, *Confessions of a Window Cleaner* (Sphere, London, 1971)

Peter Leslie, *The Extremists* (New English Library, London, 1970)

Doris Lessing, *The Memoirs of a Survivor* (Octagon, London, 1974 – pbk edn: Pan, London, 1976)

Ted Lewis, *Jack's Return Home* (Michael Joseph, London, 1970 – pbk edn: *Carter*, Pan, London, 1971)

Ted Lewis, *Plender* (Michael Joseph, London, 1971)

Graham Lord, *The Spider and the Fly* (Hamish Hamilton, London, 1974 – pbk edn: Sphere, London, 1977)

Robert McKew with Reed De Rouen, *Death List* (Futura, London, 1979)

James Mitchell, *Russian Roulette* (Hamish Hamilton, London, 1973 – pbk edn: Corgi, London, 1975)

Eric Morecambe & Ernest Wise, *The Morecambe & Wise Special* (Weidenfeld & Nicolson, London, 1977)

Frederic Mullally, *Split Scene* (Arthur Baker, London, 1963 – pbk edn: Pan, London, 1966)

Robert Muller, *The Lost Diaries of Albert Smith* (Jonathan Cape, London, 1965 – pbk edn: *After All, This Is England*, Penguin, Harmondsworth, 1967)

Andrea Newman, *A Bouquet of Barbed Wire* (Triton, London, 1969 – pbk edn: Penguin, Harmondsworth, 1976)

G.F. Newman, *Sir, You Bastard* (W.H. Allen, London, 1970 – pbk edn: NEL, London, 1971)

Christopher Nicole, *The Face of Evil* (Hutchinson, London, 1971)

David Nobbs, *The Death of Reginald Perrin* (Victor Gollancz, London, 1975 – pbk edn: *The Fall and Rise of Reginald Perrin*, Penguin, London, 1976)

Philip Oakes, *Experiment at Proto* (André Deutsch, London, 1973 – pbk edn: *The Proto Papers*, Quartet, London, 1974)

Dillibe Onyeama, *The Book of Black Man's Humour* (Dillibe Onyeama Publishing, London, 1975)

Ingeborg Pertwee, *Together* (Hamish Hamilton, London, 1974 – pbk edn: Tandem, London, 1976)

Jack Ramsay, *The Rage* (Sphere, London, 1977)

Frederic Raphael, *The Glittering Prizes* (Penguin, Harmondsworth, 1976)

Ruth Rendell, *A Guilty Thing Surprised* (Hutchinson, London, 1970 – pbk edn: Arrow, London, 1980)

Ruth Rendell, *Some Lie and Some Die* (Hutchinson, London, 1973 – pbk edn: Arrow, London, 1974)

Ian Rosse, *The Droop* (New English Library, London, 1972)

John de St Jorre & Brian Shakespeare, *The Patriot Game* (Hodder & Stoughton, London, 1974 – pbk edn: Coronet, London, 1974)

Donald Seaman, *The Committee* (Hamish Hamilton, London, 1977 – pbk edn: Futura, London, 1979)

George Shipway, *The Chilian Club* (Peter Davies, London, 1971 – pbk edn: Granada, St Albans, 1972)

John Summers, *The Rag Parade* (New English Library, London, 1972)

Julian Symons, *The Players and the Game* (Collins, London, 1972 – pbk ed: Penguin, Harmondsworth, 1974)

Peter Van Greenaway, *The Man Who Held the Queen to Ransom and Sent Parliament Packing* (Weidenfeld & Nicolson, London, 1968 – pbk edn: Penguin, Harmondsworth, 1972)

Alec Waugh, *A Spy in the Family: An Erotic Comedy* (W.H. Allen, London, 1970)

Auberon Waugh, *A Bed of Flowers* (Michael Joseph, London, 1972)

Dee Wells, *Jane* (Blond & Briggs, London, 1973 – pbk edn: Pan, London, 1975)

Gordon Williams, *Big Morning Blues* (Hodder & Stoughton, London, 1974 – pbk edn: Coronet, London, 1976)

Colin Wilson, *The Schoolgirl Murder Case* (Hart-Davis, MacGibbon Ltd, London, 1974 – pbk edn: Granada, St Albans, 1975)

Arthur Wise, *Who Killed Enoch Powell?* (Weidenfeld & Nicolson, London, 1970 – pbk edn: Sphere, London, 1972)

P.G. Wodehouse, *Aunts Aren't Gentlemen* (Barrie & Jenkins, London, 1974 – pbk edn: Penguin, Harmondsworth, 1977)

P.B. Yuill (aka Gordon Williams & Terry Venables), *Hazell and the Menacing Jester* (Macmillan, London, 1976 – pbk edn: Penguin, Harmondsworth, 1977)

Films and Television Programmes
Note: Films are listed by director, TV programmes are credited to their creators.

Hazel Adair & Peter Ling, *Crossroads* (ATV/Central, 1964–88)

Jim Allen, *Days of Hope* (BBC TV, 1975)

Elizabeth Beresford, *The Wombles* (BBC TV, 1973–75)

John Boulting, *I'm All Right Jack* (British Lion, 1959)

Eric Chappell, *Rising Damp* (Yorkshire TV, 1974–78)

James Kenelm Clarke, *Hardcore* (Norfolk International Pictures, 1977)

John Cleese & Connie Booth, *Fawlty Towers* (BBC TV, 1975 & 1979)

John Cleese, Michael Palin, Eric Idle, Graham Chapman, Terry Jones & Terry Gilliam, *Monty Python's Flying Circus* (BBC TV, 1969–74)

Dick Clement & Ian La Frenais, *Whatever Happened to the Likely Lads?* (BBC TV, 1973–74)

Dick Clement & Ian La Frenais, *Porridge* (BBC TV, 1974–77)

Barney Colehan, *The Good Old Days* (BBC TV, 1953–83)

Sid Colin, *On the House* (Yorkshire TV, 1970–71)

Reginald Collins, *Special Branch* (Thames TV, 1969–74)

Gerry Davis & Kit Pedlar, *Doomwatch* (BBC TV, 1970–72)

John Esmonde & Bob Larbey, *The Good Life* (BBC TV, 1975–78)

Albert Fennell & Brian Clemens, *The New Avengers* (Avengers Enterprises, 1976–77)

Graeme Garden, Bill Oddie & Tim Brooke-Taylor, *The Goodies* (BBC TV, 1970–80)

Gerard Glaister & N.J. Crisp, *The Brothers* (BBC TV, 1972–76)

John Hamp, *The Comedians* (Granada TV, 1971–74)

Robin Hardy, *The Wicker Man* (British Lion, 1973)

George Inns, *The Black and White Minstrel Show* (BBC TV, 1958–78)

Derek Jarman, *Jubilee* (Megalovision, 1977)

Bob Kellett, *Girl Stroke Boy* (Hemdale, 1971)

Ian Kennedy-Martin, *The Sweeney* (Thames TV, 1975–78)

Nigel Kneale, *The Stone Tape* (BBC TV, 1972)

Nigel Kneale, *Beasts* (ATV, 1976)

Nigel Kneale, *Quatermass* (Thames TV, 1978)

Stanley Kubrick, *A Clockwork Orange* (Warner Bros, 1971)

Mike Leigh, *Abigail's Party* (BBC TV, 1977)

Jeremy Lloyd & David Croft, *Are You Being Served?* (BBC TV, 1972–85)

John Lloyd & Sean Hardie, *Not The Nine O'Clock News* (BBC TV, 1979–82)

Jonathan Lynn & Antony Jay, *Yes Minister* (BBC TV, 1980–84)

Philip Mackie, *The Naked Civil Servant* (Thames TV, 1975)

Philip Mackie, *Raffles* (Yorkshire TV, 1977)

Ian Mackintosh, *The Sandbaggers* (Yorkshire TV, 1978–80)

Jean Marsh & Eileen Atkins, *Upstairs, Downstairs* (LWT, 1971–75)

Philip Martin, *Gangsters* (BBC TV, 1976–78)

James Mitchell, *Callan* (ABC/Thames TV, 1967–72)

Johnnie Mortimer & Brian Cooke, *Man About the House* (Thames TV, 1973–76)

Johnnie Mortimer & Brian Cooke, *George and Mildred* (Thames TV, 1976–79)

Terry Nation, *Survivors* (BBC TV, 1975–77)

Terry Nation, *Blake's 7* (BBC TV, 1978–81)

Andrea Newman, *A Bouquet of Barbed Wire* (LWT, 1976)

Sydney Newman, *Doctor Who* (BBC TV, 1963–89)

David Nobbs, *The Fall and Rise of Reginald Perrin* (BBC TV, 1976–79)

Sam Peckinpah, *Straw Dogs* (ABC Pictures, 1971)

Lance Percival, *Up the Workers* (ATV, 1973–76)
Jimmy Perry & David Croft, *Dad's Army* (BBC TV, 1968–77)
Jimmy Perry & David Croft, *It Ain't Half Hot Mum* (BBC, 1974–81)
Dennis Potter, *Brimstone and Treacle* (BBC TV, 1976 – first broadcast 1987)
Dennis Potter, *Pennies from Heaven* (BBC TV, 1978)
Vince Powell & Harry Driver, *Love Thy Neighbour* (Thames TV, 1972–76)
Vince Powell, *Mind Your Language* (LWT, 1977–79)
Trevor Preston, *Out* (Thames/Euston Films, 1978)
Roger Price, *The Tomorrow People* (Thames TV, 1973–79)
Jack Pulman, *I, Claudius* (BBC TV, 1976)
Jack Rosenthal, *The Dustbinmen* (Granada TV, 1968–70)
Jack Rosenthal, *Another Sunday and Sweet F.A.* (Granada TV, 1972)
Jack Rosenthal, *There'll Almost Always Be an England* (Granada TV, 1974)
John Schlesinger, *Sunday, Bloody Sunday* (United Artists, 1971)
Howard Schuman, *Rock Follies* (Thames TV, 1976)
Anthony Simmons, *Black Joy* (Kastner-Milchan, 1977)
Johnny Speight, *Till Death Us Do Part* (BBC TV, 1966–68, 1972–75)
John Sullivan, *Citizen Smith* (BBC TV, 1977–80)
Eric Sykes, *Sykes* (BBC TV, 1972–79)
Julien Temple, *The Great Rock 'n' Roll Swindle* (Virgin Films, 1980)
Gerald Thomas, *Carry On at Your Convenience* (J. Arthur Rank, 1971)
Gerald Thomas, *Carry On Abroad* (J. Arthur Rank, 1972)
Pete Walker, *Frightmare* (Peter Walker Ltd, 1974)
Pete Walker, *House of Whipcord* (Peter Walker Ltd, 1974)
Tony Warren, *Coronation Street* (Granada TV, 1960–)
Keith Waterhouse & Willis Hall, *Budgie* (LWT, 1971–72)
Ronald Wolfe & Ronald Chesney, *The Rag Trade* (BBC TV, 1961–63; LWT, 1977–78)
Bill Wright, *Mastermind* (BBC TV, 1972–97)
Fred Zinnemann, *The Day of the Jackal* (Warwick Productions, 1973)

Websites
All Music Guide (allmusic.com)
British Board of Film Classification (bbfc.co.uk)
By-Elections (geocities.com/by_elections)
Internet Movie Database (imdb.com)
The Knitting Circle (knittingcircle.org.uk)
Lenny Henry (lennyhenry.com)
Leonard Rossiter (leonardrossiter.com)
Margaret Thatcher Foundation (margaretthatcher.org)
New Economics Foundation (neweconomics.org)
Oxford Dictionary of National Biography (oxforddnb.com)
The Prince of Wales (princeofwales.gov.uk)
Project Gutenberg (gutenberg.org)
Socialist Labour Party (socialist-labour-party.org.uk)
Trash Fiction (trashfiction.co.uk)
Urban 75 (urban75.net)
Vault of Evil (vaultofevil.suddenlaunch3.com)
Wikipedia (en.wikipedia.org)

Credits

Chapter subtitles are taken from the following songs: Jam, 'This Is the Modern World'; Who, 'Won't Get Fooled Again'; Sparks, 'This Town Ain't Big Enough for Both of Us'; Hollies, 'All I Need Is the Air That I Breathe'; Mott the Hoople, 'Violence'; Strawbs, 'Part of the Union'; Gary Glitter, 'Hello, Hello, I'm Back Again'; Rod Stewart, 'Maggie May'; Radio Stars, 'Dirty Pictures'; Eno, 'Driving Me Backwards'; Sylvia, 'Y Viva España'; Marmalade, 'Falling Apart at the Seams'; Stranglers, 'I Feel Like a Wog'; Sex Pistols, 'Anarchy in the UK'; Tom Robinson Band, 'Glad to Be Gay'; Police, 'Message in a Bottle'; David Bowie, 'Fantastic Voyage'. The titles for the three main sections are taken from the titles of tracks by David Bowie.

Acknowledgements

I must express my gratitude to the following, who spoke to me and provided assistance in various ways:

Alan Williams, Austin Mitchell, Biddu, Bob Blackman, Brian Freeborn, Chris Redburn, Craig Austin, Dan Atkinson, David Van Day, Dennis Skinner, Don Smith, Eddy Amoo, Florette Boyson, Gillian Bennett, Graham Coster, Harvey Hinsley, Ian Covell, James Herbert, Jennie Bird, Jill McGregor, John Goriot, John Summers, Ken Andrews, Michael Butterworth, Michelle Coomber, Mike Pearn, Nanette Wise, Norman Tebbit, Peter Jenner, Piers Burnett, Rachel Forster, Richard Pain, Roger Crimlis, Russell Mael, Sally Carr, Shirley Williams, Stephen J. Chibnall, Stephen P. McKay, Steve Jones, Steven Thomas, Tony Benn, Tony Burrows, TV Smith, Vic Gibbons, Vicki Stevens and Zandra Rhodes, as well as those who asked not to be named.

Obviously none of the above should be considered to condone the contents of this book. Apologies too to everyone whose work I've quoted in such a cavalier fashion, probably missing all the important points.

I would also like to thank my editor, Natasha Martin, copy editor, Merlin Cox, indexer, Ian Craine, and Chris Shamwana for the cover, as well as Nithya Rae, Graham Eames, Melanie Cumming and Liz Rowe at Aurum.

And this seems as good an opportunity as any to offer belated thanks to four people who have taught me a great deal over the years, whether they knew it or not: Andrew Husband, Clare Wayland, Elizabeth Imlay and Roger Sears.

Thamasin Marsh has lived with this project since its inception, and has provided invaluable thought and support.

This book is dedicated to Gordon Turner, whose contribution is appreciated more than he realizes.

Index